A History of Modern Morocco

Morocco is notable for its stable and durable monarchy, its close ties with the West, its vibrant cultural life, and its centrality to regional politics. This book, by distinguished historian Susan Gilson Miller, offers a richly documented survey of modern Moroccan history. The author's original and astute interpretations of the events, ideas, and personalities that inform contemporary political life are testimony to her scholarship and long association with the country. Arguing that pragmatism rather than ideology has shaped the monarchy's response to crisis, the book begins with the French invasion of Algeria in 1830 and Morocco's abortive efforts at reform, the duel with colonial powers and the loss of independence in 1912, the burdens and benefits of France's forty-four-year dominion, and the stunning success of the nationalist movement leading to independence in 1956. In the postindependence era, the book traces the monarchy's gradual monopolization of power and the resulting political paralysis, ending with the last years of Hassan II's reign, when Moroccan society experienced a sudden and radical opening. A postscript brings events up to 2012, covering topics such as Morocco's "war on terror," the détente between the monarchy and the Islamists, and the impact of the Arab Spring. This concise, readable book will inform and enthrall students coming to the history of North Africa for the first time, as well as those in other disciplines searching for the background to present-day events in the region.

Susan Gilson Miller is Professor of History at the University of California, Davis. Her research interests focus on Islamic urbanism, travel and migration, minorities in the Muslim world, and the historiography of colonialism and nationalism, with a special emphasis on North Africa. Her most recent publications are *The Architecture and Memory of the Minority Quarter of the Muslim Mediterranean City* (2010) and *Berbers and Others: Beyond Tribe and Nation in the Maghrib* (2010).

A History of Modern Morocco

SUSAN GILSON MILLER
University of California, Davis

CAMBRIDGE
UNIVERSITY PRESS

32 Avenue of the Americas, New York NY 10013-2473, USA

Cambridge University Press is part of the University of Cambridge.

It furthers the University's mission by disseminating knowledge in the pursuit of education, learning and research at the highest international levels of excellence.

www.cambridge.org
Information on this title: www.cambridge.org/9780521008990

First published 2013

A catalogue record for this publication is available from the British Library

Library of Congress Cataloguing in Publication data
Miller, Susan Gilson.
A history of modern Morocco / Susan Gilson Miller.
p. cm.
Includes bibliographical references and index.
ISBN 978-0-521-81070-8 (hardback) – ISBN 978-0-521-00899-0 (paperback)
1. Morocco – History. I. Title.
DT324.M545 2012
964–dc23 2012014471

ISBN 978-0-521-81070-8 Hardback
ISBN 978-0-521-00899-0 Paperback

Contents

Maps and Illustrations

MAPS

ILLUSTRATIONS

Acknowledgments

Friends, colleagues, and family have helped me over the years and made the writing of this book possible.

Moroccan scholars provided me with the informal education necessary to study the history of their country. I especially want to thank Jamaa Baïda, Khalid Ben Srhir, Mohamed Kenbib, Abdelahad Sebti, Mohamed El Mansour, Ahmad Taoufik, Mohamed Kably, Maâti Monjib, Mohamed Dahbi, Mohamed Hatimi, Nadia Erzini, Simon Lévy, Mina Elmghari, Mokhtar Ghambou, Halima Ferhat, Rahma Bourqia, Mohamed Mezzine, Abdelfattah Kilito, and Fatima Sadiqi for generously sharing their deep knowledge of Moroccan state and society with me. My first Moroccan mentor was the impeccable Si Muhammad al-Manuni, who introduced me to the intricacies of modern Moroccan historiography. Special thanks to Said Mouline and Mia Balafrej, who offered me superb hospitality during my many visits to Rabat, and to Sonia Azagury and Rachel Muyal, my sentinels in Tangier.

I am grateful to the Moroccan American Commission for Educational and Cultural Exchange, Jim Miller, Director, which provided funding support via successive Fulbright grants, as well as to former MACECE Director Ed Thomas. In Tangier, Elena Prentice and Thor and Elizabeth Kuniholm, former directors of the Tangier American Legation Museum, provided a friendly and welcome base.

A host of North African specialists have been advisers and collaborators over the years: Wilfred Rollman, Julia Clancy-Smith, William Granara, Jonathan Katz, Michael Willis, Susan Slyomovics, Kenneth Brown, Norman Stillman, Katherine Hoffman, James McDougall, Thomas Park, Harvey Goldberg, John Entelis, Mark Tessler, Dale Eickelman, André

Levy, Susan Ossman, Joelle Bahloul, Daniel Schroeter, Gregory White, Lucette Valensi, Yolande Cohen, Bruce Maddy-Weitzman, and Michel Abitbol have at one time or another come to my aid. My thanks to one and all.

Former students, now colleagues, shared their work with me, enriching my own. Their friendship is especially treasured: Sahar Bazzaz, Jonathan Smolin, Emily Benichou-Gottreich, Ilham Khuri-Makdisi, Lisa Bernasek, Amira Bennison, Hannah Louise Clark, Amy Young, Tom de Georges, Jessica Marglin, Eric Calderwood, Aziza Chaouni, Etty Terem, Moshe Gershovich, Stacy Holden, Abby Krasner Babale, and Lamia Zaki are at the center of a new generation of Maghribi scholars who are changing the state of the field. David Stenner and Lily Balloffet, history graduate students at UC Davis, have more recently lent a hand.

My warmest appreciation to Gérard Lévy of Paris, who generously gave me unpublished photos from his personal archives, and to the Center for Middle Eastern Studies at Harvard University, my platform for pursuing Moroccan studies for nearly twenty years. My heartfelt thanks to a series of supportive CMES directors who made a place for Maghribi studies at Harvard: William Graham, Cemal Kafadar, and Steven Caton among them. In a special category of her own is Susan Kahn, Associate Director of CMES.

My new colleagues in the History Department at UC Davis have been a source of unstintingly warm encouragement. I am also grateful to the interlibrary loan section of Shields Library, UC Davis, always receptive to my requests, and to the faceless and nameless heroes of the Widener Library Scan and Deliver service. My thanks, too, to Marigold Acland of Cambridge University Press, a woman of infinite patience, and Joy Mizan and Sarika Narula, who have ushered me though the final stages of the editorial process.

Finally, thanks to my family, which has put up with my historical passions over the years with patience and good humor: Daphne, Ross, Arlen, Emet, Sam, and Max, and most of all, to David, to whom this book is dedicated.

Note on Transliteration and Translation

The transliteration of Moroccan personal and place names poses difficult problems. French spelling is predominant throughout the Maghrib, but unfortunately, it does not always render well into English. Generally speaking, I have used the French spelling for place names, making use of the glossary of toponyms found in J-F. Troin, ed., *Maroc: Régions, pays, territoires* (Paris: Maisonneuve & Larose, 2002). Exceptions to this rule are place names that are commonly found in English: Marrakesh, Tetuan, Tangier, Fez.

Personal names call for a different approach. When the name has a common French spelling and the individual may be otherwise difficult to identify, I use the French spelling (Laroui, for example, instead of al-ʿArawi). When a name gains greater clarity by using the *International Journal of Middle Eastern Studies* (*IJMES*) method of transliteration from Arabic, that method is applied: ʿAbd al-Qadir instead of Abdel Kader, Muhammad instead of Mohamed. Admittedly, this is often a matter of personal choice.

Arabic terms are transliterated using the *IJMES* method, with the modification that I have dropped all diacritical marks except for the *ʿayn* (ʿ) and the *hamza* (ʾ), indicating the latter letter only when it is in the middle of the word. (Hence *Qurʾan* but not *shurafaʾ*.) In some cases, I write the plural of an Arabic word by adding an "s" to the singular, such as *fatwas*. Finally, Arabic words that now appear in the *Oxford English Dictionary* – for example, ulama – are spelled accordingly.

All translations from Arabic and French to English are my own, unless otherwise indicated.

Chronology

1830, July 5	French landing in Algiers
1844, August 14	Moroccan defeat at the Battle of Isly
1859–1860	Tetuan War against the Spanish
1863, December 11	British Jewish philanthropist Sir Moses Montefiore arrives in Tangier
1873	Sultan Hassan I enthroned
1880, May 19–July 3	Conference of Madrid affirms the legal right of protection
1894	Sultan ʿAbd al-ʿAziz enthroned
1900, May 13	Death of the regent Ba Ahmad
1904, April 8	French-British agreement giving France a free hand in Morocco
1905, March 31	Emperor Wilhelm II lands at Tangier
1906, January 7–April 6	Algeciras Conference places conditions on Moroccan independence
1907, August 7–12	Bombardment of Casablanca by the French
1907, August 16	Sultan ʿAbd al-Hafiz proclaimed in Marrakesh
1908, January 4	*Bayʿa* of Sultan ʿAbd al-Hafiz at Fez
1909, May 4	Death of Shaykh Muhammad b. al-Kabir al-Kattani
1911, November 4	Franco-German treaty; Germany concedes Morocco to France
1912, March 30	Treaty of Fez, French Protectorate begins
1912, April 27	Lyautey is named Résident Général of the Protectorate
1912, August 13	Proclamation of Sultan Yusuf

1912, November 27	French-Spanish treaty institutes Spanish control in the north
1914, November 13	Middle Atlas Berbers defeat French at Battle of el-Herri
1921–1925	Rif War and declaration of the "Ripublik" of the Rif
1925, September 24	Lyautey is replaced by T. Steeg and departs Morocco
1927, November 18	Sultan Muhammad V is enthroned
1930, May 16	Berber Dahir
1933, 18 November	First Throne Day celebrated
1934, December 1	Reform Plan of the CAM (Moroccan Action Committee)
1937, September	Meknes riots lead to pro-nationalist demonstrations
1942, November 8	Allied landings in North Africa
1943, January 22	Anfa Conference, Roosevelt–Muhammad V meeting
1943, December 10	Creation of the Istiqlal Party
1944, January 11	Manifesto of Independence
1945, November 14	Creation of PCM (Moroccan Communist Party)
1946, June 20	ʿAllal al-Fasi returns to Morocco from Gabon to head Istiqlal
1946, September 11	Istiqlal founds party newspaper *al-ʿAlam*
1947, April 9	Sultan Muhammad V's speech at Tangier
1952, December 5–8	Anti-French riots in Casablanca
1953, August 20	Sultan Muhammad V deposed and exiled to Madagascar
1954, November 1	Start of Algerian war of independence
1955, March 20	Creation of UMT (Moroccan Workers' Union)
1955, August 22	Conference of Aix-les-Bains
1955, November 16	Sultan Muhammad V returns to Morocco
1956, March 2	French-Moroccan declaration of independence
1956, May 14	Foundation of the FAR (Royal Moroccan Armed Forces)
1956, October 8	Tangier is reintegrated into Morocco

1956, December 26	First congress of the UNEM (Moroccan Students' Union)
1957, January 21	Revolt of Addi Ou Bihi in the Tafilalt
1957, July 9	Crown Prince Hassan declared heir to the throne
1957, August	Muhammad V takes the title of King
1957, December 21	Creation of University Muhammad V in Rabat
1958, May 12	Istiqlal government headed by Ahmed Balafrej
1958, May–November	Rif Rebellion repressed by FAR under Crown Prince Hassan
1958, October	Morocco joins the Arab League
1958, December 24	Government of Abdallah Ibrahim
1959, September 6	Istiqlal splinters; left-wing forms UNFP
1960, February 14	Arrests of UNFP militants accused of plotting against the Crown Prince
1960, February 29	Earthquake in Agadir
1960, May 27	King Muhammad V takes over the government
1960, May 29	First municipal elections
1961, February 26	Death of Muhammad V
1961, March 3	Hassan II becomes King
1962, July 5	Algerian independence declared
1962, December 7	First Moroccan Constitution adopted
1963, January 2	The Istiqlal leaves the government and joins the opposition
1963, February 6	Death of ʻAbd al-Karim al-Khattabi in Cairo
1963, May 13	First legislative elections
1963, June–July	Arrests of UNFP; Ben Barka flees Morocco
1963, August 21	Birth of Sidi Muhammad, future King Muhammad VI
1963, October 15	"War of the Sands" with Algeria
1963, November 9	Mehdi Ben Barka is condemned to death in absentia
1964, March 14	Trial and death sentence for leaders of UNFP, later commuted
1965, March 22	Casablanca uprising of students and workers
1965, March 29	Hassan II amnesties political prisoners
1965, June 7	Constitution of 1962 suspended, state of emergency declared

1965, October 29	Ben Barka kidnapped in Paris
1967, June 5	Morocco sends troops to aid Arab side in Six-Day War with Israel
1967, June 5–11	Anti-American demonstrations; attacks on Jews in Meknes
1969	Agreement of association with the EEC
1970, July 31	Second Constitution ends the state of emergency
1970, August	Ila al-Amam splits from Communist Party (PCM)
1971, July 10	Attempted coup at Skhirat palace is subdued by Oufkir
1971, July 13	Ten ranking army officers are executed by firing squad
1972, February 12	Trial of soldiers implicated in the Skhirat coup opens in Kénitra
1972, March 1	Third Constitution is promulgated
1972, August 16	Second failed coup, death of Oufkir
1972, November 6	Execution of 11 detainees accused of planning the August coup
1973, January 24	Arabization of the Faculty of Letters, Rabat
1973, March 3	King announces the program of "Moroccanization"
1973, May 10	Founding of the Polisario
1973, October	Arab-Israeli war; price of oil and phosphates soars
1974, May 13	Death of ʿAllal al-Fasi
1974, June	Shaykh Yassine's letter to Hassan II, "Islam or the Deluge"
1974, November 6	The Green March begins
1975, December 18	USFP leader Omar Benjelloun is assassinated
1976, January 27	War with Algeria in the Sahara
1976, May 20	SARD is declared (Sahrawi Arab Democratic Republic)
1977, May	Trial of members of Ila al-Amam
1977, November 26	CDT created (Democratic Confederation of Workers)
1979, January	Tan-Tan is seized by the Polisario
1979, March	Driss Basri becomes Minister of the Interior

1979, June 24	AMDH (Moroccan Association of Human Rights) is created
1980, July	Amnesty of members of USFP jailed since 1973–1974
1981, June 6	Casablanca bread riots
1981, September	Foundation of Shaykh Yassine's al-ʿAdl wa-l-Ihsan
1984, August	Treaty of Oujda, Moroccan-Libyan Union
1984, November 13	Morocco quits the OAU after SARD is admitted
1985, August 19	Visit of Pope John Paul II to Casablanca
1986, July 22	King Hassan II and Israeli PM Shimon Peres meet in Ifrane
1988, May 6	Diplomatic relations with Algeria are resumed
1988, December 10	OMDH (Moroccan Organization of Human Rights) is created
1988–1993	Construction of the Hassan II mosque in Casablanca ($600 m.)
1989, February 17	Creation of the UMA (Maghreb Arab Union)
1990, May 8	CCDH formed (Consultative Committee of Human Rights)
1990, August 2	Persian Gulf War begins
1990, September	*Notre ami le roi* is published in Paris
1991, February 3	Massive pro-Islamist demonstrations in Rabat
1991, August 5	The Charter of Agadir is signed by six Amazigh associations
1991, September 6	Cease-fire in the Saharan war
1991, September 13	Abraham Serfaty is freed and exiled from Morocco
1991, October 23	Liberation of the survivors of Tazmamart prison
1992, August 21	New Constitution is presented for referendum
1993, February 6	Arrest of Police Commissioner Tabit
1993, September 15	Israeli PM Yitzhak Rabin visits Rabat
1994, August	Closing of the border with Algeria after Marrakesh bombing
1995, December 24	"Cleanup" campaign of Minister of the Interior Basri

1996, September 13	Constitutional revision calling for a bi-cameral legislature
1998, March 14	Government of "Alternance" under A. Youssoufi
1999, July 23	Death of Hassan II
1999, July 30	Muhammad VI is enthroned
1999, September 30	Abraham Serfaty returns from exile
1999, November 9	Minister of the Interior Basri is fired
2000, March 1	The Berber Manifesto
2001, October 17	Dahir of Ajdir creating the IRCAM
2002, March 21	Marriage of Muhammad VI and Salma Bennani
2002, September 27	Parliamentary elections, PJD emerges as main opposition party
2003, May 8	Birth of heir-apparent, Prince Hassan
2003, May 16	Casablanca bombings followed by mass arrests
2003, May 31	Banning of satirical *Doumane*, editor Ali Mrabet jailed
2003, December	ERC formed, headed by human rights lawyer Driss Benzekri
2004, January	New Family Code (*Mudawwana*) is enacted into law
2004, February 24	Earthquake in El Hoceima (seven hundred killed, fifteen thousand homeless)
2004, June 15	Free trade agreement with the United States signed
2004, December 15	Public testimony of victims of "years of lead" by ERC begins
2006, January 6	King announces termination of the work of the ERC
2006, December 16	Closing of the magazine *Nichane* for attacking "Islamic values"
2007, March	Suicide attacks on targets in Casablanca
2007, June	Morocco and Polisario hold talks at UN but fail to reach agreement
2007, September 7	Parliamentary elections, only 37 percent of eligible voters take part; Abbas El Fassi (Istiqlal) named Prime Minister

2009, July 30	Celebration of tenth anniversary of Muhammad VI on the throne
2010, August	Tension with Spain over border incidents near Melilla
2011, February 20	Mass rallies for political reform and a new constitution
2011, April 28	Bomb blast in a Marrakesh café kills fifteen, including ten foreigners
2011, July 1	New constitution approved in a referendum, winning 98 percent of the vote
2011, November 25	PJD wins a plurality in parliamentary elections, Abdelilah Benkirane is named Prime Minister

Who Is Who?

Ababou, M'hamed (d. 1971) Head of military academy at Ahermoumou, leader of cadets in abortive Skhirat coup

ʿAbd al-Aziz, Sultan (d. 1943) Reigned 1894–1908, deposed by his brother ʿAbd al-Hafiz

ʿAbd al-Hafiz (d. 1937) Reigned 1908–1912; signed Treaty of Protectorate with France, 1912

ʿAbd al-Qadir al-Jazaʾiri (d. 1883) Hero of resistance to French in Algeria, 1832–1847

ʿAbd al-Rahman, Sultan Reigned 1822–1859; modernizer and reformer

Aherdane, Mahjoubi Berber military chief, leader of 1957 Rif uprising; founder of the *Mouvement populaire* (MP)

Arslan, Shakib (d. 1946) Druze pan-Islamist, visited Morocco in 1930, inspired young nationalists

Azoulay, André Counselor to Hassan II and Muhammad VI on financial, political, and Jewish affairs

Azziman, Omar Legal expert, human rights advocate, Minister of Justice 1997–2002

Balafrej, Ahmed (d. 1990) French-educated leader of Istiqlal, Secretary-General of the party (1944), Prime Minister (1958); served in other top posts before retiring from public life (1977)

Basri, Driss (d. 2007) Minister of the Interior 1979–1999, dreaded symbol of the "Years of Lead," removed by Muhammad VI

Bekkaï, M'barek (d. 1961) Head of the first government of independent Morocco, appointed December 1955

Belarbi, Aïcha Sociologist, diplomat, author, women's rights activist

Ben ʿArafa, Mawlay Muhammad (d. 1976) Puppet ruler imposed by French, 1953–1955

Ben Barka, Mehdi (d. 1965) A founder of UNFP, condemned to death in absentia, "disappeared" in Paris.

Benaïssa, Mohamed Journalist, politico, Ambassador to United States (1993–1999); Minister of Foreign Affairs (1999–2007)

Benjelloun, Omar Trade unionist, head of USFP, assassinated 1975

Benkirane, Abdelilah Head of PJD, appointed Prime Minister in November 2011

Benlyazid, Farida Filmmaker, director of *A Door to the Sky* (1989)

Bennani, Salma Wife of Muhammad VI (2002), known as Princess Lalla Salma; mother of Prince Hassan (b. 2003), heir to the throne

Berrada, Hamid Student leader, journalist, condemned to death in absentia 1963

Bouabid, Aderrahim (d. 1992) Economist, founder and leader of USFP

Bu Himara (El Rogui) Rebel chief and royal pretender in the Taza region, 1902–1909

Chraïbi, Driss (d. 2007) Author, voice of postcolonial generation

Daure-Serfaty, Christine French human rights activist, reported on secret prisons during the "Years of Lead"

Dawud, Muhammad (d. 1984) Historian, nationalist, author of multi-volume *A History of Tetuan*

Dlimi, Ahmed (d. 1983) Security head, Hassan II's right-hand man after death of Oufkir; died in auto crash

al-Fasi, ʿAllal (d. 1974) Founder, chief architect of the Istiqlal party, coauthored Plan of Reforms, favored a constitutional monarchy

al-Fasi, Malika (d. 2007) An author of the 1944 Manifesto of Independence; nationalist; symbol of early political activism for feminist movement

el-Fassi, Abbas President of UGEM (1961); human rights activist; head of Istiqlal (1998); Prime Minister 2007–2011

Ghallab, Abdelkrim Leading author, novelist, political commentator, editor of Istiqlal newspaper *al-ʿAlam*

al-Glawi, Thami (d. 1956) Pasha of Marrakesh, allied with French in colonial period, opposed Muhammad V and then relented, famous for his venality

Guedira, Ahmed Reda (d. 1995) Lawyer, adviser to Hassan II, held many government posts; organized pro-royalist FDIC as alternative to Istiqlal (1963)

al-Hajwi, Muhammad (d. 1956) Religious scholar, reformer, propagandist for Protectorate

Hassan I, Sultan Reformer and consolidator; reigned 1873–1894

Hassan II, King (d. 1999) As Crown Prince, chief of FAR; after enthronement in 1961, wielded near-absolute power

al-Hiba, Ahmad (d. 1919) Son and successor of Ma al-ʿAynayn, led unsuccessful 1912 revolt against French occupation

Hicham b. Abdallah el-Alaoui, Prince Pro-democracy intellectual, cousin of King Muhammad VI, lives in the United States

El-Himma, Fouad Ali Technocrat, close adviser to Muhammad VI, founder of PAM (2008)

Ibn Musa, (Ba) Ahmad (d. 1900) Grand Vizir and Regent for young Sultan ʿAbd al-ʿAziz

Ibrahim, Abdallah (d. 2005) Head of opposition government 1958–1960, a founder of the UNFP

Jamaï, Abubakr Economist, political activist, editor of *Le Journal* (now defunct)

Jettou, Driss Technocrat, Minister of Interior (2001); Prime Minister 2002–2007

al-Kattani, ʿAbd al-Hayy (d. 1962) Scholar, bibliophile, ally of al-Glawi, favored deposition of Muhammad V, disgraced and died in France

al-Kattani, Muhammad b. ʿAbd al-Kabir (d. 1909) Sufi shaykh and political rival of Sultan ʿAbd al-Hafiz, accused of treason and flogged to death

al-Kattani, Muhammad b. al-Jaʿfar (d. 1927) Sufi shaykh, author of *Salwat al-Anfas*, history of the notables of Fez

al-Khattabi,ʿAbd al-Karim (d. 1963) Berber chief, journalist, head of Rifian Republic 1922–1926; hero of anti-colonial resistance

Laâbi, Abdellatif Poet, founder of *Souffles*, political prisoner in the 1970s

Laanigri, Hamidou Security chief abruptly removed from power in 2006

Laroui, Abdallah Public intellectual and nationalist historian

Lyautey, Louis Hubert Gonzalve (d. 1934) French aristocrat, first Résident Général of the Protectorate (1912–1925), preserver of the makhzan, and architect of Moroccan modernity

Lyazidi, Mohamed Ahmed (d. 1990) Chief propagandist of the pre-independence Istiqlal

Ma al-ʿAynayn (d. 1910) Saharan religious scholar, leader of resistance to French occupation before 1912

al-Madghari, Muhammad (d. 1892) Chief of Darqawa brotherhood, called for jihad against French in the 1880s

el-Malki, Habib Economist, minister, member of USFP

al-Manabhi, al-Mahdi (d. 1937) Minister of War under ʿAbd al-ʿAziz, exiled to Tangier after 1912

el-Mandjra, Mahdi U.S.-trained economist, diplomat, human rights advocate

Medbouh, Gen. Mohamed (d. 1971) Chief of Royal Household, killed after failed Skhirat coup

Moutiʿ, ʿAbd al-Karim Founder of Islamic radical group al-Shabiba al-Islamiyya in 1969; in 1975, accused of killing labor leader Omar Benjelloun

Muhammad V, Sultan and King Reigned 1956–1961; revered as liberator of Morocco from colonial rule

Muhammad VI, King Current ruling monarch, son and successor to Hassan II, enthroned July 1999

al-Muqri, Muhammad (d. 1957) Makhzan official

al-Nasiri, al-Makki (d. 1994) Member of CAM, journalist for nationalist press

Noguès, Charles (d. 1971) Résident Général of the French Protectorate in Morocco, 1936–1943; implementer of Vichy-inspired race laws during World War II

al-Ouezzani, Mohammed Hassan (d. 1978) Founder of PDI, rival of ʿAllal al-Fasi

Oufkir, Mohamed (d. 1972) General, Minister of Interior, died in mysterious circumstances after 1972 failed coup

Rachid b. Hassan, Prince brother of King Muhammad VI and second-in-line in succession to the throne

al-Raysuni (Raisuli), Ahmed (d. 1925) Local chieftain and sharif of the Jebala region; mounted campaign of kidnapping Europeans, 1903–1904, that received world attention

Sbihi, Abdellatif (d. 1965) Leader of "Young Moroccans"; organized resistance to the Berber dahir, 1930

Serfaty, Abraham (d. 2010) Mining engineer, founder of Ila al-Amam, jailed during the "Years of Lead"; released in 1991 and exiled; returned home in 2000

Taoufik, Ahmed Historian, novelist, Minister of Islamic Affairs (2002–), architect of a reformed religious establishment

Torres, Abdelkhalek (d. 1970) Nationalist leader in the Spanish zone

Yassine, Abdessalam Royal admonisher, founder in 1987 of al-ʿAdl wa-l-Ihsan pro-Islamist Party

Yata, ʿAli (d. 1997) A founder of the PCM (Communist Party) in 1943 and later its head; in 1974, founded the socialist PPS

Youssoufi, Abderrahmane Founding member of the UNFP; Prime Minister of the government of "Alternance," 1998–2002

Yusuf, Mawlay, Sultan (d. 1927) Reigned 1912–1927; father of Muhammad V

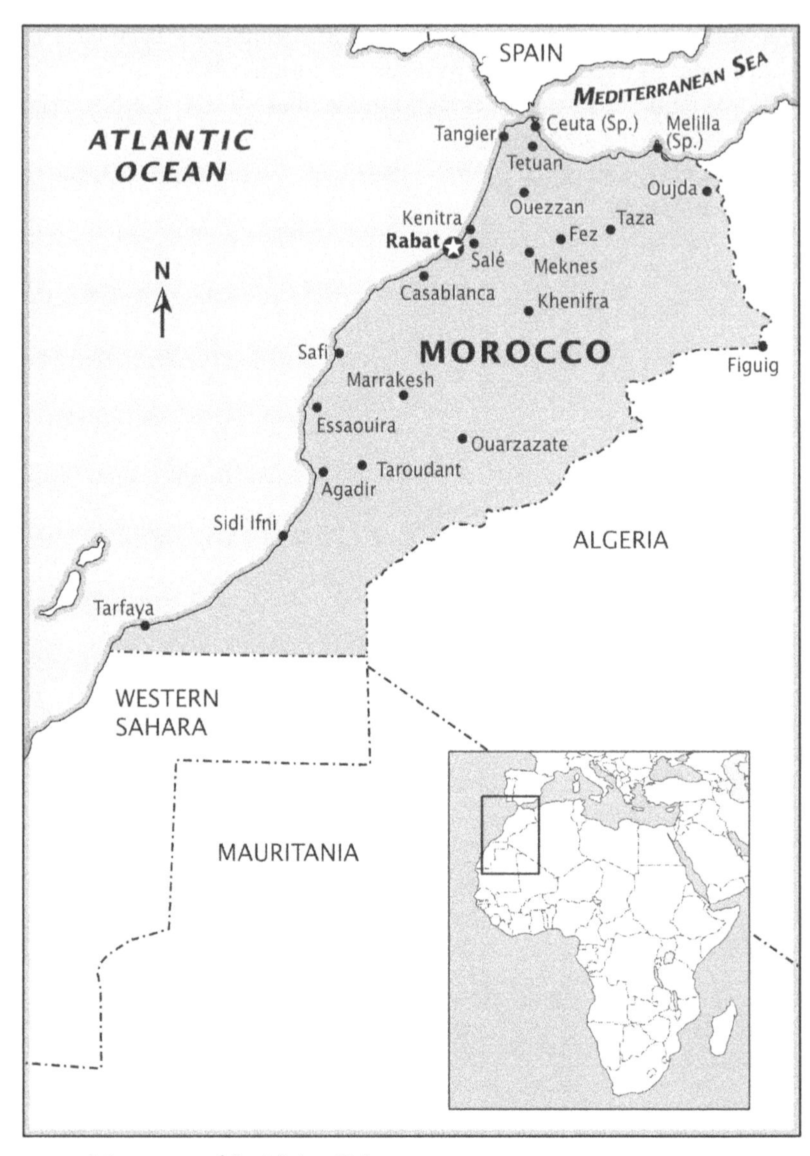

MAP I Morocco and Its Major Cities

Introduction

The present work retells the story of state-societal relations in Morocco over the long expanse of nearly two hundred years, beginning with the French conquest of Algeria in 1830 and ending with the death of King Hassan II in 1999. This history is arranged chronologically and falls into three large tranches: the period 1830–1912, before the coming of the French Protectorate; the period of the Protectorate between 1912 and 1956, when Morocco was a dependency of France; and the post-1956 years, when Morocco became an independent state under a monarchy. Writing across this broad swath of time has necessitated painful choices about what to include and what to leave out. While the desire to be comprehensive is a worthy one, it is in reality a losing cause: the pertinent fact, the delicious quotation, the choice observation, the nutty conclusion, all selected at the discretion of the author, may not always satisfy the reader. The expert will undoubtedly find many inexcusable absences in this book. The sweeping optic has opened the way for integrating the results from many different areas of social science research that might otherwise not have found a shared home.

This narrative presents a "writing against" earlier histories of modern Morocco, whether they are in French, English or Arabic. It is inspired by recent and profound changes within the field of Moroccan historiography, in turn influenced by the political opening of the 1990s that motivated Moroccan intellectuals to "liberate" their own history from the strictures of an earlier period. Furthermore, the exposure of the crimes of the "years of lead" via testimony given to the Instance Equité et Reconciliation (the ERC, or Commission of Equity and Reconciliation) in the first years of the twenty-first century has not only seized the public mind, but also forced people to confront a past they might have preferred to forget. Suddenly the historical profession in Morocco has become a vortex of ideas about what constitutes "authentic" history, and who is responsible for writing it. The personal histories and memories of ordinary people that welled up in the context of the ERC are valuable historical sources of the first order, filling in yawning gaps in the official record. But they are also controversial, and have set in motion a heated debate within Moroccan society about how and to what extent memory (in the absence of more conventional sources of documentation) ought to be mobilized for producing history. As a further consequence of the revelations of the "years of lead," the need to write contemporary history, or *l'histoire du temps present*, has been foregrounded as a major concern of Moroccan historians who have finally acknowledged that the recent past – and especially the period since 1956 – is practically a blank slate. Moreover, when considering the existing corpus, it becomes clear that earlier historical production – both native and foreign – is badly in need of revision, augmentation, and reinterpretation.

What are some of the problems that have bedeviled the writing of recent Moroccan history? What are the presuppositions that have informed it? What are the blockages that inhibit the production of a viable contemporary history? Silences that are politically motivated, myths about the sanctity of the nationalist cause, the inviolability of the monarchy, the state monopoly over representations of authenticity, the violence of state-societal relations, the occultation of sources, fears of retribution, all have played a role in shaping the contours of contemporary historical discourse. The identification of those blockages and the effort to overcome them is the endeavor that inspired this book. An overriding difficulty stems from the fact that the long middle period of the present account, the Protectorate years, have been a source of contention, included within the grand narrative of Moroccan history only on the condition that they be recognized as a time of deviation, a kind of historical "mistake." This point of view is primarily a product of the immediate postindependence years when the fervor to write a "national" history cut loose from the weight of colonialist thinking was a driving force, but it has inexplicably endured beyond its time. Various intellectual positions have converged around the idea that the Protectorate was an aberration not especially worthy of study; in fact, for many years, it was shunned by Moroccan researchers (with one or two exceptions) as a contaminated subject to be placed in isolation. The enormous impact of the Protectorate years organizationally, administratively, culturally, and politically on the postcolonial state has been minimized, or even denied. Moreover, the deep connecting currents between the precolonial and the colonial periods have also been obscured, which is ironic, given the fact that many of the outstanding Moroccan political personalities of the interwar period were born and schooled in the nineteenth century and their intellectual formation was decidedly of that era. As a consequence, the continuities that tie one stage of modern historical development to the next have not come together, making for a fragmented and disjunctive history rather than a cohesive, nuanced, and contextualized one. This blockage is not only a methodological error but also a conceptual one, preventing us from seeing modern Moroccan history as an unfolding, variegated, often discontinuous and textured canvas, yet all of one piece. Our critique does not constitute an argument in favor of teleology, for the errors of that approach are amply clear; rather, it is a plea for recognizing the ill effects of a discourse of total rupture, the reasons why it came about, and why it should be overcome.

A second blockage we have encountered relates to the practice of imagining the monarchy as the main symbol and arbiter of Moroccan "authenticity." In this scenario, the Protectorate period is seen as a wasteland from which the Moroccan people emerged unscathed because of the mantle of protection thrown over them through their mystical identification with a spiritualized monarchy. This position asserts that despite its immense intrusion into every aspect of Moroccan life, colonization had little effect on Moroccans, who came out of the experience with their "pure and essential" qualities intact. The danger here is manifold. First of all, when Moroccan history is subsumed under monarchical history, other institutions in society are deprived of their agency; tribal loyalties, religious loyalties, bonds to work, to neighborhood, to other social organizations, become subsumed under the monarchical principle, where they are submerged and eventually forgotten. Moreover, the hybridity that was a by-product of the colonial experience is lost. Many of the examples we give in this account of the interpenetration of two worlds that colonialism brought about – in social customs, laws, politics, in intellectual life – are invalidated by adopting such a narrow perspective. Also filtered out are the luxuriant varietals produced by the colonial experience – social deviants, border-crossers, and experimenters of all types who enliven historical studies. Alternatively, denying the importance of the exportation of Moroccan influences abroad that were unmediated by the royal center – through expositions, world fairs, architecture, migration, and other forms of diasporic activity – is the other side of this constricting narrative. Seeing Moroccan history solely through the prism of monarchical history is a distorting practice that begs to be superceded.

A third blockage concerns the nationalist movement and the tight grip the political parties have held on recent Moroccan historiography. There are many reasons for this: the hegemony of the nationalist parties over the daily press, the myth of an all-encompassing national "unity," the concept of nationalists as "heroes of the revolution." Nationalist leaders, especially those on the left, have been enveloped in a cloud of hagiography that is difficult to penetrate, and the closer one gets to the relationship between Muhammad V and the nationalists, the thicker is the wrap. Myths surrounding the history of the nationalist movement are deeply embedded in the popular imagination: for example, the misleading idea that Fez dominated the nationalist movement in the 1930s and 1940s dies hard, as does the contention that the nationalists made no headway in rural areas, or that its leadership was of a single mind. Studying the regional basis of nationalist organizations, the role of women in the resistance, the relations between nationalists and communists, between nationalism and Berber ethnicity, and other pertinent topics would help us understand the incessant infighting, personality clashes and violence engendered by the nationalists among themselves and later, in the late 1950s, between the liberation armies and the state's forces of order. These topics are only now emerging from the halo of mythologizing that surrounds the nationalist movement allowing them to be explored in greater depth.

The question of violence that is a subtheme of the nationalist endeavor must also be examined more carefully. The tendency toward violence in the Moroccan state is not necessarily explained by the struggles that accompanied its birth; rather, violence in itself calls for explanation, particularly in light of the connection between the war of liberation, the growth of a security apparatus in the independent state, and the eventual emergence of all-powerful police and intelligence services in Hassan II's makhzan. The history of institutions of violence, like any other history, is best understood through an analysis of the events that surrounded their formation, and by placing less emphasis on ideologies of domination, or on suspected character flaws in the Moroccan "personality," or on culturally learned behaviors, and more emphasis on the specific circumstances, fears, and assumptions of decision makers as they went about the business of state-building.

Furthermore, I have tried to bring an international dimension to this story and to situate it within the setting of regional and global events, in the belief that we cannot understand the context in which everyday decisions are made without a sense of the surrounding political landscape. This history is not informed by theories of globalization or by Marxist dialectics, but it does implicate a dimension of Moroccan history that is often forgotten; namely, Morocco's relations with the outside world as a reflection of its domestic concerns. In the nineteenth century, global powers with their thirst for colonies determined Morocco's fate. In the 1930s, the global economic crisis impacted heavily on colonial ambitions as well as native expectations. In the immediate postwar period, the perturbations in French politics, and the growing ties between Moroccan nationalists and their European, Asian, and American friends, formed the matrix for the coalition-building that helped bring about independence. In the age of Hassan II, the monarch's vision of Morocco's place in the world, his quest for international support through subtle diplomacy that relied mainly, but not exclusively, on the West, his courting of African allies, his role in the Middle East peace process, make explicit the importance of overseas efforts in managing internal affairs. In order to understand the success of the movement for liberalization in Morocco of the 1990s, one must make note of the external actors who effectively publicized the makhzan's hidden human rights abuses to the world, forcing their recognition at home. If Morocco had lived in a closed bubble, its standing in the world today – surely not arrived at by dint of its wealth – would never have come about.

The question of sources is of perennial concern to the historian. The argument has been made often that certain periods in Moroccan history are difficult, if not impossible, to study because of an absence of written sources. While it was true for a very long time that the sources for studying the Protectorate period were not accessible, that has not been the case for nearly a decade. For some time now, excellent monographs have been produced based on the colonial archives in Rabat and Nantes. For the precolonial period, that is to say, the nineteenth century, the Moroccan and European sources are voluminous and hardly exploited. For many years, the Moroccan state archives were the atelier of the very few, selected either for their innocuous politics or their poor command of Arabic; today, they are generally open to everyone. Official documentary sources for the period of Hassan II are not, however, available, and for this most recent period scholars must resort to often inaccurate newspaper accounts, the memories of participants, and the foreign press; as a result, the writing of the history of the *temps présent* is a particularly challenging venture. The controversy surrounding the historical value of personal memory raised by the testimonies to the ERC is indicative of the problematic nature of this sort of material and the passions raised by it. It is a widely accepted fact that while memory can be misleading, it can also be treated as any other historical source by using methods of comparison, fact-checking, and common sense.

Finally, it should be noted that this study is a synthetic history covering a long stretch of time, and archival sources figure into it mainly through the use of monographs, articles, dissertations, and other studies that rely on original documents. Arabic chronicles form the substance of the early chapters of the book; specialized books and articles by both Moroccan and non-Moroccan researchers are the foundation on which the later chapters are built. This variety of material in several languages and from various disciplines brought together for the first time in one volume will hopefully increase our appreciation for the complexities of the recent Moroccan past, and offer the curious reader a refreshing lesson in history.

1

The Closing of the Era of Jihad (1830–1860)

In 1830, Morocco found itself under attack by an assertive and expansive Europe, in the shape of France's massive and well-planned attack on the city of Algiers. With this event, Morocco was ineluctably drawn into an economic and political maelstrom that would absorb its energies and color its outlook for years to come. Europe for Morocco was a familiar adversary. Morocco had lived in Europe's shadow for centuries, sometimes amicably, at other times in a state of violent confrontation. Their histories were intertwined due to proximity and political necessity. Traders from Marseilles set up a *funduq* (merchants' inn) in Ceuta in 1236; in the fifteenth century Jews banished from Iberia after centuries of settlement found a safe haven in Fez; and in the seventeenth century, Moriscos – Muslims who had adopted Catholicism but were forced to leave Spain by the Inquisition – transformed Morocco's maritime economy into a corsairing one, returning the confrontation with the Christian West to Europe's shores. From the mid-eighteenth century onward, Europe's slow and steady march toward what historians call "modernity," meaning greater degrees of state integration, capitalist development, and technological progress, inevitably shaped its attitudes and actions toward Morocco. Meanwhile, Morocco responded by adopting ploys and stratagems that it hoped would mitigate foreign influence and allow it to preserve its independence.[1]

The year 1830 marks the beginning of a transition to a new phase in which Europe is no longer an intermittent factor in Moroccan affairs, but an omnipresent reality looming over political events, the economy, and even social life. Yet, at the same time, the European factor was not all-determining; other salient features of Morocco's interior landscape continued to evolve, change and confront one another, testing the capacity of the state to meet challenges at home and abroad. Factors that moved quite independently of the European encounter remained in play, such as the struggle for quotidian existence against the forces of nature, changes in intellectual life, the tension between the sultanate and the ruling classes, and the arrival of new ideas from the Muslim East that swept over society. These themes constitute the backdrop to the drama of Morocco's tumultuous confrontation with the West in the early nineteenth century. In order to fully understand the events of 1830 in their fullest context, we must first reach back into the eighteenth century to uncover some of those factors that determined how Morocco composed its response to European aggression.

REBUILDING THE MOROCCAN STATE

Unending civil war following the death of Sultan Isma'il in 1727 led to a dispersal of state power, a damaged reputation for the ruling 'Alawi dynasty, and a devastated economy. Sultan 'Abdallah (intermittently reigned 1729–1757), son of the great state builder Isma'il, suffered the ignominy of being deposed five times during his thirty year reign; these convulsions were a harsh lesson for his own son and successor, Muhammad III (reigned 1757–1790), who was convinced that in order to preserve the dynasty, a new approach to statecraft was required.[2] Chronic problems produced unending troubles: a fractious, tribal-based countryside that required constant policing; a subsistence economy plagued by inadequate reserves of capital; a lack of infrastructure in the form of roads, bridges and other methods of communication. The population in the last quarter of the eighteenth century hovered between four and five million, kept stagnant by periodic waves of disease, drought, and famine.[3] Other endemic problems blocked the path to the consolidation of state power, creating a permanent deficit of capacity at the center: the army was ill-organized, poorly disciplined, and made up of a rebellious praetorian guard and unreliable tribal contingents, the bureaucracy was undisciplined and corrupt, and the religious classes, or ulama, were notoriously independent. Finally, the navy had been disbanded, leaving Morocco's coastline denuded of protection.

Grandson of the illustrious Isma'il, Muhammad III realized that in order to bring greater stability to his rule, he had to rebuild the state from its foundations. He carried on a lively correspondence with the Ottoman court and exchanged emissaries with them. His most trusted envoy was the historian ʿAbd al-Qasim al-Zayani, who brought home from Istanbul first-hand news about the Ottoman way of doing things – their order, rationality, and organizational strength.[4] Following the Ottoman example, Sultan Muhammad III first revamped the state bureaucracy, extending it to the local level; then he reorganized the army, making it more responsive to his command. Finally, he revised the financial basis of the state with new methods of tax-collection that depended on customs duties derived from overseas trade. These bold reforms distinguish Sultan Muhammad III as the initiator of a new age in Moroccan history, influenced by intimations of modernity filtered through practices arriving in Morocco mainly from the East. The scope of the Sultan Muhammad III's ambition was so wide that Moroccan historian Abdallah Laroui has called him "the architect of modern Morocco."[5]

In order to carry out this ambitious program of reform, the sultan had to find a balance among interests that competed with and sometimes counteracted one another. On the political front, he had to give up the idea of recovering the Spanish-held territories of Melilla and Ceuta, enclaves on Morocco's Mediterranean coast held by Spain since the fifteenth century, knowing full well that such a move would expose him to the complaint from religious quarters that he was abandoning the jihad. But he had resolved that peaceful commerce with Europe was a far wiser course than engaging in fruitless warfare: "Ceuta is the heart of Morocco," he avowed, "but only a crazy man or a fool would consider attacking it ... nothing will come of it except the disgrace of Islam."[6] On the economic front, he rebuilt the Atlantic ports, most notably, the town of Essaouira (al-Sawira) on Morocco's Atlantic coast, for the purpose of promoting overseas trade.[7] He created monopolies over goods for export and levied heavy duties on imports that dramatically increased the revenues of the state, but in so doing, raised the ire of foreign merchants. He filled his treasury by imposing a new, non-Qur'anic tax (the *maks*) that was widely condemned by both the ulama and ordinary folk, not only because its legality was in doubt, but also because the hand of the state now reached into the substance of daily life. People had to pay taxes when making the ferry crossing between Rabat and Salé; when they butchered a sheep; or when they used the public scales in the marketplace. Finally, in order to mitigate the corrosive effect of these unpopular measures, he refurbished mosques and *zawiyas* (religious lodges) throughout the land, hoping to win over the affection of the "men of the pen" as well as the hearts of the common people.[8]

The campaign for reform embraced even the most sacrosanct elements in society. Muhammad III intervened "where no sultan had ventured before," organizing the ulama into classes, depending on their responsibilities, and paying them accordingly. He personally revised the teaching curriculum in the mosques, prescribing the works to be studied, giving emphasis to simplified texts that demystified legal practice. He seized his prerogative as chief *imam* (religious leader) of the Moroccan Muslim community to reinterpret existing laws and make new ones by issuing *fatwas* (legal opinions) and *dahirs* (official decrees) that buttressed his policies. Finally, he established lists of the religious nobility (*shurafa*), purging those who made false claims of kinship with the family of the Prophet in order to reap the benefits of tax exemption.

These sensible changes shook Moroccan society to its roots, and the reaction was not long in coming. In the vanguard of the opposition was his own son, Yazid, who became his father's archenemy. Building his credibility mainly on the basis of his father's "neglect" of the jihad, Yazid was joined by disgruntled others who had lost ground through Sultan Muhammad's reforms: religious elites stripped of their special privileges, brotherhoods that found their income reduced, and ordinary people who deplored the *maks* as a contravention of religious law. For two years after the death of Muhammad III in 1790, the country was thrown into turmoil, as Yazid raged from north to south, trying to undo the innovations instituted by his father.

When Sultan Sulayman, a second son of Muhammad III, acceded to the throne in 1793, the populace was in a black mood; they looked to him for relief from the excesses of Yazid, but were disappointed. Early on, Sultan Sulayman showed personality traits that impaired his ability to rule. His contemporaries remarked that he was obstinate and a poor judge of people, he paid no heed to the advice of his ministers, and he even forbade his scribes from correcting the grammar of his letters.[9] This unbending personality was thrust into power at a delicate moment, when fears of a clash with the West were growing. News of the French invasion of Egypt in 1798 reached Morocco, along with reports of French soldiers looting, killing, and abusing Egyptian women.[10] The pilgrimage to Mecca was momentarily suspended, and Moroccans felt cut off from the rest of the Islamic world. The crux of the problem, it was widely believed, was that foreigners were causing the grief and placing the *umma* (the nation) at great risk.

Sultan Sulayman responded by putting Europe at arm's length. First, he reversed the policy of Muhammad III of making overseas trade the bedrock of state finances. Commercial ties with Europe dried up and foreign businessmen were encouraged to leave: "All [foreigners] are welcome to leave the country," he said, "as one of my Jews can import whatever commission I order."[11] Then, armed with fatwas from the ulama, he forbade his countrymen from traveling to Europe on the grounds that it was contrary to the Holy Law. Finally, he dropped all pretence of continuing the jihad by sea; in 1820 he delivered the last two ships of the Moroccan navy to the Dey of Algiers. His response to the perceived threat from Europe was to close the doors and seek shelter until the storm had passed.

At he same time, he tried to put his own house in order, but with a misguided zeal that soon destroyed his relations with key elements in society. Early in his reign he abrogated the hated maks, thus lifting the heavy burden that fell especially hard on urban households. Believing that the surest source of wealth was hidden in the mountains and valleys of his own country, he turned to the Moroccan heartland, milking the tribes through the traditional Qur'anic taxes of *zakat* and *'ushr*, and extending his control into areas once thought beyond the reach of the state. This policy worked for a time, but after 1817, a series of natural disasters destroyed crops and upset the basis of his fiscal plan. Yet Sulayman stubbornly continued to tax the rural areas heavily, turning the last phase of his rule into one of chronic strife and rebellion.

In no area did his obstinate personality show itself more clearly than in the sphere of religion. A spiritual revival led by followers of Wahhabism was sweeping the Maghrib, and Morocco was caught in its wake. Founded at the end of the eighteenth century in the Arabian Peninsula, Wahhabi doctrine preached a purity and asceticism that appealed especially to the intellectual classes. The sultan became an adept of this new creed. Sulayman's deep piety, now fortified by Wahhabi fervor, produced in him a bitter contempt for the popular Islam practiced by his people – their worship of saints and their extreme reverence for the Prophet's family. He used his authority to attack these practices, condemning the use of music and dance in religious ceremonies, and banning pilgrimages to saintly shrines and religious festivals that were the economic lifeblood of the religious orders. He even had the *qubba* (dome) over his father's tomb removed, arguing that it was excessive ornamentation. The relentless campaign to suppress what he considered heterodox practices placed him in fierce contention with primary social groups – the nobility, the brotherhoods, and even the ulama – who were ordinarily allies of the sultanate.

Even as the chasm between the sultan and society widened, Sulayman blindly plunged ahead. In 1819, in the midst of a raging epidemic of the plague, he marched into the Middle Atlas at the head of a hastily assembled Berber force to collect taxes and was shocked when his troops melted away and rejoined their mountain kin. Stripped of his royal guard, the sultan was seized and held prisoner by the Ait Umalu tribe for three days before being released. Although treated with respect – the royal tent was torn into squares that were distributed among his captors as religious talismans – Sulayman never recovered from this painful humiliation.[12] Nearing the end of his reign, he faced a general uprising that began in Fez but soon engulfed the entire country. A self-imposed abdication and a mortifying defeat at the hands of the petty shaykhs of the Chérarda zawiya in the region of Marrakesh reduced his dwindling prestige to the vanishing point.

Sultan Sulayman's policies – the attack on the brotherhoods, the effort to limit the special privileges of the shurafa, the self-righteous Puritanism – had brought the state and the sultanate to a nadir of prestige and authority. The reversal of his father's efforts to set the country on an even keel had been nullified, setting back the clock on reform for a generation. A near-total dependency on local taxes had proven to be ill conceived, for the sources of internal wealth were unreliable and governed by forces beyond his control. Mounting a jihad to distract attention from the severe problems at home was also a futile endeavor, for the army was weak and the prospects of military success were dim. Thrown back on his meager assets, Sulayman found himself hemmed in on all sides; deaf to the sounds of popular protest, having sullied the image of the sultanate, Sulayman lacked the political skills to balance the competing elements that composed the body politic. His contestation with society – for indeed, he seemed to have declared war on the Moroccan people – severely weakened the state, just as it faced the challenge of a new and unprecedented foreign threat, this time very close to home.

THE FALL OF ALGIERS AND THE PEOPLE OF TLEMCEN

The French landing at Sidi Ferouch near Algiers on July 5, 1830, caused panic in Morocco. The Moroccan reaction was immediate because the frontier between the two states had always been a fluid one, with people and goods moving in both directions, particularly along the trade corridor between Fez and Oran that passed through Tlemcen. Cross-border religious ties were also strong, with Moroccan-based brotherhoods such as the Wazzaniyya and Darqawiyya maintaining important lodges in Western Algeria that provided a steady flow of income. In fact, precise sovereignty over this corner of Algeria was not at all clear, from the Moroccan point of view, because the ties between it and the sultanate were so strong. Moreover, the ruling class in Algiers was not especially beloved in the western provinces. In the years preceding the French landing, in order to replace revenue lost through the demise of piracy, the Deys (the Ottoman-appointed heads of the Regency of Algiers) had raised taxes, turning the native population against them. The problem of mixed loyalties became even more acute after the French landing. As French forces pushed deeper into the interior, the tribes and city dwellers of the province of Oran turned to Morocco for help.[13]

Suddenly, the new Moroccan sultan, ʿAbd al-Rahman (reigned 1822–1859), nephew and successor to the discredited Sulayman, saw an opportunity to restore the badly tarnished image of the sultanate by converting long-standing ties with Oran into much-needed political currency. He advanced cautiously, unwilling to offend the Ottomans or to provoke the French, even as he strategized about how to profit from the unexpected turn of events. Carving out a role as "protector of the Muslims" of western Algeria, in the summer of 1830 he accepted boatloads of Algerian refugees arriving in the ports of Tangier and Tetuan, ordering his governors to find them housing and settle them into new work. The Algerians, many of them highly skilled and well educated, were progressively integrated into Moroccan society.[14] Slowly and deliberately, Sultan ʿAbd al-Rahman began rebuilding his credibility as an alternative to the Turks throughout western Algeria.

Meanwhile, Western Algeria was in an uproar, and the city of Tlemcen was torn apart by infighting between the remnants of the Turkish military, the local religious leaders, and the tribal-backed nobility. When the people of Tlemcen offered ʿAbd al-Rahman the *bayʿa*, the oath of allegience that would legally establish ʿAlawi rule over their region, it was a tempting invitation. It offered ʿAbd al-Rahman the chance to extend his authority eastward to fill the vacuum left by the retreating Turks. Hesitant to give a hasty answer, and fearful of offending the mighty Ottomans, the sultan temporized and consulted the ulama of Fez for their opinion. The response of the ulama was mixed, some in favor, but others warning against an Algerian adventure on the grounds that Tlemcen was still under Turkish rule. Meanwhile, the notables of the beleaguered city kept pressing for a Moroccan intervention, reminding ʿAbd al-Rahman that the defense of Islam was the duty of the just ruler.[15]

Once again, a Moroccan sultan found himself in a dilemma at the center of which was the question of jihad. In October 1830, ʿAbd al-Rahman decided to seize upon the war option, and sent quantities of matériel to Tlemcen, along with a mobile column (*mahalla*) of five thousand cavalry and footsoldiers. Once on the scene, the Moroccans discovered that the Turkish remnants of the old regime were still in a fighting mood and had barricaded themselves in the town citadel, refusing to withdraw. In March 1831, frustrated by the stalemate, the undisciplined Moroccan soldiers rampaged through the streets of Tlemcen, looting and fighting among themselves.[16] The sultan was forced to order a retreat, exposing his scheme to use the Algerian crisis as a platform for his own political fortunes as a complete failure. Meanwhile, popular feeling in Morocco had been aroused; now ʿAbd al-Rahman was caught in the middle of the perennial problem of balancing people's enthusiasm for holy war against his own sense of impotence.

MOROCCO AND ʿABD AL-QADIR'S RESISTANCE

With the Moroccans in retreat, the field was left open to the Amir ʿAbd al-Qadir, an Algerian marabout (*murabit*) of the Qadiriyya brotherhood with a flair for military leadership and strong backing from the neighboring tribes. ʿAbd al-Qadir b. Muhyi al-Din al-Khattabi (1807–1883) was by all accounts an extraordinary figure. His father was a scholar of repute and head of the Qadiriyya brotherhood in Western Algeria; the son ʿAbd al-Qadir was a Sufi scholar and a follower of the teachings of the famous mystic Ahmad b. Idris. Reportedly, ʿAbd al-Qadir could recite the entire Qur'an by heart by the age of fourteen.[17] The Moroccan historian al-Nasiri described him as "not the oldest, nor the wisest, nor the most virtuous, but he was decisive and courageous."[18] He showed exceptional physical grace, and was an accomplished horseman and swordsman, fearless in close combat. In 1825, while still in his teens, he accompanied his father on the *hajj*, the pilgrimage to Mecca, stopping in Alexandria and Cairo, visiting the Holy Cities, and proceeding from there to Damascus and Baghdad, where he prayed at the shrine of ʿAbd al-Qadir al-Jilani, patron saint of the Qadiriyya order. Deeply affected by this experience, he returned home in 1828 intending to devote the rest of his life to study and prayer.

But the contemplative life was not to be his. As son of the most powerful saintly family among the Arab tribes of Western Algeria, when the French expanded their foothold into the interior, ʿAbd al-Qadir arose as the natural leader of the resistance. Anointing himself with the mantle of a *mujahid*, or holy warrior, he took charge of the struggle, after having received the bay'a from the local chiefs. It is said that when the young mujahid accepted their offer, the tribal leaders "sprang to their feet, shook their spears, clashed their swords, wept aloud, and with frantic cries yelled out, Jihad! Jihad!!"[19] 'Abd al-Qadir was careful, however, not to appear to challenge 'Abd al-Rahman's own claims of suzerainty, and made it known that he was acting merely as the Moroccan sultan's *khalifa*, or deputy. Still in theory a vassal of the Moroccan sultan, 'Abd al-Qadir continued to treat 'Abd al-Rahman with deference; but in fact, from that moment onward, he decided to become master in his own house.

The Amir's motives in launching a holy war were far more nuanced than a simple desire to drive out the French. While waving the banner of jihad, he also decided to collect regular taxes, appoint officials loyal to himself, check lawlessness, and assert an unaccustomed discipline over the loosely federated tribes of western Algeria. In other words, he intended to adopt the trappings of a state-in-the-making. At the same time, he adopted a policy toward France that was flexible and realistic, moving deftly between modes of attack and retreat, aggressiveness and rapprochement. French soldiers had to be supplied from local sources in order to survive, and 'Abd al-Qadir quickly took advantage of that weakness. When he was not fighting the French, he was busy making large profits by trading with them. Yet he remained mindful of his own needs. The Treaty of 1832 called a temporary halt to the fighting and allowed him to import arms from abroad and to hire French drill instructors for his own fledgling army.[20]

At this moment in the long Algerian war, known as "the period of incertitude," France became ambivalent about its future role in Algeria. On the one hand, it was desirous of exploiting such a rich and potentially fertile territory; but, on the other hand, government officials in Paris shrank before the costs, both human and material, that possession would entail. In the breach, France adopted a nebulous policy of "limited occupation."[21] When the truce between the Amir and France was broken in 1835, Prime Minister Adolphe Thiers expressed the general doubt: "It is not occupation on a large scale," he declared, "it is not occupation on a small scale. It is not peace; it is not war. It is war badly made."[22]

THE REVOLT OF THE WADAYA

Meanwhile, Sultan 'Abd al-Rahman faced a humbling situation at home after his abortive Algerian adventure. The withdrawal from Tlemcen sharply diminished his popularity and in no time at all, dissidents rose up in the countryside, using his humbling defeat as a pretext for contesting his rule. At the heart of the opposition was the Sultan's own elite guard, the Wadaya. Created in the seventeenth century by Sultan Isma'il, the mounted Wadaya cavalry, along with the infantry corps known as the 'Abid al-Bukhari, formed the nucleus of Morocco's permanent standing army (*jaysh*, or in the dialect, *gish*). A longstanding rivalry separated the two groups; the Wadaya, garrisoned at Fez, was composed of freemen, while the 'Abid, headquartered in Meknes, were recruited largely from slaves coming from sub-Saharan regions. But far more important than their legal status at birth, or their skin color, was the oath of loyalty they took, and their "common destiny as servants of the makhzan."[23] Over the years, both units had taken on the aspect of tightly bound kinship groups, jealous of their privileges and maintaining a self-interested solidarity that often deflected even the will of the sovereign. They were given housing and land, a more or less regular salary, and a ration of food for their families, making a military appointment a privileged one in an economy of scarcity. Beyond these two standing units, the army was filled out by contingents recruited as needed from tribes friendly to the makhzan, who were not paid, but received exemption from taxes in return for their service.

Under Sultan Sulayman the army became increasingly unruly and defied efforts at reform. In 1816, the Wadaya refused to relocate from Fez to Meknes, where they could be more closely watched; in 1818, a plague decimated their ranks, bringing the army to the verge of collapse. Their low morale was reflected on the battlefield where they formed "a disordered multitude and reckless horde lacking order [and] discipline," according to one observer.[24] Even before the Algerian misadventure, during which the Wadaya were implicated in the looting of Tlemcen, their reputation was clouded; after Tlemcen, their disgrace was complete.

The Algerian debacle was the spark for an open rebellion that broke out among the Wadaya in the summer of 1831, after Sultan 'Abd al-Rahman demanded that they return their stolen booty. The revolt began in the north and spread throughout the country, escalating into a crisis that threatened the foundations of the regime. When the sultan got wind of the uprising, he tried to flee Fez for the safety of Meknes, where he felt better protected by the 'Abid infantry, but he was stopped on the road and forced to return to Fez by rebellious troops. The anger of the Wadaya was not directed at 'Abd al-Rahman alone, however, but also toward his chief minister and the paymaster of the army who skimmed from their wages. 'Abd al-Rahman dismissed his chief minister, denuded him of his wealth, and used it to compensate the Wadaya with a generous bribe. But none of these actions ended their insubordination; the tissue of mutual loyalty and respect that had bound the Wadaya and the sultanate together since the time of Sultan Isma'il was now badly frayed. Confined as a prisoner in the palace, Sultan 'Abd al-Rahman reached a low point in his reign.

In the months that followed, the sultan managed to escape from Fez and resettle in Meknes, from where he slowly rebuilt the army by adding new recruits from among the tribes of the Middle Atlas and the Rif. Surrounded by this restored force, he marched on Fez, and after a forty-day siege, compelled the Wadaya to surrender. Acting swiftly and decisively, the sultan ordered their two most important leaders to be executed in the most brutal fashion; both were shot, and the cadaver of one was "thrown on a pile of manure where it was eaten by dogs."[25] 'Abd al-Rahman then dispersed the units of the Wadaya to Marrakesh, Larache, and Rabat. By 1834, the revolt of the Wadaya was over, but the extended crisis had exposed the fundamental weaknesses of a military system unchanged for nearly two centuries: incompetent and corrupt officers placated by gifts and rewards; low levels of training and equipment; unruly troops composed of diverse, often rival, units who resisted centralized control; a chronic deficiency of funds. The lesson that Sultan 'Abd al-Rahman carried away from these events was the acute need for far-reaching military and fiscal changes. The breaking of the tyranny of the Wadaya was a small but significant step toward a more encompassing plan for reform that would emerge in the last years of his reign.

THE BATTLE OF ISLY AND THE WAGES OF DEFEAT

The Tlemcen affair did not end Morocco's involvement in Algeria. The Amir 'Abd al-Qadir continued to cultivate his standing among his followers by pursuing the holy war. He called on Moroccan tribesmen of the eastern Rif Mountains to join his resistance, and he entreated the sultan to help him with military supplies. At the outset of the struggle, 'Abd al-Rahman complied, recognizing 'Abd al-Qadir as a "champion of Islam" and maintaining a steady stream of horses, arms, and money flowing to him. But over time, 'Abd al-Qadir began assuming the airs of an independent sovereign, minting his own coins and imposing special taxes in the name of jihad. When the conflict with France resumed in 1839 after a long truce, relations between the two leaders deteriorated rapidly. Vacillating between his duty to defend the borders of Islam on the one hand, and his fear of attracting retribution from the French on the other, Sultan 'Abd al-Rahman decided to distance himself from the Algerian conflict. This led him into difficulties not only with ʿAbd al-Qadir, but also with his own people, who saw his withdrawal as a clear abrogation of his religious responsibilities.

Despite his reluctance, the sultan could not ignore the French presence in Algeria; ineluctably, he was drawn into a direct confrontation with France. In a bid to crush once and for all the Amir's stubborn resistance, the French government, declaring their objective to be one of "total occupation," assigned the task of defeating ʿAbd al-Qadir to the battle-hardened General Thomas Bugeaud. A tough campaigner who had risen through the ranks and had taken part in the Napoleonic wars, Bugeaud was not about to fail in his assignment. The French launched a vicious campaign of scorched earth and "methodical devastation" aimed at breaking the Algerian resistance and bringing the war to a quick conclusion. Angered by the Moroccan sultan's aid to ʿAbd al-Qadir, and by the presence of Moroccan soldiers in the ranks of the Amir's army, Bugeaud ceased to respect the inviolability of the borderlands. Time and time again, he forced the Algerian mujahid and his followers over the border into Morocco. In 1843, the French began building a fort close to the holy shrine of Lalla Maghnia near Oujda, well within Moroccan territory. With the French at the eastern gates of the Empire, ʿAbd al-Rahman felt compelled to mobilize his troops and to declare holy war, bringing popular feeling to a fever pitch. British consul Drummond Hay reported in April 1844, "the whole population of Morocco is in a state of great ferment."[26]

Squirmishes began in May 1844, but it was not until August 14, 1844, that a decisive battle took place near the banks of the Isly river, northeast of Oujda, between French forces and a larger Moroccan army under Sidi Muhammad, son and khalifa of Sultan ʿAbd al-Rahman. Employing ancestral methods of combat, the Moroccan army marched into battle "arrayed in ranks as far as the eye could see." Sidi Muhammad, wearing a bright purple mantle, rode in their midst mounted on a snow white steed, the imperial parasol over his head. When the tide of battle turned against him, an alarmed Sidi Muhammad folded his parasol, donned a less conspicuous robe, and changed his mount, but these stratagems only made matters worse. His troops now failed to distinguish him in the thick of the battle, and thinking he had been killed, lost heart. Despite their vastly superior numbers, the sultan's forces could not hold up against the disciplined and well-armed French. By noon, the battle was over. The Moroccan army fled in panic, some stopping to pillage their own camp and the sultan's treasury, while others escaped to the safety of tribal lands. "It was a huge calamity and a great misfortune, the like of which the

Moroccan state had never previously experienced," pronounced the historian al-Nasiri.[27] Memorialized as the antithesis to the great Moroccan victory over Christians at another river, "The Battle of the Three Kings" at Oued al-Makhazin in the sixteenth century, the defeat at Isly was widely interpreted as an eschatological happening, a sign of Islam's changing fortunes vis-à-vis the rising West.[28]

Meanwhile, on the morning of August 6, 1844, a French fleet under the command of the Prince de Joinville, third son of King Louis Philippe, pounded Tangier from the sea, raining down a torrent of shot "so tremendous, so uninterrupted, so destructive " that after two hours, "the walls of the town looked like lace." Terrified by the onslaught, inhabitants of the town fled to the hinterland or escaped by sea to Cadiz or Gibraltar. The few who remained in the town cowered in their houses like "a flock of sheep being led to slaughter," waiting for the storm to pass.[29] The young prince then ordered the French fleet down the Atlantic coast to Essaouira, where it wrought similar havoc. The rout at Isly and the bombardment of the Moroccan ports was another brutal reminder of the yawning military disparity between Morocco and France. Reluctantly, the sultan signed the Treaty of Tangier (September 10, 1844) that ended hostilities and the treaty of Lalla Maghnia (March 1845), that defined the border between their two territories, knowing full well that by doing so, he was accepting France's permanent presence in Algeria. But ʿAbd al-Rahman had no choice: his army was in shambles, his commanders disheartened, and popular feeling in need of a dose of reality. The stunning defeat wounded national pride and brought closer to home the fear that Islam itself was under threat.

ʿAbd al-Qadir, now an outlaw, crossed the border into Algeria rather than commit himself to a Moroccan internment. Two more years of aimless wandering, punctuated by bitter fighting and unspeakable atrocities, left him worn out and destitute. At the end of 1847, surrounded by his family and a handful of survivors, he surrendered to the French General La Moricière, yielding up his saber in exchange for the promise that he and his family would be permitted to go to Acre or Alexandria. But this promise was never fulfilled; instead, with his small retinue, he was loaded onto a warship headed for France. In January 10, 1848, his party disembarked at Toulon and were taken to the chateau at Pau, the first stage of a long exile that would last until his death in 1883.[30]

Today, in the retelling the story of this first period of colonialism, the figure of ʿAbd al-Qadir stands out more brilliantly than that of ʿAbd al-Rahman, whose reputation became mired in the muddy banks of the river Isly. The Moroccan sultan was dismissed as a leader who failed in

FIGURE 1. The Amir ʿAbd al-Qadir in exile, 1865, a *carte de visite* by the French photographer Eugène Disdéri (1819–1889), who pioneered this genre of portraiture. Among his many decorations is the Grand Cross of the French Legion of Honor, seen hanging from the rosette on his left side, awarded for his help in rescuing Maronite Christians during the 1860 war on Mount Lebanon. (Adoc-photos/Art Resource, NY)

his mission, and no contemporary monument or historical monograph vaunts his name; meanwhile, ʿAbd al-Qadir has become a known as the foremost hero of the Algerian resistance, and in 1966, his remains were returned home to Algeria amidst a display of collective joy. In 1987, an imposing statue of him astride a lunging stallion was erected in a main square in downtown Algiers, replacing the statue of General Bugeaud hastily removed after the Algerian revolution. Apotheosized as a saint, holy warrior, social reformer, and "precursor of a modern, free Algeria," his life and career have been appropriated to signify the forging of the Algerian people into a single independent nation.[31] The mythologized ʿAbd al-Qadir is a far less interesting character than the historical one, whose motives were more complex. In the crisis following the French landing in

1830, he emerged as a star performer, a leader capable of resisting but also yielding, of negotiating and then refusing to negotiate. Even his capitulation was staged with a self-conscious dignity and an awareness of posterity. Diplomacy, cooptation, cruelty, and assassination were all part of his extensive repertoire.

Resistance, as historian Frederick Cooper has pointed out, takes on many forms, contesting, deflecting, and sometimes even engaging with the invader, while colonial authority also assumes multiple aspects, including a confusion of aims and an absence of focus, especially in the initial stages of occupation.[32] ʿAbd al-Qadir and the French were locked in an agonistic bond, each seeking to overcome the other not only on the field of battle, but also in the realm of ideas, reputation, and historical memory. Understanding very well how to exploit the concept of jihad to vanquish his adversaries as well as to mobilize his own camp, ʿAbd al-Qadir managed his meager assets with skill and imagination. At the same time, he challenged the authority of his Moroccan overlord by assuming both the comportment and mystique of the warrior-saint, in stark contrast to ʿAbd al-Rahman's cautious maneuvering and fumbling capitulation. If ʿAbd al-Qadir is a hero of anticolonial resistance today, and if ʿAbd al-Rahman is a forgotten monarch, it is only incidentally because of France. Rather, it is due to the way that historians have measured the success of each in manipulating the symbols of power, and to the peculiar way that memory works.

ENGAGEMENT WITH THE OUTSIDE WORLD

Late in 1845, in the aftermath of the defeat at Isly, the sultan sent the *pasha* (governor) of Tetuan, ʿAbd al-Qadir Ashʿash, as ambassador to Paris to negotiate border issues and to have a first-hand look at the situation of his rivals. The account of this mission, as recorded by his secretary Muhammad al-Saffar, placed in focus the immense disparities between the two societies. Fifty days in Paris opened Moroccan eyes to French achievements in science, business, education, communications, agriculture, war, and the art of living. Going out of their way to astonish and impress, their French hosts rolled out all the tricks and gimmicks of the new era: the telegraph, experiments with electricity, the Diorama, the mechanical printing press. The Moroccans reacted accordingly; aware they were a captive audience at an especially brilliant show, they responded with amazement and unabashed admiration. It was only in the religious sphere that the French were seen as irreparably deficient. "How confident they are," al-Saffar the scribe wrote, "how impressive their state of readiness, how competent they are in matters of state, how firm their laws, how capable in war and successful in vanquishing their enemies – not because of their courage, bravery, or religious zeal, but because of their marvelous organization, their uncanny master over affairs, and their strict adherence to the law."[33]

In a long report that reached the hands of the sultan, al-Saffar prudently but unequivocally reinforced the message of Isly; Morocco had fallen dangerously behind, and the security of the state was in peril. Moreover, educated people like al-Saffar perceived that the challenge from the West was on the ideological as well as material plane, requiring a reappraisal of almost every facet of public life, from rethinking the structure of the economy, to reorganizing the military, to defending Moroccan territoriality, and even to the definition of a specific national identity based in Maliki Islam. While none of these perceptions was entirely new, it was the gravity of the situation, coupled with a firsthand vision of Europe's patent superiority in matters of state-building, and its rapid progress toward that elusive condition known as "modernity," that so frightened the Moroccans. While characterizing the accomplishments of his hosts within the literary framework of *aja'ib*, or "wonders" – the stock-in-trade of the traditional Arabic travel account – al-Saffar understood that he was indeed witnessing something unprecedented. These innovations were not the two-headed dogs or sea monsters of the Arabic travel accounts of old; rather, they were signs of a new age in which Europe's power would be projected onto the rest of the world not only in military and economic affairs, but also in the realm of ideas, methods and ways of doing things that would impinge on every sphere of daily life.

Following the capture of 'Abd al-Qadir in 1847 and the progressive "pacification" of Algeria, the Great Powers turned to less violent and more scalpel-like assertions of power, opening the era of what some historians have labeled the quest for "informal" empire.[34] The period 1848 to 1865 saw pertinent manifestations of a growing competition among Britain, Spain and France for influence in Morocco, as each looked to that country as a fertile ground for realizing its overseas ambitions. The key actors in this scenario were the British, now recognized as the preeminent Mediterranean power after Lord Nelson's spectacular victory at Trafalgar in 1805. Morocco drew British interest for three main reasons: because of its geographical position at the entry to the Mediterranean, gateway to the shortest route to India; for its role in supplying the British garrison at Gibraltar; and for its potential as a trading partner.[35]

In the first quarter of the nineteenth century, spearheaded by the rapidly accelerating industrial revolution, the rise in the doctrine of free trade, and a belief in the efficacy of the "open door," British determination to expand its commercial sphere of influence in Morocco grew noticeably. Britain was also motivated by political objectives; namely, keeping their French rivals, now positioned in Algeria, at a comfortable distance from Morocco's northern coast, and placating the Spanish who were in an increasingly aggressive mood. Understanding the close interaction between economic activity and political influence, Britain's talented representative in Morocco, John H. Drummond Hay (1816–1893), used aggressive diplomacy to convince an enfeebled Sultan ʿAbd al-Rahman that Britain should be Morocco's "protector" against less friendly nations, if he would agree to a new commercial treaty that would substantially increase British economic influence. After many months of haggling, the sultan capitulated and instructed his chief negotiator, Muhammad al-Khatib, to "swallow … the bitter medicine … do the best you can [to come to] terms that do us no harm."[36]

In two Anglo-Moroccan conventions of "friendship, navigation, and commerce" signed in 1856, Drummond Hay was able to convince the sultan to accept conditions that Morocco had long refused: the dramatic decrease in customs duties to ten per cent of value, an end to royal trading monopolies, and the opening of Morocco's doors to a larger volume of overseas trade. Britain also gained special advantages, such as the right to extend legal "protection" to individuals, both native and foreign, who came under its jurisdiction. Known in the Ottoman Empire as "capitulations," treaties of "protection" had been permitted in the past by Moroccan sultans in order to promote trade, but they were usually tightly controlled and limited to foreign merchants who lived in the port towns. The status of "protégé," or protected person, allowed a foreigner involved in a legal matter to have his case heard in his own consular court, rather than in a Moroccan court presided over by a Shariah-trained judge, or *qadi*. After the 1856 treaty, the practice of foreign representatives granting "protection" (*himaya*) grew by leaps and bounds, and protégés now included Moroccan subjects employed by foreign enterprises, with dire consequences for the stature and authority of the makhzan.[37]

Meanwhile, the opening up of trade for Britain proved to be advantageous: in the years 1861–1865, the average annual imports into Britain from Morocco were three times the imports for the years 1852–1854; the average exports during those same years were double the amount for 1852–1854. Britain now commanded the lion's share of Morocco's overseas trade, providing more than three-quarters of Morocco's total imports, and receiving more than two-thirds of its exports.[38] British manufactures flooded the markets; in lieu of handcrafted domestic products, Moroccans purchased all sorts of cheaply made manufactured items, from Manchester cottons to copper teakettles. As a result, rather than stimulating the economy, the "opening up" of Morocco undermined the fragile mechanisms that had kept prices stable, causing rampant inflation.

Now other European states lined up to take advantage of Morocco's all-too-apparent vulnerability. At the front of the queue was Spain, itself in turmoil, riven by infighting between dedicated pro-monarchists, on the one hand, and irate liberals, on the other, who wanted to end a reactionary regime founded on Church wealth. Political life in Spain was ruled by a military oligarchy engaged in an all-out effort to protect its own privileges. Driven by a deep-seated national passion for "African conquest," the ruling junta saw a Moroccan military adventure as a means of maintaining a grip on power while distracting public attention from the ceaseless turmoil at home. A jingoist press aroused popular opinion to a fever pitch, reminding one observer of a "revival of the medieval crusades." In preparation for combat, Spanish investors offered the government loans at zero percent interest and bullfighters donated their prizes to the war effort. In this overheated atmosphere, it is not difficult to understand how Prime Minister O'Donnell, head of the military junta, was able to launch an African campaign that rode a wave of patriotic enthusiasm.[39]

THE WAR OF TETUAN AND ITS BURDENSOME LEGACY

A brief but murderous three-month war between Spain and Morocco centered in the north near Tetuan began in late 1859, during which Moroccan troops again demonstrated their incapacity to confront a better-organized European foe. The war was initiated when Anjera tribesmen from the periphery of the Jebala Mountains raided the Spanish garrison at Ceuta, provoking a thunderous response. Disregarding Britain's plea for a peaceful settlement, the Cortes in Madrid declared war on October 22, 1859, when Spain attacked Moroccan troops camped in the vicinity of Ceuta. After putting up a valiant defense, according to the historian al-Nasiri, the sultan's army was pushed back toward Tetuan, with the Spanish troops "fighting in a line and following a solid order" in close pursuit. On February 3, 1860, the Spanish force paused briefly before the gates of Tetuan. Defensive artillery mounted on the walls of the town remained strangely silent; one Spanish observer called them *arqueológicos*, relics from the seventeenth century that belonged more properly in a museum than in battle. It was toward the end of the Jewish Sabbath, and as the Spanish force paused at the main gate, swarms of enraged Rifian mountaineers entered the town from another direction, headed for the Jewish quarter and intent on pillage. Al-Nasiri describes the ghastly scene that ensued:

> A tumult broke out in the town, ... the hand of the mob stretched out to plunder, and even [normal] people took off the cloak of decency.... People of the Jabal, and the Arabs, and the riffraff began to pillage and steal; they broke down the doors of the houses and the shops ... keeping at it the whole night until the morning ...[40]

Pedro Antonio de Alarcón, a young Spanish soldier-writer who was part of the Spanish force, was equally nauseated by the devastation; he noted that the desolate streets reeked of "perfume ... [for] the soil is full of broken flasks of essence of roses, of aromatic herbs and spices, resulting from the sack of the [shops] and houses ..."[41] Two days later, General O'Donnell entered Tetuan and began to restore order, taking steps that made it appear as if the Spanish stay would be open-ended. Meanwhile, the local Jewish population, Spanish-speaking descendents of fifteenth century refugees from the Inquisition, seized the opportunity to recover their losses by serving the invading army as interpreters and moneychangers, muddying their relations with the Muslim population for years to come. Alarmed by the threat to the status quo that a Spanish occupation posed, Britain reacted quickly, bringing pressure to bear on both the Moroccans and the Spanish to come to an agreement. As the price of withdrawal, Spain demanded a huge indemnity of twenty million *duros*, about $4 million in 1861 U.S. dollars, an amount far greater than the balance of the Moroccan treasury. Eager to see the war brought to a swift close, Britain guaranteed a £500,000 loan funded by private investors to help Morocco meet the Spanish demands. Both the British loan and the amount due directly to Spain were to be repaid from customs revenues; Spanish agents were to be stationed in the ports to supervise the collection of the tariffs, inflating the number of foreign merchants already living there.[42]

The crippling settlement that followed the Tetuan war exhausted the financial reserves of the state, inhibiting its capacity to pay for much-needed reforms and driving the makhzan more deeply into debt.[43] Moreover, with this defeat, the door to Europe swung open even wider. The effects of the financial drain took on various forms in the coming years, including disruptions to the balance of trade, the

FIGURE 2. British Representative Sir John H. Drummond Hay greeted by Sultan Muhammad IV at the palace in Fez, 1868. Mrs. Hay and Miss Hay remain discreetly out of sight in the doorway. (*A Memoir of Sir John Drummond Hay*, London, 1896)

ruination of native crafts, and the undermining of a stable currency. It was a landmark moment; for the first time, Morocco borrowed funds from abroad to meet its debt obligations, signaling a new stage in its dependency on the West. Even more than the Battle of Isly, the Tetuan war was a watershed moment in Morocco's growing entanglement with Europe.

The historian al-Nasiri captured the humiliation of the moment when he said: "The Tetuan war removed the mantle of respect (*hijab al-hayba*) from Morocco, allowing the Christians to run roughshod over it, and the Muslims were broken as never before."[44] Sultan ʿAbd al-Rahman's relationship with British representative Drummond Hay was symptomatic of the new era in Morocco's relations with the West. In turn threatening and cajoling, dispensing largesse and well-meaning advice, Drummond Hay won a position of exceptional authority at the Moroccan court; in his own words, he was astonished at the degree of "blind confidence" the sultan had placed in him.[45] The age of jihad was now definitively over, as

Morocco was transformed into another subaltern state feeding European expansion by offering raw materials, cheap labor, and unprotected markets.[46] By deftly manipulating the twin tools of creating dependency while promoting an atmosphere of good will, Britain had implicated the sultanate into an expanding system of international power and money.

2

Facing the Challenges of Reform (1860–1894)

Sultan ʿAbd al-Rahman died suddenly on the eve off the Tetuan war in 1859, bringing his son Muhammad IV (reigned 1859–1873) to the throne. Commander of the Moroccan troops at the ignominious defeat at Isly while still his father's *khalifa* or deputy, Sultan Muhammad IV was no stranger to crisis, and was said to feel "very strongly his past humiliations." His determination to set a new course for Morocco after the disgraces of Isly and Tetuan led him to firmly embrace a policy of reform. While new measures were at first introduced slowly and tenuously, over time their cumulative effect began to be felt widely, and soon a more radical approach to change took shape that was counterbalanced by the reality that Moroccan society was still largely rural, agrarian, conservative, deeply traditional, and wary of rapid transformations.

THE CONTOURS OF REFORM

In recent years, the notion of "reform" in the Islamic world as a response to Western interference has undergone modification. While earlier generations of historians spoke of the decline and degradation of Muslim societies in the process of confronting the challenges of modernity, contemporary historiography has revised this image of deterioration. That the political contours of much of the Muslim world were reshaped in the second half of the nineteenth century by European imperialist designs is no doubt correct, but the Muslim reaction to this aggression was not nearly as passive or bungling as some would have us believe. Morocco in the late nineteenth century also offers an occasion for revisionist thinking. Writing from a Western perspective and using sources that were ideologically suffused with the notion of failure, colonial and postcolonial historians made judgments about the inevitability of independent Morocco's demise that are now being revised. The discourse of decline was not only pervasive but also one-sided, for there were pockets of growth, patterns of success, and even moments of triumph, unevenly distributed yet worthy of consideration. Thus current research focuses more on the ideas of resiliency, of cautious yet strategic thinking, and on the selective appropriation of new technologies that helped the sharifian state to follow an independent course long after neighboring Algeria (1830) and Tunisia (1881) had fallen to the imperial sword. Viewed within this framework, the reform period in Morocco was not a series of abortive attempts to "catch up" that ended in failure, but rather a selective adaptation to innovations and ideas aimed at stabilizing and maintaining the ʿAlawite dynasty in power.

Unlike the highly centralized Ottoman Empire, where *Tanzimat* (the Ottoman reform movement) emerged as a fully developed state-sponsored program embracing an array of administrative, legal, and military measures, in Morocco, change unfolded in a piecemeal, contingent, and multicausal manner. It took place more in response to specific events than as a concerted and centrally directed effort to move the state rapidly into a Westernized orbit. Yet it was evident that certain aspects of governance had to be radically remade and that remnants of the *ancien regime* had to be updated, in order for reforms (*islahat*) to make headway. Just as in the Ottoman Empire, the reform movement had to break the back of the old order and make way for new styles of absolutism that would inflict an all-too-familiar pain on the population. In Morocco, reform created a cadre of "modernizers," or "new men" committed to change, but their numbers were very small and their influence limited. Indeed, the chief agent of reform was the sultan himself, coordinating, directing, cajoling, and sometimes figuratively whipping the bureaucracy into action. Moreover, while many aspects of the process were flawed, others showed surprising strength and innovation. By viewing this period from multiple perspectives, by examining the specific measures adopted to meet external and internal threats, we shall see that the simplistic view that the makhzan was implacably opposed to change and fought it at every level is indeed false. Instead, it is clear that the makhzan acted with vigor and determination in areas where it exercised strength and unrivaled control, such as administration, taxation, and the military. It is equally apparent that it struggled to achieve a balance between those who opposed change, and its own inclination to move ahead using models taken from both Europe and the Islamic East, and in particular, from Muhammad ʿAli's Egypt. The reform period, roughly embracing the years 1860 to 1912, should be seen as a complex, contentious, and extended period of interaction among various internal and external actors from which Morocco's leadership emerged far more familiar with the ways the modern world.[1]

What were those inner strengths? First of all, the longevity, prestige, and stability of the ʿAlawi dynasty that, by the mid-nineteenth century, had ruled Morocco for more than two hundred years. The roots of the ʿAlawi sultanate ran deep, and the personal charisma of the monarch coupled with his religious prestige enhanced his legitimacy and his capacity to turn the cumbersome wheels of change. Morocco never achieved the "depersonalized" rule of large bureaucracies such as the Ottoman state, and the figure of the sultan was always at the core of the construct of the nation. Chosen by the court and then publicly confirmed by the *bayʿa*, the nineteenth-century sultans ascended to the throne with relatively little opposition.[2] Sultan Muhammad IV had already served a long apprenticeship under his father when his moment arrived, and his only rival was a distant cousin from the far reaches of the south who was easily set aside. His son and successor, Hassan I (reigned 1873–1894) was universally acclaimed and his incumbency lasted more than twenty years.[3] Not that opposition to either monarch did not exist: upstarts, rebellions, and a constant policing of city and countryside were mandatory to retain the seat of power. But on balance, the makhzan's solidity, coherence, and continuity throughout the long nineteenth century served, almost to the end, as the main engine of transformation. Only after 1900, when converging foreign interests viciously attacked the foundations of the state that were already weakened by internecine warfare, was Morocco finally overtaken by the tide of imperial expansionism that had inundated its neighbors decades before.[4]

ECONOMIC POLICIES

After the 1860 Tetuan War, according to historian Germaine Ayache, "the history of modern Morocco begins."[5] Starved for revenue and blocked by treaty from substantially raising port revenues, Sultan Muhammad IV looked to the countryside to lighten his load of debt, and in particular, to the fertile breadbasket of Morocco, the coastal plain stretching from Casablanca to Safi, comprising three important tribal confederations: the Chaouia, the Doukkala, and the Abda. These regions were the main producers of Morocco's agricultural wealth and its steadiest source of agricultural taxes. Sultan Muhammad moved aggressively to exploit this wealth by abolishing the old Qur'anic tax based on the size of the harvest and by replacing it with a fixed sum imposed on each tribal faction to be paid in cash. As a result, the system was made more efficient, but the cost was high. The old system took into account the vicissitudes of nature, while the new one, though brutally efficient, ignored practices that had been in place for centuries that were geared to the environmental reality of good years and bad years that followed one another in unpredictable succession.

This change in the makhzan's relationship with rural areas would entail major consequences. By squeezing an agricultural economy already operating at subsistence level, the government removed the thin layer of reserve that held rural society together and kept it from starvation. A severe drought in the years 1867–1869 experienced across the land meant that agriculturalists were without seeds or food stocks to see them through to the next harvest. In order to get by, farmers borrowed from local middlemen who lent cash at exorbitant rates, creating a crisis "that penetrated to the pores of society."[6] Faced with economic ruin, some peasants began to sell off their holdings piece by piece; others abandoned the land altogether and fled to the cities. Thus a conjuncture of factors – heavy state taxes, the venality of local officials, and natural disasters – led to a disaggregation of rural society that worsened over the following years.

The growth of cities and expansion of trade was another economic factor that came into play after the Tetuan War. The increase in the population of the major urban centers was dramatic: from a village of eighty-five hundred in 1857, Tangier blossomed into a city of forty thousand in 1904. Not all the growth was due to a foreign influx; native rural elites set up urban households in the major towns and cities across the empire and attracted relatives and retainers from afar. Towns were places where new mercantile interests congregated, eager to share power with traditional elites. An urban bourgeoisie became visible in places such as Fez, Rabat, and Tangier, led by a rising class of entrepreneurs often involved in business deals with foreign enterprises. The newly rich became an engine of modernity, consuming at unprecedented levels, introducing higher standards for education, and demanding "quality of life" improvements. Jews emerged from their *mellahs* (quarters) and were now visible in the urban landscape; postcards from that era show market scenes peopled by Jewish men in their distinctive dress. The Tangier-Fez axis was especially active, carrying people and goods from the hub of Morocco's precolonial industry in Fez to its only working Mediterranean port at Tangier. As we shall see, cities were also the setting for a host of oppositional activities, in the form of revolts, riots, and demonstrations against the regime and its increasingly intrusive tax collection system. And while some sectors of urban society enjoyed unprecedented wealth and opportunity, especially (but not exclusively) in the port cities, others resented the ascendancy of social inferiors and "subordinates," seeing it as clear evidence of the corruption of mores that the foreign presence had introduced.

Establishing the financial stability of the state was clearly the necessary foundation of any successful program of reform. Yet despite evidence of a thriving trade with the outside world and growing revenues flowing into the coffers of the state – the heavy cost of the Spanish indemnity notwithstanding – Morocco found itself in the midst of a monetary crisis by mid-century. The root cause was a precipitous decline in the value of the Moroccan currency. Historically, Morocco's monetary system was simple: the *mithqal*, a gold piece, was divided into ten ounces (*uqiyas*), a silver coin; each uqiya was worth four *muzunas* (also a silver piece), and each muzuna was equal to forty-eight *fils*, (flous) a copper or bronze coin. For centuries, this monetary system held steady, but in the mid-nineteenth century, locally minted coins began to lose their value as European coins flooded the Moroccan market in quantity. Unable to stem the tide, the makhzan realistically allowed foreign coins to serve as legal tender, and Moroccans began to use them as if they were "native"; as a result, comparable Moroccan coins having higher silver content disappeared from circulation. Meanwhile, the bronze coins that were most commonly used depreciated in value, making goods more expensive for the average person.[7] These trends gained momentum during the Tetuan War when Spanish soldiers made a profit from changing money at favorable rates. Pedro Antonio de Alarcón noted that currency trading became their informal pastime: the Spanish currency had "a floating value ... *napoleons* are good today for 25 *reales*, tomorrow 18, the day after tomorrow 30, according to their abundance or scarcity."[8]

Monetary instability had especially dire consequences for Moroccan peasants, for whom every decline in the value of bronze coins meant an increase in their cost of living. Sultan Muhammad attempted to stabilize the currency by issuing a new silver coin called the *muhammadi dirham* and fixing its exchange rate relative to bronze coins. He ordered that the new dirham be used in all commercial transactions, including the payment of taxes. But this measure worked for only a short time and soon this coin also disappeared from circulation. Later sultans followed a similar strategy, issuing new coins with new names, readjusting the rates of exchange to cover the rate of inflation, and imposing new taxes, so that the long-term damage to makhzan finances was contained and revenues remained more or less constant. But the mass of people who had less ability to regulate their finances were not so fortunate, and they often had to "eat" the costs of rising inflation by going into debt. The historian al-Nasiri noted that in the year 1864, the price of basic foodstuffs rose to new heights, to the point where people had to sell their valuable goods and jewelry "at a fraction of their price, which came down heavily on the weakest elements of society."[9]

Perhaps the most devastating effect of the ongoing monetary crisis was a psychological one; in the popular mind, currency troubles were somehow linked to the more general problem of foreign intrusion into the local economy. But as Thomas Park argues, the perception that the makhzan was on the verge of financial collapse that some historians have forwarded is actually false. In fact, he says, the makhzan was fully cognizant of the extent of its financial troubles and the mechanisms needed to overcome them; the sultan and his advisers responded to the problem by manipulating exchange rates to maintain fiscal control.[10] These efforts show that the Moroccan economy was undergoing an evolution necessitated by the movement to a monetarized, cash economy. The influx of revenues from the ports, the need to calculate expenses and prepare a rudimentary budget, the adoption of cash salaries for the growing bureaucracy, all pointed to rapid changes in the way that Moroccans measured and distributed wealth that were far more in accordance with modern practice than previously.

ADMINISTRATIVE REFORM

Over the course of the century, the central administration was progressively professionalized and regularized. While not as institutionalized as Ottoman officialdom, the Moroccan ruling class was nonetheless built on a meritocratic model, with promotion contingent on loyalty, achievement, and family ties. Muhammad al-Saffar is a good example of how promotion through the ranks operated; son of an aristocratic Hispano-Moorish family ("al-Andalusi" was one of his surnames), educated at the Qarawiyyin University in Fez, he became a notary, or *ʿadl*, who fulfilled both administrative and religious functions in the judiciary. Chosen for the embassy to Paris because of his literary skills, his elegantly written travel account caught the attention of Sultan ʿAbd al-Rahman who brought him to the court to educate his sons. Helped by his proximity to the royal center, al-Saffar quickly rose through the ranks to the upper reaches of the state bureaucracy, becoming a minister and close adviser to three successive sultans.[11] Nor was his story atypical; other middling ulama followed the same track, as the bureaucracy expanded and the need for educated men with a good command of Arabic grew. Despite chronically inadequate finances, Sultans Muhammad IV and Hassan I introduced structural reforms modeled on the bureaucratic innovations ushered in by the *Tanzimat*, including a hierarchically ordered state apparatus that by the end of the century included ministers with specific portfolios for finance, war, justice, and foreign affairs.[12] Ministers were salaried, and during the reign of Hassan I, the very top levels of government were organized into formal bureaus each having a well-defined set of tasks. Muhammad al-Saffar became the first *wazir al-shikayat*, comparable to a Minister of Justice, hearing grievances from *qaʿid*-s (local governors) and tribal leaders and redirecting them to the appropriate department for a hearing. Muhammad IV created a school in Rabat (*al-madrasa al-makhzaniyya*) for training personnel in techniques of modern administration and the proper forms of written communication. A voluminous correspondence with the foreign diplomatic corps was perhaps one reason for the expansion of the secretarial corps; another was the widening scope of the bureaucracy into new areas, such as the more meticulous management of the royal estates.

The process of restructuring was an incremental one, geared to the practical necessities of raising revenues to support the expansion of the state. A body of inspectors (*umana*) was formalized after 1862 to supervise the garnering of fees in the ports, at the town gates, and in the markets, and this cadre eventually became the backbone of the state's fiscal operations. Bright young men recruited mainly from elite families in Fez, Tetuan and Salé were sent out to the hinterland to collect taxes. At the head of these cadres was the *amin al-umana*, the inspector-general, who was in fact a Minister of Finance.[13] Each agent was given a set salary and was forbidden from engaging in commercial activities on the side.[14] The close relationship between the inspectors in the ports who were both servants of the makhzan as well as counterparts to the European merchants who gathered there, introduced a cosmopolitan factor into urban society. This development blurred the strict separation between natives and foreigners in the commercial sphere, empowered wider groups of natives to grasp the subtleties of international trade, and opened new avenues for information and cultural exchange.[15]

By 1870, the greater degree of organization within the bureaucracy was palpable. Sultan Hassan I (reigned 1873–1894), with his talent for authority and his knack at choosing competent subordinates, pushed administrative reform even further. He mandated the hours of work (6 AM to 10 AM, then

3 PM until sunset, with Thursday for rest and Friday morning for prayer).[16] The professionalization of the administration undergirded an already existing *esprit de corps* among the servants of the makhzan. With their own strict codes of conduct, their adherence to court protocol, their own forms of dress and own varieties of worship (in 1900, most were members of the brotherhood headed by the Saharan Shaykh Ma al-ʿAynayn), they constituted a self-confident and privileged elite. Another of Sultan Hassan's strategies was to replace or supplement provincial officials who had overstayed their tenure with "new men," often selected from the ranks of the *ʿaskar nizami*, the reformed or "new" army, hand-picked by him. In the Doukkala region, for example, five governors mushroomed to eighteen. Hassan's main tactic in governing was "divide and rule" in order to enhance his control from the center, a strategy later exploited to near-perfection by the French.

In spite of all these measures, the countryside remained unpredictable, and complete control over the rural areas eluded Sultan Hassan I, just as it had eluded previous sultans. Rural insurrections of a millenarian cast would often break through the façade of a subdued countryside, usually in the aftermath of a *mahalla*. News of the revolt of the Mahdi Muhammad Ahmad, the charismatic religious figure who stymied the forces of British colonialism in the Sudan in 1881, reached the Moroccan hinterland, rousing enthusiasm for jihad and raising anxiety in the palace that distant events would become an exemplar for a homegrown variety of rebelliousness. While tribal uprisings, the opposition of brotherhoods, and urban insurrections were a common feature of nineteenth century Morocco, the rise of a mahdi was a threat of a different order, as we shall see in the reigns of the last two pre-Protectorate sultans, ʿAbd al-ʿAziz and ʿAbd al-Hafiz, raising the specter of *fawda* (anarchy) that millenarian movements had often provoked in the past.

INTEGRATING THE NATIONAL SPACE

The rural world was coming more under the thumb of the central government, but did the balance of power between center and periphery really shift, or were other mechanisms at work that altered the relationship? In the early nineteenth century, the state did not have complete mastery over its territorial space, making it exceptionally difficult to manage outlying areas. The premodern makhzan was a patchwork of jurisdictions that operated with minimal coordination, with the countryside presenting a particular set of problems. The cliché of a "tribal mosaic" contains more than a grain of truth.[17] Molecularized by vast regional differences in terms of climate, language, ethnicity, and geography, the rural world was a universe unto itself. Yet here, too, we see signs of a greater degree of integration between the makhzan and its outlying areas, particularly under the reign of Sultan Hassan I, whose expeditions to the Souss (1882) and to the Tafilalt (1883) expanded the perceptual boundaries of the state.

"The throne of the emperor of Morocco is his horse; his canopy is the sky," one minister reportedly said.[18] Sultan Hassan's annual expeditions (*harkas*) were part of an overall plan calculated to project the aura of a well-run sultanate into every corner of the empire. By personally leading these expeditions, he transformed the figure of the sultan into the symbol of a disciplined and encompassing authority. The harka was fundamentally a military column, often as many as fifteen thousand men, made up of infantry, cavalry, and artillery. The slow progress of this enormous living wave of soldiers, animals, court officials, traders and suppliers, wives and concubines across the landscape – in addition to the massive amount of matériel needed to sustain them – made an unforgettable impression.[19] The sultan's visits to tribal chiefs were the occasion for both fear and rejoicing: fear that new fiscal demands would be made, that livestock would be confiscated, granaries emptied, tax evaders jailed; joy that the moral ascendancy represented by the personhood of sultan had come to bless this or that corner of the empire. Criss-crossing the Moroccan territory from one end to the other for years on end, appearing one season in the north, the next in the south, the court of Sultan Hassan I took on the aspect of nomadic encampment constantly on the move.[20]

The peripatetic makhzan was a force for integration, bringing into the fold of the nation distant territories that had previously not been identified with it. The great qaʿids of the High Atlas, the Goundafa, the M'tougga and the Glawa, each of whom owed his rise to power to his control over a pass through those lofty mountains, were drawn into a tenuous relationship with the ruling monarchy for the first time. In a letter to his provincial governors announcing his diplomatic success in winning over the "Lords of the Atlas" and gaining their cooperation in supplying his army with tribal contingents, Sultan Hassan I took credit for this achievement:

> We have sheathed our swords in their scabbards, and stemmed the flow of blood ... we have brought honor to them, substituting words of diplomacy for words of war. ... We have conquered their lands in their entirety, both the valleys and the uplands, from the craggy hillsides to the towering peaks that are companions of the moon and greet the stars whenever they appear ...[21]

Rather than speaking of a weakened tribal structure vis-à-vis the growing military power of the makhzan in the later nineteenth century, or of an already contentious relationship made more acute, we should better imagine the emergence of new kinds of linkages – economic, political, and military – between center and periphery in which each tightened its hold on the other, bringing the "tribal" element to the center, and projecting the "makhzan" into the farthest reaches of its territory.[22]

MILITARY REFORM

Finally there was the question of military reform. Modernizing the army along European lines was a central objective of the state following the crushing defeats of Isly and Tetuan.[23] For centuries, the Moroccan army had been based on a core of professional soldiers, the *gish* (Ar.*jaysh*) units, complemented by irregular tribal contingents (*na'iba*). Both groups had grown increasingly volatile in the course of the nineteenth century, fiercely resisting any reduction in their privileges despite their mounting failures, in a manner reminiscent of the insubordination of the Ottoman janissary corps earlier in the century. Starting with ʿAbd al-Rahman's first tentative efforts to create a new army, the ʿaskar nizami, until the imposition of French colonial rule in 1912, sultans grappled with the question of how to bring the military to a new level of preparedness, so that it would become an instrument of internal order and a wall of defense against outsiders. The implications of the word *nizam* were clear: it meant a rational chain of command, creating units of well-equipped infantry and modern artillery, and teaching coordination in the battlefield that required a machinelike discipline rather than individualized displays of heroism. It also meant a closer relationship with Europe as the source for modern weaponry and for the recruitment of foreign military advisers. Yet another aspect of military reform was the sending of student missions to the West as a means of learning new methods of training and command.[24]

Over the course of sixty years, between 1845 and 1905, the fighting capacity of the Moroccan military improved dramatically. But at the same time, military reform was plagued by a host of problems that slowed its progress. The "new order" evoked the darker side of European-induced modernity that eventually reached into all levels of the Moroccan state. Among the questions it raised were those concerning the relevance of infidel models to the Islamic polity, whether the makhzan could manage the heavy financial obligations and unending hemorrhage of wealth that an upgrading required, and what would be the effect of change on key groups in society who depended on the status quo for their well-being.

It should be noted that the "new order" –a term borrowed from the modernization efforts of the Ottoman Sultan Selim III in the 1790s, and later used to describe the modernized armies of Muhammad ʿAli Pasha in Egypt and Ahmad Bey in Tunis – did not imply a complete break with the past. Unlike the Ottoman Empire and Egypt, where ancient corps like the janissaries and the Mamluks had to be crushed in order to clear the path, in Morocco the core army units of gish and naʾiba were left intact when the first *tabors*, or battalion-strength units of the ʿaskar nizami, were created in 1845. However, there was no mistake about the difference between the new units and the old guard. First of all, there was a totally new nomenclature for ranks and organization, often provided by Ottoman and Egyptian military manuals. Moreover, the men looked different: they wore European-style uniforms and carried flintlock rifles made in England. Finally, the new units were infantry, as opposed to the old-style mounted cavalry, enabling the Moroccans to replicate the tactics that had produced the concentrated firepower the French had displayed at Isly. Unfortunately, the first adversary against whom they were deployed in the 1840s was the immensely popular resistance hero ʿAbd al-Qadir, hounded around western Algeria by Moroccan auxiliaries. This use of the ʿaskar nizami against the native hero dampened popular enthusiasm for the new army, and in the course of time, many soldiers deserted. The ʿaskar nizami were an insignificant unit within a pathetically disorganized regular army when Moroccan troops were defeated by Spanish forces before the gates of Tetuan in 1859.[25]

This situation began to change when Sultan Muhammad IV came to the throne. The new sultan hardly looked the part of a modernizer with his flowing white robes and mane of curly black hair, but he was in fact immersed in the language of reform and fully aware of the technological transformations taking place elsewhere in the region. He had reportedly perused military manuals translated from Turkish and European languages into Arabic, and he had a lively curiosity about technical innovations. An Englishman hired to build a steam engine in the palace in Marrakesh in 1863 recounted how one day the sultan visited the work site. That evening, the sultan ordered the engine room to be furnished with carpets and invited the ladies of the harem to a sumptuous feast, simultaneously astonishing and terrifying them by turning the blasting engine on and off.[26] Sultan Muhammad knew a smattering of French and Spanish, engaged in building projects to improve the roads and ports, initiated sugar and cotton plantations in the Haouz region, and imported European machinery to process the raw materials.[27] Perhaps his most daring innovation was the introduction of a state-sponsored printing press, the first of its kind in Morocco, in 1865. By 1868, more than three thousand books, mostly manuals of religious instruction, had been printed on the lithographic press in Fez. In appearance they resembled hand-written manuscripts and in content they were hardly revolutionary; but a line had been crossed and the long-standing monopoly of the scribal classes over the reproduction and transmission of the written word had finally been breached.[28]

In the sphere of military reform, Sultan Muhammad was equally ambitious. He reconstituted the ʿaskar nizami, equipping it with up-to-date weapons supplied by a munitions factory in Marrakesh. He created a ministerial post equivalent to a Minister of War (*al-allaf al-kabir*) to oversee military affairs, and he expanded the social base of the army by conscripting men through regular call-ups directed to every level of society. He established a military training school at Dar al-Makhzan in Fez, and he sought out Muslim military instructors from Algiers and Tunis to train the new corps, preferring them to Europeans. By the end of his reign, Sultan Muhammad IV handed on to his son and successor Sultan Hassan I a fighting force trained and armed to a degree his internal adversaries could no longer match, giving the makhzan a preponderant edge in controlling the national territory.[29]

In much the same way that military reform had transformed the Egyptian state under Muhammad ʿAli, the ʿaskar nizami in Morocco proved to be a force of primal change. Through the conscription process, it sought out recruits from the all parts of the country and from every social class; it made the state visible through the distribution of supplies, uniforms, food, fodder and equipment; it created new medical practices for sanitizing the troops; it fostered codes of discipline, service and accountability, as well as new standards of cruelty in the punishment of those who refused to comply. Conscripts in the sultan's new army were tattooed between the thumb and the forefinger in order to identify them in case of their desertion. While riddled with inefficiencies, the reformed army was at the same time a model for a new variety of state power that reached into society and made its influence felt in ordinary lives.[30]

Surprisingly, Sultan Muhammad's reforms encountered minimal opposition from the ulama, who were ordinarily inclined to reject innovations that originated in the West. But largely because of his solicitous attention to the opinions of his key religious advisers, Sultan Muhammad headed off the possibility of turning them into a party of opposition. The handful of mid-century religious figures who wrote about the nizami army took the attitude that it was an instrument for repelling the infidel, shoring up the foundations of the state, and fulfilling the religious duty of jihad – all considered acts of piety.[31] As foreign incursions on Morocco's borders increased in the decades of the 1870s and 1880s, discussion over the correctness of adopting reforms from the infidel ceased. French incursions into the Guir Valley (1870), the creation of a French military outpost on the Moroccan-Algerian border at Aïn Sefra (1881), and the installation of a British trading post at Cap Juby (Tarfaya) in 1882, required a military response and convinced the governing elites as well as the ulama that it was time to act boldly.

The chronicler al-Nasiri's analysis of the situation rejected the superficial notion that reform was simply a Moroccan adaptation of Western methods of making war. Writing toward the end of the century and evaluating the "new order" retrospectively, he expressed acute insight into the far-reaching consequences of military reform. He was himself a cautious "modernizer," and he understood that the creation of a new army was a complex operation laden with cultural signifiers. He perceived reform as the leading edge of a broader reconstruction of relations within Moroccan society based on the idea of the individual's responsibility to serve the state. The ʿaskar nizami, in his view, was a school for practicing the arts of a new brand of Islamic modernity, where recruits learned the fundamentals of religious practice, the principles of rational organization, and the meaning of rank and hierarchy:

> The first thing [the soldier] should learn is to appreciate the blessings of his religion and to direct his efforts toward protecting Muslims. The purpose of this army (*jund*) is to protect the faith and if it fails in this regard, then how can it render service to the Muslim people? Furthermore, [the soldier] must learn manly virtue, the importance of proper decorum and dress, worthy speech, respect for superiors, and compassion for the less fortunate. He should understand that the finest quality before God and man is zeal for religion and country (*watan*), as well as love of the sultan and his wise counsel. If the fanatical foreigner is ready to defend his false religion, then why not insist also that the believing Arab should protect his own religion, his state (*dawla*) and his homeland (*watan*)?[32]

While the ʿaskar nizami may have been undertaken initially as a means of improving the state's capacity for self-defense, it had since grown into something much broader. It was now the organizing frame for the state's primacy over its subjects, providing the model for a disciplined society cohering around the idea of a Moroccan "nation." If this concept was not yet fully developed, if the implications of reform were not yet fully understood, they nevertheless pointed in the direction of an acute awareness that certain institutions had now become the means for imposing a vastly expanded form of state authority capable of reaching down to the cellular level of everyday life.

Hassan I continued to expand the military reforms instituted by his father. His efforts moved along several axes at once, but were mainly directed toward an increasing professionalization of the military. During his reign, the ʿaskar nizami was expanded to the unprecedented size of twenty-five thousand men.[33] His military projects included shoring up the coastal defenses with batteries of large caliber cannon, the founding in 1888 of a small arms factory in Fez (the "*Makina*"), the recruitment of top-flight military instructors from both Europe and the Ottoman empire, and the dispatch of students missions for study abroad. Between 1874 and 1888, three to four hundred students, chosen from the *jaysh* and *ʿabid* as well as from among the civilian population, were sent to academies of war in Britain, France, Italy, and Belgium to study mathematics, engineering and military science.[34]

Not all of these innovations were a success: production at the Makina was miniscule and the cost of each unit produced much greater than the price of comparable imported weapons. Moreover, the ability to maintain the more sophisticated equipment eluded the men placed in charge of them. The three batteries of eighteen-ton British Armstrong guns installed on the ramparts of Tangier did not function properly, and were never fired in anger. Many of the returning students disappeared into the bureaucracy, but some, like Muhammad Guebbas, who was sent to the Royal School of Military Engineering at Chatham in 1875, learned respectable English and on his return, joined the upper ranks of the makhzan, serving every sultan from Hassan I to Yusuf, when he became Prime Minister.[35]

Raising the revenues to pay for these projects required that the government be constantly on the move. Every year from spring until fall, Sultan Hassan was on campaign, leading expeditions to all parts of the country organized with great care and at enormous expense. The *mahalla*, or mobile encampment, traveled throughout the countryside, collecting back taxes, extracting expressions of fealty from local chiefs, winning over reluctant allies mainly through persuasion but occasionally through a show of force. Often the planning and execution of the campaign was in response to internal political events, demonstrating that the "new army" was as much an instrument of internal policing as a bulwark against the foreigner. For example, the volatile brotherhood of the Darqawa led an uprising in the name of jihad in the fall of 1887 near Figuig, ostensibly to protest French incursions in that border region. Alarmed by the uprising, the sultan immediately responded. Deploying a combination of force and diplomacy, he squelched the rebel action by claiming that "unofficial" proclamations of jihad posed a danger to the state; in a letter to the obstinate chief of the Darqawa brotherhood, Muhammad b. al-ʿArbi al-Madghari, who was advocating for a locally-led jihad, the sultan warned that he alone had the right to raise the flag of holy war.[36] Sultan Hassan quickly followed his warnings by launching an expedition to those regions, heading off what might have been a general uprising.

Likewise, his campaign to the Tafilalt in 1893, just months before he died, was most likely motivated by internal political causes. Sensing the end was near, he expressed the wish to visit the tombs of his ʿAlawi forbears buried in that remote southern oasis. But the mahalla had other purposes as well. The appearance of the sultan in the far corners of the state helped to establish makhzan supremacy over the trans-Saharan trade routes that bisected the Tafilalt, at that moment being closely watched by the French from across the frontier with Algeria. And through face-to-face contact with the local chieftains, the mahalla reestablished the ancient ties of fealty between the ʿAlawi sultan and his desert minions. More than a military maneuver, the system of the mahalla, according to Daniel Nordman, was "specifically related to the exercise of sovereignty," by sketching on the ground the limits of the Moroccan national territory.[37]

DIPLOMACY AND THE PROBLEM OF PROTECTION

During the second half of the nineteenth century, the state and its activities became entangled in a web of relations in which internal and external policies could no longer be separated. Morocco's engagement with the outside world was now an established fact, and the necessity to build a cadre of professionals who could deal with Europeans was imperative. Moroccan embassies had never been stationed permanently in European capitals, but now the number of special envoys sent abroad to negotiate issues such as trade, frontiers, and the purchase of equipment increased dramatically. The office of the sultan's diplomatic representative in Tangier (the *niyaba*), established in 1851, became an important outpost for the exchange of information with Europeans, and the holder of that position (the *na'ib*) became in reality a Minister of Foreign Affairs. The immense amount of correspondence between the na'ib and the makhzan preserved in the royal archives is proof of the intensifying diplomatic activity that required the direct involvement of the sultan, as the Great Powers increasingly viewed Morocco as a fertile field for their imperial ambitions.

Another area in which entanglements with Europeans grew was that of "protection." Begun in the eighteenth century as a means of stimulating commerce by releasing foreigners from the jurisdiction of Moroccan law, including the payment of taxes, the granting of "protection," or what we might call "diplomatic immunity," metastasized in the nineteenth century into a corrupt and abusive practice that embraced hundreds of people and undermined the authority of the makhzan. Known as the regime of "capitulations" in the Ottoman empire, the idea of "protection" appeared first in a treaty signed between Morocco and France in 1767, but remained a rather benign legality while the number of foreigners in Morocco was small. The list of protected people grew exponentially following the signing of the Free Trade agreement between Morocco and Great Britain in 1856; it now included not only foreign merchants in the ports, but also official consular representatives (often native Jews) along with their employees and their families, servants and friends, as well as the Moroccan partners or "associates" of Europeans – indeed, anyone who had access to a European could potentially negotiate or even purchase protection and become exempt from taxes, renounce his debts, or refuse to appear in a Muslim court.[38]

Many protégés were *tujjar*, or merchants, because of their key role as intermediaries, but other natives were also accorded protection and refused to pay taxes for less obvious reasons: chiefs of zawiyas, ministers of state, the unofficial native escort of J. H. Drummond Hay, and one entire village in the environs of Tangier whose inhabitants were employed as beaters in boar hunts organized by the U.S. Consulate.[39] The practice grew despite the warnings of the ulama that protection was tantamount to "wallowing in the mud of the infidel."[40] Certain European agents even had the audacity to put patents of protection up for sale, and some Moroccans reportedly bought multiple titles of protection, just to be on the safe side.[41] While the aim of the reform movement was to open a new era in state-societal relations founded on order and rationality, the practice of protection proposed a different option riddled by corruption and special privileges. Dubbed the "bridgehead of imperialism" by one observer, the granting of protections penetrated deeply into the social fabric.

On the one hand, one might say that protégés were "proto-entrepreneurs" acting as the leading edge of a new, capital-intensive exploitation of Morocco's agricultural and mineral wealth, energizing the economy by launching new projects on an unprecedented scale, such as the manufacture of luxury products, the processing of raw materials, the extension of agricultural lands, and the stimulation of trade and other basic industries. On the other hand, they were a source of disruption and economic grievances. Some protégés used their status to engage in banned activities, such as ignoring restrictions on imports and exports, purchasing tribal lands and illegally privatizing them, lending money at exorbitant rates, and by eluding the Shariah court whenever they were called to account. They also used their extraterritorial status to demand redress of "losses," both real and imagined, in the commercial sphere, forcing the makhzan to pay large fines. While Jews figured disproportionably among the protégés, they were by no means the majority. Most Jews who benefited from the practice were bankers and wealthy merchants, while the mass of Jews – poor artisans, shopkeepers, and laborers – were not affected at all. In fact, they were not only excluded from protection, but often became victims of it, when Muslims ruined by debts to avaricious Jewish money-lenders turned their anger against others who were innocent of such practices. The net effect was to exacerbate class divisions within the Jewish communities, placing rich and poor in opposition, and undermining a sense of communal solidarity.[42]

All these anxieties came to a head when the British aristocrat Sir Moses Montefiore, a Sephardic Jew, undertook a mission to Morocco in 1863 to procure guarantees for the security of his Moroccan coreligionists. Sir Moses was a wealthy British financier and politician with close ties to other powerful European Jews as well as to the non-Jewish world. He was one of the architects of a new international solidarity movement led by elite European Jews aimed at improving the conditions of their coreligionists in the "Orient." Appropriating the language of social justice emanating from the French Revolution, and making use of modern tools of journalism and propaganda, Montefiore and his associates pursued a two-pronged mission: to combat the abuse of Jews wherever it might occur, and to introduce legal guarantees similar to those that had improved the status of Jews in the West. In 1840, following the notorious "blood libel" case in Damascus in which Jews were unjustly accused of having committed ritual murder, Sir Moses extracted from the Ottoman sultan a *firman* (royal decree) assuring Jewish rights and granting "the same advantages" to Jews as other subjects of his empire. This success inspired Montefiore to seek other venues for his well-financed and morally driven humanitarian activities.

In 1860, a group of French Jews founded the Alliance Israélite Universelle (AIU) in Paris, adopting a program of education and humanitarian "good works" aimed at building strong links between Europe and the Jews of the Middle East.[43] Morocco had suddenly appeared on the map of Jewish philanthropy during the Tetuan War of 1859–1860, when the plight of the hundreds of Jewish refugees who fled northern Morocco for the safety of Gibraltar and Cadiz was broadcast in the European Jewish press, launching an international effort dubbed "The Moroccan Relief Fund." This campaign advertised the condition of Moroccan Jewry to the rest of the Jewish world. In 1862, the AIU established its first primary school for Jewish children in Tetuan, following with more schools in Tangier (1864), Essaouira (1866), and Safi (1867).[44]

Eager to bolster his reputation as a champion for Jewish rights, and despite his advanced age, Sir Moses now turned to Morocco, where news of the torture and imprisonment of Jews in the coastal town of Safi on dubious charges had reached European ears. Seizing on this incident and working hand in hand with British representative Drummond Hay as his reluctant consort, Montefiore – who had a keen sense of the theatrical – decided to repeat his success of twenty years before and personally petition Sultan Muhammad IV to grant "equality" to all *dhimmis* (non-Muslims), Christians and Jews alike.[45] Arriving in Tangier on December 11, 1863, Sir Moses' reputation in defense of Jewish interests had preceded him, and he received a tumultuous welcome. It was widely believed that the purpose of his visit was to succor the poor, and a century later, people in Tangier still recalled how he rode into town on a donkey, a pannier of silver coins at his side, casting fistfuls to the crowd as he passed.[46]

After successfully gaining the freedom of the Jewish prisoners in Safi, Montefiore's mission changed and began to take on a different cast. Traveling down the Atlantic coast on a British warship, the portly octogenarian arrived in Essaouira and from there was carried overland in a sedan chair to Marrakesh. His audience with the Sultan Muhammad IV went according to plan, with the sultan obligingly issuing a dahir that promised "Jews who live throughout our dominions receive their rightful measure of justice equal to others according to the law," employing modern liberal expressions such as "equality" (*taswiya*) and "justice" (*mizan al-haq*). Speculation about the motives for this surprising move center on at least two possibilities: first, that the sultan may have been anxious to please Great Britain, his principal European ally, by showing his open frame of mind and by rewarding this semiofficial envoy with the prize for which he had come so far; second, that the sultan was sincerely concerned that Jews be treated fairly in his dominions, and by enforcing this measure, he would win over to his side the small but economically important Jewish middle class.

In fact, Sultan Muhammad IV followed up the dahir with a circular letter to all provincial governors urging them to halt abuses against Jews.[47] The dahir did not constitute any change in Shariah law, only the manner in which the law might be applied. Nevertheless, it was a stinging rebuke to the ulama, who felt it was their exclusive right to interpret matters regarding dhimmi status. Jews, by contrast, felt as if the dahir constituted an important sea change, and copies of it were immediately translated into Hebrew and posted on the doors of synagogues throughout Morocco, even in the most remote mellahs.[48] When news of the proclamation spread internationally, Montefiore's already lofty reputation reached new heights. But in reality, the dahir did little to change the status of Jews in Morocco. Indeed, it might have had the opposite effect, as is evident in al-Nasiri's vexed comments, where he complains that "certain Jews" tried to unfairly exert political pressure on the sultan in order to gain concessions "like the Jews of Egypt."[49]

Montefiore's mission was a watershed event on several counts: it demonstrated the nascent political power of an "emancipated" international Jewry; it forged a bond between Moroccan Jewry and world organizations ready to intervene on its behalf; and it made the "Jewish question" an ongoing theme in the makhzan's dealings with the West. The question of Jewish rights reappeared in 1870, when the entire Jewish population of Algeria was given the legal status of citizens of France through the promulgation of the Crémieux Decree, a decision that reverberated strongly throughout Morocco's mellahs.

The visit of Montefiore, recorded in Moroccan memory as the visit of "the Jew Mushi," continued to reverberate long after, especially among the ulama who regarded the dahir as an affront to their preeminent role in shaping legal discourse.[50] Thereafter, European diplomats regularly mingled the question of Jewish rights in their discussions with the makhzan, even when broaching matters such as slavery and prison reform, using the topic as a convenient lever for intervention in Moroccan affairs. The Montefiore episode exposed an unexpected side to the program of reform, pointing out to makhzan officials that any change in the status of dhimmis was an acutely sensitive point with Europeans that could unleash demons impossible to contain.

The topic of protection continued to trouble the makhzan throughout the reform era. It was a preoccupation of Sultan Hassan, who internationalized the question and tossed it into the hopper of topics that stirred up Great Power rivalries. He was skillful at dealing with the entreaties of foreigners and raised to perfection the art of playing off one representative against another. He believed that an international meeting bringing together all the interested parties could work to his advantage. Indeed, each of the powers had distinct objectives in Morocco: Britain's aim was to stimulate commerce and increase its market share of Morocco's exports, while the French were obsessed with protecting their investment in Algeria. Moreover, the occupation of Tunisia by France and the declaration of a "Protectorate" over that former Ottoman dependency in 1881 had raised France's stake in North Africa.[51] Only Morocco continued to elude its grasp, but fierce opposition from other European states was assured if it were to make a move at this time. Protection was a safe means of extending French political influence inside Morocco without risking a confrontation with the other Great Powers. Spain held similar goals, but was handicapped by internal dissention and instability. Both Spain and France preferred a weak makhzan while the British hoped for the opposite – a "reformed" Moroccan state that could stand on its own.

Aware of these distinctions, Sultan Hassan thought it would be a good moment to settle the problem of protection and called for an international conference on the issue. But the results were not at all satisfactory, and the regime of protections went on. The Treaty of Madrid (signed July 3, 1880) was negotiated in part to limit the practice, but instead of reducing foreign interference, the makhzan was forced to make even more concessions that further limited its sovereignty, such as granting foreigners the right to own land in the countryside, something that Great Britain in particular had been pushing for all along.[52]

The upward-spiraling number of Moroccans now exempt from Muslim law angered the ulama, who regarded foreign intervention as the main reason for the country's moral decline. Prominent personalities with important positions in society were being seduced by the allure of protection, furthering the impression of a state under siege. Sharif and head of the zawiya of Ouezzane, Mawlay ʿAbd al-Salam, owner of vast estates in northeast Morocco and chief of a rich brotherhood with branches in Algeria and one of the staunchest supporters of the makhzan, was granted France's protection in 1884, as part of a wider French strategy to co-opt important religious figures as political allies. Mawlay ʿAbd Salam returned the compliment by ignoring French incursions in the southern region of Touat, considered Moroccan territory and a place where his zawiya had many followers. To compound the insult, the sharif posed proudly for a photograph wearing a French military uniform festooned with medals.[53] His defection was a great psychological blow to the makhzan, revealing the extent to which foreign influence had penetrated the traditional power structure.

FIGURE 3. The "Emperor of Morocco," presumably Sultan Hassan I, a *carte de visite* by the E. & H. T. Anthony Company of New York, manufacturer of these early photographic gems. Photographs of Sultan Hassan I are extremely rare; this is the only known photographic portrait of him. (Courtesy of Special Collections, Fine Arts Library, Harvard University)

Protesting against the abuses of protection was now a political necessity, as well as a religious one. ʿAli b. Muhammad al-Simlali, a scholar and a servant of the court, was no doubt acting as the spokesman for Sultan Hassan when he wrote in 1891 that foreign protections had brought about "the disorder and breakup of the people of Morocco."[54] Whether the guilty party was a hereditary aristocrat, like the Sharif of Ouezzane, or a *dhimmi* moneychanger, seeking protection was seen as a traitorous act.

Despite the storm of opposition, the practice continued unabated; it was a constant thorn in the side of the makhzan, a reminder of the danger of outside interference and of its own vulnerability to foreign pressure.

THE RISE OF AN ASSERTIVE BOURGEOISIE

The death of Sultan Muhammad IV in 1873 and the ascent of his favorite son, Hassan I, marked a new era in Moroccan statecraft. Thirty-seven years old, Hassan had been indoctrinated into the subtleties of court politics at a very early age. "Courage and perseverance were his dominant traits," according to French observer La Martinière, yet a quiet modesty permeated his disposition.[55] The worldly Italian traveler Edmondo de Amicis confessed he was "enthralled" by Sultan Hassan's appearance when saw him outside the palace in Fez:

> This Sultan ... was the handsomest, most attractive young man who ever won an odalisque's heart. He was tall, active, with large, soft eyes, a fine aquiline nose, dark, oval face, and a short, black beard. His expression was at once noble and melancholy. A white *haïk* [cloak] enveloped him from head to foot ... the large and entirely white horse he rode had green housings, and the stirrups were of gold. All this whiteness and the long, full cloak lent him something of a sacerdotal air. ... His graceful bearing, his expression, half-melancholy, half-smiling; his subdued, even voice, sounding like the murmur of a brook; in short his entire appearance and manner had a something [*sic*] ingenuous and feminine, and yet, at the same time, a solemnity that aroused instinctive admiration as well as profound respect.[56]

The combination of solemnity and intelligence that de Amicis felt was corroborated by others. Sultan Hassan's subjects were convinced of his saintly qualities. It was said that he rarely reacted with force if other means were at hand. Although violence was indeed in his arsenal of responses, he used it with restraint and an eye to increasing his authority; nevertheless, he did not shrink from displays of rank brutality, and foreigners took notice of the heads of his enemies hanging from the gates of Bab Mahruk in Fez. He was cautious in all things, even to the point of appearing indecisive, according to sociologist Jacques Berque, but his intentions were clear. He carefully guarded the patrimony he had inherited from his ancestors, yet he approved of the reforms initiated by his father, and under his guidance, the country entered an era of prosperity. The Spanish indemnity was paid off in 1884, and thereafter, all customs receipts went directly into the Moroccan treasury.

Sultan Hassan knew how to deflect the incessant demands of Europeans while harboring no particular affection for them, so that foreign visitors were treated with courtesy but kept at a distance. His strategy was to fend them off through dilatory responses and "inexhaustible diplomacy"; British envoy Charles Euan-Smith was kept waiting for weeks in the sizzling summer heat of Fez in 1892 in the hope of negotiating a new commercial treaty with the makhzan. The treaty was endlessly discussed, and when a compromise was finally reached, the text was so watered down that Euan-Smith reportedly tore it up in disgust.[57] When Sultan Hassan gave in to foreign demands, it was always couched in terms of a one-time concession rather than as an established rule. He adhered closely to court protocol – the *qa 'ida*, or rules of behavior – that determined the dress, decorum, and daily routine of those around him. Under his rule, ceremonial traits of power were preserved with a rigor and exactitude, and nothing escaped him. Most letters passed through his hands, and he often added his own notations; he saw everything and knew everything. During the autumn of 1887 he fell ill and was unable to attend to his duties, thus bringing the bureaucratic apparatus to a complete standstill. His qualities of attention, consistency, and adherence to past models brought him the high regard he enjoys today as one of Morocco's great sultans.[58]

His first crisis was a test of these qualities, foreshadowing the manner in which he would deal with similar social upheavals throughout his reign. The "abominable" (in the words of the historian al-Nasiri) *maks*, or "gate tax" was reimposed by Muhammad IV in 1864 after a long hiatus. This tax was levied on goods entering the city, as well as on goods sold in the market, such as wool, animal hides, and foodstuffs, causing hardship among the artisans and working people, and consternation among the ulama, most of who considered this tax as illegal.[59] The *maks* was not the only source of discontent; foreign goods introduced after the free trade agreement of 1856 competed with handmade manufactures of local artisans, raising prices and cutting into their traditional markets. Only a small group of rich Moroccans who served as middlemen to Europeans benefited from this trade. Reluctant to stir up trouble with the wealthy urban bourgeoisie who were one of its main pillars of support, the makhzan looked the other way. Meanwhile, popular resentment, especially among the militant crafts guilds like the tanners (*dabbaghin*), began to fester. Increased taxes and competition from foreign goods had hit these artisans and their families especially hard.[60]

The anger of the urban working classes reached a boiling point just after Sultan Hassan I succeeded his father to the throne in October 1873. The tanners rose up in protest against the maks, "raging like lions and tigers" through the streets of Fez and ransacking the house of Muhammad Bennis, the *amin al-umana*, or Minister of Finance, who was seen as chief agent of the onerous tax. Bennis fled and took refuge in a nearby public bath. One rioter was reportedly so enraged that he single-handedly tore the massive door from Bennis' house and carted it off down the street, finally collapsing under its weight. Fez was turned into a battleground as frightened burghers barricaded themselves behind closed doors. The sultan, who was on campaign, sent solicitous letters calling for calm. The hated tax collectors were momentarily withdrawn, and the rebellion ceased.

But the maks collectors soon reappeared in the markets, causing the insurrection to break out once again, this time in an even more violent manner. Local Fez militiamen, egged on by prominent citizens, took up positions in the minarets of Old Fez and fired down on the ʿaskar nizami, called out by the makhzan to face the fury of the mob. The opposition of the townspeople was an act of insubordination the sultan could not ignore. The insurrection finally ended when Sultan Hassan ordered the ʿaskar nizami to pillage the town at will, a measure calculated to shock the people of Fez back to their senses. Among the leaders of the revolt were prominent citizens – a sharif, a secretary of the makhzan, a Muslim jurist – who were punished, but then quickly restored to favor. Each party to the dispute had made its point: the bourgeoisie led by the *umana* asserted its new-found militancy; the working classes demonstrated the limits of their patience; and the sultan drew a line on his willingness to negotiate with the people of Fez.[61]

This incident exposed many of the fault lines opening up in state-societal relations stemming from the makhzan's insatiable thirst for cash. It laid bare the difference in attitude between the working poor, suffering from excessive taxes and Europe's entry into the local economy, and the new bourgeoisie, including the tax collectors, many of whom were being enriched by their dealings with foreigners.[62] In the course of these changes, the social equilibrium in Fez had become destabilized. The people of Fez had a longstanding reputation for rebelliousness, and the revolt of the tanners was an expression of popular dissatisfaction with changing geographies of urban power. At issue was the extent to which the makhzan could allow pockets of local authority to challenge the centralizing goals of the state. Finding a balance between entrenched special interests and the centripetal ambitions of the sultanate was an ongoing theme of Hassan's reign, evident in his actions in rural as well as urban contexts. As the center of gravity gradually shifted, Sultan Hassan acted with determination to reassure his subjects that the rudder of the state was holding steady.

Typically, the peripatetic Hassan I met his death while on the march. His mahalla had left Marrakesh and was passing though a remote region near Tadla in July 1894, when the sultan succumbed to the illness that had debilitated him during his last years. Because the army was still in enemy territory, his chamberlain Ba Ahmad kept the death a secret, ordering the ministers who accompanied the mahalla not to reveal the news. The harem was also entreated to keep silent, and the usual you-yous that are a sign of lamentation were suppressed. The camp was wrapped in silence as Ba Ahmad plotted his next moves. The body of the sultan was washed and dressed in fresh linen, and propped up daily in an enclosed litter until the mahalla reached Rabat, when his death was revealed. And none too soon, for the heat of the summer had rendered a telltale corpse.[63] The greatest sultan of the age of reform was instantly regretted, as Moroccans feared what would follow without his judicious leadership. The strong personality of Hassan I held the state together during his lifetime and maintained an illusion of cohesiveness; as we shall see, with his death, centrifugal tendencies inherent in the Moroccan polity reemerged once again.

THE BALANCE SHEET OF REFORM

Was the movement for reform a success or a failure, or something in between? Obviously it did not halt the aggressive tendencies of Europe, nor did it increase the capacity of the state to block European interventions. The results of the reform movement were hardly uniform. The old continued to coexist with the new. New coinages did not replace ancient economies of barter; the ʿaskar nizami operated alongside traditional tribal contingents; a bureaucracy chosen on merit did not supplant one based on family and kinship; a sultanate inclined to consultation did not overrule an authority derived from divine right. On closer examination, it appears the changes introduced never penetrated deep enough to alter the fundamental structures of the state, nor did they extend far enough outward into the public sphere to change popular attitudes. The modernizing element was not consolidated in any one institution, but rather weakly diffused throughout the system. The "new army" was not sufficiently strong to impose its will; the rising middle class was too embryonic to seize its due; the educated youth, often an engine of revolution, were still too scattered and strung between poles of social differentiation; the rural notability that presented the only real challenge to reform eventually threw in its lot with the makhzan and remained loyal to its absolutist tendencies, but without endorsing a spirit of change; and finally, the ulama remained indifferent or openly hostile to innovation, making concessions only when coerced.

Paradoxically, the potency of the state had increased because of military reforms that now gave the army a monopoly over coercive force. Meanwhile, Hassan, the exemplary sultan, never considered devolving his authority, nor did he see a way of escaping his confinement within a tight web of moral expectations and religious dogma. This is not to say he was deaf to the wishes of his subjects. But there was no regularized mechanism for hearing them, other than the *shikayat* system that was not widely accessible. Caught between his dual roles of secular monarch and religious guide, the sultan was unable to break through the wall of intellectual conservatism that enveloped the seat of power. The culture of the makhzan would not allow for a revision of the norms that governed political life. Lacking were the conversations, debates, and exchanges of ideas that would have stimulated a genuine rethinking of the underlying social and political structures that historians have recognized as part of the progression to modernity in other parts of the world.[64]

The end of the nineteenth century in Morocco was a time of increased tension between state and society. On the economic front, the vicissitudes of the agricultural sector and swings in the world market disrupted the macro-sphere, sending shock waves down to the village level. The fluctuations of the prices of basic goods were a main source of widespread social discontent. While some were able to pay the elevated prices for expensive imported goods and suffered hardly at all from periodic scarcities, others were laid low by them and endured horrible deprivation. Growing inequalities in the class system due to expanded contacts with Europe and the influx of foreign capital exacerbated the impact of environmental disasters such as drought and famine.[65] The frustrated desires of the new middle class to change its relationship with power weakened further whatever was left of the old social consensus but did not produce a new one, as the revolt of the tanners demonstrates. Ironically, in the coastal city of Tangier, an integral part of the empire geographically, with its mixed population of Jews, Muslims and Europeans, the period of 1870–1900 saw the refashioning of political institutions based on new consensual methods of decision making that were Moroccan in style yet influenced by European institutional forms. But the adoption of such models by the makhzan of the interior was beyond anyone's imagination. Tangier's liminality, the omnipresence of the odious foreigner there, its large Jewish population, in sum, its complete exceptionalism, eliminated its potential as a model for a more open, popular-based, and integrative form of rule.

FIGURE 4. The main street of Tangier in 1890, called the Siyaghin after the many Jewish goldsmiths [*suyyagh*] who lined its upper end. V. Hell, photographer. (Postcard collection, Gérard Lévy, Paris)

Only the Islamic sphere offered some hope, because here the modalities of change were deeply and innately engrained in the public consciousness. Here alone was an opportunity for introducing elements of a modernity that might stick and ramify to embrace all levels of society, endowing them with the prestige of a just program for social change. But here too, there was failure, since the traditional ulama, the experts in religious law, were already in a state of pusillanimity and nothing had risen to take their place. The leaders of Islamic modernity that arose in Egypt in the late nineteenth century did not have their counterparts in Morocco, although, as we shall see, a Moroccan parallel to the Levantine religious revival propelled by intellectuals such as Muhammad ʿAbduh and Rashid Rida did eventually emerge in figures such as Muhammad b. al-Kabir al-Kattani and Ma al-ʿAynayn, who appeared in the first decade of the twentieth century. These movements had a specifically Moroccan character, based on respect for the religious nobility and admiration for the charismatic figure. But they were fragile affairs, easily crushed, and soon fell victim to the paranoiac tendencies of a dying sultanate.

Challenged on the one hand by ideas flooding in from the West, and, on the other hand, by the obdurate resistance of the masses and scattered segments of the elite, the sultans of the era of reform had little room to maneuver, yet they would tolerate no infringement of their prerogatives, nor could they find the means to lead society forward. Europe was changing as well: the growth of liberalism, the increase in imperial appetites, the articulation of the "civilizing mission" and Europe's growing tendency to assume the right to intervene on behalf of subjugated peoples everywhere, were driving a new militancy. The example of Algeria next door, where France was building a modern society while ignoring its native population, was frightening to Moroccans. Reforms in Egypt and Turkey were equally threatening, and their outcomes were considered unsuitable for Morocco. The historian al-Nasiri, that incomparable seer, ended his magisterial *Kitab al-Istiqsa* with these words of warning:

> You should know that the situation of this generation is completely different that of the one that came before. The habits of the people are completely reversed, the behavior of merchants and craftspeople is unlike what it used to be in regard to money, prices and the conduct of affairs, to the point where people are in dire straits and have great difficulty finding a way to satisfy their daily needs. If we compare the situation of the generations that preceded us with our own, we find it to be totally different, mainly because of the close contact with Europeans, their mixing with us, and their proliferation in Islamic lands, so that their ways and customs have overtaken ours and absorbed them completely. ... And you should know also that the authority (*'amr*) of these Europeans in recent years has reached an odious level and an unprecedented openness ... so that it is almost at the point of immorality (*fasad*). The knowledge of where this will end and what will be the outcome is God's alone.[66]

3

The Passing of the Old Makhzan (1894–1912)

At the death of Hassan I, the groundwork was already laid to bring to the throne his favorite son, ʿAbd al-ʿAziz. Only fourteen years old at the time, the young prince was kept in the shadow of the regent Ahmad ibn Musa, popularly known as Ba Ahmad, the former palace chamberlain, who shamelessly doled out patronage for personal gain and filled the most responsible posts in the makhzan with his closest relatives. A clever and ruthless man commonly known as "the steel wire," Ba Ahmad was worried that the new sultan's legitimacy might be compromised because of his young age, so he carefully orchestrated his image to make him acceptable to a skeptical public. When the tribes of the south rose in revolt in 1895, cutting Marrakesh off from the rest of the country, the teenaged ʿAbd al-ʿAziz was placed at the head of a hastily composed mahalla stiffened with reinforcements from the immensely powerful tribe of the M'tougga, one of the great Berber confederations of the Atlas, and sent to the south. The expedition was a success, and ʿAbd al-ʿAziz triumphantly entered Marrakesh in March 1896 with Ba Ahmad at his side, leading an endless procession of captured horses, camels laden with booty, and a straggling column of prisoners, their chains jangling in the dust as they labored through the streets of the city.[1] The staging of these early years was mainly theatrics; but with the passing of time, the Moroccan people began to peek behind the scenes and to observe the confused choreographies of a dynasty in distress.

AN AGE OF CRISIS

Sultan ʿAbd al-ʿAziz was not without imperial demeanor or talent as a ruler, but he was at the mercy of the same problems that had plagued his predecessors: insufficient revenues, tribal revolts, and now, because of unbridled spending, a mounting foreign debt. But, unlike his father, he lacked the strong character to engage with, and much less overcome, these formidable obstacles. Moreover, perhaps because of his youth and naiveté, he was lured into distractions pressed on him by courtiers who plied him with expensive toys and extravagant entertainments.[2] When word of these pastimes leaked outside the palace, his reputation suffered. Added to this troubling mix was ongoing pressure from France, relentlessly chipping away at Morocco's borders, especially in the southeast. Soon most of Sultan Hassan's accomplishments in shoring up the administration and the economy came unraveled, baring the chronic ills that had plagued the makhzan for years and allowed foreigners to intervene in the first place.

In the colonial and postcolonial literature, the short reign of the mature ʿAbd al-ʿAziz (1900–1907) is often referred to as the "prelude to Protectorate," the period when, in the words of Moroccan historian Abdallah Laroui, "anarchy became the leitmotif" of makhzan politics. To the French diplomat Eugène Aubin, writing in 1903, it seemed that "the makhzan is falling to pieces, and its authority is crumbling away. The little order that reigned in the country is giving place to universal anarchy. Brigands are clearing the mountains and occupying the highways ... [and] horsemen are pillaging at the gates of cities. It is a favorable opportunity for settling old scores ..."[3] Laroui offers two possible approaches to analyzing this disastrous scenario: the first, an "anthropological" one, sees anarchy as an innate attribute of Moroccan social behavior, and the second, a "political" one, blames Europe and the weakness of the makhzan for the corrosive practices such as protections, loans, and other exactions that undermined the authority of the state.[4] Neither explanation is all encompassing, while both undoubtedly contributed to the dramatic series of events that gradually diminished the sultan's ability to rule, culminating in a dynastic crisis and the eventual imposition of the French and Spanish Protectorates in 1912.

Historians both pre- and postcolonial have written about this period as if the fall of the makhzan was inevitable, as a result of an accumulation of forces that defeated efforts at reform. Without making a case for inevitability, it is no doubt true that key factors converged at this moment and served to accelerate Morocco's submission to the West. Foremost among these factors was the unfortunate personality of Sultan ʿAbd al-ʿAziz himself, who, because of his character and circumstances, was unable to seize the reins of power and pursue an independent political course. Also significant was the cynical manipulation of events by foreign diplomats and schemers who stood ready to reap the benefits of every political setback they managed to contrive. Finally and most tellingly, we must not discount the mounting tensions within the country itself that created deep divisions and a widespread mood of impending calamity.

We should remember it was also a decade of innovation, a time when many in the Moroccan elite developed a new sense of their place in the world, a period of expanding cultural relations with Europe and the Islamic sphere, an era of striking achievements in literature, law, and religious thought. Intellectuals, bureaucrats, reformers, travelers to Europe and the East, social dreamers with a cautious enthusiasm for change, are the less well-known figures of this period. Their portraits are only now coming to light, as well as their impact on the social and cultural life of their times. Our study of the period 1900–1912 is refreshed by the lives of near-forgotten figures who shaped the course of events – even as they watched the makhzan collapse – and whose actions inflect and modify the handed-down image of a society bent on self-destruction.

PORTRAIT OF A MISGUIDED RULER

When Ba Ahmad died suddenly in a cholera epidemic in 1900, ʿAbd al-ʿAziz was finally free to follow the path of reform laid out by his father, but he was handicapped by his age – he was twenty at the time – and his lack of experience. Seeking assurance, he turned to a small and motley circle of courtiers inherited from the days of Ba Ahmad to help him conduct the business of state. His attraction to foreigners gave them unusual access to the intimate side of palace life. French diplomat Eugène Aubin, arriving in Fez in the midst of a political crisis in 1903, became friendly with people in "official positions" . . . whose lips were unsealed "by the emotional stress of the moment."[5] According to Aubin, the young sultan lived in isolation within the palace, and unlike his father, rarely ventured out among his subjects. "He has shown no disposition to become like his ancestors, either a religious or warrior sultan."[6] The sultan reportedly loved sports such as rugby and polo, introduced by his Scottish military adviser, Harry (Kaid) Maclean, and he was intrigued by gadgets and modern inventions. Gabriel Veyre, a young French cinematographer, introduced to the court in 1901, was hired to instruct the sultan in the use of "modern discoveries" such as "telephones and the telegraph, cinematography and phonography [*sic*], bicycling and motoring, and anything else that pleased him." Veyre found a room in the palace at Marrakesh filled with photographic equipment,

FIGURE 5. "The only man in Southern Morocco with his Bradbury bicycle"; perhaps the cyclist is Budgett Meakin, editor of the *Times of Morocco*, who travelled from Tangier to Marrakesh on a bicycle in 1897, giving a mixed crowd of curious onlookers a first look at this "modern" invention. Hayton Yates and Co., Photographers, Mogador. (Postcard Collection, Gérard Lévy, Paris)

"of all brands, forms and dimensions from the smallest Kodaks to a large darkroom" ... as well as "all sorts of plates, basins, and flasks – a fully equipped photography shop!" But unfortunately, all of this material was "abandoned to the sun, the rain ... playthings for the sheep that wandered freely around the palace, using [the heaped up goods] as a mountain on which to gambol with their young, most of it already reduced to rubbish."[7] According to Veyre, the sultan was surrounded mainly by women – over two hundred in his harem, including a dozen favorites. They were his constant companions and the main subjects of his experiments with photography. Some of them learned to ride bicycles, and were even allowed to pilot the motorcars parked around the palace grounds. Veyre, a devotee of early cinema, often held showings of the latest films from Europe for the sultan also attended by the women of the harem, who sat hidden behind a screen.[8]

Other personalities with whom the sultan had close contact were noted for their physical beauty rather than their probity. Foremost among them was al-Mahdi al-Manabhi, a striking young *muhazni* (soldier) from obscure rural origins who had caught the attention of Ba Ahmad and became his aide de camp. When the government of Ba Ahmad was decimated by cholera in 1900, al-Manabhi rose to the position of Minister of War.

Dynamic and fun loving, he was "like a fish in water," soon displacing the grand vizir as chief counselor to the young sultan.

A rogue character often in attendance was military adviser Maclean, the Scottish drill sergeant who had fled the Gibraltar garrison after an amorous misadventure. Landing in Morocco, he soon became one of the trusted inner circle, providing the sultan with amusements and whatever else he desired from abroad. One of Maclean's tasks was to stage royal entertainments:

> ... the immense gardens of the Agdal [in Marrakesh] were given over to hare and gazelle hunts, the salukis forcing them to bound among the trees like arrows. Nearly every night were fireworks displays, a luminous shower of multi-colored stars that suddenly lit up the gardens and were reflected in the vast basins of water, while musicians played and slaves served milk sweetened with the perfume of almonds or a syrup of pomegranates and raisins ...[9]

Distracted by these lavish displays, ʿAbd al-ʿAziz grew increasingly remote and out of touch with his subjects. In the popular mind, his reputation was clouded because of his intimacy with foreigners, and because of his self-imposed distance, his character and intentions were known only through gossip and word of mouth. At court, his reliance on favorites and his disdain for official business created an atmosphere of jealousy and suspicion. Aubin remarked that under ʿAbd al-ʿAziz, there "has arisen a weak makhzan – a makhzan of professional politicians, intriguing against one another, adopting different attitudes, and playing on the inexperience of the sovereign."[10] As the internal and external threats that had dogged the country for years mounted, an irremediable gap opened up between a darkening reality and the capacity of the state to cope with it.

THE ECONOMY IN TRANSITION

Fiscal troubles were at the heart of the growing crisis. The eternal problem of raising enough revenue to meet the growing needs of the state seemed insolvable. When ʿAbd al-ʿAziz assumed full power in 1900, the treasury contained, according to Dr. Weisgerber, the equivalent of sixty million francs, that is to say, "enough to cover normal expenses for four budgetary years." But that surplus soon vanished, as the expenses of the state grew disproportionately to its income, rising from six million francs in 1882, to twenty million in 1893, to forty million by 1900.[11] More than half of the revenues went abroad, to pay indemnities, to purchase arms and military supplies, or to buy European manufactured goods; the annual trade deficit alone reached 14 million francs annually between 1902 and 1909.[12] On a visit to the port of Larache in 1903, Aubin saw the results of the capricious buying habits of the sultan: "Half a dirigible balloon, the hull of a steam launch, a heap of rails, cases of glassware, gun carriages, agricultural machines ... [were] lying casually dotted on the wharf or in the custom-house stores, bearing lamentable witness to royal aberrations."[13] Not only had the spending habits of the sultanate become excessive, but the traditional means of raising revenues through coercion, such as the mahallas to the countryside, had fallen into disuse.

ʿAbd al-ʿAziz's plan to stem the hemorrhaging of the treasury by reinstituting the *tartib*, a tax first mentioned at the Madrid Conference in 1880, was his solution to the crisis. Unlike the Qurʾanic taxes such as the *aʿshar* and the *zakat*, from which many were exempted, the tartib was a universal capital tax imposed on everyone, including Europeans, protégés, tribesmen, urban dwellers, and even the religious nobility, to be paid in cash and without exception. In return, foreigners for the first time were allowed to buy land on the perimeters of port cites open to overseas trade. Such uniform taxes were not an innovation in the Muslim world; the Ottomans had tried this method as early as 1839, and found it impractical without a standardized currency and an efficient bureaucracy to administer it. For a variety of reasons, Sultan Hassan I had never implemented the tax.[14]

ʿAbd al-ʿAziz was drawn to the notion of a single tax imposed on all his subjects as a direct, simple, and efficient method for introducing fiscal reform. It was also decidedly "modern," in that it supposedly treated every subject anonymously and equally, without regard to position, kinship or any other mark of status. Some said it was "a British idea," brought to the court by journalist Walter Harris who reached the sultan's ear through his friend Kaid Maclean: others saw it as the brainchild of Minister of War al-Manabhi. The tax rolls were prepared with great attention to detail, evaluating land and livestock, leaving no material goods unaccounted for, making this exercise a high point of administrative competence in the Azizist period. But regardless of the care given to its preparation, once imposed, the new tax immediately stirred up immense opposition, especially among the most powerful, who labeled it "anti-religious, unjust, and offensive." Not only was the tartib not sanctioned by the Qur'an, they argued, and hence implicitly unjust; it also enraged local qaʿids who habitually sequestered part of the tax revenues for themselves. Local officials were in the habit of demanding "two dollars instead of one," it was said, one for the makhzan, and one for themselves.[15]

According to Dr. Louis Arnaud, who recorded the memories of Moroccan soldier Hajj Salem el Abdi, the tax was irremediably harsh:

> [It] was imposed on everyone and everything. Sheep, goats, donkeys, horses, mules, camels, olives, and dates; the trees that gave fruit and those that gave nothing; even the earth and stones paid a sum fixed in advance. Nothing was exempt but the air to breathe and water to drink.... The rich and the poor, those who owned hundreds of olive trees and troops of she-camels, and those who had only a donkey and a few sheep; pashas as well as qa'ids, men of the shurafa as well as marabouts; those who possessed baraka and those who had none; everyone had to submit.[16]

As a result, the tax was universally hated. A second attempt under 'Abd al-'Aziz at instituting the tartib fared no better than the first. The tax was especially noxious to the French and other foreign interests, who feared its ill effects on the protégé system. Because of the ubiquity of protections and the incorporation of most commercial activity within their scope, the makhzan had little space to maneuver and had to bend to Europe's will. By 1903, the experiment was declared a failure, leaving state finances in worse shape than ever, for now state coffers were truly empty. In the final analysis, foreign and internal interests worked in concert to sabotage the new tax and to eventually defeat it.[17]

In search of a quick remedy to fix the fiscal dilemma, the makhzan tried minting coins with a lesser intrinsic value, but the public refused to accept them. A 25 percent depreciation in the value of the currency between 1896 and 1906 further diminished the resources of the state.[18] The makhzan had to turn to other sources, and foreign creditors were always ready to lend a hand. The first major loan for 7.5 million francs at 6 percent interest was negotiated with French banks in December 1901; more loans followed from British and Belgian sources, making the makhzan financially dependent on Europeans.

The Anglo-French accord of 1904 removing Britain from its traditional role of informal protector of the makhzan was a watershed, changing the nature of the diplomatic game. It gave France the lead in negotiating a major bailout of the flailing makhzan, tying its hands even further. Seeing the handwriting on the wall, upper echelons of the government split into two warring factions – those who favored the loan, and those who saw it as a dire threat to Morocco's independence. Greasing the wheels of decisionmaking with generous "gifts," the French finally completed the signing of the loan contract in June 1904. With a face value of 62.5 million francs, the loan carried an interest rate of 5 percent, and like the Spanish indemnity of 1860, it was guaranteed by a portion of the customs revenues. With the British now out of the picture, and France controlling the major source of state revenue, the removal of all obstacles to a French takeover was complete.[19]

The extent to which the governmental financial crisis of 1901–1904 caused the impoverishment of the masses is a topic worthy of debate. Postcolonial authors, building a case for a picture of economic ruin caused by Europeans, argued that the inflation that appeared at century's end caused dislocation and suffering on a broad scale. Bolstered by lurid descriptions from European travelers of widespread penury, they spoke of the "impoverishment" of the working classes, arguing that craftspeople in particular were dragged down into a "precarious" existence by competition with European-made goods. "The more those at the top borrowed, the more those at the bottom were impoverished," observed Abdallah Laroui, but without providing substantive evidence.[20] While it is certainly true that poverty grew, it was not universally the case. Evidence points to the fact that urban and the rural economies were not uniformly shrinking in the years immediately leading up to the Protectorate. Historian Stacy Holden has shown how the makhzan took charge of the food supply during the 1903–1907 famine by developing sophisticated mechanisms to increase the amount of flour for sale in urban markets. Nicholas Michel has vigorously challenged the notion of end-of-century economic collapse by producing data to show that although extreme poverty may have existed, it was found only in isolated pockets. More common, according to Michel, are signs of a growing prosperity in both town and country, based on stable prices for subsistence items, improvements in the standard of living, a rise in the consumption of luxury goods like tea and sugar, and an increase in land under cultivation. This is not to disallow the fact that the makhzan itself was in a fiscal crisis and out of money, for that was surely the case; but the extent to which that crisis spread out into the wider society is the subject of debate.[21]

INTERNAL POLITICS: MAHDIS, INSURGENTS, AND REBELS

By 1904, it was widely believed that ʿAbd al-ʿAziz had lost control of the government and was in the grip of Euromania. The antimakhzan reaction burst out at all social levels, but especially in the countryside, where local strongmen suddenly rose up to challenge the legitimacy of the regime. Rural insurgencies were not a new phenomenon in Morocco; chronicles from earlier eras are filled with tales of banditry and rebellion marked by pillaging, kidnapping and assassination, usually between rival rural factions, but also between tribal groups and the makhzan. Indeed, pillaging was not a monopoly of country warlords but also a strategy of the state as well; in the time of Sultan Hassan I, the "eating up" of dissident tribes was a way of winning back economic advantages as well as symbolic ones by recouping taxes and other badly needed resources while reinforcing respect for the ruling authority. Brigandage in the Moroccan context, according to sociologist Rahma Bourqia, was not a marginal activity, but an innate part of the social and political process in which discontented groups could make a claim on the makhzan's monopoly of power. It was far more common in times of environmental crisis, when food supplies were short; moreover, it rose and fell with the makhzan's political fortunes, making the years 1903–1907 a prime moment for social upheaval in the countryside.[22]

The language used in the Arabic sources to describe bandits is emotional and violent – *fussad* (miscreants), *qutta' al-turuq* (highway robbers), *awbash* (riff-raff) and *munharifin* (deviants, outcasts) – revealing the anxiety of a state in distress. However, from the popular point of view, rebellious figures

FIGURE 6. "The Civil War in Morocco," *Le Petit Journal*, January 18, 1903, graphically illustrating the turmoil and popular strife caused by Bu Himara's uprising in the Taza region. (Courtesy of Widener Library, Harvard University)

such as Bu Himara and Ahmed al-Raysuni, both operating far from the reach of the makhzan in the north, were political entrepreneurs on a mission, engaging in recognized forms of social protest against an oppressive regime. Among their objectives was the negotiation of a new relationship with the central power based on a redistribution of honor and material goods. Indeed, historically speaking, acts of brigandage often became occasions for a kind of public theater, especially when the confrontation between the sultan and the upstart ended in a ceremony of punishment and pardon that restored balance to the makhzan-tribal relationship. These subtle means of reapportioning power and renegotiating social control were at the heart of the phenomenon of banditry and rebellion that reared its head with particular virulence in the first decade of the twentieth century.[23]

The most notorious example of the bandit-as-political upstart in this period was a disaffected student who took on the title of El-Rogui (Ar.: al-Ruki, or "The Pretender"), but was popularly known as Bu Himara, or "the man on a donkey." Bu Himara first appeared in the northeast region of Morocco in 1902, claiming to be the sultan's older brother and rightful heir to the throne. His given name was Jilali b. Idris al-Yusufi al-Zarhuni, from the region of Jebel Zerhoun. Earlier in his career he had spent time in Fez and picked up all the gossip of the court, tales of the sultan's entertainments, and the in-fighting and pointless intrigues of his ministers. He capitalized on the mood of popular agitation, and using his claim to sharifian descent, surrounded himself with "a halo of miracles, prophecies and dreams." His face supposedly changed color three times a day, green in the morning, yellow at noon, and black at night, a testament to his supernatural powers. He went so far as to constitute a rival makhzan, with all its trappings and protocol, centered in the far north in Selouane in the remote region between Melilla and Oujda, far from the reach of the sultan's armies, where he controlled a vital stretch of the Mediterranean coastline. There he entered into commercial relations with Europeans, collected customs duties, imported firearms, and even granted mining concessions to the valuable iron and lead deposits in the nearby Rif Mountains. Draping himself with the mantle of the *mahdi*, or "rightly guided one," Bu Himara declared a jihad against the infidel (a category in which he included the sultan) and rampaged through the north for seven years, supported by disaffected tribes. He easily defeated the poorly organized mahallas sent to crush him, and even threatened Fez for a time, before he was finally captured in the summer of 1909 and executed by Sultan ʿAbd al-Hafiz.[24]

The makhzan's inability to crush this rival was due to a number of factors, foremost among them a decrease in the capabilities of the sultan's army.

The energetic reforms carried out by his predecessors slowed under ʿAbd al-ʿAziz, mainly due to the ongoing fiscal crisis and the sultan's inability to assert his leadership over the military corps. Minister of War al-Manabhi proved to be an incompetent general, and as his mistakes accumulated, the officer corps became demoralized and massive desertions took place among the rank and file.[25] In addition, thousands of rifles entered the country from abroad, much of it as contraband, and soon found their way into rural areas, giving tribal chiefs access to weaponry equal to or superior to that of the makhzan. In the most remote parts of the country, tribal warriors were exchanging ancient flintlocks for single-shot breechloaders such as the American Remington (*mashuka*), the French Chassepot (*sasbu*), and the British Martini-Henry (*bu hafra*). The rearming of the countryside not only changed the internal military balance of power; it also opened the makhzan to the critique that it was not in control of its territory and was teetering on the brink of collapse.[26]

The rise of the Rogui gave the signal to other rebels to openly defy the makhzan. In the region of Tangier, a local warlord named Ahmad al-Raysuni gripped the town with fear during the winter of 1903–1904. Al-Raysuni was the scion of a well-known sharifian lineage of the Jebala, a hilly region south of Tangier with a long history of opposition to foreign invaders.[27] As a young man, al-Raysuni entered the netherworld of brigandage, surrounding himself with a band of outlaws who rustled cattle and carried out other forms of extortion. He was caught and thrown into a dungeon at Essaouira in 1894, where he was kept chained to a wall, leaving deep scars on his wrists and ankles; when he was set free in 1900, he promptly returned to his old ways. Noting the success of upstarts like Bu Himara, al-Raysuni decided to build an independent power center in the north by kidnapping Christians. At the head of his band of well-armed mountaineers, he invaded Tangier's posh garden suburbs and snatched wealthy Europeans from their palatial homes – Greek-American Ion Perdicaris, British journalist Walter Harris, and Scottish drill instructor Harry Maclean were among his victims – holding them for ransom and stirring up an international uproar that stoked the anger of U.S. President Theodore Roosevelt, who took the capture of Perdicaris as a personal affront. The Perdicaris affair alone netted al-Raysuni $70,000, prompting an outraged telegram from the famous Rough Rider that bugled: "I want Perdicaris alive or al-Raysuni dead."[28]

Al-Raysuni survived this incident, as he did so many others, with the outlaw's knack for the quick escape, and eventually he retired with his booty to his mountain fastness of Tazrout in the tribal region of the Beni

Arous. British travel writer Rosita Forbes spent weeks there in 1923, interviewing the aging miscreant about his life for her romantic exposé entitled *The Sultan of the Mountains*. She concluded "... He believes in the luck which invariably turns the most adverse circumstances to his advantage, and is not above staking his remarkable immunity from danger against the credulity of his followers, but below this is the conviction of divine right."[29] Al-Raysuni used his notoriety to build a political base in the north that paralleled, in many ways, the vast fiefdom the Glawa clan were consolidating in the south. Like them, he realized that Morocco was headed for foreign domination and that the time was ripe for staking out an alliance with its future rulers. His dealings with the Spanish, the eventual masters of the north, began in 1911 when he was awarded the governorate of Assilah southwest of Tangier, thus acquiring a political legitimacy once denied to him. A shrewd strategist, al-Raysuni had converted banditry into political capital, a transition that would have been unthinkable under Sultan Hassan I, who drew a clear distinction between charlatans and men of honor.[30]

This situation of moral confusion made possible the rise of a charismatic leader of a different sort who aspired to lead Morocco out of its troubles. A noted scholar of Fez, Muhammad b. ʿAbd al-Kabir al-Kattani, emerged from the ranks of the ulama at the end of the nineteenth century to head a movement of Islamic revival aimed at halting the drift of Morocco toward Europe. Al-Kattani was a member of an illustrious family with sharifian roots, known for its independent stance vis-à-vis the makhzan. The al-Kattanis founded a zawiya in 1853 in Fez that attracted men of all social classes, but especially the working poor who were drawn to Sufi teachings. Like others in the Fez elite, the al-Kattanis were appalled by the influx of European advisers, diplomats and adventurers who invaded the court of ʿAbd al-ʿAziz and seemed to be directing the course of events. In 1895, Muhammad al-Kattani, only thirty-four years old but already famous for his saintly qualities and his oratory skills, rose to leadership of the zawiya and began to preach renewal on the basis of *ijtihad*, or the reinterpretation of Shariah law freed from the confines of tradition (*taqlid*). He called for resistance to Europeans and their banishment from the precincts of power, but without directly attacking the sultan. Moreover, he used his zawiya to attract disciples whom he indoctrinated into mystical practices that rejected set norms and redefined the limits of orthodoxy, thus placing himself in direct confrontation with the religious establishment. Recognizing in him a threat to their authority, leaders of the Fez ulama branded al-Kattani a heretic and put him on trial, but through clever diplomacy, he was able to return to favor by drawing closer to the sultan, who appropriated al-Kattani's critique of the ulama to his own advantage, using it as a reference point for reining in the overly independent doctors of law.[31]

After charges against al-Kattani were dropped, he returned to preaching, determined to present himself as an alternative to the reactionary ulama. He broke with tradition in other ways, too; he understood the power of the printed word and published and distributed religious tracts and political pamphlets produced on the lithographic press in Fez attacking moral corruption. He also founded a short-lived Arabic newspaper called *al-Taʿun* ("The Plague") that preached opposition to the growing Western influence, established a Tangier branch of the Fez zawiya at the nerve center of Morocco's communications with the outside world, and used it as a platform to expand his contacts deeper into the Maghrib and the Mashriq, spreading news of his reformist agenda far and wide.[32]

Operating according to "politics in a new key," to adopt a phrase of historian Sahar Bazzaz, al-Kattani built a coalition of forces seeking an alternative to the failing regime. Disheartened by the sultan's ineptitude, al-Kattani eventually dropped his support for ʿAbd al-ʿAziz and defected to his brother and rival ʿAbd al-Hafiz, when the two began a countrywide struggle for dominance in 1907. Al-Kattani's role in the *Hafiziyya* of 1907–1908, the movement to replace the ruling ʿAbd al-ʿAziz with his brother, was instrumental. Lending ʿAbd al-Hafiz his prestige as a sharif and head of a brotherhood, al-Kattani rode the wave of enthusiasm for the royal challenger and helped bring him to power in 1908. But these two formidable and in many ways antipodal personalities – the sufi shaykh and the new sultan – soon had a falling out, especially when it became apparent that ʿAbd al-Hafiz would be no more successful than his brother in confronting foreigners. Meanwhile, al-Kattani's influence in both the urban and tribal areas kept growing thanks to his "charm and passionate eloquence," according to his contemporary, the Moroccan scholar Muhammad al-Hajwi, raising the possibility that this much-admired popular figure might lead a coalition of tribal forces that would independently proclaim jihad.

The specter of an al-Kattani-led uprising no doubt motivated ʿAbd al-Hafiz in the next stage of their relations.[33] In March 1909, feeling himself in dire danger, al-Kattani fled Fez with his family and disciples; however, they were swiftly recaptured and paraded through the streets of Fez like common criminals with their hands tied, their beards shaven, their heads bare. Taken to the palace, al-Kattani's band were punished in the cruelest manner possible, their hands cut off and the wounds rubbed with salt. To complete the humiliation, the master himself was beaten before his wives and children until he expired, and his corpse was thrown into an unmarked grave to head off the possibility of a post-mortem cult of veneration.

The tragic story of Muhammad al-Kattani has been intentionally "forgotten" by later generations of Moroccan historians, perhaps because of its powerful motifs of royal injustice, bitter vengeance, and unspoken martyrdom. But at the time, details of the tragedy sank deeply into the Moroccan psyche, making this episode an important turning point in the slow but steady dissolution of makhzanian authority. This event also brought into the open the widespread hatred of Europe and its representatives and the precipitous decline in the prestige of the shurafa and ulama, once considered the guardians of the public trust, but now seized by mental paralysis. The excessive cruelty used to bring down the al-Kattani family exposed beyond a doubt the makhzan's fundamental weaknesses. Lastly, the extreme violence employed against a revered religious leader cast a shadow over the sultan's moral stature, contributing to 'Abd al-Hafiz's final disgrace and leaving permanent scars in the collective memory.

Each of these "outlaws" whose portraits we have drawn appear to be unique, but on closer examination, they had much in common. They represent a new strain in political life that redefined how opposition to the state could be expressed. Bu Himara created an independent principality adapting methods copied from Western statecraft, such as taxes, control of the economy, and military conscription. Using violent means, al-Raysuni exploited foreigners to fatten his treasury and to legitimize his bid for political authority. Muhammad al-Kattani was also shaped by European ideas – the printing press, newspapers, and other new forms of communication were tools he used to spread his message of political renewal. Each of these "upstarts" was influenced by aspects of modernity filtering into Morocco from abroad; each combined elements of the old-style *mujahid* with new skills of propaganda and mobilization that transformed local protests into a countrywide awareness of impending disaster. Though the danger they posed to the *ancien regime* may have been more symbolic than real, in the confused circumstances that preceded the coming of the Protectorates, their resistance contributed greatly to the disequilibrium that made the difference between the makhzan's survival and its fall.

DIPLOMACY AND WAR

In the situation of upheaval that characterized the Moroccan scene after 1903, European powers – with France in the lead – acted quickly to exploit the makhzan's weakness. Repositioning themselves through a series of dramatic moves, they swiftly sealed Morocco's fate. The attack came from a variety of directions, military, diplomatic, and financial. In the military sphere, France mounted an aggressive campaign to absorb key areas of the Moroccan desert along the ill-defined frontier with Algeria in the southeast. Arguing that the makhzan had "neglected" this distant zone, French troops began to trespass. For a long time, the colonial party in France, backed by Algerian settlers, had been pushing for annexation of this region as the future land link between Algeria and the French colony in Senegal. While the makhzan's presence in the desert region was indeed weak, it was nevertheless considered part of the Moroccan patrimony, especially the oasis of Tafilalt that was the home of the ʿAlawi shurafa. Another important center in the southeast was the populous oasis of Figuig, a bustling regional market, about seven hundred kilometers distant from Fez. Both Tafilalt and Figuig shipped their products – mainly dates and skins – via the long and tortuous route across the Atlas Mountains to the commercial center of Fez, receiving in return imported goods such as tea, sugar, and manufactured cloth.[34]

By 1897, the French-built trans-Saharan railroad reached as far as Aïn Sefra on the Algerian side of the border, and soon Figuig merchants were shipping goods to coastal Oran on the railroad in preference to sending them via the long mountainous route to Fez. After 1900, the French military stepped up their operations in the southeast, and took over the sprawling oasis of Touat, prompting a renegotiation of the border with the Moroccans in 1901 that brought little clarity. Nor did French ambitions end there. Prodded by a militant Algerian settler lobby that scorned the more cautious government in Paris, the army moved further south after 1903 under the leadership of an ambitious colonial officer named Louis Hubert Gonzalve Lyautey, who occupied the Béchar oasis southwest of Aïn Sefra inside Moroccan territory and rebaptized it Colomb to hide its precise location from Paris. Operating with full freedom at the edge of the empire, Lyautey advocated a policy of "suppleness, elasticity, and conformity to place, time and the circumstances," with a sharp eye to both the military and political consequences of his forward actions.[35] (See Map 2, page 97.)

The response of Sultan ʿAbd al-ʿAziz to Lyautey's artful strategy was weak and indecisive; instead of encouraging resistance from local chiefs to confront the French, he tried to suppress it, fearing that attacks by the tribesmen would only incite France to penetrate further. Indeed, by 1911, the French had reached the river Ziz, two hundred miles inside Morocco from the Algerian border, bringing much of the pre-Saharan southeast of Morocco under French control. Meanwhile, in the southwest, the French launched an expedition from Saint-Louis on the Senegalese coast into the Saharan interior, with the aim of eventually reaching the region of Adrar in Mauritania. A local Sahrawi shaykh named Ma al-ʿAynayn, a much-venerated religious figure of the region of Saguia el Hamra, became alarmed at the loss of territory to non-Muslims, and rallied his "blue men" followers to defend their ancestral lands. Courted by ʿAbd al-ʿAziz and supplied with money, arms and ammunition by the makhzan, shaykh Ma al-ʿAynayn undertook a self-proclaimed jihad in the southwest that kept the French at bay until the last days of Moroccan independence.[36]

FIGURE 7. "The Dreaded Guest." A Moroccco-bound Kaiser Wilhelm II of Germany is shown making his way south as other heads of state look on with rising apprehension. An alarmed French President Emile Loubet looks out from the tricolor-draped window. *Puck Magazine*, New York, August 1905. (Library of Congress Prints and Photographs Division)

Meanwhile, on the diplomatic front, Britain stepped away from its longstanding support of a neutral and independent Morocco, clearing the way for French ambitions. The Entente Cordiale of 1904 between Britain and France settled their outstanding differences over colonial territories; France gave Britain a free hand in Egypt, and in return received the right to "preserve order ... and provide assistance in Morocco." The French stranglehold on Morocco tightened. France deliberately followed a stealthy diplomacy calculated to narrow Morocco's options to the vanishing point. Secret agreements between France, on the one hand, and Spain and Italy, on the other, eliminated these lesser rivals from the race. The only remaining roadblock was France's archenemy, Germany. When Kaiser Wilhelm II made a surprise visit to the port of Tangier on March 31, 1905, throngs of jubilant Moroccans met him. His declaration of support for Moroccan sovereignty was calculated to show Germany's determination to be counted in as a major player in the swiftly moving game of international politics. Though the Kaiser's visit momentarily derailed French ambitions, it was merely a sideshow to Germany's main purpose, which was to gain an advantage in the intensifying struggle for continental supremacy. As for the "Moroccan Question," it was once again put on the table for consideration by the Great Powers, but with France now in the lead, pushing for a long list of reforms that would assign it a preeminent role in the military and economic restructuring of the Moroccan state.

As the noose tightened and France's list of demands lengthened, Sultan ʿAbd al-ʿAziz decided to call for a "consultation" (*shura*) with carefully selected members of the urban and rural elite representing all parts of the country. The convening of the fifteen-member "Council of Notables" (*majlis al-aʿyan*) in January 1905 was calculated to appeal to European liberals while giving the Moroccan regime the façade of unity to strengthen its hand in the coming negotiations. Though hardly the first sign of a "modern representative government" – as nationalist leader ʿAllal al-Fasi would later claim – the council did serve as a sounding board for developing a response to French demands. With French public opinion sharply divided, and Germany showing renewed interest in Morocco after the Kaiser's visit, the makhzan felt its best card would be another round of international negotiations in which no one country would predominate. This strategy, however, proved to be a grave miscalculation; with the loss of Great Britain as an ally, and Germany's wavering commitment, the sultan was deprived of champions who could neutralize France and block her ambitions.[37]

FIGURE 8. Bab al-Suq, gate to the main market in Casablanca, c. 1907; French soldiers, European housewives, Jews in traditional garb, and small children mingle with the crowd. Note the advertisements for European manufactured goods posted on the walls of the madina surrounding the gate. (Postcard Collection, Gérard Lévy, Paris)

At the international conference held in the southern Spanish coastal town of Algeciras in January 1906, the gathered diplomats reluctantly acquiesced to France's now dominant position, allowing her to continue the process of "peaceful penetration." The United States argued strenuously that the Powers should retain international control, quietly advising Germany that in the American view, France was simply a "mandatory" of the other powers and acting "under responsibility to all of them" to assure an "open door" to foreign commercial interests. But in the end, the "internationalism" President Theodore Roosevelt desired was ignored; while Morocco's territorial integrity and sovereignty were reaffirmed, large areas of the sultan's authority were ceded to France, especially in the port cities. A port police was created, composed of Moroccans but commanded by French and Spanish officers, and a state bank was founded under the watchful eye of the foreign powers that essentially took over the country's fiscal administration. When news of the accords reached Fez, it was clear that the government of Sultan 'Abd al-'Aziz had been betrayed and was now in deep trouble.[38]

Stirred into action by the Treaty of Algeciras, opposition within the Council of Notables hardened; in the deteriorating political climate, ordinary Moroccans began to show their anger in the streets. Since the conference of Madrid in 1880, the number of westerners in Morocco had increased dramatically, not only in the cities on the coast, but also in communities of the interior. Missionaries, doctors, military advisers, businessmen, travelers, sportsmen, explorers and adventurers, including women, were no longer an unusual sight in Morocco's inland cities. Their presence was a source of agitation and controversy, for not everyone accepted them gladly. Writing in 1885, French military officer Jules Erckmann complained that foreigners were the targets of stones and insults, and householders did everything possible to prevent Christians from lodging among them. Misunderstandings were rife on both sides. As Morocco suffered setbacks in the diplomatic arena, popular resentment toward foreigners grew.[39]

In the forefront of foreigners regarded as unwanted interlopers were Christian missionaries. Spanish Franciscans had resided in Tangier since the seventeenth century, where they ministered to the tiny Christian population and kept on the fringes of Moroccan society. As the tempo of European intervention increased, more missionaries arrived. After the 1859 war, a victorious Spain erected two churches, one in Fez and the other in Tetuan. Later in the nineteenth century, Cardinal Lavigerie's Catholic crusade in Algeria spread to Morocco, and ordinary Moroccans became fearful that their closest neighbor would soon become a source of spiritual contamination. By 1875, more Christian missions were established along the coast, from Tetuan to Essaouira; in this last town, synagogues, mosques, a Protestant temple and a Catholic church nestled side-by-side in the *madina*, the older, walled part of town. Jews were a particular target of the "London Society to Promote Christianity Amongst the Jews," a missionary relief effort that drew converts during the severe famine of 1877–1879. In 1882, the Protestant "British and Foreign Bible Society" began distributing Bibles throughout the country, and in 1887, the "North African Mission" appeared in Fez and Sefrou, represented by four English ladies who dispensed medical advice along with Christian teachings.

The makhzan greeted this wave of zealous foreigners with a cautious wariness rather than hostility, and even tried to conciliate Christian interests. In 1888, Sultan Hassan I sent a goodwill embassy to the Vatican headed by Minister of Foreign Affairs Muhammad Torres. But among the common people, the missionaries and their activities were regarded with suspicion, and many feared their aim was conversion rather than good works. In October 1902, a young English missionary named David Cooper was assassinated in the streets of Fez by a deranged man, who was immediately seized upon and executed by the authorities, enraging the populace even further, for he had sought refuge after the event in the tomb of Mawlay Idris, patron saint of Fez, a *hurm* (religious sanctuary) that was supposed to be inviolate. The execution of Cooper's killer on orders of the sultan simply exacerbated the growing fear that Christian missions were being officially "protected" and that Europeans were getting the upper hand.[40]

But the most spectacular episode in this angry escalation of popular feeling was the killing of Dr. Emile Mauchamp, an eccentric French doctor living in Marrakesh, who was repeatedly stabbed and beaten to death by a frenzied mob in March 19, 1907, at the doorstep of his house. Eulogized as a "martyr to civilization" by his French compatriots, Mauchamp's death became a *cause célèbre* demonstrating the growing gulf between European aims and Moroccan sensibilities. The French press represented the murder as an unprovoked and random act of barbarous cruelty; but recent reappraisals of the event suggest that the killing of Mauchamp was most likely a calculated political act, designed to send a message to foreigners that they were unsafe, and to the sultan, that his days were numbered.[41]

Shortly after Mauchamp's murder and supposedly in retribution for it, a French force occupied the Moroccan city of Oujda on the border with Algeria, and held it for ransom until a series of exorbitant French demands were met. Tensions rose even higher in July 1907, after eight Europeans

FIGURE 9. Victims of the 1907 street fighting in Casablanca are taken away for burial; especially hard hit was the *mellah*, where dozens of people were killed during the bombardment and subsequent looting. (Postcard Collection, Gérard Lévy, Paris)

riding on a newly constructed railroad line in Casablanca were murdered by native tribesmen. In the confusion that followed, the guns of the off-shore French cruiser *Galilée* were turned on the town, setting off a general insurrection. Parts of the city were destroyed and many were killed; especially hard hit was the mellah, which turned into a scene of wild mayhem. The French responded by sending a two thousand man expeditionary force to Casablanca under General Drude and occupying the city, raising the stakes even higher. Clearly, the period of "peaceful penetration" was over; the only element lacking to complete the montage of disarray was a dynastic crisis. Sadly, this too was in the making.

THE HAFIZIYYA

By the summer of 1907, Morocco had reached a point of no return in its struggle to maintain self-rule. Deeply alarmed by the inability of Sultan ʿAbd al-ʿAziz to hold the country together, responsible elites looked elsewhere for a leader who could solder the bits of a disintegrating state. ʿAbd al-Hafiz, elder brother of the sultan and *khalifa* in Marrakesh, seemed the best candidate for this prodigious task. He possessed a maturity of intellect and a political cunning his younger brother lacked, and he had the support of spiritual authorities such as the al-Kattanis. Since 1901, he had been the makhzan's man in the south, building close relations with the so-called Lords of the Atlas, a loose collection of Berber clans who ruled the High Atlas region with impunity. Foremost among them were the Glawa family, headed by Madani al-Glawi, a powerful local chieftain acquainted with the wider world and cunning enough to understand the dangers of the French threat. The alliance between ʿAbd al-Hafiz and the Glawa took shape in 1906–1907, and became the nucleus of an elaborate scheme to overthrow ʿAbd al-ʿAziz and capture the throne. With this union, a spirit of revolt was ignited that soon took on the appearance of a full-scale jihad, mingling religious excitement, anti-French sentiment, and a profound dislike of the ruling monarch. Supported by his southern allies, ʿAbd al-Hafiz quickly assumed the trappings of rule. Dr. Arnaud described a ceremony in which he accepted gifts from the people of Marrakesh:

> ... the customary presents were handed over, including negresses and fully decked out horses; then came the Jews with Isaac Corcos at their head, depositing mounds of cloth and silks. Mawlay ʿAbd al-Hafiz was seated on the throne of his brother, in the room that had served as the Sultan's bureau. He had the Glawi standing to his right ...[42]

FIGURE 10. Rural tribesmen are rounded up by force to serve in the Army of Sultan ʿAbd al-ʿAziz in his losing battle with his brother, ʿAbd al-Hafiz, who succeeded him in 1908. Album Brémond. (Collection Gérard Lévy, Paris)

A *bayʿa* pronounced in favor of ʿAbd al-Hafiz was offered in Marrakesh in September 1907, plunging the country into a civil war, pitting south against north, and splitting public opinion into two opposing camps over the question of succession. In Fez, the news of ʿAbd al-Hafiz's coup was greeted with dismày, not because people were opposed to replacing the incompetent ʿAbd al-ʿAziz with his more forceful brother, but rather, because of the air of illegality that surrounded the effort. They especially disliked the fact that they had been circumvented in certifying the new sultan's election in Marrakesh, and how he had taken the unusual path of leaning on southern Berbers rather than seeking legitimacy from the ulama of Fez.

In January 1908, the Fez ulama, prodded on by Muhammad al-Kattani and his followers, reluctantly declared ʿAbd al-ʿAziz's "moral death" and issued a "conditional" bayʿa in support of ʿAbd al-Hafiz as his successor. The bayʿa made a series of demands: that the new sultan should undertake the jihad neglected by his predecessor; that he abolish the hated gate taxes (*maks*); that he liberate the occupied cities of Oujda and Casablanca; that he put an end to protections; and that he confine Europeans to the port cities. In other words, the bayʿa was conditioned on ʿAbd al-Hafiz revoking Morocco's consent to the Act of Algeciras. In daring to impose terms on the naming of the sultan, the Fez bayʿa was unprecedented in the

Moroccan experience. The assent of the Fez ulama turned the tide for ʿAbd al-Hafiz, and soon other imperial cities followed suit. Yet the war of succession dragged on for another six months as ʿAbd al-ʿAziz continued his resistance, egged on by the French. The end came on August 19, 1908, on the road between Rabat and Marrakesh, when the deposed sultan's mahalla was ambushed by partisans of his brother, and his soldiers melted away in the torrid summer heat. Abandoned by his men, his *jallaba* shredded by bullets, the ex-sultan fled to the safety of French-held Casablanca, where he announced his abdication two days later. He spent the rest of his very long life as a pensioner of the state, living in Tangier, where he died in 1943.[43]

The fragile coalition that brought ʿAbd al-Hafiz to power soon disintegrated. Despite his intelligence and keen political skills, the new sultan managed in very short order to alienate the pillars of society: the urban bourgeoisie, the shurafa, and the rural nobility. By reinstating unpopular taxes, by adopting an ambivalent attitude toward jihad, and by failing to curtail European influence, ʿAbd al-Hafiz's ambition to restore the prestige of the sultanate had the opposite effect. Chronically short of funds, he reinstated the tartib and resorted to expropriations, the sale of offices, and other exactions against the rural population that destroyed whatever good will toward the sultanate was left. According to Dr. Weisgerber, "soon Mawlay Hafiz ... found himself in the same situation as his predecessor: without prestige, without authority, faced with an empty treasury and a mounting debt."[44] Moreover, the two French bridgeheads in Oujda and Casablanca were taking on an aspect of permanency, and ʿAbd al-Hafiz was forced to reopen negotiations with an enemy now firmly planted on Moroccan soil. Left with a rump territory only tenuously under his control, he was the sultan of a Morocco that was neither politically nor economically viable. As the historian Ibn Zaydan later observed, "The tear was beyond repair."[45]

Early in 1911, fed up with unending rounds of new taxes and news of yet another huge foreign loan, the tribes of the Middle Atlas besieged Fez and the sultan found himself a prisoner of the palace. In a moment of panic, he appealed to the French for relief. Seizing the opportunity, a large French expeditionary force entered Fez on May 21, 1911, ending the fiction of Moroccan independence. On August 15, 1911, ʿAbd al-Hafiz signed over control of his army to France who now provided the soldiers' pay. French advisers quickly took charge and displaced the Moroccan officers. Both Spain and Germany registered a weak protest; after a half-hearted showing of the flag by the German gunboat *Panther* in the port of Agadir on July 1,

FIGURE 11. Defeated Sultan ʿAbd al-Halfiz was exiled to France in the summer of 1912, following the signing of the Treaty of Fez and his forced abdication. Servants of the ex-Sultan collect his baggage after his arrival in the southern French port of Marseilles. Cliché Rol. (Collection Gérard Lévy, Paris)

1911, Germany dropped its objections to the French coup and accepted territory in the Congo as compensation. On March 30, 1912, Sultan ʿAbd al-Hafiz signed the Treaty of Fez, abrogating power and creating a French Protectorate over most of Morocco; with this decisive act, the last missing piece in France's vast North African empire was finally set in place.

Might Morocco have stayed independent, had this divisive internecine struggle not beset the country? Surely, the civil war dispersed the last shreds of popular support for the old regime, making it ripe for foreign takeover. Yet, for all that, the Hafiziyya might also be viewed as a moment of strength, when diverse elements of the nation finally cooperated in an effort to repel the foreign danger. There is no doubt that the Hafiziyya was a time of national reawakening, similar to heroic moments of the past when Morocans had joined together to repel unwelcome invaders. Some historians have even argued that the Hafiziyya was a pivotal moment in the formation of the modern state, representing a new turn in political life. For it was indeed the case that novel ideas about the limits of royal absolutism were taking hold, even if only in their infancy, among a narrow group of reformers deeply influenced by ideas coming mainly from the

East. The notion that public opinion should influence policy, that the leadership should demand bureaucratic accountability, and that rulers ought to adhere to the contracts that lent them legitimacy, were abstractions now being seen in a new light. The idea that consultation and power-sharing should be central to the governing process was also emerging as an explicit theme. Many of these concepts had already taken root elsewhere in the region. In 1906 the Persians and in 1908 the Turks had forced constitutional governments upon their absolutist rulers; now these ideas were reverberating throughout North Africa and reaching Morocco. Events of this period were portents for the future, when Moroccan nationalists were looking for models of popular participation. Rather than throwing a veil of silence over the Hafiziyya as a shameful episode of fratricidal warfare, as contemporary Moroccan historiography has tended to do, or treating it as an anomaly, (in the manner of "official" accounts of the period), the Hafiziyya might better be seen as a bridge between the old makhzan and a new one that arose later during the nationalist period, driven by the need to recompose fundamental structures of power while preserving the symbolic assets of the state.

Nonetheless, concepts of popular sovereignty and parliamentary rule were still far from the collective thinking of this pre –World War I generation of Moroccan intellectuals. Late-nineteenth-century reformers held fast to the principle of Shariah-based rule, not only because of their fundamentally conservative outlook, but also because reform of the old makhzan, rather than its overthrow, seemed the most pragmatic means of making the transition to a more modern polity. At the same time, they were steeped in ideas coming from the Arab East, especially the thoughts of the Egyptian reformer Muhammad 'Abduh. Copies of his journal *al-'Urwa al-Wuthqa* advocating political renewal through the medium of a revitalized Islam passed from hand to hand in cafés and were read at social gatherings. Like their Egyptian counterparts, Moroccan reformers called for political innovation expressed in Islamic terms; but in order for change to be legitimate and consistent with prevailing norms, they argued, it had to be overseen by a pious sultan who was kin to the Prophet.

Morocco of 1912 was not the Morocco of 1870. The public sphere was in the midst of a process of transformation. Evidence of European styles and tastes were everywhere: cigarettes and steam-powered flour mills, telephones and the telegraph, cameras, bicycles, sewing machines and pianos, and even the occasional motorcar. Methods of mass communication were becoming part of the fabric of daily life. During the Hafiziyya, the contending parties wrote petitions and letters, meant to be read in public places to rally popular support. News from outside circulated in the port cities, and foreign newspapers made the rounds. In Morocco, as in Egypt, Syria, and elsewhere in the Muslim world, a cultural revolution was taking shape. Young men sent abroad to study in Europe and the Ottoman Empire returned home armed with foreign languages and novel epistemologies, while institutions such as the "new army" and the reformed bureaucracy drew on recruits from all sections of the country, broadening their social base and contributing to an expanded sense of national identity.

Moreover, there was new thinking about religion and its role in politics following the drama of the Hafiziyya: Did Islamic thought and law provide a viable vehicle for change, and if so, who was most qualified to direct and interpret it? Engaging in doctrinal disputes over this question was the domain of a new generation of scholars inspired by tenets of Sufi mysticism, who plumbed the sources of faith and invented new modes of religious discourse. Calling themselves *salafis*, but without belonging to any formal movement, they were in fact inquiring minds seeking to engage with modernity by replotting the contours of the received canon in the spirit of reform. They operated in an atmosphere in which political change was the overriding concern, but in fact, the thrust of their ideas was directed more toward a moral reawakening inspired by the values of the their pious ancestors (*al-salaf al-salih*), including the Prophet himself. Their attitudes against corruption (*fasad*), against superstition, and against certain extreme religious practices placed them in a position to wield moral influence over men of authority, including the sultan himself. Even before the watershed events of 1912, the feeling that Morocco stood poised at the threshold of a new era was already in the air.[46]

In the political sphere, even though the makhzan was badly broken, it still claimed legitimacy on the basis of dynastic loyalty. The term *watan* (nation) had entered popular discourse, but it was not yet imbued with the qualities of exclusivity that would inform later expressions of the national idea. Still, European intervention had promoted a sense of countrywide unanimity and attachment to the homeland. The more Europe threatened, the more Moroccans responded to the call for jihad and committed acts of violence, like the Mauchamp murder, in order to remove the stain of humiliation associated with submission to foreign influence. The unanimity inspired by the Hafiziyya was fleeting, but it foreshadowed a spirit of solidarity that would be remembered and built upon at later stages in Morocco's struggle for independence.

FIGURE 12. Ex-Sultan 'Abd al-Hafiz made the rounds of Parisian society after arriving in France in 1912. Here he is in deep conversation with French ecclesiasts. (Collection Gérard Lévy, Paris)

SIGNS OF MODERNITY: CHANGES IN CULTURE AND MATERIAL LIFE

In much of the non-Western world in this era, the impact of industrialization is the key to understanding local manifestations of rapid social and economic change, especially on the urban level. Though large-scale industrial development in the European sense was absent from Morocco, as it was from much of the Middle East, the spread of capitalism was having an effect, especially in the coastal cities. Beirut, Alexandria, Tunis, and Oran were "bulking points" for goods coming from or going to the rapidly industrializing economies of the West. In Morocco, both Tangier and Casablanca fell into this category of the port city that served as a distribution point, and whose elites were deeply involved in the business of realizing profitability from trade with Europe. In the absence of a strong central or municipal government, town fathers took the lead in deciding what a modern city should look like, making key decisions about urban growth that would determine the course of the future.[47]

Tangier – a port city straddling the Strait of Gibraltar on Morocco's northern coast – offers a fine example of a Moroccan town that showed signs of a transition to a Western-style modern urbanity well before the era of colonization. Since the mid-nineteenth century, Tangier had grown exponentially as a commercial node because of its role as the country's busiest port, with the best customs and storage facilities, as well as easy access to the interior by road. Europeans flocked there because of its proximity to Europe and the presence of a diplomatic corps who played a leading role in town politics, for it was Tangier – at a safe distance from the interior – that the makhzan had designated as the place where foreign relations would be conducted. The number of Europeans in the town grew exponentially; from an estimated one thousand in 1872 (out of a total population of fourteen thousand), to eight times that number in 1904, out of a total of forty thousand – 20 percent of the town.

Also noteworthy in Tangier was the presence of a native Jewish population in which capital and expertise in trade were concentrated. Most of the leading Jews had been educated at the French-oriented school of the Alliance Israélite Universelle founded in Tangier in 1864, after the visit of Sir Moses Montefiore. Skilled in languages and the art of dealing with foreigners, many of them served the diplomatic missions in Tangier as interpreters, or "dragomans." Along with Muslims of similar talent, this native Jewish elite was an engine of urban growth, investing its wealth in property, construction, and speculation in land, and transforming a "sleepy Arab town" into the likeness of a southern Mediterranean port city, with its red tiled roofs, winding streets, and garden suburbs.[48]

The city was a slate on which an appreciation for things European was etched; spacious Italianate villas, schools run on a European model, a hospital with Western-trained doctors, apartment houses, tourist hotels, a local telephone system, daily connections with Europe by sea, restaurants, bars, cafés and dance halls, and even a municipal theater, built in 1913. By 1890, class divisions had begun to replace ethnic ones, and a city once segregated into ethnic quarters was now known for its cosmopolitan mix, with Jews, Muslims, and Christians living "promiscuously" side by side, in the words of one foreign observer. Along with the intermingled living conditions came a spurt in the growth of associational life in which natives and foreigners joined together in sporting clubs and charitable organizations, musical groups and theater troupes, even in ladies' circles and auxiliaries. While these new cultural activities were confined to a narrow

FIGURE 13. The Moroccan embassy to France, 1909, headed by Minister Muhammad al-Muqri (center), accompanied by translator Si Kaddour Ben Ghabrit (far right), and other makhzan officials. Official embassies to Europe brought home firsthand accounts of European industrial development. Album Brémond. (Collection Gérard Lévy, Paris)

elite of wealth and education, their effects necessarily filtered downward and outward.[49]

Tangier was also a center for newspapers and a modern press. In 1883, the first French-language newspaper – *Le Reveil du Maroc* – appeared in Tangier, managed by a Jew from Essaouira named Levy Cohen for the purpose of spreading French language, culture, and political ideas among his co-religionists. About the same time, *al-Moghreb al-Aksa*, published by G. T. Abrines in Spanish, was directed toward Tangier's burgeoning Spanish-speaking community that included refugees from the political turmoil in Andalucía. Later *al-Moghreb al-Aksa* joined forces with the English-language *Times of Morocco*, edited by Budgett Meakin, an Englishman whose crusading mission was to "expose abuses committed by Europeans availing themselves of Moorish corruption, and to arouse a greater interest abroad in the development of Morocco."

While Tangier was the epicenter of foreign influence, signs of a non-native presence soon appeared in other cities – Casablanca, Tetuan, and Rabat also had European colonies before 1912. More than a dozen or so foreign-language newspapers sprang up in the first decade of the twentieth

FIGURE 14. The 1909 Moroccan embassy to France donned workman's togs to visit the arms factory at St. Étienne. Minister al-Muqri is standing to the left of the young boy, and translator Ben Ghabrit stands directly behind. Album Brémond. (Collection Gérard Lévy, Paris)

century, reflecting the views of their patrons on the so-called "Moroccan Question." Some Moroccans knew foreign languages and could read the newspapers; others had them read to them. Mahammad Jibbas (Guebbas), who rose to the post of Grand Vizier in the early years of the Protectorate, was fluent in English, and Muhammad al-Muqri, also a Minister, knew some French. It was said that Sultan ʿAbd al-Hafiz's children were taking French lessons for several hours each day.[50]

During the Hafiziyya, the role of newspapers had become pivotal and articles in the press represented the polarized factions. An Arabic newspaper called *al-Saʿada* appeared in Tangier in 1904, its Syrian editor a follower of the literary awakening known as the *Nahda*. In 1908–1909, *al-Saʿada*, reflecting the position of France, supported ʿAbd al-ʿAziz, and was violently attacked by the al-Kattanis, who were pro-Hafiz. By 1909, at least three other Arabic newspapers were in circulation; one of them, *Lisan al-Maghrib* ("The Voice of the Maghrib") achieved notoriety in 1908 when it published the text of a liberal constitution that was backed by an anonymous group of Moroccan intellectuals. The editors of this newspaper, refusing to be intimidated by the makhzan, also printed a series of "open letters" to Sultans ʿAbd al-ʿAziz and ʿAbd al-Hafiz that evoked novel concepts such as freedom of speech, affording their readership access to progressive ideas circulating elsewhere in the Arab world.[51] According to Abdallah Laroui, the Syrian-edited Arabic newspapers introduced educated Moroccans to "a liberal conception of popular sovereignty very different from the notion of *shura*"; although these efforts were mostly stillborn, they provided the raw material for a new mode of political discourse.[52]

Westernizing tendencies radiated outward from Tangier to the rest of Morocco, contributing to the atmosphere of political ferment. Familiarity with European material culture remained a class-based phenomenon, confined to the upper echelons of government and a handful of the elite initiated into its codes and practices. Western ideas, on the other hand, traveled in far wider circles and had a ripple effect throughout society that stimulated innovative forms of creativity. In the field of history, Ahmad al-Nasiri led the way in the 1880s when he used non-Muslim sources, contextualized documentation, and cited precise quotations to write his monumental *Kitab al-Istiqsa*, the first national history of Morocco. Government recordkeeping also improved, and maintaining detailed account books (*kunnash*) became good bureaucratic practice. Narratives of travel to Europe circulated among the literati, bringing home the pleasures of Paris, London, Marseilles and Strasbourg to a small but avid readership. While most of this production remained in manuscript form, some of it was printed in Fez and reached a broader audience. Most books printed between 1865 and 1920 dealt with religious subjects such sufism and jurisprudence, but others touched on subjects that had more mundane appeal. While the Moroccan novel was not yet born, literary works having a didactic purpose became more common. They took up the burning questions of the day, such as the advisability of jihad, the dangers of cooperating with Europe, and whether or not to consume foreign-made products such as tea, sugar, candles, and tobacco. The best example of this sort of literature was the immensely popular *Nasihat ahl al-Islam* ("Advice to the People of Islam"), a fiery exhortation by Muhammad b. Jaʿfar al-Kattani published in Fez in 1908, calling on Moroccans to unite and to purge themselves of the noxious foreign influences that had seeped into society. The al-Kattanis seem to have grasped, more than any of their contemporaries, the power of the printed word and its ability to shape public discussion through the medium of books and pamphlets written in simple and direct language.[53]

The first decade of the twentieth century witnessed a cultural awakening led by precursors of a modernist trend in intellectual life whose full contours would only emerge after World War I. Included in this category was the legal scholar Muhammad al-Mahdi al-Wazzani (1849–1923), who corresponded with the Egyptian Muhammad ʿAbduh on questions of religious practice and introduced reformist ideas into Morocco. Al-Wazzani's great legal compendium, the *Miʿyar al-Jadid*, showed deep humanistic insight, bridging the gap between Shariah law and social reality at a time when questioning the sources of religious authority was uppermost in people's minds.[54] Another figure of this incipient modernity was the Tangier historian Muhammad Skirij (d. 1940), informant to French social scientist Edouard Michaux-Bellaire; Skirij penned a seven-volume chronicle of Tangier's history that closely adheres in style and format to Muhammad b. Jaʿfar al-Kattani's monumental history of Fez, *Salwat al-Anfas*.[55] These years also saw the first appearance of the savant Muhammad al-Hajwi (1874–1956), polymath, propagandist, and later, Minister of Education under the Protectorate, who wrote more than fifty books on diverse subjects such as travel, women's education, Islamic law, and history. Also the al-Azhar trained Abu Shuʿayb al-Dakali, who was an outspoken advocate for reformist ideas in Morocco, exceeding in influence even ʿAbduh himself, according to the historian Abun-Nasr.[56] Each of these men demonstrated a keen if selective understanding of key aspects of modernist thought. Adept in the techniques of propaganda and mass appeal (al-Hajwi used the radio in the 1930s to call for the reform of family law), they developing the art of skirting entrenched conservatism by reaching out to a new generation of readers and listeners. In sum, we could view the period 1900–1912 in the usual manner, as representing the limitations of the pre-modern state, anticipating the coming of the Protectorate as a result of the breakdown of authority through mismanagement and a poverty of ideas. Or we can adopt a fresh perspective that takes into account the long-forgotten and largely ignored nonstate actors who rose up in the interstices of society and seized the opportunity created by the vacuum of power to advance a different vision of how Morocco's past and future might be joined.

4

France and Spain in Morocco

The Early Years of the Protectorates (1912–1930)

The signing of the Treaty of Fez on March 30, 1912, ushering in the French Protectorate, was a mournful finale to ʿAbd al-Hafiz's reign. Over the preceding decade, large segments of the Moroccan heartland had fallen into French hands; it was only France's reluctance to alarm other European states that kept her from declaring full dominion over Morocco before 1912. A secret Franco-Spanish agreement of 1904 acknowledged Spain's "historic" claim to the entire north of Morocco, with the exception of Tangier, whose "special" character was recognized by the Great Powers in the 1906 Treaty of Algeciras. In the final division of Moroccan spoils between France and Spain in November 1912, Tangier's future was left up in the air. Britain wanted the city and its hinterland to become an international zone where no one foreign power would prevail, while France wanted Tangier to remain among the assets of its Protectorate. Posing a host of difficult issues, the question of Tangier was set aside for the time being. Then World War I intervened, and it was not until 1923 that France, Spain, and Great Britain – noticeably without the help of the newly formed League of Nations – finally agreed on a multi-tiered international administration for the city under the nominal headship of the sultan. This agreement acknowledged Sharifian sovereignty, as France greatly desired, while preserving Tangier's international character, as Britain wished. The Tangier question was settled for the time being to the satisfaction of Britain and France, but not of Spain, who quietly grieved over its loss.[1]

A TROUBLED BEGINNING

Despite all the diplomatic maneuvering, France's hegemony over Morocco in 1912 was still far from complete. A countrywide insurrection broke out as soon as the Treaty of Fez was signed, starting in Fez itself. Moroccan troops garrisoned in the madina rose up against their French military instructors and went on a rampage, killing Europeans and looting at will. As the city erupted in chaos, rebel militiamen entered the *mellah*, or Jewish quarter. A woman resident recounted the anxiety of those terrible days: "We closed the doors of our houses, our hearts pounding with fear ... the enemy entered and stole everything ... they pointed their weapons at us and said: 'Your riches or your life, you bastards!' Terrorized, we gave them what they wanted ... " After a devastating fire and a severe pounding from the French artillery, the fighting stopped, but hundreds were dead and the Jewish quarter was devastated. During the insurrection the Jews of Fez, about twelve thousand in all, fled their homes and took refuge on the nearby palace grounds, sheltering in the royal menagerie alongside the lions and panthers.[2] Meanwhile, in the southern region of the Tafilalt, the insurrection continued under Ahmad al-Hiba, a son of Ma al-ʿAynayn, who resumed the jihad after the death of his father and even claimed the sultanate at Marrakesh before he was crushingly defeated by a smaller but better armed French force under Lieutenant Colonel Charles Mangin.

Providing direction during this chaos was the man now emerging as the Protectorate's chief figure – soon-to-be Résident-Général Louis Hubert Gonzalve Lyautey, who immediately took decisive measures to seize the levers of power. Resurrecting the disgraced ʿAlawi dynasty and preserving the sultanate as the reliquary of Moroccan sovereignty was now the centerpiece of French policy, but no one was fooled. The real master of events was Lyautey. In August 1912, he forced an uncooperative ʿAbd al-Hafiz to abdicate and with the endorsement of the ulama, replaced him with his more pliable younger brother, Mawlay Yusuf, whose main virtues were his quiet reserve, his piety, and his bland personality. Realizing that an era had ended, the embittered ʿAbd al-Hafiz, as a final act, broke the royal parasol and smashed the imperial seals before departing for a permanent exile.[3]

LYAUTEY LAYS THE FOUNDATIONS OF THE FRENCH PROTECTORATE

Lyautey was an extraordinary personality whose policies and personal vision laid the groundwork for the institutions that informed France's forty-four year tenure in Morocco. Born into a Catholic family with royalist leanings and trained at the elite French military academy of

St. Cyr, Lyautey was deeply imbued with a respect for tradition while at the same time burning to leave his mark on the world through bold action. After years in the colonial service in Indochina, Madagascar, and Algeria, Lyautey carried with him a well-honed set of ideas about the exercise of colonial administration. Morocco in 1912 was the perfect canvas on which he could limn his inspiration; immensely conservative in its societal makeup, it was in dire need of a top-to-bottom "regeneration." Charged with energy and a passion for work, Lyautey now set out to achieve the reorganization of the makhzan. Like many colonialists of his generation, Lyautey believed that the Protectorate formula gave France the opportunity to bring Western progress to the subject peoples under its sway, but without changing their fundamental "soul." An unremitting romantic, Lyautey believed that Morocco, unlike Algeria, should not to be annexed to France, nor should it be considered a "colony"; rather, it was to remain sovereign but "protected" until that undefined moment when, in his own words, it would be "developed, civilized, living its own autonomous life, detached from the metropole."[4] He vowed to "offend no tradition, change no custom, and remind ourselves that in all human society there is a ruling class, born to rule, without which nothing can be done . . . enlist the ruling class in our service . . . and the country will be pacified, and at far less cost and with greater certainty than by all the military expeditions we could send there."[5] With that mission before him, he gathered a group of exceptionally talented young men – social planners, educators, architects, and military men – who subscribed to his goal of building a new Morocco without disrupting what they considered its basic values: a love of hierarchy, a respect for nobility and birth, loyalty to family, a consummate religious piety. Lyautey's formula was concise–complete control, but no direct rule. There was an idealistic strain to his vision, perhaps even a heroic one; it involved a deliberate return to a chivalrous world of pure intentions, yet it was firmly planted in a setting of power plants, railroads, concrete and steel. On the whole, in the early years of his administration, his ideas met with success; it was only later, after the first decade, that the delicate balance between the anachronistic and the modern was thrown off, and the scale tipped asymmetrically in a dangerous leaning toward the past.

The Treaty of Fez offered few restrictions on the scope of Lyautey's ambition. Modeled after the Protectorate set up in Tunisia in 1881, its formal purpose was to establish a "proper" government of order and security that would allow for the introduction of reforms that would ensure Morocco's economic development. Unlike the government of Algeria that had "turned to dust" even before the coming of the French, Lyautey asserted that precolonial Morocco was "an independent empire with a history, jealous to the extreme of its independence, rejecting all servitude . . . looking like a structured state, with its hierarchy . . . its foreign representatives, its social organisms . . . " His plan was to return the makhzan to its former glory, while strictly limiting its authority, and to restore the sultan as the respected symbol of the state. To this end, he set about retrieving the makhzan from the ruins of the closing years of ʿAbd al-Hafiz's reign and refurbishing its image. In Lyautey's Protectorate, the sultan retained his formal powers: he issued decrees over his own signature and seal and preserved his religious status as first imam of the nation. He was surrounded by the trappings of power and every detail of courtly ceremony was kept intact. "At the Moorish court," Walter Harris wrote, "scarcely a European is to be seen, and to the native who arrives at the Capital there is little or no visible change from what he and his ancestors saw in the past." To the chagrin of the colonial party, Lyautey openly prided himself on being "the first servant of Sidna," and did not hesitate to hold the stirrup of the sultan's horse when he dismounted at state occasions. "In Morocco," he argued, "there is only one government, the *sharifian government*, protected by the French."[6]

But behind the scenes, in modern office buildings away from the palace and its pageantry, a second and almost completely separate government would grow up, efficiently French, and holding the actual reins of power. Each part of this two-headed hydra would evolve along its own track: an indigenous, Moroccan-manned "government of the people," simplified and stripped down, held in respect, concerned largely with religious, cultural and educational affairs, on the one hand, and a complex, multi-layered, French technocratic bureaucracy, tasked with the running of a modern state on the other. From his new capital of Rabat, Résident Général Lyautey was de facto the Protectorate's highest authority; immediately beneath him in the hierarchy was the Secretary General, his confidant Henri Gaillard, the liaison between the Moroccan and French sides of the administration. This post was the nerve center of the Protectorate, serving as a clearinghouse for every matter that touched on administrative, judicial, and political affairs. In 1912 it consisted of two departments, finance and public works; it eventually expanded into eight departments that included agriculture, commerce, education, health, communications, and native affairs – the basic structure of a government-in-the making. This last department was charged with the sensitive task of taking the pulse of the Moroccan people and monitoring the minutiae of their daily life, from vetting appointments, to enforcing the payment of taxes, to shaping educational policy – but without dropping the mask of "indirect rule." The top level of administration was assigned to a Native Policy Council that acted as the right hand of Lyautey, overseeing all aspects of Protectorate rule. But in fact, the bureaus, sub-bureaus and multiple services of each department were the workhorses of the regime, carrying out the complex day-to-day operations of rule. It was here that the actual business of government took place, where projects were planned and staffed, where budgets were conceived, and vital decisions made.

Following the shift in the mechanisms of control, little was left of the old makhzan. The *baniqas* (benches) where the sultan's advisers had once sat patiently awaiting for his summons were vacant, and the sultan was left with only a few officials under his direct charge. Among them were the grand vizier, a minister in charge of Islamic justice and the high courts of appeal, who was also head of the *habus*, or the Islamic endowments, and the director of Islamic education at the mosque-university of the Qarawiyyin at Fez. The sultan was now anointed as the guardian of "Islamic Affairs," while the French administration controlled everything else.

As his capacities increased, Lyautey implemented an extensive program of reform that filtered into every area of public life. The goals he set were impossibly high: cajoling, insisting, verbally flogging his underlings and his critics in Paris, brooking no opposition, he set about rationalizing the bureaucracy, integrating the tribal areas, reforming the legal system; building roads, dams, railways and a power grid; redesigning the cities; improving sanitation and health; promoting business; creating a narrow but effective system of education; preserving the impressive architectural patrimony; exploiting agricultural and mineral wealth by controlling land use; and finally, securing the necessary funds to carry out these vast and expensive improvements. His record of success in achieving this ambitious and far-reaching program, though far from perfect, elicits our admiration, even after calculating its high cost.[7]

MODERNIZING MOROCCO'S CITIES: THE WORK OF HENRI PROST

Lyautey's first task was to gain control over Morocco's untamed physical space through a subtle combination of military conquest and political seduction. He began by establishing secure zones around the cities, reassuring urban notables that "business as usual" would follow. Then he took on the task of rethinking the design of Morocco's main population centers to accommodate the expected influx of Europeans who would staff the Protectorate administration. Architecture, urban design, and the protection of the Moroccan patrimony were particular concerns of the Résident-Général, and he invested important resources in them. Technocrats trained in modern methods of city planning were recruited from France to work under Lyautey's close supervision. Architect and urbanist Henri Prost, winner of the prestigious Grand Prix de Rome in 1902, was put in charge. Armed with a set of draconian dahirs that empowered him to "scandalously" expropriate whatever he needed, Prost went to work; in the period from 1914 to 1923, nearly every major Moroccan city was radically reshaped by his hand. New quarters were built separate from the old, characterized by a geometric sparseness associated with the latest modernist style. Municipal services such as water and sewage were installed where none had existed before; industrial zones were located distant from residential areas but close to transportation hubs; broad avenues for the circulation of traffic were drawn across empty fields; elegant apartment blocks were carved out of checkerboards of ramshackle housing. Cities like Casablanca became a "laboratory" for testing out the most recent ideas in city planning that were as yet untried in the metropole. Prost's work was profoundly modern but also characterized by a deep respect for the traditional Moroccan building arts. Using motifs such as tile work, arches, and the open courtyard design, he designed cities of classic proportions whose aesthetic appeal has withstood the test of time. The singularity of his vision is evident today in the monumental tree-lined boulevards of Fez, in the majestic arcades of central Rabat, and in the simple forms of the "Habous" quarter of Casablanca, an entire neighborhood constructed by using modern infrastructure beneath a neo-Mauresque façade.[8]

Behind this architecture was a particular understanding of Moroccan urbanity based on a perception of the city as the focal point for *hadariyya*, roughly translated as "civic culture." When French planners studied Morocco's cities, they discovered a refined social life conducted behind closed doors, kept alive by a Moroccan elite immersed in the inherited forms and practices of the every day: a particular mode of eating, dressing, conducting business, entertaining, and spending leisure time. Enamored with this discovery, they viewed the domestic scene as the warp and woof of social life, and decreed that the native habitat – the old madina – should be left alone, unaffected by the exercises in modernism taking place elsewhere in the city. As Lyautey said: "The Arab and the Jewish quarters, I will not touch them. I shall clean them up, restore them, supply them with running water and electricity, and remove the waste, but that is all . . . And out in the *bled* (countryside), I shall build another town . . . "[9]

Modern quarters were built for Europeans in cities both large and small, usually within a stone's throw of the old city. Both parts were hierarchical and carefully controlled; the new quarters had their precise zones for living and working, segregated by function and socio-economic standing, while the old town was kept frozen in the grip of the indigenous patrician class whose status and privilege remained intact. Municipal organization – regularized by a 1917 dahir – left the hierarchies of the pre-colonial order untouched. In each large city, a *pasha* was named as the head of municipal affairs, assisted by a municipal council composed of representatives of the urban elite. The pasha received orders directly from the sultan who was, as the French incessantly repeated, "the source of all authority in Morocco"; in Rabat, Salé and Casablanca, this façade of "indirect rule" was scrupulously maintained. But in fact, the powers of the pasha were gradually reduced over time and overall management of the city was incrementally transferred to the "Chief of Municipal Services," a French bureaucrat who reported directly to the Secretary-General of the Protectorate and wrestled with such mundane matters as taxation, water supply, and school budgets. This figure was closely shadowed by a municipal commission that reflected mainly settler interests. Lyautey's purist conception of how Moroccan cities should be run reflected a practical approach to existing problems, but also a blind romanticism that paid insufficient attention to the dynamic forces that the new era had unleashed. It was not long before the madinas that had been "left to themselves" were bursting at the seams, transformed by a rampant increase in population that neither Prost, nor Lyautey, could have possibly imagined.[10]

TRACING THE PATHWAYS OF RESISTANCE

While Moroccan cities took on more complex forms, the bled was also reconceived to fit the colonial imaginary. Rural Morocco was divided into military regions and a slow process of conquest began. In areas that were subdued, the Office of Native Affairs (Direction des affaires indigènes) sent out young officers carefully chosen for the job of local administration; it was a question of "finding the right man for the right place," according to Lyautey. The Résident-Général demonstrated extreme flexibility in his choice of personnel, recruiting loyalists from military intelligence, among other places. In this regard, he followed a pattern established many years earlier by the *Bureaux arabes* in Algeria, whose liberal-minded officers steeped in St.-Simonian ideas had acted as the vanguard of the "civilizing

FIGURE 15. Colonial infantry departing from the Gare de Lyon train station in Paris, July 1912, on their way to Morocco to reinforce French troops preparing to launch an assault against Berber tribes in the Middle Atlas Mountains. Cliché Rol. (Collection Gérard Lévy, Paris)

mission." Speaking Arabic and often personally dedicated to Lyautey through years of shared service, his appointees were charged with facilitating the transition from military to civilian control by "educating and guiding" local qaʿids and pashas to bend to the finer points of France's unfolding master plan. Working hand-in-hand with the local qaʿid to realize "indirect rule" (that could not have been more direct), each officer aspired to be a petty chieftain in his own right. The stories of French officer Maurice Le Glay captured the powerful emotions felt by these men who formed the vanguard of conquest as they placed their imprint on the rural scene. Their aim was to make French authority absolute; in places where their control was tentative, the work of "pacification" (the euphemism generally applied) was considered incomplete.[11]

The bravery and single-mindedness of these officers were legendary; a certain Captain Ayard was captured by the Berbers of Bekrit and held prisoner for two years; at the end of his captivity, he persuaded the tribe to surrender and make peace with France. Using punitive military measures on the one hand, and tactics of persuasion and even bribery on the other, Lyautey's "right men" launched a campaign to control the "untamed"

Moroccan rural space. Within days of an officer's arrival, a rudimentary market, a clinic, and a school were usually established. Road building quickly followed, along with new wells and dams, pumping stations and vaccinations; after years of hard work, an indissoluble bond would develop between the French officer and "his" people, who often bestowed upon him the title of *hakim* – a capable and wise man.[12]

But the high-minded qualities of the individual colonial officer could not mask the brutality of the spreading occupation. In the Middle Atlas, the French imposed a state of siege, with the aim of subduing the major tribes living in this mountainous region, and in particular, the Zayan tribal confederation who had a reputation for ferocity. The policy of "a drop of oil" (*tache d'huile*) became Lyautey's signal invention, falsely suggesting the quiet nature of the spread of French influence; this clever catchphrase was directed at the home front in order to show that the submission of rural Morocco would be speedy, low-cost, and unopposed. But, in fact, the opposite case was more often the reality.

In the spring of 1913, for example, French troops moved into the Middle Atlas region but made little headway, finding that every push forward was met with determined resistance. Berber chiefs of the Zayan confederation united under the leadership of a grizzled old warrior, Moha ou Hamou, who fought every inch of the French advance with "an absolute scorn for death." At the famous battle of el-Herri that took place near Khénifra in November 1914, Moha's forces overcame a poorly organized French column, killing over six hundred officers and men. This stunning victory for the Moroccan side shocked the French command into recognizing the offensive capacity of the Berber tribesmen. French forces regrouped and began using aerial reconnaissance and artillery. Bombarding villages at will, they ranged across the plains and foothills, but dared not enter the steep heights where the Berbers had an advantage. Instead, they imposed an economic blockade, depriving the tribesmen of access to their traditional markets, and they employed scorched earth techniques to destroy their crops. These tactics, coupled with unremitting and often brutal military pressure, finally broke the back of the Middle Atlas tribes. By the summer of 1918, even the son of Moha ou Hamou had had enough, and with his capitulation, the Zayan front collapsed; after years of a cat-and-mouse game, France had finally achieved some success in the vital spinal cord of the country.[13]

But the slow pace of conquest and its escalating costs did not win over the politicians and bureaucrats in Paris. With World War I raging in Europe, critics complained that Lyautey's gradualist approach was not sufficiently

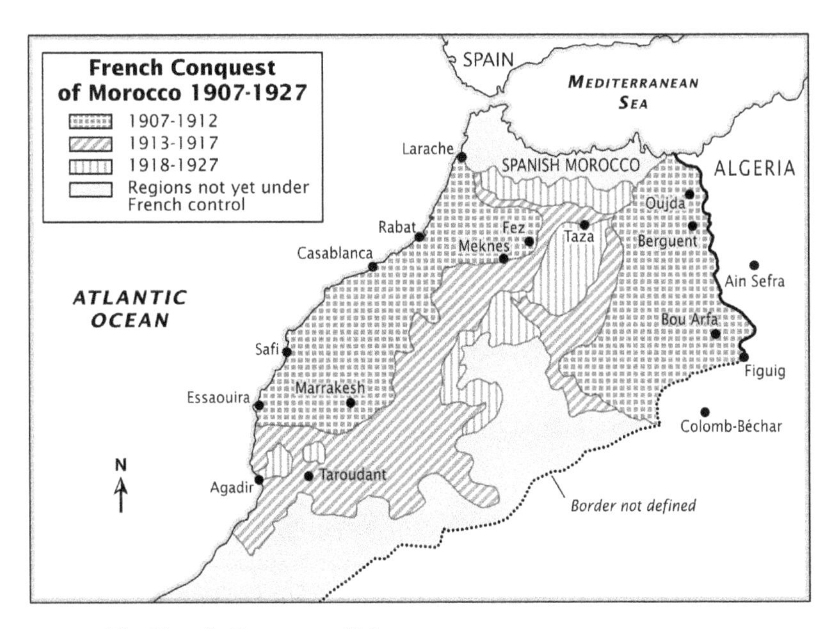

MAP 2. The French Conquest of Morocco, 1907–1927

bold, and that the Moroccan adventure was draining away resources badly needed in France. In response, Lyautey invented new language that turned defeat into victory and setback into progress; he argued that it should be France's aim not to possess all of Morocco, but only *le Maroc utile*, or those areas that were "useful" by dint of their military, economic, or strategic importance. Thus he reset the parameters of the colonial mission while justifying his own slow, and sometimes vacillating, approach to conquest. It was not until 1924, after more than a decade of bloody struggle in which many French troops died, and many more Moroccan lives were sacrificed, that the entire Middle Atlas region was finally subdued.[14]

In the South, Lyautey exercised a different strategy that took into account the local chiefs, the same "Lords of the Atlas" who had supported ʿAbd al-Hafiz's uprising. Three Berber clans – the M'tougga, who held the Tiz-n-Test pass, the Goundafa, who controlled Oued N'fis, and the Glawa, who commanded the mountain peaks of Telouet near the Tiz-n-Tishka pass – derived their power from their strategic perches atop the High Atlas range. Instead of confronting these powerful seigneurs directly, Lyautey adopted a policy of cooptation that he believed would save money and French lives. The so-called *politique des grands caïds* recognized the local warlords in return for their rendering service to France. French allies

FIGURE 16. Sultan Mawlay Yusuf, handpicked by Résident Général Lyautey to succeed the deposed Sultan ʿAbd al-Hafiz, enters Casablanca under the royal parasol, traditional symbol of sultanic authority, in November 1913. Cliché Rol. (Collection Gérard Lévy, Paris)

included Haïda ou Mouis, the pasha of Taroudant, who worked tirelessly on their behalf, relentlessly pursuing the indomitable al-Hiba throughout the anti-Atlas. When the pasha Haïda was killed in the line of fire near Tighanimine near Agadir in 1916, he was hailed by the colonial press as "the heart and soul of makhzan resistance to Hibist schemes in the Sous."[15] By using surrogate fighters, by supporting them with money, equipment, advice, and occasionally troops, Lyautey could proclaim that "indirect rule" was indeed working, and that the conquest of the south was bought cheaply. "At no point did they let us down," he wrote to Minister of War Painlevé: "They made themselves the instruments of our policy [and] proved themselves to be clear-sighted as well as courageous leaders of men." But in fact, France had made a bargain with the devil, for these independent warlords in the south were often so abusive and tyrannical to their own people, that their behavior gave Moroccans yet another reason to abhor their French masters.[16]

Lyautey's strategy of working through tribal leaders and urban elites was based in part on his sense of *realpolitik* and finding others to do the job, and in part on his own innate appreciation for rank and tradition. The lavish displays of pomp and circumstance, the uniforms decked with glitter, the decorations and prizes, the reification of the sultanate as near-sacred, reflected a state of mind that in many ways returned Morocco to an imaginary point in the past. Despite these regressive tendencies, change was perceptible everywhere. Even in the seemingly untouchable sphere of religion, the passion for reform had taken hold, bolstered by the desire to build respect for the revivified sultanate. Religious affairs clearly belonged in the restored makhzan's portfolio, but only after being subjected to the same kind of rationalization as other affairs of state. The rich religious endowments were restructured and placed under the French administration's eagle eye, while publicly remaining in the hands of the ulama; new judicial standards were set for the posts of qadi and notary, and the distinction between "civil" and "criminal" cases was redefined.[17]

Finally, there was the question of the zawiyas, or sufi brotherhoods, that so fascinated French social scientists, who believed that they contained "the secret to the historical constitution of Morocco." Their rootedness in society had impressed the policymakers of the Residency as much as it had influenced ethnographers; hence, the desire to neutralize them politically. Aware of their pivotal role, Lyautey courted them, showered them with attention, and tried to rally them to his side. A small group of sufis from among the Fez elite, refusing to collaborate, chose instead the long road of exile and left for the Muslim East. As for the rest, they were free to continue to conduct ceremonies and receive pilgrims; however, at the same time, they were gradually being coopted as "agents of the makhzan" through the renewal of the precolonial practice of granting the *tanfida*, a license allowing the brotherhoods to receive lucrative donations. The blurred lines between secular and religious, the need to exert control over the Muslim sphere, the insertion of the sacred into the architecture of a modernized state, all taxed the ingenuity of French policy makers. The challenge of preserving the ancient patrimony of the makhzan (for which France was now the self-appointed caretaker) while meeting the requirements of a new kind of absolutism was daunting.[18]

EDUCATION FOR THE ELITES, WORK FOR THE MASSES

Finding the right balance between the forces of tradition and contemporaneity was especially acute in the sphere of education, where the measures of class and ethnicity entered the picture and were used to determine who would have access to a modern education, and who would not. European, Jewish, and Berber and Arab Muslim students were each directed to a separate school system; primary schools for Muslims, Jewish-run schools for Jewish students, and after 1912, separate schools for French and European children. After 1916, five "schools for the sons of notables" were created to educate boys from elite families, while the majority of Muslim students were sent to vocational schools to prepare for manual trades. Girls were almost completely excluded from this highly restrictive schema. Two *collèges*, or high schools, were also established, one in Fez (1914) and the other in Rabat (1916). These Eton-like boarding schools fulfilled Lyautey's notion of turning out Moroccan "gentlemen" of a "double culture" who would enter the ranks of the makhzan immersed in traditional values while being conversant with modern bureaucratic practice. It was not until 1930 that the students at these collèges were permitted to prepare for the high school diploma (*baccalauréat*) in Morocco in order to have access to higher education in France. After 1920, special schools for Berber-speaking children in rural areas were created where French *instituteurs* (teachers), specially trained for the dual tasks of teaching and intelligence gathering, were assigned after a year of rigorous training in a Berber dialect. One of these schools, Azrou in the Middle Atlas, became a *collège* after 1930, providing Berber youth with a step forward to higher posts in the administration; the best of them would go on to the elite military academy at Dar el-Beida near Meknes, where they were trained to become officers in the colonial army. This integrated policy had one purposeful goal: to put in place a hierarchical system of social reproduction that would guarantee an indigenous elite loyal to France and ready to enter its service. But, as Mohammed Benhlal has shown, the school system was far more porous than its architects intended and pupils entered it from a variety of social levels, not only from the rich but also from the middle and working classes, ultimately turning the Berber educational system into a "vehicle of social mobility."[19]

The majority of Muslim children who went to school, a mere fraction of the total schoolage population, attended Qur'anic schools that were outside of Protectorate supervision altogether. Most Jewish children attended the secular and privately run primary schools sponsored by the French-based Alliance Israélite Universelle (AIU) that had branches all over the country. Before 1912, Jewish girls' schools not only imparted basic subjects such as reading and writing, they also trained girls for the workplace by teaching them tailoring, laundering, and, eventually, typing, shorthand, and other vocational skills.[20] In 1913, a similar program was established for Muslim girls in Salé by the French authorities, where the girls learned various handicrafts; later the curriculum was broadened to include French language. This model soon spread to other cities, and by 1917, over 450 girls were enrolled in French-run handicraft schools that served mainly working class families. Finally, in the period 1919–1924, reformist-minded intellectuals, fearing that the French system presented a cultural threat and that the traditional Qur'anic schools did not meet the needs of a modern society, founded privately funded "free-schools" where Arabic language was taught along with other subjects. The student population of the free schools were mainly sons of the well to do.

Protectorate officials were leery about schooling for the masses, fearing that an educated proletariat would become a source of discontent and eventually supply recruits for an anticolonial opposition. Lyautey's elitist sensibility marked the system. That quality, along with what Daniel Rivet has called a "wary Malthusianism" that embraced selectivity as a matter of principle, impregnated the educational structure from top to bottom. The fear of drowning in a sea of well-educated, militant Moroccans haunted the authorities and justified in their minds a highly restrictive approach to schooling the masses.[21]

The capstone of Lyautey's efforts as an educational innovator was the Institut des Hautes Études Marocains (IHEM) which he founded in Rabat in 1920. The purpose of this institute, housed in the graciously designed Bibliothèque Générale close to the Residency, was to serve as a "school" for colonial administrators eager to advance their knowledge of Moroccan society and history. Lyautey himself attended meetings at the IHEM, which flourished under his patronage.

Lyautey's support of the IHEM was consistent with the tradition of French scholarly research on North African society that moved in tandem with the colonial project. As France's interest in Morocco mounted in the late nineteenth century, so did the pressure from the colonial party to gain detailed knowledge of the country. In 1890, the Paris-based Comité du Maroc, a pro-colonial lobby founded by Alfred Le Chatelier, occupant of the chair in Islamic sociology at the Collège de France, campaigned in favor of a stepped-up effort to study all aspects of Moroccan society. Le Chatelier was the moving spirit behind the *Mission scientifique*, a research unit established in 1904 in Tangier whose flagship scientific publication was the authoritative *Archives marocaines*.[22]

With the coming of the Protectorate, Lyautey proposed to create a new research institute structured according to his own design. His ambition was to train colonial officials to be as at home in Moroccan society as he was, speaking one or more of its languages, knowing its customs and people. Under Lyautey's patronage, the IHEM developed a vigorous intellectual agenda that included the journal *Hespéris*, that continues today as *Hespéris-Tamuda*. Leading French scholars of the Maghrib such as Evariste Lévi-Provençal, Henri Terrasse, and Louis Brunot served as directors, while Henri de Castries, Pierre de Cénival, Roger Le Tourneau, and Robert Montagne were on its roster of instructors, making the IHEM a highly selective and "embryonic university" and a pathway to advanced studies.

In the decade of the 1920s, the IHEM held annual congresses attended by Moroccan luminaries such as the historian ʿAbd al-Rahman ibn Zaydan and the educator Muhammad al-Hajwi, who lectured in Arabic. But participation of native scholars was subject to the political climate and did not survive the tensions of Rif War. Moreover, only a handful of privileged students – mainly Europeans – were permitted to study inside its hallowed walls. Until World War II, none of its graduates were Muslims; practically speaking, this elite institution contributed not at all to the formation of the first generation of nationalist leadership. Like other institutions founded by Lyautey, the IHEM was fundamentally an instrument of political control, meant to reinforce through research and teaching the structures of domination imposed by the Protectorate regime.[23]

WORLD WAR I: THE MOROCCAN ROLE

World War I interrupted Lyautey's plans for a speedy end to conquest. The European population in Morocco greeted the outbreak of the war with a patriotic wave of enthusiasm, filling the streets of Casablanca and shouting "À Berlin, À Berlin!" In a very short time, men and matériel began to flow back to France, leaving Lyautey with a skeleton staff and diminished resources. The Résident Général saw his closest collaborators recruited for military service, his budget cut, and his reinforcements reduced to a trickle. Five battalions of Moroccan infantry (*tirailleurs*) retrained after the Fez mutiny by French officers were sent off to France with a message from Lyautey to the Minister of War: "They are marvelous; you will ask me for more." Sultan Yusuf immediately and unhesitatingly threw his support behind the French cause, ignoring a fatwa from the Ottoman sultan – now allied with Germany – calling for jihad, and was lavishly praised by Lyautey for his "absolute loyalty." Over the course of the war, the Moroccan forces in France, all volunteers, won fame as a first-class fighting force, recognized by their commanders as "intelligent, maneuverable, courageous, passionately warlike ... tough, sober, and good marchers."[24] By war's end, Morocco had supplied about forty-five thousand regular infantrymen and auxiliaries to the war effort, had suffered nine thousand men killed or missing in action, plus another seventeen thousand casualties caused by sickness and battle wounds. The situation was ironic. While tens of thousands of Moroccan soldiers were fighting and dying alongside Frenchmen in the trenches of the Western Front, their brothers and cousins were battling other Frenchmen in the valleys of the Middle Atlas, in the Rif Mountains, and in the High Atlas.[25]

Who were these footsoldiers and what did this wartime experience mean to them? French sources depict them as rural, poor, and often illiterate. Their motive for joining the army was usually economic, and they often joined up in family units. Qaʿids were ordered to scour the villages and suqs looking for recruits, who came from all over Morocco, enticed by a recruitment bonus of fifty francs per year. Initially eager to enlist, news of the bloodbath in France soon dampened their enthusiasm. Moreover, the Moroccans were subject to rank discrimination in pay, a lack of promotions, limited rights to a pension, and benefits that were far inferior to those of the metropolitan troops. They were also subjected to the institutionalized racism of the French army; common wisdom decreed that they were "inferior" to French troops, ignorant of the French language, with "deplorable" sexual morality, harboring an "instinct for piracy," and "unsuited" to perform certain military tasks. We know little of their impressions of Europe; the few letters that have survived speak of beastly weather, unfamiliar food, and a burning desire to return home.[26]

Moroccans also went to France as civilian workers during the war, about thirty-eight thousand in all, filling places left vacant by men serving at the front; many stayed in France after the conflict ended, despite the distresses of living in a foreign land. They filled menial jobs as dockworkers, laborers, and fieldworkers, often earning less than two francs a day. Housed in the worst possible conditions, deprived of nourishment because of severe rationing, they had few of the comforts of home. Life in France was not to their liking, as summed up by Jilali ben Thami, a worker in the region of Paris who wrote home to his family: "Oh dear brother, I find myself in the land of infidels . . . it is God who wanted me to leave the land of Islam to come . . . to this land where I find neither joy nor profit. We ask God for one thing, which is to deliver us from here."[27] The discipline of the factory, the meeting with men from other colonized nations, the exposure to French modernity, raised their political awareness. Racial discrimination, differences in pay, and poor living conditions led to strikes and work stoppages by North Africans that alarmed French officials. During and after the war, Moroccans joined leftist parties, especially the dockworkers from Tangier and Casablanca who were already acquainted with socialist ideas from home. Furthermore, in France Moroccans encountered Algerians whose anticolonial political ambitions were ahead of their own, and became "infected" with their militancy and passion. The Moroccans' sudden immersion in techniques of political organization and their growing recognition of their rights as workers would have important implications for the future.[28]

During the war, Lyautey refused to cede "a single inch" of conquered territory and adopted instead the policy of "an empty shell," maintaining forward posts while withdrawing from the rest of the countryside. After the defeat of Germany in 1918, France turned its full attention once again to the arduous task of conquest, pouring war-hardened soldiers of the Foreign Legion and the latest war-tested equipment – tanks, machine guns, airplanes, mortars – back into Morocco. More native troops, including veterans of the European conflict, were enlisted on the French side. By the early 1930s, so many Moroccans were engaged in combat that the "war against Moroccans" was transformed into "a war between Moroccans." Still the Berber resistance held on, retreating even deeper into the mountains; local leaders, some now forgotten, such as M'barak b. Husayn al-Tuzunini, rose up claiming to be leaders of the jihad. Al-Tuzunini created a reign of terror in the distant south, assassinating French officers and the chiefs of rival brotherhoods until his murder by a disgruntled follower in 1919.[29] It was not until 1934 that such old-style resisters were finally brought to heel, and France could claim that the entire country was under its control.

ʿABD AL-KARIM AL-KHATTABI AND THE RIF WAR

The most serious test of colonial will came in the confrontation with Muhammad ibn ʿAbd al-Karim al-Khattabi, known as ʿAbd al-Karim, leader of a rebellion in the years 1921–1926 centered on the Rif Mountains. Northern Morocco (with the exception of the Tangier Zone) was ceded by France to Spain in November 1912, in an arrangement called a "sublease." Spain's portion was hardly the choicest cut, "the bone of the Jebala and the spine of the Rif," according to one observer.[30] Yet Spain had high hopes for its Moroccan stakehold. The traumatic loss of the remnants of its New World Empire at the end of the nineteenth century caused a wave of critical self-examination about Spain's position in a still unabashedly imperial world. While other European nations were accruing colonies, Spain's were falling away. Was Spain in decline, with no hope of regeneration, or did she have a future as a colonial power? Led by the belligerent King Alphonso XIII, known as "El Africano," Spain looked to Morocco to revive her imperial fortunes and restore her claims to greatness.[31]

FIGURE 17. Spanish King Alfonso XIII, champion of his country's expansion in northern Morocco and known as "El Africano" because of his imperial ambitions, directing military operations in the Rif Mountains, around 1911. (Collection Gérard Lévy, Paris)

Recently industrialized and slowly modernizing, Spain saw Morocco as a source of raw materials, cheap manpower, and unobstructed markets. The rich mineral deposits of the Rif held promise, but the roughness of the terrain and the lack of roads made their exploitation difficult. In its first eight years of dominion, Spain made little headway into the interior, but its intentions were clear. The Rifians, for their part, became increasingly alarmed, for they were neither isolated nor ignorant of European ways: the proximity of the *presidios*, the Spanish enclaves on Morocco's northern coast, a tradition of seasonal migration to the heavily hispanicized region of Oran in Algeria, offshore fishing and dealing in contraband, had familiarized Rifians with their Spanish neighbors. However, now that Spain was no longer a visitor but a permanent resident and the Rifians were colonial subjects, the relationship changed radically. By the time that General Dámaso Berenguer was appointed High Commissioner for Spanish Morocco in 1920, a resolute Rifian resistance movement had coalesced under the brothers ʿAbd al-Karim, leaders of an impromptu force made up of tough tribesmen known for their fearlessness in battle and their stunning accuracy with a rifle.

The ʿAbd al-Karim family consisted of a father and two sons, Muhammad, the elder, also known as Mohand, and M'hammad, the younger. The patriarch was qaʿid of the powerful tribe of the Beni Ouariaghel who gave his sons a modern education, but did not neglect their religious training. Muhammad (1882–1963) finished his studies at the Qarawiyyin in Fez, went to work for the Spanish in Melilla, and then became a journalist, editing the Arabic section of the local Spanish newspaper, *El-Telegrama del Rif*. A complex person with a heteroclite education, Muhammad ʿAbd al-Karim spoke Spanish and Arabic and was also learned in Islamic law – prized achievements in the eyes of the Berber-speaking Rifians. Both brothers were angered by Spain's fumbling attempts to exploit the Rif's rich mineral deposits, and watched with growing concern as the Spanish army penetrated deeper into their homeland.[32]

Muhammad ʿAbd al-Karim was jailed for preaching sedition in 1916, an experience that instilled in him a fierce desire for revenge. On leaving prison in 1917, he returned to his homeland at Ajdir and began building an armed force organized around his tribe of the Beni Ouariaghel. Meanwhile, Spanish forces numbering about seventy-five thousand men were advancing deep into Rifian territory, dislodging the most powerful tribes of the Central Rif, such as the Beni Saʿid, the Temsamane, and the Tafersit. The Spanish force was large, but the rank-and-file were unreliable; the men were woefully undertrained, badly equipped and underfed, supplementing their meager rations with frogs and turtles caught in the watercourses. Moreover, the officer corps was arrogant and incompetent, the lines of communication with bases on the coast overly long, the roads were primitive tracks, and medical help was "beneath contempt," according to eyewitness Walter Harris, who saw wounded soldiers waiting days for treatment.[33]

Clashes in the mountains continued throughout the spring of 1921, with Rifian fighters overrunning Spanish outposts, but these encounters were not taken seriously by the Spanish. In July, the Rifians attacked and decimated a Spanish force of vastly superior size at the tiny outpost of Anwal in the eastern Rif, winning a stunning victory. When General Manuel Silvestre, commander of Spanish forces in the Rif, received news of the attack on Anwal, he hurried to the battle front, but it was too late. Harassed on all sides, Silvestre and his men held out until all were either killed or committed suicide in shame. This defeat led to a general panic, with the entire Spanish army fleeing cross the waterless and burning landscape of the central Rif in the heat of summer – a complete rout in which artillery, transport, heaps of arms and ammunition, along with the wounded, were abandoned on the roadside. At the garrison town of Monte Arruit near the coast, the fleeing Spanish soldiers finally made a stand; but here, too, they were completely overrun. In all, the Spanish lost about nine thousand men killed in the battle of Anwal and its aftermath, with hundreds taken prisoner; in addition, they left behind a huge quantity of rifles, machine guns and artillery. Moreover, Spain was forced to abandon five thousand square kilometers of countryside – a dozen years of effort to implant its presence in those inhospitable mountains gone to waste. When news of the catastrophe reached Madrid, rumors of ineptitude and corruption in the army spread, precipitating a parliamentary crisis. The establishment of a military dictatorship under General Primo de Rivera (1870–1930) swept aside the liberal constitutional regime that was still in its infancy, setting the stage for fifty years of authoritarian rule, much of it under the dictatorship Generalissimo Francisco Franco, who first gained national attention as a result of his heroic role at the battle of Anwal.[34]

After this spectacular victory, explained by the Rifians as due to divine intervention, ʿAbd al-Karim tightened his hold on his political organization and laid the foundations of a separate state. He founded the "Rifian Republic" (*al-jumhuriyya al-rifiyya*), a political entity with its own cabinet, currency, tax and judicial systems. In addition, the Rifians formed themselves into a regular army, headed by ʿAbd al-Karim, who imposed compulsory conscription and even pressed women into service. After assuring his political ascendency, he then launched an international campaign to win his territory's independence. Abroad, he used modern expressions of self-determination to mobilize liberal support in Spain and France; in the domestic sphere, he employed the language of Islamic revival to win adherents to his cause.[35]

Following a two-year hiatus in which each side withdrew to regroup, the Rif war entered a new phase in which France entered the fray. By 1924, the French had subdued the tribes in the eastern region of Taza. The railroad line between Fez and Oujda, the sole practical means of communicating by land between Morocco and western Algeria, ran through this territory. Defending this territory was a primary French goal. During World War I, the Germans had tried repeatedly to disrupt the railroad, bribing Rifian contingents to cross the border from Spanish into French Morocco to cut the railroad line; to prevent this, France had installed a string of military outposts along the frontier between the two zones that reduced but did not entirely eliminate the Rifian threat. Lyautey was careful not to let his men cross the wide no-man's-land that separated Spanish from French Morocco. But as ʿAbd al-Karim boldly moved further south, extending his authority among the tribes who lived near the border separating the two zones, anxiety in the Residency increased. The Rifian leader, for his part, was angry that France and Spain were playing the imperial card, drawing imaginary lines across a territory where they had few interests or past history – only the knowledge that their authority was being challenged by a "native" upstart.

Fearing the Rifians' vaulting ambitions, and dubious about Spain's ability to contain them, Lyautey was drawn into the Rif War against his will. Earlier, he had famously warned: "Don't set foot in the Rif. It's a hornet's nest; moreover, it is not ours ... ".[36] Now in the final year of his pro-consulate, aging and in ill-health, he recognized that the uprising in the Rif could be a source of a contagion that would spread southward and poison his thirteen years of effort in French Morocco. On the larger scale, it seemed that the supremacy of Western civilization was being challenged by a bunch of fanatical country bumpkins. With this thought in mind, Lyautey mounted a major counteroffensive, sending troops across the poorly demarcated border that separated the two zones, cutting off ʿAbd al-Karim from his new acquisitions. ʿAbd al-Karim saw no choice but to defend himself, for acquiescing in the loss of this region would have been a sign that he was stepping back from his pledge to rid the Rif of colonial rule. Yet he knew he could not sustain a two-front war against the Spanish on the coast and the French in the south; nevertheless, he went forward, bringing together his own Rifians with men from the Jebala and the border tribes.

Armed with the latest weaponry, including machine guns, hand grenades and field artillery taken from the Spanish, the combined Rifian forces gathered for a fight. In a series of stunning attacks led by ʿAbd al-Karim in April 1925, the string of well-fortified border posts built by the French were overrun and their defenders routed. ʿAbd al-Karim's men, four thousand strong, broke through the French defenses and rushed toward Fez; it was reported that bands of armed Rifians were roving within twenty miles of the city. The French now realized that it was far more than Spanish incompetence that had created the Rifian success.

Fully aroused, France dispatched its most distinguished war hero, General Philippe Pétain, to take charge of the fighting. Lyautey was relegated to the sidelines by his superiors in a humiliating démarche that permanently blunted his prestige. Writing home to Paris, Pétain confessed that from his point of view, "we were unexpectedly attacked by the most powerful and best armed enemy that we have ever met with in our colonial campaigns."[37] In response, the French unleashed a barrage of modern weaponry perfected during World War I with terrifying effect – aerial bombardment, poison gas, and armored tanks and cars. In the summer and fall of 1925, Pétain directed a joint French-Spanish effort that crushed ʿAbd al-Karim's main force and cut it off from its food supply. Meanwhile, Spain successfully landed troops on the coast at Alhucemas in September, 1925, giving Spain a foothold from which it could strike at ʿAbd al-Karim's inland capital at Targuist. The Rifians found themselves caught in a pincer movement, with Spanish forces pressing downward from the coast, the French moving cross-country from the south, and a separate Spanish force approaching from the east. Meanwhile, Primo de Rivera vowed "to break ʿAbd al-Karim's power" in the Central Rif, and laid plans for his unconditional surrender. In the spring of 1926, the war entered its final stages.[38]

In France, news of the plight of the Rifian forces and the crisis facing their "Ripublik" stirred an antigovernment outcry. Thousands of irate French socialists and communists marched through the streets of Paris

FIGURE 18. ʿAbd al-Karim al-Khattabi, hero of the Rif War, preferred surrendering to his French adversaries rather than to the Spanish. Here he is pictured (in the center) on his way to exile on the Isle of Réunion in the summer of 1926. Photo Coutanson. (Collection Gérard Lévy, Paris)

protesting the conduct of hostilities and condemning France and Spain as colonial "slave masters."[39] But the French government was determined to finish with ʿAbd al-Karim, and on May 23, 1926, Targuist fell and the Rifian chief became a fugitive. On the night of May 26, 1926, accompanied by a small group of wives and family, he slipped across the lines and surrendered to the French, apparently preferring a Gallic imprisonment to a Spanish one. It had taken more than 158,000 colonial soldiers against a combined Rifian force of 40,000 men to bring him to heel.[40]

It was the desire of Lyautey's successor, Résident Général Théodore Steeg, that ʿAbd al-Karim would be "neither exalted nor humiliated, but in time forgotten."[41] But such was not the case; the Rifian warrior remained politically active throughout his entire life in exile, writing and commenting on the course of events in his homeland, first from the Island of Réunion in the Indian Ocean, and later from Cairo, where he became a rallying point for the Moroccan nationalist cause and an inspiration to a younger generation of Maghribis seeking models of anti-colonial resistance. Having become the beacon of the nascent nationalist movement, he was branded *persona non grata* by the Protectorate administration and his banishment made permanent. ʿAbd al-Karim returned to Morocco briefly after independence in 1962, but he was already gravely ill, and died in Cairo the following year without ever seeing his tribal homeland again.[42]

ʿAbd al-Karim and his war pose many problems for the historian. Was his effort a reversion to old-style jihad, a final, abortive attempt to throw out the "infidel," or was he a modern politician, motivated by the vision of a unified state? Or was he something else, perhaps: an opportunist, first a Bolshevik and then a capitalist, playing with one side or the other depending on the benefits that accrued? Jacques Berque observed that ʿAbd al-Karim "was no local marabout, promising paradise to those who fought the infidel, but a political chief whose ambitions now included the idea of nationhood, and even a share in the international game."[43] Within the realm of Morocco historiography, the Rif War is embedded in a larger and even more controversial question: At what point did resistance to the colonial powers actually began, who should take credit for it, and who were its "true" leaders? Was it a grassroots and popular uprising, as Germain Ayache has argued, or was it a tribal vendetta, driven by jealousy and offended honor? Some have claimed it was the first truly anticolonial war, the struggle of an oppressed people attempting to wrest their freedom from imperialist tyrants. On another plane, the memory of the "Rifian Republic" was a constant reminder to those in power in Morocco – whether they were colonial administrators, Moroccan nationalists, or the

ʿAlawi monarchy after 1956 – of the ability of this proudly self-reliant region to raise the banner of revolt in defiance of the claims of the state. The legacy of ʿAbd al-Karim still agitates and disturbs – an unresolved and contrapuntal note in the narrative of the nation.[44]

THE GROWTH OF COLONIAL CAPITALISM

Even though the "pacification" had not been completed, settlers began arriving in numbers after World War I, changing the human composition of colonial Morocco. What new elements did they introduce into the life of the country, and what sort of a society did they help create? To what extent did they mingle with, influence, and in turn were influenced by, the Muslim majority? A subject of riveting interest, whose barest outlines can only be sketched here. The current of migration was not uniform, but proceeded by fits and starts. Nor was it all French, but a mixture of Mediterranean peoples, dominated by the French, but also including Italians, Greeks, Spanish, and Corsicans, with many coming from other parts of French North Africa. In some periods, departures outnumbered arrivals. The settlers' mode of life was in many ways similar to that of the native Moroccans, as were their food and habits, and perhaps even their appearance; but they were Christian, modern, disproportionately male, urbanized, politicized, and imbued with a sense of their own cultural superiority. They were ready to pitch in and drive the colonial engine, now moving forward at breakneck speed, by assuming work as construction workers, farm hands, small shopowners, bakers, carpenters, plumbers, tailors, florists, sellers of shoes and thread. Their contribution, as well as their primal error, was their willingness to exploit a land that was not really theirs, by providing the economic and social cement between a French managerial class and bedrock of Moroccan unskilled labor.[45]

The influx also brought a smaller but not insignificant number of professionals with access to capital: lawyers, doctors, architects, building contractors, owners of newspapers, and some large landowners who frequently made the circuit Paris-Rabat. In 1918, at the end of the war, the European colony numbered about sixty thousand, with forty thousand arriving in the expansion that took place between 1919 and 1922. Immigration stagnated in the mid-twenties, and then spiked again during the "boom" years of 1926–1929. It continued to increase until 1931, aided by the loans offered in French financial markets to underwrite large infrastructure projects such as the railroad and the electric grid. The capitalization of these projects stimulated employment and changed the face of the land: civic buildings and residences, road construction, railroads and port construction, leaped upward in these years. After 1931, the flow was reduced to a mere trickle because of the Great Depression; at that point, approximately 162,000 Europeans lived in Morocco, sixty percent of them of French origin.[46]

Both public and private investment were behind this surge of activity. Lyautey's insistence on the rapid development of infrastructure related to ideology as well as to economics; he wished to show the world that France could single-handedly manage the exploitation of Morocco and thus join Britain in the pantheon of great imperial powers. He shared with Albert Sarraut, perhaps the most influential voice within the French government on colonial policy, the belief in the doctrine of *mise en valeur*, or the encouragement of massive investment in colonial development, preferably, but not exclusively, from state funds.[47] French companies that won the coveted contracts to finance these giant projects were able to walk away with handsome profits. The new port of Casablanca was the first rosette in Lyautey's chestful of achievements, with its long jetty extending two kilometers into the sea; by 1925, it had surpassed Tangier (now inside the Spanish zone) to become the principal port of the Sharifian Empire, followed distantly by Kénitra.

The next great project was a railroad system that knit together much of the country from Oujda to Marrakesh, supplemented by thousands of

FIGURE 19. The *Compagnie de Transports au Maroc*, or CTM, was created in November 1919 with the aim of reaching "all of Morocco" with its fleet of buses that traveled along a new colonial road system planned to connect all major towns and cities. (Collection Tangier American Legation Institute and Museum)

kilometers of paved road. "The automobile is a last resort that we are glad to have, but it will never constitute true commercial transport," Lyautey announced in 1919. Meanwhile, hordes of Moroccans of every social class embraced *la-tren*, with the number of voyagers riding on the rough metal benches of fourth class reaching 620,000 in the year of 1926.[48] Mining concessions, dam construction, and a massive electric grid rounded out the tableau of major infrastructure projects. France's achievements were showcased in a series of international fairs staged by Lyautey during and after the war that attracted foreign visitors and shone the spotlight on progress in all sectors of the colonial economy. The first fair was held in Casablanca in 1915, inaugurated by Lyautey with Sultan Mawlay Yusuf at his side.

Yet it was widely believed that the "true fortune" of Morocco resided in the promotion of modern agriculture. Lyautey was sharply opposed to intensive rural colonization in Morocco, fearing a replication of the situation in Algeria, where (in his words) the "riff-raff" of southern Europe swarmed to take advantage of a giveaway of land that reduced much of the native peasantry to a rootless proletariat. A small number of "choice" settlers who would impart a strong French flavor to the bled was his goal. Recognizing that some colonization was inevitable, Lyautey tried to confine it to a "superior" class of "gentlemen-farmers" who would grow cereal crops on farms located in the coastal areas of the Chaouia and the Gharb, near Fez and Meknes, and in the region of Marrakech. Planting cereals, it was believed, would restore Morocco to its historical role as "the granary of ancient Rome," while securing for the metropole a guaranteed supply of basic foodstuffs. More to the point, however, was the oft-invoked and misguided image of a Moroccan "Far West" – an empty land, an unutilized space, ripe for exploitation by the pioneering spirit. Armed with subsidies and offered generous quotas that guaranteed them a niche in French market, privileged colonials were to be "an example" to the peasantry by introducing new farming techniques while exuding a mystical love for the soil.

Conforming to Lyautey's wishes, the influx of settlers wishing to farm the land was not great. The number of handpicked "official" settlers arriving in the period 1917–1925 was a modest 692, even as the area under cultivation began to expand, demonstrating an overwhelming preference for the *grande propriété*, or large estate, usually measuring about one thousand acres, as the ideal size for colonial exploitation. The number of migrants who worked the land was not great; in the years 1917 to 1931, sixteen hundred people settled on 620,000 acres, and after 1931, the number of new settlers completely dried up.[49]

What drove these people to come to this strange land? Often the dream of easy riches and of achieving the wealth and status that had eluded them at home. Though Morocco was "no El Dorado," as one French observer admitted, it could be a land of opportunity, free from the blockages that impeded advancement in less fluid societies. It was a place for exercising the imagination and pursuing high ambitions. The case of Madame Garnier, a silk maker from Marseilles, emerges from the archives and shows the progressive attitude of some of those who came: a devoted disciple of the liberal French economist Charles Gide, she was appalled by the condition of women in Morocco and decided to build a silk cooperative in the Haouz that would employ women and provide a shelter for the sick and exhausted. Not all immigrants were so high-minded; some were simply seeking a *boulot* (job). In the remote oasis town of Ouarzazate, Dmitri "the Greek" opened a small café that everyone frequented "without distinction or segregation," day and night, a convivial spot boasting wooden tables and a cement floor.[50]

For most settlers, and especially those working the land, life was hard. Malaria and dysentery were endemic, conditions in the countryside were rudimentary, the sole comforts being "the warmth of anisette and the ardor of the sun." Harassed by meddlesome bureaucrats and in charge of unwilling workers, the *petit colon* or small farmer often lived in a state of high anxiety and morbid resentment, intensified by a deep racism that colored all relations with the *les indigènes*, the pejorative term for native Moroccans. Some struggled to bridge the gulf of incomprehension separating worker from boss, while others retreated into a closed self-pity. Moïse Nahon, settler, essayist, schoolteacher, native Moroccan and adviser to Lyautey, captured the mood of frustration that characterized life in the bled in his slim collection of essays, *Notes d'un colon du Gharb: 2 juillet 1920–décembre 1924*. In a series of vignettes, he represents with pristine clarity the paternalism the settler felt to toward his workers and the vitriolic anger he directed toward an obtuse officialdom. Putting aside their republican sentiments, most settlers considered the Protectorate administration as a necessary evil, useful for squelching whatever hopes Moroccans might have had to recover their own soil.[51]

To accommodate this wave of migration, most of it destined for rural areas, a massive transfer of land ensued, with makhzan, tribal, and even privately held land, shifting from Moroccan to European ownership. The lure of quick cash was too much for many impoverished peasants to resist. Even though French law tried to protect farmers, unscrupulous local officials found ways to circumvent the regulations. Much of the newly acquired land was put into grain production, with the intention of turning Morocco into the breadbasket of France; cropland planted to grain increased sixty percent in the decade between 1919 and 1929, without regard for the fact that growing grain in drought-prone Morocco was an expensive and risky plan. Meanwhile, thousands of acres of collectivized land changed hands, leaving whole tribes without a means of livelihood.

The thirst for land reached new levels after 1930, just as the world price of grain plummeted, and Moroccan wheat, propped up by protective tariffs and guaranteed quotas in the French market, became absurdly expensive. Moreover, farmers in the metropole were producing bumper crops of grain at a far cheaper price. It became clear that if Moroccan farmers were to profitably export their crops, they would have to abandon grain production and turn to something else. The stake in the heart of Moroccan cereal growing was a massive plague of locusts in the summer of 1930 that left the roads covered with a thick, black, moving carpet that devastated cropland. As famine loomed, planners abandoned the dream of recreating "the granary of Rome," and turned instead to the model of a "French California" that entailed the cultivation of high-value citrus fruits and vegetables on irrigated land. In addition to recuperating land previously considered inferior, the shift from grains to fruits and vegetables required the setting up of farmer cooperatives to market the product using modern techniques of branding, packing and quality control. It was a shift that would have important consequences for Morocco's agricultural future.[52]

Preparation of the land for such intensive, mechanized agriculture called for large amounts of capital and a degree of organization beyond the capacity of most native farmers. Unable to compete, they abandoned the countryside and sought work in the cities, following the periodic cycles of boom and bust in the colonial economy. A severe drought in the years 1936–1937 accelerated the rural exodus. The face of Morocco's cities began to change; unable to find places to live in the urban core, migrants settled on the periphery, throwing up substandard housing and ringing the cities with shantytowns called *bidonvilles*. In 1931, more than half the residents of Casablanca were Moroccan; by 1954, three quarters, or 500,000, were Moroccan, with 150,000 living in bidonvilles lacking good sanitation or clean water.[53] The influx of rural people was the foundation of a new urban underclass unfamiliar with city ways. These workers periodically went back home to the bled, constituting a mobile and restless proletariat prone to volatility. Lyautey's concept of a "native" city and a "European" city existing side by side in harmony receded into the past, as cities became a cacophonous mélange of native and foreigner, rich and poor, longtime residents and newcomers from the countryside, all muddled together in an explosive mix.[54]

The exploitation of Morocco's riches was not limited to agriculture; mineral resources were also subsumed under schemes for exploitation. The Sharifian Office of Phosphates (OCP), created in 1920 to extract the immense phosphate reserves in the Khouribga region, rapidly became the most profitable mining enterprise in Morocco. With its up-to-date plant and a direct railroad line to Casablanca port, the Khouribga mines readily responded to rising world demand for phosphates (thirty-three thousand tons exported in 1921, nearly two million tons in 1930). However, Moroccan miners did not benefit from this success; forbidden to organize, with no social protections, and salaries at a fraction of European wages, they were cogs in the wheel of the extractive colonial economy. Industrial workers fared no better. Fearful of competing with the metropole, French planners kept manufacturing at a low level; canneries, sugar refining, a brewery, and flourmills producing for local consumption comprised the limited investment in industry in the interwar years. All other necessities for life came from outside.

The growing population of manual workers was slowly drawn toward the nascent Moroccan trades union movement. Founded in the aftermath of World War I, syndicalism in Morocco was an outgrowth of the French-based General Confederation of Labor (CGT). Initially, union members were French nationals employed in the public sector, many of them seasoned by experience in Algeria and Tunisia – postmen, teachers, policemen, administrators of every type. Work in the colonies had its attractions: advancement was usually more rapid than in the metropole, and housing allowances, costs of travel, and even periodic trips back to France were part of the terms of employment. The effervescent political climate after the World War I, the Russian Revolution of 1917, and other global events inspired these workers to organize. In May 1919, employees of the French administration, working quietly in a "fragmentary, hesitant, and furtive" manner, under the cover of names such as "Mutuality" and "Association," formed the first labor union in Morocco, the Association Générale (AG) in 1919. Its various subunits represented groups such a engineers, bank employees, hoteliers, postal employees, and teachers – the salaried bourgeoisie. Influenced primarily by the labor movement in France, the main objective of the AG was to improve working conditions in Morocco to reach the level of the metropole. None of its members were Muslim. Largely oblivious to the conditions under which native Moroccans worked, the "salaried employees" pushed their own middle class agenda. In fact, according to labor historian Albert Ayache, "they did not understand the singularity of the country where they worked and did not understand the true nature of the colonial situation."[55]

With the departure of Lyautey in 1925 and the end of the Rif war, leftist political groups consolidated and formed workingmen's clubs in the major cities of Morocco, and their militancy increased. The trial and execution of Italian anarchists Sacco and Vanzetti in Boston in August 1927 incited thousands of demonstrators to gather in protest in front of the American consulate in Casablanca. Still, none of these manifestations included Moroccans, formally excluded from organizing by the Residency, who feared the politicization of the "native worker" through an association with socialists, radicals and communists. In the words of one official, "the native masses are amorphous and easily led astray by agitators with bad intentions." But the drift toward unionization could not be held back. The great capitalist expansion of 1926–1929 brought many more Moroccans into the work force, and it was only a matter of time before they were "infected" with radical ideas.[56]

Yet it would take another decade for Moroccan workers to form their own associations. Oppressed by shrinking salaries and rising prices, weighed down by fines, restrictions, and a lack of rights, the Moroccan proletariat entered the political shoals of the 1930s ripe for insurrection. By 1934, it was clear that both the Residency and the European-dominated labor organizations had lost control of the Moroccan worker, who had moved into the magnetic field of a powerful new phenomenon that we shall explore in Chapter 5; namely, the country-wide uprising led by young men dedicated to the nationalist cause.

THE END OF THE PROCONSULSHIP OF LYAUTEY

By 1925, when he left the country for the last time, Lyautey's plans for Morocco were close to fulfillment. It seemed that it was well on the way to becoming the obedient client state he envisioned, moving slowly down the path of progress while preserving its cultural distinctiveness in the modern world. This image, however, was deeply flawed, because it excluded the main actors in Morocco's future, namely, the majority of the Moroccan people. Out of touch with a rising generation of "young Moroccans" (*jeunes marocains*) who were politically and socially attuned to a new age, Lyautey realized that his notions of governance by "indirect rule" had been swamped by an expanding bureaucracy swollen to many times its original size. This hyper-centralized "Leviathan state" from which Moroccans were systematically excluded was exactly the inverse of the governing order he had envisioned in 1912; moreover, it was the substratal cause for a rising tide of local resentment. His belief that he could "manage" Moroccan society with kid gloves and "drops of oil" dissolved as his charisma faded and his closest advisers departed, to be replaced by impatient hardliners who pushed for more aggressive interventionism – to "do what was needed" for Moroccans, without their participation or assent. Some argued that this shift was necessary due to an innate "incapacity" of the natives to contribute to a modern state; others suspected Islam and its "debilitating" effects; still others blamed the failure on Communist influence, or Egyptian reformers, or the nefarious effects of Pan-Islamism; but in the end, it was the French colonial system itself that had turned Moroccans against the Protectorate.

Lyautey's final legacy is an ambivalent one, vacillating between the positive achievements of a techno-organization that produced a beneficial modernity, on the one hand, and that same organization's capacity for brutal control, on the other. His accomplishments were manifold, but not always as he would have intended: he ended the opposition to the colonial state, but in its place, he opened the way to a new form of resistance – a vibrant patriotism nurtured on the hope that someday, the burden of foreign rule would be lifted from the backs of the people. Through his policy of the *grands qaʿids*, he brought an end to *siba*, or tribal dissidence, putting in its place a corrupt and archaic chiefery who oppressed the rural masses and held them perennially in check. He raised the standards of health, built modern cities, introduced new methods of transport, of work, of communication, while maintaining a Protectorate "with a human face," but at the same time, he did all this without the assent of those he governed. His love of rank and hierarchy, of royal princes and sons of the elite, perfumed Morocco with an oligarchic scent that lingers to this day. Finally, he snatched the sultanate from the dross of history, restoring it to a position of respect, eliminating all contenders to its monopolistic claim on religious authority, and in so doing, positioned it to reach for absolute power when the dust of decolonization had finally settled.

Meanwhile, Lyautey himself remained stoic, despite his disgrace in the Rif War, and stayed at his post like an aging gladiator knowing his final days were near. He sent his official letter of resignation on September 28, 1925, but stayed in Morocco for several more weeks, making a pilgrimage to the sites and symbols of his greatest successes: Casablanca port, the Funduq al-Najjarin in the Fez madina, the cadets at Dar el-Beida, and a sentimental visit to Sultan Yusuf, during which both were overcome with emotion. He knew "that a world had come to an end."[57] Then he left for his manor in Lorraine, in northeast France, now transformed into a Moroccan palace, never to return.

Four years after his death in 1934, when the Protectorate was still in full season, a monumental equestrian statue of Lyautey was erected in the central square of Casablanca, a city he planned and had built. Sitting astride a splendid horse, Lyautey's figure surveyed the urban scene like a proud *condottiere*. Later, in 1955, on the eve of Moroccan independence, the statue was mysteriously removed from its pivotal spot and relocated in a nearby garden of the Consulate of France, behind a protective iron fence, where it stands today. The evaluation of Lyautey's heritage in contemporary Morocco, like the relocation of his monument, is tinged with an undercurrent of strong emotion, and precisely where he ought to be positioned is a subject of heated debate.[58] For the time being, however, his achievements are not widely appreciated by the mass of Moroccan people. It may take decades, if ever, for the story of the beginnings of the Protectorate and his role in it to be rewritten by Moroccan historians in the liberal spirit he so much admired.

5

Framing the Nation (1930–1961)

It is difficult to pinpoint the precise moment when the concept of nationalism entered the Moroccan political consciousness. We know that the idea of a Moroccan nation as a framework for political life appeared in writing in the mid-nineteenth century, as a way of distinguishing "Moroccans" from other peoples. The scholar-scribe Muhammad al-Saffar, traveling in France in 1846, spoke of "the people of Morocco" as a definable entity, different from others, with their own particular cultural, religious, linguistic and political qualities. Later in the century, the lexicon of historian Ahmad al-Nasiri included the word *watan*, or "homeland," suggesting a distinct Moroccan territory, separate from its neighbors. But the notion of a Moroccan "nation" as the centerpiece for an ideology of exclusivity or a rallying point for people's aspirations did not yet exist, nor would it for some time. In this chapter, we shall trace the trajectory of the Moroccan nationalist movement from its obscure origins in the madina of Fez and the streets of Paris to a hard-won independence – an objective achieved within the space of a single generation.

THE ORIGINS OF MOROCCAN NATIONALISM

The moment of transition to a new world order in which "nationalism" became an ideological preoccupation of colonial peoples occurred after World War I. Out of the wreckage of the Great War, new states emerged on the periphery of Europe, inspired by notions of parliamentary democracy, rule of law, and constitutionalism as governing norms, all within a clearly defined national space. President Wilson's Fourteen Points, first articulated in January 1918 and then reiterated at the Paris Peace Conference of 1919, carried the hope of national "self-determination" for all peoples, regardless of who they were or where they lived. These ideas influenced many on the European left and soon spilled over into the non-Western world, much of it still under colonial rule, inspiring a rising generation to articulate its own vision of the future. The effect of this new mood was nothing short of epic; countries from India to Morocco emerged from the war with energized native elites – teachers, writers, public figures – who aligned themselves with an awakened bourgeoisie ready for change. Thanks to improved education, new modes of communication, and the integrative effects of the post-war economy, their thoughts moved in tandem with Europe's own, inciting a torrent of political activity across the globe.[1]

How were Moroccans affected by talk about political freedom coming from Europe, and how did they imagine its impact on their own lives? The establishment of the Protectorate in Morocco in 1912 constituted a sharp break with the past by expanding the limits of state control and testing people's toleration for foreign rule. The colonial order dispatched the makhzan and other traditional structures of authority to the periphery of political life, creating a vacuum soon filled by a parallel, secular, and unfamiliar Protectorate authority inspired by the principles of republican France, but operating according to the rules of naked self-interest. World War I quickly followed, upsetting everyday routines – shortages of food and matériel, the absence of able-bodied men sent to France for combat or work, the destabilization of social life. These ruptures induced widespread suffering, particularly among poorer classes who were victims of the war economy and its devastating aftermath. Less than ten years into its hegemony, French power was already passing through its zenith, moving into a new stage of contestation with a gathering opposition. "During the whole inter-war period," says Jacques Berque, "France's power dwindled in proportion to the growth of her appetites and responsibilities ... she asked more than she received, she promised more than she performed, she undertook more than she accomplished."[2]

For the native elite the break with the past that World War I offered was liberating and brought a new sense of hope, especially among the few in the younger generation who were being trained to become the vanguard of a new ruling class. For these Moroccans, the postwar turmoil represented an opportunity to act, not as subalterns being led to "maturity" under the tutelage of France, but as architects of their own destiny. It took another decade for the resistance to colonialism to coalesce into a full-blown movement for independence, but hints of future insurrection were already in the air before Lyautey left Morocco in 1925.

Signs of a change were evident in a variety of settings. The highly selective education system that was the centerpiece of Lyautey's plan for transforming the next generation into a vector of modernity was already under fire. The crisis came in 1922, when the "sons of notables" attending the two *collèges musulmans* revolted against the tightly controlled curriculum intended to prepare them for middling jobs in the administration. Comparing their own limited choices with the course of study being offered to Europeans at the French *lycées*, they concluded that their education was inferior. Some sought schooling elsewhere: Tuhami al-Muqri, son of Grand Vizir Muhammad al-Muqri, went to Beirut to study with the Jesuits, and pronounced it a life-changing experience. Others went to the al-Azhar University in Cairo where modern subjects were combined with an Islamic course of study, without the usual heavy dose of French cultural superiority. Lyautey already spoke of "inevitable aspirations," and in 1922, he told the Native Policy Council that the young elite was changing with "disconcerting rapidity," and that he feared that their "political awakening" would soon have dire consequences.[3]

To combat the narrow access to education, committed Moroccan intellectuals went outside the system and created "free schools" as an alternative to the elitist French system, with the aim of educating children in Arabic language, literature, and Islamic history. Still, the level of schooling remained pathetically low; in 1934, out of a native population of between seven and eight million, with half a million children of school age, only eleven thousand were in school.[4] The select few who acquired a primary education joined with graduates of the Muslim *collèges* and the Qarawiyyin University to form the nuclei of cultural associations and literary clubs that sprang up in every major city. These associations, some of them secret, served as centers for intellectual exchange and political discussion that was decidedly pro-nationalist. In 1928, members of the "Islamic Literary Club" of Salé presented a modern Egyptian play directed by one of their own members about the Abbasid caliph Harun al-Rashid that contained blatantly political themes, demonstrating their ability to adapt cultural products emanating from Cairo, the capital of progressive Arab thinking, to the local situation.[5]

Meanwhile, future nationalist leaders Ahmed Balafrej, Mohammed Hassan al-Ouezzani, and al-Makki al-Nasiri, sought higher education in France. Soon the streets of the Latin Quarter became familiar terrain for young men who were sons of the Moroccan upper bourgeoisie. In the intensely cosmopolitan environment of postwar Paris, where émigrés from all parts of the colonized world met and intermingled, the Moroccans became politically sensitized and began to question the *raison d'être* of the Protectorate. In 1927, they helped found the Maghribi student association AEMNA (North African Muslim Students Association), where they came into contact with militants from the Arab East, such as Shakib Arslan, a champion of Arab nationalism and disciple of Muhammad ʿAbduh. The far-ranging discussions, the heady freedom, the meeting with radicalized youth from other countries, produced a sense of political intoxication that traveled homeward with them.[6]

On their return, they joined with other activists whose roots were in the salafi circles that had grown up around the Qarawiyyin University in Fez. Foremost among the homegrown nationalists was Muhammad ʿAllal al-Fasi, son of a distinguished Andalusian family, who became leader of a clandestine opposition centered in Fez in 1927. Possessor of a golden tongue, al-Fasi sensitized his comrades to the importance of ʿAbd al-Karim's uprising in the Rif, tirelessly stressing themes such as liberty and resistance to authority in speeches he made in mosques, schools, clubs and other social gatherings. Under his direction, the Fez group seized the leadership of the young nationalist movement. The growth of this movement did not go unnoticed by French officialdom in Rabat, who deplored the activities of these "intellectual dropouts and talkative dreamers ... whose only concern was to speak, write, and preach against the great work of France in Morocco and to propagate ... the mental weaknesses of the educated classes ... " in the words of one bureaucrat.[7]

Meanwhile, other grievances roiled the surface of public life, disturbing the image of a smoothly working, well-oiled, and efficient colonial machine. Economic troubles headed the list. The old pre-Protectorate agricultural tax, the tartib, was an ongoing source of irritation in the countryside. Government inspectors made an annual census of crops and herds with the collaboration of the tribal *jamaʿa*, or ruling council. Local qaʿids would retain 6 percent of the tax as their due, linking the tartib in the minds of farmers with extortion and venality. This obnoxious impost that produced ready cash for the coffers of the Administration was not abolished for another fifty years, until the reign of Hassan II. The *patente*, a tax imposed on urban shopkeepers, was equally hated; pashas pocketed a fixed portion of the income from this tariff as their reward. Instead of introducing rationality and efficiency, the French promoted a tax system that spawned corruption and mismanagement. By the mid-twenties, two important sectors of the economy, the peasantry and the urban business classes, were moving headlong toward an anticolonial stance.

Other restrictions imposed by the Protectorate strangled freedom of speech and limited the possibilities for political expression. Moroccans were prevented from attending large political gatherings for fear that they would "hear things beyond their capacity to understand," and Arabic newspapers were forbidden to write about politics, provoking cries of censorship.[8] Paternalistic and illiberal policies emanating from the

FIGURE 20. A young Sultan Muhammad V, not yet a symbol of nationalist resistance, arriving at the Élysée Palace, home of the French president in 1930, accompanied by his personal secretary, Muhammad al-Mammeri. (Collection Gérard Lévy, Paris)

administration, now scoffingly referred to as the *himaya* (literally, the "protection") raised the political temperature and created conditions for a confrontation.

THE "BERBER DAHIR" ELECTRIFIES THE NATION

The opportunity to vent the ill will incubating under an increasingly oppressive Protectorate administration came in the spring of 1930, with the promulgation of what was popularly known as the "Berber dahir." Coincidently, 1930 was also the year of the centenary of French Algeria, celebrating one hundred years of occupation, as well as the year of the Eucharist Congress held in Carthage, Tunisia; both events were perceived by Maghribi people as an assault on their religious and cultural sensibilities, provoking the fear that the underlying intention of France was to evangelize and convert all Muslims to Christianity. The widely publicized conversion in 1928 of Muhammad Benabdeljalil, the son of a prominent Fez family, deepened the sense of foreboding. The "Berber dahir" and the passionate response it elicited took place in an atmosphere of mounting popular anxiety.

The roots of the concept of "Berber separatism" on which the dahir was based reached deep into the French colonial experience in North Africa. The belief that Arabs and Berbers were each distinguished by an essential otherness that went far beyond the obvious linguistic differences was firmly held among colonial officials. The origin of this belief can be traced back to the nineteenth-century soldier-scholars of colonial Algeria, who embraced the idea that the two were in fact distinct "races," each having its own language, physical characteristics, habits of mind, social organization, and relationship to Islam. The "vulgate" went as follows: Berbers were industrious, Arabs languid; Berbers were indifferent to religion, Arabs were fanatically orthodox; Berbers respected hierarchy, Arabs were anarchical; Berbers were reticent, Arabs were prolix; and so on, in an unending litany of oppositions. This polarization played itself out in common parlance, in scholarly literature, and in the practices of governance. Ignoring evidence to the contrary, Protectorate officials in Morocco (many of whom were raised in the "nursery" of Algeria) insisted on recategorizing Moroccans in starkly binary terms that paid no attention the subtleties of ethnic and cultural variability. Practices of separation and "divide and rule" became a fixed feature of Protectorate policy, introducing miscalculations that were reproduced over and over again throughout the colonial administration.[9]

The distinction between the two groups was inscribed with special clarity in the legal domain, where a series of "Berber dahirs" – for there were several of them – defined the juridical status of Morocco's Berber peoples as different from the rest of society. Colonial officials took as a given that Berbers were by nature more "civilized" and democratic than Arabs and that their system of justice should reflect this difference. Noting that in the pre-Protectorate era, each Berber community had its own independent Council of Elders, or *jama'a*, "not unlike the councils of the Teutonic peoples in the age of Charlemagne," French officials proposed a return to this archaic form of organization. It was decided to revive the jama'a and to endow it with special powers based not on the Shariah but on Berber customary law. Sultan Mawlay Yusuf, surely against his better judgment, for the measure undermined his own authority as imam and guardian of the Muslim community, signed the first Berber dahir into law in September 1914, even while most Berber areas were still outside of French control.[10]

By 1930, the tribal jama'as had been operating smoothly for some years, but without a permanent statute spelling out their specific powers. With Lyautey gone, and with the passing of Sultan Mawlay Yusuf in 1927, the overall situation radically changed. The young and timid Sidi Muhammad b. Yusuf (1909–1961) ascended to the throne at age seventeen, just as the Residency was pushing for a more assertive "native policy." The time seemed propitious for instituting a new Berber statute resting on a more solid footing. On May 16, 1930, the French administration promulgated a dahir announcing that Berber tribes would thereafter to be governed "according to their own laws and customs," making explicit the distinction between Berber law (now to be written in French) and the Shariah law that applied to everyone else.[11]

The revolt against the dahir burst out almost immediately, and began in the town of Salé. Abdellatif Sbihi, an interpreter in the colonial administration and graduate of the School of Oriental Languages in Paris, quit his post to devote himself to speaking out against the measure. Meeting at clubs, on the beach, and in the mosque, he and his young and mostly upper class friends decided to use the *latif*, a prayer recited in times of communal distress, as an expression of protest, understanding that the mass of Moroccans were unequivocally attached to religion, whereas their nationalist sentiment was still weak. His recruits shared his belief that the dahir was the opening wedge in an insidious attempt to undermine the notion of a single Moroccan nation united under Qur'anic law. They suspected, not without good reason, that the dahir was a means of imposing a policy of "divide and rule," and that the French were preparing Berbers to become full-fledged members of colonial society, while leaving the Arabic-speaking population far behind.

In the weeks after the dahir was announced, protests broke out in Salé, Rabat, Fez and Tangier. The latif was pronounced in the mosques, but with the addition of a special ending: "Save us from the miseries of fate and do not separate us from our Berber brothers!" On July 18, 1930, after the conclusion of the Friday prayer in Fez, the crowd spilled out into the streets and joined a demonstration organized by Mohammed Hassan al-Ouezzani, graduate of the École des Sciences Politiques in Paris. Al-Ouezzani was immediately arrested and brought to the Pasha's palace where he was subjected to a public flogging. This humiliation not only radicalized al-Ouezzani, who went on to became one of the more militant nationalist leaders; it also gave momentum to the protest and advertised its goals. In secret meetings throughout the country, "young men without beards" persuaded – sometimes through trickery – older and more conservative imams to allow public recitations of the special prayer. Organizers contacted members of the foreign press, and the story of the insurrection spread overseas, even appearing in the *Times* of London.[12] Now fully awakened to its meaning, French officials were helpless to stop the recitation and reacted with beatings, deportations, and prison, giving many young activists their first lesson in the cost of civil disobedience. The Residency soon realized that its actions were having the opposite effect from what was intended, and retreated. In August, when the sultan issued a conciliatory letter allowing Berber tribes to opt out of the conditions of the dahir and submit instead to the rule of Shariah if they wished, the furor subsided.

The angry reaction to the Berber dahir helped internationalize the Moroccan problem, signaling its emergence as a new focus of anti-imperialist agitation. The Emir Shakib Arslan, a pan-Islamic activist resident in Geneva, also known as "the *mujahid* (warrior) of the pen," was notified by Moroccan students Ahmed Balafrej and Muhammad al-Fasi about the uprising, and in August, Arslan appeared in the Spanish zone, where he gave a series of fiery talks attacking the Protectorate regime for its plan to "de-Islamicize" Morocco. His visit, in the flowery rhetoric of the times, formed "a pure pearl in the historical chain of the emerging Moroccan awakening."[13] News of his appearance in Morocco reverberated throughout the Arab world as newspapers in Cairo, Damascus, Tunis, and Tripoli picked up the story, and messages of protest flowed into the Quai d'Orsay.

Gradually, the tide of anger provoked by the Berber dahir receded, but not before its organizers created a countrywide network aimed at combating an increasingly oppressive colonial administration. Mohammed Hassan al-Ouezzani exulted that "the movement surpassed all our hopes and expectations." But within the corridors of the Residency, its importance was downplayed. Georges Hardy, adviser to the Protectorate administration on educational matters and a highly influential voice, dismissed it as a display of "puerile behavior" by "showoffs (*enfants terribles*) who have aroused simple souls and pulled off some pointless demonstrations." But others recognized that a milestone in French-Moroccan relations had been passed: "Morocco, too, has now felt the thrust of nationalism," noted one pro-colonialist critic.[14] Meanwhile, the project to reform the system of

FIGURE 21. Grand Vizier Muhammad al-Muqri was a deeply conservative pillar of the "old guard" who served the makhzan for fifty years in various important posts. Initially rejected from the Protectorate administration for his "panislamic" tendencies, he proved to be indispensible and was eventually restored to his former position. (Collection Gérard Lévy, Paris)

Berber justice was discreetly dropped, and when it was again reviewed in 1934, the role of the French courts in Berber affairs was vastly reduced, making the expansion of the "Berber policy" through judicial reform a dead letter. It was a victory for the *jeunes marocains* and gave an energetic boost to their nationalist ambitions.

By all accounts, the 1930 revolt was the seedbed out of which the embryonic nationalist movement emerged. However, it is important to note that crucial elements were missing that would have implications for the future. Most notably, the leadership of the antidahir revolt was largely urban, young, aristocratic, and Arab; absent were rural peasantry and tribal-based Berbers who were the subjects of the dispute. While it was indeed a moment of mass mobilization, this absence raises the following questions: Did Berbers favor the dahir, or reject it? Did they have any attachment to the nascent ideas of national unity the uprising implied, and if so, how did they imagine the Berber place in it? Which was the greater threat? The loss of religious identity, through an association with France, or the loss of ethnic identity, through absorption into the Arab mass? What was *their* picture of the ideal nation, and how was it to be constructed? At this time, we do not have answers to these questions, which require further immersion into the archives and other written and oral sources.

However, we do know that in the popular imagination, the "Berber dahir" of 1930 represents a foundational event in the unfolding story of Moroccan nationalism, satisfying the need for "a myth of origin" from which a linear history of the nation could evolve. Etienne Balibar has noted that such foundational events are particularly susceptible to reinterpretation over time, as ideological needs change and new demands are placed on the construction of the nation-state. Recent readings of events surrounding the "Berber dahir" stress its integrative aspects and its success in bringing about the semblance of a unified national voice, in contrast to older readings that stressed the individual "heroism" of its protagonists. The story of the Berber dahir has become an essential part of the "clay" of national memory, to be molded and remolded over time.[15] The attention being paid to it today is testimony to its significance as a moment for gauging the strength of a movement still in its infancy yet aroused to action and ready to test its mettle against an obdurate colonial authority.

THE NATIONALISTS MOBILIZE

Inspired by their success in blocking the implementation of the Berber dahir, in August 1930 a group of activists from Salé, Rabat, Tetuan and

Fez formed "the Zawiya," a tight steering committee of the most prominent nationalist leaders from all over the country engaged in "research and study of doctrine," and a larger and less selective group called the "Ta'ifa," or "Outer Circle." Both organizations were clandestine in order to evade security surveillance, which was becoming more intense. Arrest, detention, and the police mug shot became a badge of honor among young adherents. The use of terms like *zawiya* and *ta'ifa*, borrowed from religious discourse, was no accident; radicalized by the events of 1930, the membership of the Zawiya drew on the nomenclature, structure, and emotional strength of the Sufi brotherhoods to build their own organization. A third and final level of organization was a more public committee called the CAM, or Comité d' action marocaine (*kutlat al-amal al-watani*) formed in 1933, assigned the task of writing a program for reform. Membership of the Kutla, as it was commonly called, eventually swelled to sixty-five hundred before it was disbanded in 1937.[16]

The Kutla/CAM became the vehicle for nationalist action, moving forward on two main fronts; first, to organize and mobilize the masses, especially in the cities, along the lines of the movement against the Berber dahir, and second, to develop a solid platform based on principles for negotiating with the Protectorate authorities. The aim was not independence, nor even autonomy, for in 1933 a future without France was still unthinkable; indeed, for a long time, the nationalist movement looked more to France for salvation that than it looked into itself. Rather, the CAM aimed for a top-to-bottom reform of the Protectorate regime to bring it closer to the principles of the Treaty of Fez. It also wanted to introduce more Moroccans into the administration, and to urge the adoption of the rule of law rather the self-serving interests of France as the bases for political action. It was an ambitious program, but the young nationalists, led by ʿAllal al-Fasi, the principal spokesman of the movement, were convinced of their ability to bring about change through the agency of nationalist agitation.[17]

Their first objective was to capture the imagination of the intellectual elites and convert them into a true vanguard of change. In public speeches – ʿAllal al-Fasi was an electrifying orator – a new lexicon was introduced that resonated with revolutionary fervor. It included words such as "people" (*shaʿab*), youth (*shabiba*), "nationhood" (*qawmiyya*), the "masses" (*jamahir*), and most of all, the word *umma*, which suddenly referred to all Moroccans, Jews as well as Muslims. This speechifying was more than verbal pyrotechnics. It represented a conceptual remaking of society along new lines that broke with ancient taboos, criss-crossing long-standing divisions, and reshaping the social compact by bringing together artisans, workers, students, shopkeepers, dispossessed peasants, and intellectuals into a new organization with one goal – to wrest back ownership of the nation. Speaking to the people in a language they understood, the youthful voices of the nationalist movement found a willing and attentive audience. As Jacques Berque pointed out, the old social compact was indeed "breaking down." Nationalist rhetoric of the 1930s was the medium for redrawing old boundaries and mapping out new ones.[18]

The signs and practices associated with traditional Moroccan cultural life were appropriated to reinforce the image of a politicized collectivity. Performing the Friday prayer became a civic duty. Even the subject of personal demeanor became an arena for nationalist expression. Some forms of dress were better than others: the *jallaba* (robe) and the *tarbush* (peaked cap) became the national costume for men. For women, it was the enveloping and cumbersome *haïk* (cloak).[19] New rituals were invented. In 1933, the first "Festival of the Throne" was organized by the nationalists, commemorating the accession to the sultanate of the Muhammad b. Yusuf seven years earlier. The event turned into an enthusiastic show in support of the young monarch, up to then regarded as a marionette dancing to the tune of the Residency. It was the first truly civic celebration at the level of the nation, transcending local events such as the religious festival. Early in 1934, ʿAllal al-Fasi was invited to meet with the sultan, and some weeks later the nationalists organized another popular manifestation in Fez in his honor, this time inextricably linking in the popular mind the concepts of *sultan* and *watan*. The sultan, even without his specific consent, had been effectively appropriated as a symbol of the nation.[20]

On the intellectual front, the opposition carefully gathered an arsenal of ideas that would serve as bargaining chips in a confrontation with French authority. The young activists – some of them trained in France and conversant with legal discourses of the Third Republic – had plentiful sources on which to draw. In their writings, a modernist Islamic thread inherited from reformist thinkers such as Abu Shuʿayb al-Dakali and Muhammad al-Hajwi intermingled with strands of democratic liberalism brought home from Paris and Cairo. While no one source produced the "brain" of the fledgling movement, a paradigm that drew on various points of the compass was becoming clear: in terms of a political philosophy, an unmistakable tendency toward popular sovereignty and the separation of religious and secular authority; in tactics, a de-centering of politics away from the mechanisms of colonial control through propaganda, negotiation, and the rallying of outside support.

FIGURE 22. Nationalist leader and later Foreign Minister Ahmed Balafrej in the courtyard of his house in Rabat in the 1950s. (Collection Said Mouline, Rabat)

In 1932, Ahmed Balafrej, a brilliant, Sorbonne-trained member of the opposition, a "visionary" and a "mystic" according to one observer, founded the journal *Maghreb* in Paris. This journal became the principal voice of the nascent movement, its pages filled with illuminating articles, many of them written by French-trained Moroccan intellectuals. Its editorial board – in fact a "committee of patronage," according to historian John Halstead – was made up entirely of French leftists. It was headed by socialist Robert-Jean Longuet, grandson of Karl Marx and friend and supporter of Shakib Arslan, who served as link between the Paris-based group and the young nationalists. Despite the French façade, the journal was a Moroccan project, backed by the Zawiya. Socialist themes were highlighted, but they were never a dominant tone, leading French leftists to criticize the Moroccans as the "bourgeois of Islam ... clerical, racist, and even anti-socialist." As a result, the connection between the Moroccan nationalists and the SFIO, the *Section Française de l'Internationale Ouvrière*, or French socialist party, was a tentative one – "more like a marriage of convenience than of love."[21]

Nevertheless, in its two short years of life, *Maghreb* made a powerful impression; the articles were eloquent, well-researched, and covered a wide range of topics from education, to law and justice, to the question of Palestine, to women's rights, attesting to the Moroccans' political maturity. Meanwhile, another revue, *L'Action du Peuple*, appeared in Fez edited by Mohammed Hassan al-Ouezzani, now emerging as ʿAllal al-Fasi's chief intellectual rival; this revue covered many of the same themes as *Maghreb*. The success of these journals domestically and abroad led the Residency to abruptly suspend them in the spring of 1934. However, the two revues had achieved their goal; they were the opening salvo in a protracted war of words that would engage the nationalists and the Residency for the next ten years.[22]

The next event in the nationalist campaign to gain recognition was the publication of a widely heralded Plan of Reforms (*Plan de Réformes marocaines*). Written in Fez by a small inner circle of activists in 1934, the plan first appeared in Arabic, and later in French. Couched in polite and lawyerly language – French Résident Général Henri Ponsot said that "it would make an excellent doctoral thesis" – it was a remarkable document that history has largely forgotten, despite the insight it offers into the state of nationalist thinking at the time. The main thrust of the Plan was the remaking of the French Protectorate regime. Drawing on essays published in *Maghreb*, it summarized grievances against the colonial order and pointed out practical solutions for fixing them. One hundred thirty-four pages long, the document spells out the various measures needed to overcome Morocco's "internal crisis" and to reconstitute the Protectorate on a more even-handed basis: government by committee at the local, tribal and national levels, with the last elected by universal male suffrage; a totally revised judicial system based on both Shariah and Western law; penal reform; freedom of the press and assembly; workers' rights; a progressive social policy for the aged and unemployed; elective municipal councils that would include Moroccans; compulsory primary education and one standard curriculum for the entire country; and perhaps most radically, a call for land reform and the end to the feudal ties between settler and native agriculturalist. In a sign for the future, the Plan demanded that Arabic be reinserted everywhere in public space, including the railway, where "all tickets and receipts, as well as signs on the cars and in the stations, be printed in Arabic as well as French."

FIGURE 23. President of France Gaston Doumergue (center, carrying a top hat) arrives at the sultan's palace in Rabat, October 1930, surrounded by officials of the makhzan, including the Sultan's personal secretary Muhammad al-Mammeri and a broadly smiling Si Kaddour Ben Ghabrit, diplomatic liaison between the makhzan and official France. Agence Muerisse. (Collection Gérard Lévy, Paris)

Strikingly, the Plan did not call for an independent Morocco or separation from France; instead, it aimed at "restoring confidence in the work of France in Morocco" and demanded greater Moroccan participation in government, a more cooperative relationship with the Residency, and a more faithful execution of the provisions of the 1912 Treaty of Fez. Nor did it question the limits of sultanic authority; in spite of the provision for elected governing councils, there was no discussion of how those councils would work, or how they would interact with a ruler whose authority, at least in theory, was still absolute. This question was put aside for the time being, after ʿAllal al-Fasi announced that democracy would come about after a trial period of participation.[23] The framers of the Plan considered that the legislation already in place for governing the settler population would be perfectly suitable for the natives. The decision to work within the framework of the Residency was sincere, for at that moment, the nationalist leadership still did not visualize Morocco without France. But that did not mean a relationship of servility or abuse. At a fundamental level, the Plan launched a frontal assault on the colonial mentality and the corrupt practices it had engendered; namely, the racism, discrimination, and anti-liberalism that allowed Moroccans to be treated as inferiors.

The Plan was presented to the Residency in Rabat and to Foreign Minister Pierre Laval in Paris in December 1934, as well as to the sultan, but its fate was already sealed; it was flatly rejected and shouted down by a settler lobby that was sufficiently influential to block all attempts at pro-native reform.[24] In retrospect, the Plan of Reforms was the last chance to excise the hidden decay of the colonial regime without attacking the whole body. It failed, not for the reason that it was either ill-timed or badly conceived, for it was not, but rather because the administration's vision was blinkered by settler opposition and the gathering clouds of war. With the advent of the French Popular Front in 1936 headed by socialist Léon Blum, the nationalists had hoped for an improvement in relations with Paris, but that was not to be; the new "left" government in the metropole was as indifferent to nationalist demands as the previous one. Europeans in Morocco rose up against the Popular Front with a lionlike roar, forcing the Blum government to hastily retreat from plans to accommodate nationalist demands. As politics in France veered crazily from left to right and back again, so did the equilibrium of the Protectorate.

Meanwhile, the colonial administration resigned itself to a state of perpetual confrontation with the native opposition that kept up continual pressure, reminding the French of their presence. At the same time, the nationalist movement entered a phase of vigorous expansion, opening its doors to the rural population, tightening discipline, creating a nation-wide organization, and boosting card-carrying membership to over six thousand, excluding the northern zone. Basking in its newfound strength, the old CAM was reconstituted under the cumbersome title of al-Hizb al-Watani li-Tahqiq al-Matalib, (The National Party for Realizing Our Rights), holding its first party congress in Rabat in April 1937. A surprising relaxation of press laws after the advent of the Popular Front permitted the opening of newspapers sympathetic to the nationalist cause, such as the Arabic language *al-Atlas*, and the French language *L'Action populaire*, edited by Khadija Diouri, wife of nationalist leader Muhammad Diouri. Their political activities held in check by close official scrutiny, the nationalists resorted to incitement through journalism, using the press to rile up popular feeling over the deteriorating economic and political situation.[25]

In these hyperactive times, the nationalist leadership split into several camps: the National Party (PN), headed by the exiled ʿAllal al-Fasi, on the one hand, and the Patriotic Movement (PMI) directed by Mohammed Hassan al-Ouezzani, on the other, were the two largest factions. During the war years, other groups rushed in, populating the political field. The Rabat-based conservative Independence Party (PI), and a fledgling Communist Party (PCM) whose members were mostly Europeans troubled by the growing social inequality aggravated by the Great Depression, were among the new players. ʿAllal al-Fasi's National Party, reincarnated as the Istiqlal (Independence) Party during the war, dominated the field because of its superior organization and its ability to mobilize membership on a mass scale.

The final act in the prewar confrontation between the Residency and the nationalist opposition took place in Meknes in September 1937, when the authorities announced a plan to divert part of the Oued Boufakran, the town's main source of water, to settler farms. Crowds filled the street crying "Water or Death!" and "Not a drop for the settlers!" In the police action that followed, some demonstrators were killed. The violence of the mêlée set off a chain reaction, and the protest spread like wildfire to other cities, taking on the coloration of a general uprising against the Protectorate administration. Alarmed at the level of agitation, the authorities rounded up the nationalist leadership; on November 3, 1937, ʿAllal al-Fasi was flown to a nine-year-long exile in Gabon, while others of the inner circle were imprisoned, fled, or sent to the Sahara. Ahmed Balafrej, in Paris at the time, escaped arrest and sought refuge in the Spanish zone. On the eve of World War II, the nationalist movement in the French zone, grown during the interwar years into a "well-oiled propaganda machine," appeared to have been decapitated. But its headlessness was only an illusion; its brains had simply gone underground, and its will was intact.

THE SPANISH ZONE FOLLOWS A SEPARATE PATH

In the Spanish zone, pro-nationalist activity took a very different turn. Tetuan was a charming Andalusian-style town ruled by a coterie of old families immensely proud of their Hispano-Moorish heritage. It was said, perhaps apocryphally, that in some of the houses of Tetuan hung a key to the ancestral home in Granada. There a group of young militants established a separate nationalist organization in 1930. The Tetuan group included Muhammad Dawud, Mehdi Bennouna, Abdelkhalek Torres, and Abdelslam Benjelloun, among others, and their main activities were journalistic. Their newspapers were allowed to flourish by the Spanish authorities, mainly because they spread harsh criticism of the colonial policies of France, Spain's ancient rival, while turning a blind eye to Spain's own misdeeds. Collaboration became the norm in the North. It was quite a different game from the one the southerners were playing, and it created tensions in nationalist circles between north and south.

In April 1931, the rickety monarchy of Spain's Alfonso XIII fell and after a brief republican interlude, the country became embroiled in a bloody Civil War, pitting the Republicans against a military insurgency under the leadership of Generalissimo Francisco Franco, hero of the Rif campaign and leader of the *africanistas*, Spanish army officers whose careers had been shaped by the Moroccan campaign. During the Spanish Civil War (1936–1939), Franco used northern Morocco as a staging area for his assault on the mainland, and by war's end, nearly eighty thousand Moroccan mercenaries had fought on Franco's side, lured by steady rations and a generous wage of four *pesetas* a day. The Rifian regulars, or *moros* as they were known, served as shock troops and suffered high casualties in the Spanish conflict. They were feared for their ferocity, and whole Republican units were known to have deserted their posts at the suggestion that they might be facing Moroccan troops.[26] Achieved with Moroccan help, Franco's victory turned Spain into an authoritarian regime that veered sharply to the right where it would remain for the next forty years.

The relationship between the Franco regime and the nationalists was a convoluted one, and was largely determined by Spain's attitude toward France. Franco pandered to the Moroccan nationalists by giving them legal status and allowing them to publish their newspapers without censorship, in stark contrast to French policy vis-à-vis the nationalist press. Spain's High Commissioner, the "brilliant if eccentric" Colonel Juan Beigbeder, a Spanish T. E. Lawrence according to some because of his fearless temperament and political acumen, played off one nationalist faction against the other, maintaining cordial relations with all while keeping them off balance. His friendly attitude stood in sharp contrast to France's heavy repression in the south and provided an enticing example of a "good" Protectorate power. Beigbeder curried favor with Abdelkhalek Torres – head of the northern Party of National Reform (PRN) – not out of love or gratitude, but because he wished to embarrass France, where the Popular

Front remained vehemently opposed to the Franco side in the Spanish civil war. The goal of humiliating France may have also motivated Spain's occupation of Tangier in 1940. Franco's army marched into the international city in June of that year, on the same day that Paris fell, and remained there for five years.

It has been suggested that the reason that Abdelkhalek Torres collaborated with Franco was not that he was especially drawn to Fascist ideology, but rather that he dreamed of a Moroccan caliphate of the North, united with Spain in a romantic reenactment of the *convivencia* that existed between Muslims and Christians in medieval al-Andalus. Contacts between nationalists in the North and personalities drawn into the orbit of prewar Berlin such as the Mufti of Jerusalem Hajj Amin al-Husayni, Shakib Arslan, and Rashid ʿAli al-Kaylani, suggest that at least some of the northern leadership explored building ties to the Nazis, in the naïve belief that enemies of France were the friends of theirs. Historian Amina Aouchar says that Torres himself went to Berlin in 1941 to meet with Himmler and Goering and to press the nationalist case. It should be kept in mind that the intense political rivalry between the Left and the Right in Europe in those years dominated the calculations of France and Spain in Morocco, just as the same exogenous factors shaped the strategic thinking of the nationalists. It would be simplistic to think of the northern nationalists as rabidly "pro-Nazi"; rather, they were manipulating the few assets they had in order to advance to their goal of independence.[27]

THE SUBSTANCE OF EVERYDAY LIFE: HEALTH, SOCIETY, WORK

A sharp rise in fertility after 1930, and especially after 1935, seemed to go unnoticed amidst the familiar rhythms of daily life. A vibrant growth rate rejuvenated the nation and produced new cadres of young people willing to be swept up in the nationalist cause. Annual population growth for the Jewish and Muslim population was slightly less than 2 percent between 1936 and 1951; it went from 5.8 million in 1936 to 8.4 million in 1951, including nearly a million in the Spanish zone. In the same period, the European population grew from 219,000 to 415,000.[28]

Young Moroccans differed from their elders in their willingness to take to the streets, to shout slogans, to aspire to modern values and inventions, even if they were not always within reach. Radio, the cinema, printed books and newspapers, organized sports, *kura* (football) on the *plage* (beach), were now part of the fabric of the quotidian. French-derived neologisms filled in

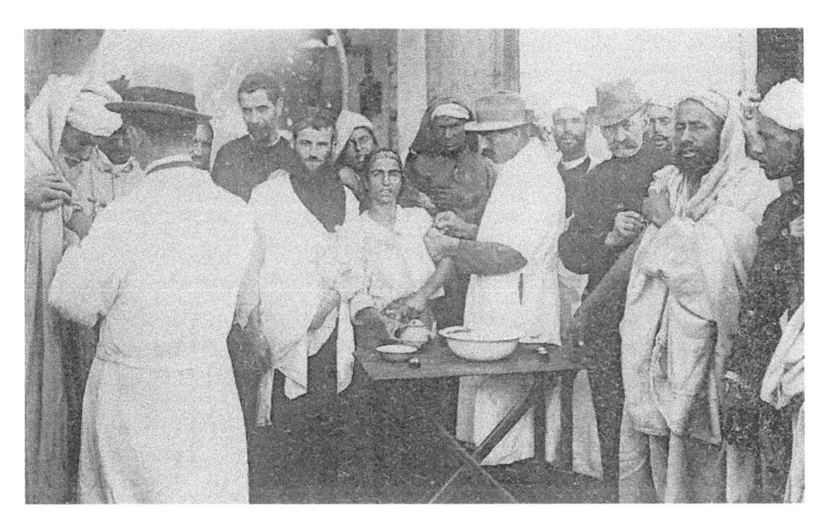

FIGURE 24. Public health was an ongoing concern of French officials, who feared the spread of contagious diseases, especially in the crowded inner city. Poor people living in the native quarters were targeted for free vaccinations in order to stem the tide of smallpox. Here residents of the *mellah* are being vaccinated by colonial health officials, Casablanca, 1920s. (Postcard Collection, Gérard Lévy, Paris)

verbal voids: *tumubil* (automobile), *firmage rumi* (French cheese), and *le tren* (the railroad) were innovations that quickly became part of the vocabulary of even the modest day laborer. In elite circles, the adoption of foreign ways and their seamless integration into local forms was even more noticeable: French language spoken at home, the "dual" salon, the dressing wardrobe divided into two compartments, one *rumi* (European), and the other *taqlidi* (traditional). Western mores were adopted selectively but with alacrity throughout all levels of society.[29]

Other aspects of the slow evolution of forms were less appealing. The state of health in Morocco at the dawn of the Protectorate was deplorable. Rudimentary health services were limited to the major cities, with few doctors and almost no hospitals or clinics. Protectorate authorities hastily introduced modern methods of disease control aimed at protecting settlers, while coincidentally improving the health of native Moroccans. Colonial fear of contamination from the "insalubrious" native quarters had an immediate effect on Moroccan living standards. Measures included combating infection, building clinics, recruiting doctors, instituting a vast program of vaccination, building closed sewer systems, assuring clean water supplies, and imposing strict rules of hygiene and sanitation, especially in urban areas. The aggressive treatment of diseases such as syphilis, malaria, and bilharzia did not have an immediate or dramatic effect and they continued to be endemic; syphilis in particular resisted control until the use of penicillin was introduced after the World War II. A vigorous campaign of vaccination against smallpox undertaken in 1925 seems to have had better success, forcing the disease into regression. Typhus was perhaps the most deadly unchecked disease, with seasonal bouts in the years 1920–1921, 1928–1929, and 1942–1943.[30]

The triumph of French medical practice was not a foregone conclusion and met with popular resistance, as traditional health practitioners continued to hold sway among the poorer classes. Blood-letters with their striped barber poles could be seen plying their craft in rural markets until the late twentieth century. Muhammad al-Hajwi, the modernizing religious scholar, speaking on Tunisian radio in 1937, assured his native listeners that their own traditional medical practices rivaled Europe's in efficacy, particularly in matters of childbirth. "Muslim women are more adept in sexual matters than Western scientists would give credit," he said. "[They] are skilled in the knowledge of herbs and potions, [and] capable of performing acts that would astonish the devil."[31] Al-Hajwi's argument for cultural authenticity did not appeal to everyone. Many women sought out Western medicine, evidenced in the rising number of hospital births. The number of clinic visits in 1912 was half a million per year, surpassed two million in 1929, and reached twenty million in 1955, 86 percent of them native Moroccan. Admittedly, these services were not evenly distributed, with most concentrated in the coastal cities. The proportion of doctors to people in the southeast of the country was a shocking one per twenty thousand. For those deprived of the healing touch of modern medicine, there was always succor in *maktub*, or "inevitable fate."[32]

Other European forms spread throughout society, changing the texture of everyday life. In the late 1920s, colonial investment in Morocco reached new heights, and many new workers entered the modern industrial and agricultural sectors. The great economic crisis that began in Europe in 1929 did not arrive in Morocco until 1931, and was initially felt only in the small modernized industrial sector. European investment fell precipitously, and the feverish speculation of the years 1927–1930 ended abruptly. Exports dried up, so that 1936 values were roughly half of those of 1929. Especially hard hit were the mining, port, and construction sectors, where drastic layoffs began after 1931 and the problem of unemployment (and underemployment) reached massive proportions. Moreover, Moroccan workers still lacked a collective awareness of their political strength and did not go on strike to defend their rights. In rural areas, they often worked seasonally, disappearing into the bled when the annual crop cycle ended; in the city, they were frequently temporarily employed, badly underpaid, hired and fired at the whim of the *patron*, fined for the least infraction, and forced to buy supplies at the "company store."

In 1934, according to Albert Ayache, half the Moroccan population of Casablanca inhabited bidonvilles such as the Carrières centrales, a festering slum area with no services, no paved streets, no running water or electricity. Living in deplorable conditions, lacking class-consciousness and possessing few professional skills, they did not hold any promise as a political factor. The Residency actively blocked workers from organizing, cheered on by extreme rightwing groups such as the militant and anti-Semitic Croix-de-Feu, whose Moroccan branch, made up mainly of businessmen, was openly bent on destroying workers' unions. In response, the working class closed ranks, joined by socialists and intellectuals, on the one hand, and artisans and shopkeepers on the other, when their income plummeted because of cheap foreign goods flooding the markets. This broad coalition between workers, craftsmen and tradesmen became the matrix for a nascent labor movement that arose in response to generally worsening economic conditions.[33]

Gradually, the syndicalists and the nationalists, at first hostile to one another, began to draw closer together. The political potential of the unions was gradually recognized by the nationalists, who overcame their fear of joining forces with people who in their minds had been "overpoliticized." The burgeoning worker-nationalist alliance struck fear in the heart of the Residency, panicked by their combined ability to organize the street. To head this off, the administration flatly refused to legalize Moroccan unions and only allowed the formation of "corporations," a traditional form of labor organization that could be more easily controlled. Finally, in 1936, after the socialist Popular Front came to power in France, the right to organize was granted, but to Europeans alone. Soon strikes broke out all over the country, with workers demanding basic rights such as a minimum wage and an eight-hour day.

In the midst of this crisis, General Charles Noguès, an old "Moroccan hand," was appointed by the Popular Front in September 1936 to take over the Residency, replacing the much-despised Marcel Peyrouton. Noguès' arrival inspired hope of change: the new Résident Général drew closer to the young Sultan Muhammad V and became his mentor, but he had little sympathy for the nationalists. When labor strife spread throughout the country, he refused to negotiate, forcing the nationalists and workers even closer together. He then moved forcefully against them, crushing their organizations and dispersing their leadership. After this round of violence, the pro-labor newspaper *Clarté* announced that the Moroccan workers' movement had finally come of age: "The Moroccan proletariat has finally shown that it has acquired a class consciousness and will stand without retreat alongside European workers to defend the right to work for its daily bread." On the eve of World War II, despite constant harassment from the Protectorate regime, the Moroccan labor movement had shown its political strength and willingness to enter the fray. Its painful education in agitation and mobilization would prove to be a valuable asset in the 1950s when the curtain rose on the last days of the Protectorate.[34]

WORLD WAR II AND THE RADICALIZATION OF THE NATIONALIST CAUSE

As Western Europe's defenses fell before the Nazi onslaught in the spring of 1940, opinion in the colonies also shifted. The "strange defeat" of France signaled an opening for North African nationalists, who saw in Marianne's broken sword an opportunity for their own cause. Maréchal Philippe Pétain, ancient foe of ʿAbd al-Karim, was appointed head of a collaborationist government centered on Vichy, while General Charles de Gaulle fled to England and formed the nucleus of the Free French forces that eventually helped to liberate Europe. The metropole was fractured and defeated and in North Africa, the interminable status quo was abruptly ruptured. As the ground shifted, native politics took on a new energy and direction.

In Morocco, tension between pro-Gaullist and pro-Pétainist forces remained acute throughout much of the war, with the majority of settlers leaning toward Pétain, and the majority of politically conscious Moroccans gradually turning their support toward de Gaulle and the Allies. Sultan Muhammad V initially pledged loyalty to the Third Republic, but with the coming of the pro-Nazi puppet regime at Vichy, his sentiments gradually shifted, especially when the Vichy authorities tried to impose their murderously harsh anti-Semitic race laws on Morocco. Mohammed V reportedly refused to sign off on Vichy's plan to ghettoize and deport Morocco's quarter of a million Jews to the killing factories of Europe, earning for himself their undying devotion. His stand was based as much on the insult the Vichy *diktats* posed to his claim of sovereignty over all his subjects, including the Jews, as on his humanitarian instincts. Over his opposition, partial race laws were imposed, with damaging effects on

Moroccan Jewish livelihoods and morale. Wedged in between an indifferent Muslim majority and an anti-Semitic settler class, Morocco's Jews were pushed to the edges of society during World War II, entering a no-man's-land from which they never really returned.[35]

The war years were a period of widespread deprivation and dislocation in North Africa, but also a time of gestation for the nationalist movements of Algeria, Tunisia, and Morocco. Despite the fact that their leadership was scattered to the four winds during the immediate pre-war years, when the Moroccan nationalists reemerged in 1944, they had undergone a transformation. The war had dramatically altered the terrain on which nationalist politics were being played out. The French colossus had fallen, an American one had taken its place. The prewar colonial politics of repression, indifference, and deception were no longer viable; world opinion, sickened by the Nazi violation of Europe and its terrifying results, turned away from imperialism as an acceptable form of rule. People crushed by Hitler's Reich in Eastern Europe in particular, were rising out of the mire of defeat and clamoring for liberation. Decolonization was at the top of the international agenda, and the desire to correct the cruelties of the immediate past was the broadly conceived goal. In this atmosphere of upheaval, the Maghribi nationalist parties regrouped, feeling that their time had finally come.

"It had become obvious since 1937," ʿAllal al-Fasi later wrote, "that an irrevocable divorce had occurred between the people on the one hand and the Protectorate regime on the other."[36] As the maelstrom of war descended on North Africa, the nationalists openly embraced the goal of independence, and sought the means to achieve it. The Allied North African campaign provided an opportunity. On November 8, 1942, in preparation for the assault on Fortress Europe, Operation Torch got underway with American and British landings near Casablanca, Oran and Algiers, turning Morocco and the rest of the Maghribi littoral into a staging area for the eventual retaking of Europe. Swaggering U.S. General George S. Patton Jr., who headed the Moroccan sector of Operation Torch, met frequently with Sultan Muhammad V after the landings to talk about the future of Morocco. Patton innocently saw Morocco "as a gateway for the Americans entering the continent of Africa."[37] The Moroccans were impressed by this first encounter with American armed might, by the well-oiled military machine, the modern equipment, and the seemingly endless supplies of food. The palace and the nationalists quickly abandoned any lingering pro-Vichy sentiments and turned toward supporting the Allied cause; eventually, thousands of Maghribis joined in the battle against the Axis, fighting bravely through Sicily, Corsica, Italy, France, and Germany, in some of the bloodiest battles of the war.

Even before the Allied landings took place, nationalist leaders were led to believe that the Americans in particular would look favorably on their project. The Atlantic Charter of August 1941 was vaguely reassuring, but hardly specific; rather, it was the Anfa Conference held in Casablanca in January 1943, where Allied chiefs gathered to strategize about the conduct of the war and the peace to follow, that gave the Moroccan nationalist cause its greatest boost. U.S. President Franklin Roosevelt met privately with Sultan Muhammad V and British Prime Minister Winston Churchill on Friday, January 22, 1943 ("no cocktails before dinner ... no pork," wrote the President's son Elliott in his diary) and announced, much to Churchill's discomfort, that "the post-war scene and the pre-war scene would ... sharply differ, especially as they related to the colonial question." According to the future King Hassan II, then a fourteen-year-old, who also attended the dinner, Roosevelt went much further, promising that in "ten years from now your country will be independent." Regardless of what was actually said, Roosevelt's conversation with the sultan became a crucial turning point, encouraging the Moroccans to work openly for complete independence.[38]

But hopes raised would almost immediately be disappointed when the American government adopted an ambivalent policy toward the anticolonial struggle. The Americans had already shown their canniness, weaving their way through the maze of competing French factions; in preparation for the Allied invasion, they reached an agreement on stockpiling supplies with the Vichy Commander-in-Chief in North Africa, General Maxime Weygand, who openly collaborated with the Nazis, while at the same time they encouraged General de Gaulle, vigorous opponent of Hitler, who headed the Free French forces. Following the success of Operation Torch, the Americans threw in their lot with de Gaulle, realizing that they needed his help in order to win the war in Europe. Previous pronouncements about American willingness to lend a hand in loosening the colonial grip were now tempered by a more cautious tone. De Gaulle, for his part, played his cards close to the chest and avoided all talk of decolonization. After his Free French forces had safely dislodged the Vichyites from North Africa in 1943, de Gaulle expressed the wish to "safeguard the Empire," turning a cold shoulder to the "encouragement" supposedly given by Roosevelt to the nationalists.[39]

Meanwhile, the nationalists, now known as the *hizbiyin*, (party members), or *hizb al-Istiqlal* (the Independence party), resumed their pressure on the Residency, taking advantage of the disarray caused by wartime shifts in command. On January 11, 1944, the Istiqlal issued a "Manifesto of Independence" that explicitly called for "the independence of Morocco in its national entirety under the aegis of His Majesty Sidi Muhammad Bin Yusuf" and the installation of a democratic constitutional government guaranteeing the rights of "all elements in society." Signed by fifty-nine of the movement's faithful, the Manifesto urged the sultan to take the lead in engaging in negotiations with "interested nations ... whose object would be the recognition ... of that independence." The Manifesto adopted the call for reforms outlined in the 1934 Plan and repackaged them with a demand for independence, making a seamless transition from one kind of activism to another. The new and revolutionary assertion underlying the Manifesto was that the Moroccan people themselves had to assume responsibility for making the changes that the Protectorate had failed to bring about.

The year 1944 represents major turning point for other reasons as well. It marks a shift in the center of gravity of the nationalist movement from Fez to Rabat, from the old cradle of bourgeois culture to a fresh and untried venue; an expansion of its membership into broader sectors of the urban bourgeoisie and into the new urban proletariat; the rise of activities aimed at building populist cadres such as a party-sponsored scouting movement and public parades; and the founding of the Arabic newspaper *al-ʿAlam* in 1946. The Istiqlal followed a specific program to stamp public space with a "modern Moroccanness" that was mimetically informed by European forms of mass organization on display during the interwar years.[40]

Although the 1944 Manifesto fell on deaf ears, it marked a major step forward in the nationalist struggle. The administration, distracted by wartime confusion, responded precipitously by arresting Istiqlal leaders Balafrej and Lyazidi, along with eighteen others, and accusing them of "consorting with the enemy." These arrests provoked widespread protests, indicating that the Manifesto had achieved the goal of rousing the masses. The fortunes of the Istiqlal continued to rise thereafter, particularly as the party gained skills in manipulating the street. By taking the lead in shaping nationalist rhetoric, by attempting to broaden its social base, by piloting the labor unionists into its fold, and by beginning to ally itself with the revered figure of the sultan, the Istiqlal had succeeded in seizing control of the movement for independence.[41]

The role of the sultan at this stage was becoming critical. In the minds of the nationalists, the institution of the sultanate – given new life under the

Protectorate – was the symbolic pole around which the revived independence movement could be organized. Not everyone agreed; some of the *hizbiyyin* saw the sultan as a useless anachronism incompatible with a modern state. But al-Fasi and others in the Istiqlal were convinced that the popular enchantment with the near-mystical image of the Sharifian ruler had immense value that could be harnessed to the nationalist cause. How this notion fit with the Istiqlal's pretensions to democratic governance was not yet clear, nor would it become clearer in the coming years; the inherent contradiction between the hard kernel of absolutism at the center of the concept of Sharifian authority stood in irreconcilable opposition to the Istiqlal's ideal of a democratic and popular sovereignty.

It is true that the Istiqlal's ideology, if it had one at all, was already an eclectic mix of ideas taken from democratic constitutionalism, Egyptian reformism, Islamic teachings, nineteenth century progressivism, and Third World anticolonialism, all broadly construed. Al-Fasi himself acknowledged the profound *bricolage* that made up revolutionary doctrine: "Every constructive revolution has been preceded by probing into the remote past; such a return, which on the surface appears a retrogression, is in fact a mighty liberator . . ." But the high value intrinsic in the symbolism of the monarchy could not be ignored. The sultan's endorsement offered cultural, religious, and emotional assets to the revolutionary cause that the Istiqlal readily seized on and incorporated into its program.[42]

POSTWAR DEVELOPMENTS: THE UNEASY ALLIANCE BETWEEN THE SULTAN AND THE ISTIQLAL

Meanwhile, a wounded France struggled to retake the advantage in the larger drama unfolding across the colonial world. Postwar efforts by the French to regain control of the Moroccan polity took the form of top-down state planning inspired by the new, globally announced values of democracy, human engineering, and a shared prosperity to eliminate economic and social disparities. In Morocco and elsewhere in North Africa, the grip of the colonial power did not lessen; it simply put on kid gloves. In urban areas, the Protectorate undertook major infrastructure projects to ameliorate the gap in living standards between natives and colonizers, especially in the housing sector. Initiating new construction targeted at reducing the number of bidonvilles, the most blatant sign of the failure of social policies, was a top priority. French modernist architect Michel Écochard arrived in Morocco in 1946 to head the Department of Urban Planning, and was given the task of building functional housing for the "greatest number possible." Ignoring cultural specifics, Écochard proposed worker housing consisting of two eight-by-eight meter rooms, a patio and a W.C. that would meet their "human needs." Never realized, his plans were symptomatic of a postwar discourse of social welfare that not only came too late, but was also disconnected from the Moroccan reality. To fill the gap between inefficient state planners and local needs, charitable organizations rallied to take care of the indigent. Soup kitchens sprang up in all the major cities, regularly feeding thousands of poor people. In Fez, a Muslim welfare society ran a popular soup kitchen in the madina at Bayn al-Mudun, feeding five thousand people a day.[43]

Another expression of state social planning took place in the rural areas. The most prominent of these new state-run social programs was the "Secteurs de modernisaton du paysannat" or SMP, a plan for rural development inaugurated in 1946 by new Résident-Général Eirik Labonne, a reformist-minded professional diplomat who replaced Gabriel Puaux when the war was over. An advocate of the "soft" approach of using economic development rather than brute force to contain pressure for change, Labonne decried the forty years of "stagnation" imposed by the Protectorate regime and proposed a "new deal" for Morocco. Touted as the opening phase of a new French social policy, the SMP employed French social scientists inculcated with egalitarian ideals, like the young Jacques Berque who later went on to a career as a distinguished sociologist of Islam. These idealistic young people helped set up programs designed to modernize farming methods that imitated the Soviet model of the *kolkhoz*, the agricultural cooperative. Several factors disrupted Labonne's plans: a policy of stubborn noncooperation emanating from the Istiqlal, a foot-dragging Protectorate bureaucracy, and a huge outcry from big landowners who were implacably opposed to Labonne's worker-centered approach. These elements combined to force Labonne to back down and disperse his cadres, diluting the project to the point of ineffectiveness.[44]

The radicalization of the nationalist movement was now an established fact; fragmented into several tendencies, the Istiqlal stood at the head in an uneasy alliance of pro-independence forces. Returning home from his Gabon exile in 1946, 'Allal al-Fasi – now surrounded with the "halo of a national martyr" – managed to heal the rift with the nationalists of the Northern zone, joining forces with Torres to maintain pressure on the Residency to negotiate the terms of independence. The ranks of the Istiqlal swelled with increasingly militant masses who were suffering from postwar inflation, the burden of heavy taxes, and the small daily indignities inherent in the condition of colonial rule.

Composed of a cross-section of the Moroccan social mosaic, membership in the party grew dramatically in the postwar years, spreading outwards from its bourgeois origins to wider social groups. According to Mehdi Ben Barka, "the extraordinarily rapid development of the industrial sector resulted in the formation of masses of workers who, little by little, were won over to the nationalist ideology."[45] While statistics are at best approximate, "reliable observers" estimated party membership at about three thousand in 1944, reaching ten thousand after the sultan's speech in 1947, and one hundred thousand after 1952. The intellectual leadership of the party working under the baton of Balafrej stressed three themes: inculcation of party discipline and consciousness-raising, devotion to the monarchy, and fixation on the goal of independence.[46]

The actions of the sultan were pivotal in the move toward a confrontation with the French. Gradually, the shy and retiring Muhammad V rose up like a lion to meet his historical destiny. In an electric speech pronounced at Tangier on April 9, 1947, the sultan – who had never before uttered a word that might suggest he would deviate from Protectorate policy – praised the march toward Moroccan "unity" and affirmed his belief in the country's "Arabo-Islamic" destiny, publicly carving out a wide space between himself and the Residency. Carefully modulating his language, the sultan now joined the duel between the Istiqlal and the Protectorate regime, turning it into a three-sided altercation. The popularity of the sultan and his family soared, as "monarchy fever" seized the Moroccan people and Muhammad V became the adored symbol of the nation. His portrait appeared everywhere, in the smallest shops of the madina to the place of honor inside the private home.

Bolstered by the surge of support, the sultan's behavior became progressively more objectionable to his former tutors.[47] In January 1951, despite repeated requests from General Juin, Labonne's successor, the sultan refused to set his seal on a dahir that would paralyze the Istiqlal; moreover, he initiated a barrage of requests to the Residency – unanswered – to "redefine the Franco-Moroccan accords to allow for Morocco's complete recovery of her independence." Finally, the Residency grew impatient and resorted to strong-arm tactics. In an ultimatum addressed to Muhammad V in January, 1951, Juin ordered the sultan to approve the repugnant dahirs or risk being deposed. He then backed up this threat by surrounding the palace in Rabat with troops and dismissing top officials of the makhzan, including the rector of the Qarawiyyin University in Fez. Under duress, the sultan stepped back, but without detaching himself from the nationalists, who responded by inviting him to form a unified national front. They were joined in 1952 by the powerful labor arm, now reorganized after the war under native Moroccan leadership. A standoff developed, with the sultan and the nationalists on one side, and the forces of order backed by the Protectorate administration on the other.

In this atmosphere of open rebellion, the alliance between the sultan and the nationalists tightened, as both became increasingly convinced that the days of the Protectorate were numbered. In fact, it was difficult at times to discern who was leading whom – the sultan or the Istiqlal. On the diplomatic front, the Istiqlal took the lead, with Balafrej and others campaigning at the newly formed United Nations in the fall session of 1951 to raise the question of Morocco. A UN mission sent to Morocco in February 1952 to investigate the situation on the ground was greeted by wild street demonstrations calling for freedom. The Moroccan question remained before the UN for several years, enmeshed in the politics of anticolonialism and backed by the emerging Third World bloc, but it never succeeded in winning enough votes to reach a favorable resolution. Nevertheless, the exposure at the UN advanced the nationalist case and gave it credibility on the world stage. Senior spokesmen for the Istiqlal – Balafrej, Laghzawi, al-Fasi himself – traveled continually to Europe, the United States, and the Arab States, seeking support for Moroccan independence, writing letters, launching publicity campaigns, meeting with important political figures. In order to win international support, the nationalists tempered their message to the world, issuing statements through their party organs that were moderate in tone. Ahmed Balafrej, playing the role of chief spokesman and theorist, continued to insist publicly on "the installation of a constitutional monarchy, whose organs are His Majesty the Sultan as head of state, an elected Assembly, and a responsible government."[48]

After 1951, the enthusiasm of the masses drove the nationalist cause and the founding fathers simply rode the wave. The tempo of protest rose in November 1952, when Farhat Hached, a prominent Tunisian labor leader and pro-nationalist, was assassinated in Tunis. In sympathy, over thirty-five hundred workers organized by the Casablanca trade unions came out in force and staged a demonstration that was brutally disrupted by French police. The event culminated in a rampage into the native quarters by irate Europeans that ended with hundreds killed or wounded. The union leadership went underground and did not reemerge until 1955 when the UMT (Moroccan Union of Workers), was founded. By that time, six hundred thousand working people had joined its ranks. For the procolonial party, the conjuncture of this bloody popular uprising with

Muhammad V's growing obstinacy won him the derisive title of "the Sultan of the Carrières centrales", a Casablanca slum; but for the average Moroccan, he had become their revered defender and champion. The mood of general insurrection was now complete.[49]

Panicked by the sultan's growing popularity and his stubborn refusal to do their bidding, French authorities decided to send him into exile. The plan to usurp the throne was led by Thami al-Glawi, Pasha of Marrakesh, one of the "Lords of the Atlas" whose personal wealth and power had grown immensely during the Protectorate thanks to his pro-French sympathies. Patently corrupt, with a taste for Cartier watches and expensive British motorcars, al-Glawi, working under French guidance, engineered a plot to dismiss Muhammed V and enthrone in his place the aging Muhammad Ben ʿArafa, the ruling sultan's uncle. Al-Glawi was joined by ʿAbd al-Hayy al-Kattani, scion of the brotherhood of the same name and brother of the murdered Shaykh Muhammad al-Kattani, who had been the victim of ʿAbd al-Hafiz's brutality in 1908. The al-Kattanis still harbored great antipathy toward the ʿAlawi dynasty, a detail overlooked by the Protectorate administration when it co-opted them because of their extensive grassroots organization.

The co-conspirators concocted a plan that unfolded with scenes worthy of a Hollywood melodrama: a petition signed by Glawi's collaborators among the pashas and qaʿids stating that the sultan's policies were incompatible with Islam; the solemn proclamation of a new imam at the holy sanctuary of Mawlay Idris in Fez; the descent of mounted tribesmen acting under al-Glawi's orders into the streets of Rabat; the royal palace invested by tanks. According to the later account by Hassan II, Résident-Général Guillaume himself entered the palace to supervise the operation, and found the Sultan still in his pajamas. The royal family was packed off to Madagascar on August 20, 1953, amid howls of protest from every segment of the population. Ordinary Moroccans were thunderstruck by this event. The nationalist cause ceased to be an abstraction and instead became the saga of a single family, uprooted from its home and sent off to a distant exile. The entire country was transfixed, and it was said that women standing on their rooftops at night could see the image of the banished sultan in the moon.[50]

French opinion was deeply divided over such a desperate act. De Gaulle denounced the deportation as "stupidity," predicting, "he will return ... I know it ... he will never abdicate," while French Foreign Minister Georges Bidault declared that France was engaged in a war of civilizations, a "fight of the Cross against the Crescent."[51] President of the Republic Vincent

Auriol invoked the bogeyman of that era: "... behind the Sultan is the Istiqlal, and behind the Istiqlal are the Communists."[52] But others sprang to the defense of the rightful occupant of the throne and the nationalist cause. Led by Nobel laureate François Mauriac, Parisian intellectuals, already up in arms over the war in Algeria, now added French Morocco to the list of die-hard colonial enclaves struggling against the tide of history. He was joined by eminent figures from the world of Orientalist scholarship, such as Louis Massignon, Charles-André Julien, and Régis Blachère, who were determined to save whatever was left of Franco-Moroccan amity. Muhammad V and his family remained in exile in Madagascar for two years and were finally allowed to return in 1955, on the eve of independence.[53]

A DRAMATIC FINALE TO FRENCH RULE

The departure of the Sultan unleashed an international storm of protest, further compounding France's troubles in a turbulent Maghrib that was squirming out of its grip. Tunisia under Bourguiba was clamoring for self-rule, and the bloody Algerian revolution that lasted eight long years (1954–1962) and cost nearly a million lives had already begun in earnest. The territory from Tunis to Casablanca was on fire. The crushing defeat of French forces in May 1954 at Dien Bien Phu in Indochina, the last outpost of its Asian dominion, seemed to support the view that France was entering the dusk of empire. Moroccan troops who participated in this disaster were totally demoralized, and on repatriation, became ready fuel for the anticolonial conflagration.[54] From his Cairo exile, Istiqlal leader ʿAllal al-Fasi reacted to the expulsion of Muhammad V by broadcasting a call for armed struggle that was picked up by a new instrument of insurgency – the radio – and delivered to every corner of Morocco. All of Morocco was tuned into the revolution. In the months of August-September 1953, eleven thousand new radio sets were sold. Violent attacks became a daily occurrence. Some, such as the abortive attempt on Mawlay Ben ʿArafa's life by house painter ʿAllal Ben Abdallah, created instant heroes of the resistance. Secret cells proliferated throughout 1954 and 1955, attacks on settlers multiplied, farms and factories were set on fire, and strikes paralyzed vital sectors of the economy. Clandestine organizations of colonial diehard "ultras" responded by carrying out the assassination of nationalist leader Tahar Sebti and liberal French industrialist Jacques Lemaigre-Dubreuil, who favored compromise. Former Prime Minister Pierre Mendès-France admitted that the Protectorate had "almost always ignored liberal

Frenchmen" and that opinion in Morocco was far more nuanced than the French public had been led to believe. Even the far right press began speaking out against *immobilisme*, realizing that change finally had to come.[55]

Following the example of Algeria, where the FLN liberation movement had spawned a paramilitary force, a Moroccan Army of Liberation (ALN) formed in the north of the country. Armed with hunting rifles and weapons pillaged from French depots, the ALN carried out attacks against police posts and offices of the *Affaires indigenes*, destroying local bases of French authority and forcing the regime to negotiate with its back to the wall. These attacks were committed with one goal in mind: the return of the sultan, "the Prince of the Believers," now transformed into the symbol of a nation clamoring for independence. On August 20, 1955, a well-planned and deadly attack by Middle Atlas tribesmen on the European population of Oued Zem, a farming community near Kasba Tadla, ended once and for all the myth of Berber "solidarity" with the Protectorate. The carnage that ensued provoked a massive and brutal military response from the French side, who used airplanes, tanks, and ground troops to subdue a resistance that left five hundred Moroccans dead. France poured troops into Morocco, many of them fresh from the killing fields of Indochina, as the situation moved increasingly out of control. The war was now being carried out on a national scale, with both sides engaging in atrocious acts, and showed no signs of letting up.[56]

Recognizing it had few remaining options and that "the whole of Morocco was in flames," the French government, torn by discord, removed Ben ʿArafa from the throne and began negotiations with the exiled sovereign. Preliminary talks at the French resort town of Aix-les-Bains in August 1955 with "representatives of Moroccan public opinion" yielded little benefit. They were followed by direct conversations between the sultan and a mixed French-Moroccan delegation in Antsirabé, Madagascar in early September. In October, a roadmap setting out steps to the sultan's return included the creation of an interim "Throne Council" composed of loyalists to France such as the ancient former Grand Vizir Muhammad al-Muqri, now close to one hundred years old.[57] The council was immediately rejected by the Istiqlal and the street.

France had run out of options and was obliged to turn to the deposed sultan to extricate itself from an impossible situation. Even the usurper al-Glawi, seeing the handwriting on the wall, recanted and called for Muhammad V's "prompt restoration." The sultan was brought to Paris to meet with French Foreign Minister Antoine Piney, and from Paris he addressed the nation. Speaking in a remarkably moderate manner, the sultan set the tone for the new era by promising reforms that would make Morocco into "a democratic state based on a constitutional monarchy" joined to France "by permanent links of interdependence." The following Friday, the mosques in Morocco filled with worshippers to hear the *khutba* (Friday sermon) in the name of Sidi Muhammad, while the national council of Moroccan rabbis met in Rabat and issued a declaration expressing "their great joy" in anticipation of his early return.

On November 16, 1955, the sultan stepped foot on Moroccan soil once again; greeted by delirious crowds, he announced the end of the Protectorate. As thousands of well-wishers encircled him, he pronounced the closing of the "minor jihad" – the pursuit of independence – and the beginning of a "major jihad," the collective effort to rebuild the nation. Implicit in his words was the message that the sultan himself, the elected head of the umma, would be the supreme leader. Yet he faced a formidable competitor in the Istiqlal, who had played the part of master architect of independence; with its sprawling network, its armed militants, its local cells in every city and town and throughout countryside, it was a state within the state that had to be absorbed in order to make the transition to independence complete.

THE DISSOLUTION OF THE NATIONALIST CONSENSUS

Morocco's politicized cadres, energized by their success in the nationalist struggle, were eager to become equal partners in planning and executing the effort of state building. During the forty-four years of French overlordship, Morocco's economy and society had been fundamentally transformed; in the cities, a salaried proletariat had supplanted the artisan class, while in the countryside, much of the peasantry, still more than 70 percent of the population, had become a landless proletariat, beholden to a small, powerful and wealthy group of native landowners who would become even richer with the departure of the French. The project of introducing modernity had come at great cost: the division of the economy into dual sectors, the modern and the outmoded; the abandonment of the majority to poverty, ignorance, and lack of advancement; the stripping away of precolonial protections that had cushioned the worst effects of a capricious natural environment; and the reinforcement of structural imbalances between classes and ethnic groups. Illiteracy in Morocco on the eve of independence was an appalling 90 percent; the expected life span for men was forty-seven years. The systematic exploitation of Morocco's riches for the benefit of a few had created a distorted pattern of abuse that was difficult to undo. The habit of the Residency was to disguise its manipulation of power behind a false façade of royal legitimacy, when in fact the monarch was hamstrung and almost until the end of France's tenure in Morocco, unable to act independently. Ostentatious displays of respect toward the throne hid a deep-seated contempt for its actual worth.

Immense problems of a practical nature faced the country at the threshold of independence. Creating and consolidating state institutions, building a national economy, organizing civil society and the nascent political parties, establishing social protections for a needy population, headed the list. Agrarian reform was imperative. The expropriation of millions of hectares of arable land by the colonial regime had left the Moroccan peasantry – more than 3.5 million of them – without land. Educational reform was badly needed; only 15 percent of schoolage children were actually in school. A university system had to be built out of the scarce resources left by the French. In the course of forty-four years, the Protectorate had produced a scant 1415 Moroccan baccalaureates, 640 of them Muslims and 775 Jews. The assets of the young nation were waiting to be mobilized and developed.[58]

In terms of efficacy, the makhzan of 1956 was not vastly different from the makhzan of 1912. The Protectorate regime had kept the native Moroccan government in a puerile stage of evolution, robbing it of the chance to benefit from the experience of engaging in practical politics by keeping it in a deep freeze. The principal dilemma facing the new regime was how to restart the engine of the state and overcome the blockages of an arrested political and social development. Members of the revolutionary vanguard, young men of the Istiqlal like Mehdi Ben Barka and Aberrahim Bouabid, who were very popular with the youth sectors of the party, were ready to assume the mantle of leadership, but their aspirations were soon frustrated. The euphoria that accompanied the return of the sultan and the granting of independence swiftly turned into political infighting among factions of the Istiqlal, and between the Istiqlal and other aspiring political parties. The polarity of views was not immediately apparent, as various interests sparred for dominance in the government of national union that took office in December 1955 under M'Barek Bekkaï, a Berber from the Oujda region who was, in the words of one observer, "a man of honor but not a politician." The appointment of Bekkaï to this post signaled the beginning of an enduring alliance between the throne and the conservative rural elite who had formerly served as the bedrock of the Protectorate administration in the countryside. The Istiqlal, to its great chagrin, was given only nine out of twenty-one ministries in this new government despite its strength and domination over the political field. The party that had fought hard and won the prize of independence now found itself shut out from key networks of patronage. The rest of the ministerial portfolios were distributed to two minor parties: al-Ouezzani's PDI (*Parti Démocratique de l' Independence*, founded in 1951) received six portfolios, while a group of independents headed by Ahmed Reda Guedira, royalist and friend of Crown Prince Hassan, received another six.[59]

The struggle for power between Muhammad V and the Istiqlal now became the principal motif of the new state's political life, intensifying in the months and years to come. Forces loyal to the monarchy rallied to counter the overwhelming weight of the Istiqlal, who had hoped to profit from its pivotal role in bringing the monarchy to power. While talk of democratic constitutionalism remained part of official rhetoric, the sultan – now known officially as the king – reconsidered his options. Instead of moving forward steadily toward governmental restructuring, he stopped the clock on introducing radical changes, and projects of reform that had been at the core of the Istiqlal's argument with the colonial regime were sidelined, replaced by an angry debate over the distribution of power. Indeed, the political process became enveloped in a miasma of distrust that engulfed society as a whole, as mysterious political assassinations of prominent individuals such as Touria Chaoui, the first Moroccan aviatrix, and Abbas Messaadi, a Berber militant, heightened the general sense of fear. The preindependence atmosphere of unity quickly dissipated, and jockeying for position rather than institution-building became the main business of the political elite.

In 1959, the Istiqlal itself sundered, with younger members under the leadership of Mehdi Ben Barka, Abderrahim Bouabid, and Abderrahmane Youssoufi forming a new, more "progressive" branch that became a separate party, the leftwing UNFP (National Union of Popular Forces). Its program of action included agrarian reform, democratic government, and the swift departure of the remaining vestiges of French rule, in other words, all the measures of far-reaching reform not prioritized by the monarchy. Representing "the revolutionary option," the UNFP moved rapidly further to the left, leaving behind a truncated Istiqlal still dominated by the figure of ʿAllal al-Fasi. Reconciling the interests of the progressives with those of the throne was proving to be increasingly difficult. Through his reticence to engage in rapid change, King Muhammad V demonstrated that he was deeply bound to a primordial concern for self-preservation and a doubtful attitude toward the political maturity of a

Moroccan people who had been "delivered to modernity by the forceps of the Protectorate."[60]

Meanwhile, other parties coalesced and chipped away at the power base of the Istiqlal. In 1957, the Popular Movement representing a mainly rural, Rifian Berber position took shape in the North, the Communist Party (PCM) reappeared after years of repression, and new life was breathed into the PDI, or Independent Democratic Party of Mohammed Hassan al-Ouezzani. Together, these competing groups now formed a disorganized opposition, warring with each other for a seat at the table. To the monarchy's satisfaction, a multiparty system was taking shape, diluting and weakening the monolithic structure and influence of the Istiqlal.

Managing this chaotic political scene with consummate skill, the monarchy emerged by 1959 as the main pillar of stability in the state. King Muhammad V captured and manipulated powers delegated to the government, keeping for himself control over the military and eventually, over security services, as well as the ministries of Justice and the Interior. Given this preponderance of royal influence over affairs, the new "left" was consistently outmaneuvered by the palace, whose strength grew incrementally as it perfected techniques of rewarding and bringing its friends closer, while undermining its adversaries through processes of divide and rule. Eventually, the competition between the king and the opposition forced the monarchy to turn away from the urban-based parties of the left and seek its base of support in the countryside, in a process carefully reconstructed by political scientist Rémy Leveau in his study of peasant politics in the immediate postindependence period.[61] The alliance between the king and the rural notability had fateful repercussions; it relegated party politics to a subordinate position, allowing the monarchy to disregard an increasingly urbanizing and radicalizing popular will; it postponed much needed agricultural reforms that would have benefited the peasantry and alleviated the entrenched poverty of the countryside ; and it set the stage for long-term agrarian policies that mainly benefited pro-royalist rural elites.[62]

A key element in this process of reasserting royal hegemony was the role being played by young Crown Prince Hassan, now his father's right-hand man, who was placed at the head of the newly constituted national army (*Forces armées royales*, FAR) in 1956, composed of units of the disbanded ALN. Crown Prince Hassan was supported by a cadre of military professionals who had served in the French colonial army, such as Mohamed Oufkir, graduate of the Berber college of Azrou and veteran of the war in Indochina. The officer class of the FAR and the rank-and-file had two things in common: at least 90 percent were of Berber and rural origin, and most professed loyalty to the throne rather than to the nationalists, whom they held in deep suspicion. Thereafter, the relationship between the monarchy and the army was an especially close one, with members of the ruling family regularly appearing in uniform.[63] However, the new army faced a confused situation in the field, where rogue remnants of the ALN continued to operate, refusing to lay down their arms until they could see the outcome of the political struggle. Angered that French troops remained on Moroccan soil, the southern branch of the ALN launched a war against the FAR, only to be defeated in 1958 with the help of French and Spanish troops after a bloody settling of scores.[64]

Another armed separatist movement arose in the ever-effervescent Rif in 1957 under Mahjoubi Aherdane, a Berber leader acting as a voice for a rural elite who felt alienated from the left-leaning, urban-centered and seemingly Istiqlal-dominated political process. Launched with the slogan "We did not achieve independence in order to lose freedom," the insurrection by the *Mouvement Populaire* (Popular Movement, or MP), as it eventually was called, was brutally crushed by General Oufkir, who was rewarded with the title of "Butcher of the Rif" for his efforts. In his own defense, Aherdane declared that his enemy was not the monarchy but rather "corrupt intermediaries," a not so subtle reference to his hostility to the Istiqlal. Following the defeat of the MP, King Muhammad V took a page from the book of his ancestor, Sultan Hassan I, and pardoned the "siba" of Aherdane and his followers, allowing the MP to be swiftly reintegrated into the political fold. The creation of yet another important political faction, the FDIC (Front de Défense des Institutions Constitutionnelles), a loyalist coalition headed by Ahmed Reda Guedira, rounded out the process of intense fissuring in this period of post-independence politics. The membership of the FDIC included urban intellectuals, rural notables, young technocrats; in other words, all those "who had been alienated by the Istiqlal"; but their real political cement was fealty to the king.

The rise of breakaway political factions who refused to submit to Istiqlal party discipline eliminated once and for all the possibility of a unified opposition that could serve as a counter-balance to the rising influence of the monarchy. By 1960, the political stage was crowded with a swirl of actors, each one competing fiercely with the others, their net impact neutralized by the political agility of the monarchy.[65] Moreover, in an ominous sign for the future, with blessings from his father, Crown Prince Hassan gradually seized control of a national security apparatus originally put in place by the Istiqlal in the early days of independence to root out its political enemies.

In July 1960, Hassan's close associate, the sphinxlike and ruthless Oufkir, his eyes perpetually hidden behind dark glasses, was appointed Director General of Security, bringing the secret service fully under the control of the palace.[66]

Fully occupied by its need to solidify its hold on politics, build up the army, and restore stability to the country, the monarchy paid less attention to the fundamental human needs of its people. Muhammad V was a liberal on international affairs, firmly aligning himself with Third World anti-imperialism, but he was a staunch social conservative at home. In the domestic sphere, he chose a strategy that carefully avoided upsetting the traditional groups that sustained him in power. A new government formed in 1958 and headed by Abdallah Ibrahim, a trade union leader and cofounder of the UNFP, seemed to auger well for reform, but the monarchy was firmly opposed to promoting broad societal interventions. Instead, the majority of Moroccans were left to cope on their own with problems such as high unemployment, scarce housing, inadequate schooling, understaffed health services, and a stagnant economy depleted by the flight of foreign

FIGURE 25. U.S. Vice-President Richard Nixon and Mrs. Nixon are greeted by King Muhammad V during a state visit to Morocco in 1957. While relations with the United States were cordial, the Moroccan sovereign generally followed a policy of nonalignment and sought friendships with neutral nations. (Courtesy of the Tangier American Legation Institute and Museum)

capital. Even nature conspired to confound social progress; on February 29, 1960, a massive earthquake destroyed much of the town of Agadir in Morocco's south, claiming up to fifteen thousand lives. To those on the left, it seemed ironic that Morocco, a beacon of political progress on the regional level, languished in the rear when it came to social advances at home. In May 1960 the king, weary of the endless political back-and-forth, summarily dismissed the government of Abdallah Ibrahim and seized the reins of power, anointing himself as his own Prime Minister.

In the arena of diplomacy, as the Cold War intensified, Muhammad V cleaved a clear path between Eastern and Western blocs. While professing strong anticommunist sentiments, he endorsed a policy of nonalignment and cultivated friendships with emerging African nations. His independence in foreign affairs did not please his American allies, nor did it win him large amounts of U.S. foreign aid.[67] The monarch's relations with France were equally murky. When the declaration of independence was signed on March 2, 1956, one hundred thousand French troops still remained on Moroccan soil, and it was clear that France would continue to play a role in Morocco politically, economically and militarily for some time to come. Moreover, an absolute disengagement from colonial status was not a foregone conclusion; negotiations in February and March 1956 between Morocco and France revealed a wide divergence of opinion about the future relationship between the two nations. France proposed "an independent state united with France by permanent ties of interdependency," while Morocco insisted on the complete abrogation of the Treaty of Fez of 1912 and full exercise of Moroccan sovereignty. As France became increasingly mired in the Algerian War of Independence, the Moroccan view prevailed. In April 1956, Spain signed an agreement to quit the northern zone, but it took twenty more years to complete the withdrawal of its forces from the provinces of Tarfaya and Sidi Ifni in the Sahara, while the cities of Ceuta and Melilla remain in Spanish hands to this day. Finally, on October 8, 1956, an international conference opened in Fedala to discuss Tangier's reversion to Moroccan sovereignty for the first time since 1912. While large chunks of the national territory that had been alienated for nearly two generations were being reunited with the national space, other sore points like Ceuta, Melilla, and the Saharan territories remained in foreign hands to fan the flames of irredentist passions.

Meanwhile, in a monumental national tragedy, the majority of Morocco's age-old Jewish community of 250,000 souls began to leave, at first in a clandestine trickle, later in a flood, leaving a painful rent in the social fabric. Treated meanly by the Protectorate regime, suffering from faltering economic conditions, displaced from their traditional role as intermediaries by the new native middle class, humiliated by the race laws of Vichy, confused by the upheavals in the Middle East, deeply disappointed with France while heeding the nationalist clarion with only half an ear, and above all, pulled by the siren call of Zionism, Morocco's Jews began a grand exodus after 1947, migrating both to Israel and the West. The Six-Day War of 1967 was the final act for Morocco's Jews, drawing away most of those who remained, ending a millennium of coexistence that had marked Morocco as the most tolerant of Muslim societies.

From its modest origins within student circles of Fez and Paris, in the space of thirty years the Moroccan nationalist movement had grown into a globalized cause having tentacles that stretched outward to Europe, the Americas, and the Middle East. Within Morocco, it reached from the great cities of the coast deep into the plains and mountains of the Berber heartland. Its cadres included Sorbonne-educated intellectuals and tribal militants, pious salafis and rough-edged industrial workers, peasants and shopkeepers. Its single-minded quest for dignity and nationhood had transformed the simple doctrines of its founding fathers, based on a rational set of legal and social principles, into a strident declaration of the unity and historical uniqueness of the Moroccan people. Strictly hierarchical, strongly anticommunist, fervently patriotic, especially when it came to the king, leaning toward tradition but open to innovation, embracing Muslims and Jews, Arabs and Berbers, the movement was as variegated as Morocco itself.

But deep cracks were appearing in its hastily constructed façade. In the postindependence years, we see signs of a political machine running out of control, ignoring principles fundamental to its founders, leaving a vacuum filled by a revival of royal absolutism. Instead of constitutional democracy, there was no constitution; instead of economic liberalism, the state took charge; instead of a nation free of the colonizer, the fingerprints of France were still found everywhere; instead of a mosaic-like and vibrant multiethnic and multipolar social organization, people were being forced into a stifling, centralizing, and homogeneous mold in the educational system, in the workplace, in the shaping of the political field. In many ways, the tenor of politics was reminiscent of the old makhzan, with its leitmotifs of patronage and gift giving, arbitration and negotiation, and patriarchal systems of kinship and family. Presiding over this swirling vortex was the king, ready to take charge through the age-old implements of authority in Morocco, deftly deploying his religious prestige, financial weight, coercive force, and convincing powers of persuasion.

This picture of a free-for-all struggle for power among rival parties is hardly the image the founders of the Istiqlal had in mind when they wrote their Manifesto in 1944. Nor does it mimic in any way the Morocco that ʿAllal al-Fasi imagined when he promised that a demotic age would engulf the Maghrib at mid-century. His projection of a revolutionary state, deeply Islamic, vaguely monarchical, resoundingly populist, and directly responsive to the voice of the people, was fading fast. Perhaps such a regime would have emerged had the progenitor of the nation, King Muhammad V, been allowed to live out the fullness of his years. Instead, as we shall see, the regime he prematurely bequeathed to his son and successor King Hassan II was a fluctuating system of transient relationships, kept loosely in order by a monarch that anthropologist Clifford Geertz cleverly dubbed "The First Machinator": a distant and enigmatic figure lacking the style of a Nasser or a Bourguiba, closed within himself, who failed to impose a true sense of national purpose.[68] Morocco did eventually inherit its own *zaʿim*, but he was a flawed one, without the monumentality, or the generosity, or the selfless conviction that the nationalists imagined. The coming phase – the age of Hassan II – frames the last chapters of Morocco's twentieth-century history, in which the personality of the ruler became the defining element in the search for a national purpose that might meet the expectations of the Moroccan people.

6

The First Age of Hassan II

The Iron Fist (1961–1975)

The sudden and unexpected death of Muhammad V on February 26, 1961, during minor surgery unleashed a torrent of grief from a people who had come to revere the shy and retiring figure who, by sheer force of will, had become father of the nation. Designated as heir apparent in 1957, the thirty-two-year-old Crown Prince Hassan was of a different temper. He stayed close to his father's side throughout the last tumultuous years of French rule, absorbing the lessons of political survival at home and in exile. Educated at the palace by a battery of French and Moroccan professors (including the brilliant Mehdi Ben Barka in Mathematics) and later at Bordeaux, where he received a law degree, he was open to the world and far more at ease with the accoutrements of modernity than his father. Yet he was also a lover of tradition and the prerogatives of power: the tinsel uniforms, the hand kissing, the palace ceremonial ordained by ancient protocol. Unlike his father, he was completely fluent in French in addition to Arabic, and spoke capable English as well. Cold-blooded and hot-tempered, an *amateur* of fast cars and sleek women, with a broad streak of ambition and a love of command, he was more than ready to rule.

THE NEW KING TIGHTENS HIS GRIP ON POWER

Hassan II's credentials were impressive but not altogether flawless. His postindependence success in organizing the FAR and repressing revolts in the Rif and the south had burnished his reputation as a decisive and effective leader. But among the common people, his worth was questioned by his supposed attraction to the forbidden pleasures of life. Viewed as a playboy whose nocturnal wanderings in the company of hard-drinking army officers cast doubt on his attachment to religious values, the young king faced the challenge of creating a public persona consonant with his role as "Commander of the Faithful." His primary objective was to convert that reserve of symbolic capital into political coin. Thus the early years of his reign were devoted to building his own signature image based on the mythic aura of his father, while setting an agenda aimed at eliminating opponents and consolidating his personal power. The later years of his rule were devoted to undoing the mistakes of the first years, guaranteeing the family legacy, and projecting forward his vision of a "new" Morocco. His character and ambitions were decisive in shaping Morocco's direction in the last third of the twentieth century. Indeed, the survival of the Moroccan monarchy in this period, when so many other Middle Eastern and North African monarchies failed, is largely due to the "the remarkable personal skills" of Hassan II, according to political scientist Rémy Leveau, who observed him closely for a half century.[1]

At the top of his agenda was the unfinished business of assuring the political supremacy of the monarchy, while playing a cautious game of engagement with the political parties. In the May 1960 municipal elections, the Istiqlal party had won a majority of votes, obliging the then Crown Prince to work with it and gain its support. After the death of Muhammad V and Hassan II's sudden ascension to the throne, ʿAllal al-Fasi, who was still the undisputed leader of the Istiqlal, returned the favor and threw his party's considerable weight behind the new and untried monarch, calling for a show of "national unity." In return, Hassan II was reluctantly compelled to pay attention to al-Fasi's demand for a constitution based on representative rule that had been promised earlier by Muhammad V. He invited al-Fasi and Ahmed Balafrej to join a new government in the spring of 1962, and at the same time issued a "Fundamental Law," a sort of provisional constitution, meant to satisfy the Istiqlal's demands for a move in this direction. This document introduced foundational issues for the Istiqlal into political discourse that had hitherto been unwritten, such as Morocco's "Arab and Islamic" character and the state's duty to reclaim its historic territories; but it did nothing to alter the balance of power in favor of representative government. In fact, rather than tempering absolutism, it made it even more pronounced. Any decision-making authority not given directly to the king was assigned to his close associates, keeping the levers of control firmly within his grasp. Historian Maati Monjib comments that the Fundamental Law "was a bad precedent that opened the door to all kinds of abuses, and it was the first step toward promulgating a constitution totally designed by the clients (*services*) of the king."[2]

The constitution that finally appeared in December 1962 was written behind closed doors by Hassan's appointees, not by a representative body. It was immediately boycotted by the parties of the extreme left, but it was cynically supported by the Istiqlal as well as by Istiqlal-affiliated organizations in an attempt to remain in power. The constitution was approved by popular referendum with 85 percent of the vote. Article Nineteen confirmed the king's position as "Commander of the Faithful," and "supreme representative of the nation," blending his political and religious roles and consolidating in the head of state near-unlimited executive powers. One leftist leader ruefully complained, "We have a king who uses all the means of the twentieth century, automobiles, airplanes, and so forth, in order to perpetuate feudalism."[3] At the same time, the constitution gave a brief nod to liberal principles by encouraging the stabilization of multiparty system that would be "democratic and social," reflecting the views of Hassan's close ally, ultra-royalist Ahmed Reda Guedira. But Hassan himself was not very interested in power-sharing or in nurturing open processes of rule. Instead, he used his extraordinary executive power, now endorsed by the new constitution, to maneuver the Istiqlal out of the government and into a situation of permanent opposition, where it would stay for nearly four decades.[4] Thereafter, political activity fell into a stable pattern in which authoritarianism coexisted side by side with plural political parties, skillfully manipulated and circumscribed by the king, thus preventing any one party or political force to come forward and challenge the throne's monopoly on power.

Hassan II made important diplomatic moves as well, orchestrating a swift turnabout in Morocco's foreign policy. He abandoned the non-aligned position his father had mapped out and instead veered sharply toward the West. Once ʿAllal al-Fasi was out of the government, Hassan II no longer felt obliged to support the nationalists' demand to recover Morocco's "historic" territories remaining under foreign rule.[5] The irredentist aspect of the Istiqlal platform had been a major thorn in the royal side, paralyzing Hassan's freedom of movement on the diplomatic front; for years it had provoked sharp anger against Morocco from Algeria, France, Spain, Mauritania, and to a lesser extent, the United States. The Saharan issue in particular vexed Morocco's relations with its African neighbors; Morocco's ambitions in the Western Sahara ran counter to a plan for Mauritania's independence that was backed by other African states. With the Istiqlal in opposition, the king could set aside the irredentist issue, at least for the time being, and concentrate on other matters. Hassan II quickly lowered his voice on territorial demands, and turned instead to mending fences with important friends in Europe, Africa, and America.[6]

France in particular was drawn in by Hassan's turnabout; in 1961, France was in the twilight of empire, in search of new relationships with its former vassals. The Algerian War was winding down and de Gaulle's plan for a definitive departure from North Africa was close to realization, including a final evacuation of France's remaining bases in Morocco. In Hassan's view, improved relations with France could bring a windfall of economic and diplomatic dividends, among them a staunching of the hemorrhage of French capital out of Morocco caused in part by the belligerent anti-imperialist speeches of the Moroccan left. This calculation proved to be correct, and Franco-Moroccan relations improved markedly in the period 1962–1965. With France now responding to his overtures, Hassan II began to lay the foundations of a foreign policy designed to reflect his long-standing desire to firmly establish himself as an ally of the West. A precedent had already been established when, in December 1959, Muhammad V negotiated an agreement with the United States to withdraw from its five military bases in Morocco acquired at the height of the Cold War as a part of America's Strategic Air Command (SAC) anti-Soviet early warning system. With the advent of a new generation of long-range bombers, the Moroccan bases were deemed no longer essential by the U.S. military and the withdrawal was completed by 1963. This amicable exchange over the shutdown of the bases became the cornerstone for the warm and increasingly close Moroccan-American friendship that developed over the course of Hassan's reign.[7]

While soothing relations with France, Hassan purposely disrupted them with his closest neighbor, Algeria. Morocco's border with Algeria, inherited from the colonial past, was ill-defined, especially in the southeast, where France had begun chipping away at Moroccan territory even before 1912. The area around Tindouf became especially important when oil reserves were discovered there in the 1950s. King Hassan II mistakenly believed that Algeria's new national leadership, having wrested its freedom from France in 1962 with Moroccan help, would agree to a realignment. But when a dispute broke out over the disposition of the tiny border outpost of Hassi Bayda, newly elected Algerian President Ahmed Ben Bella stubbornly refused to discuss any border revisions. This altercation arose at a time when politics in both countries were in turmoil: Hassan was wrestling with an uprising on the left, while Ben Bella was faced with smoothing out the nasty internal rivalries left over from the Algerian Revolution.

In this hypertensive and over-heated atmosphere, the face-off between Morocco and Algeria quickly escalated, producing the sad spectacle of the two recently decolonized and once-amicable states fighting each other in "a war of the sands." Later, Hassan II would call it "a stupid war . . . a real setback"; however, at the time, the struggle with Algeria served to test the leadership skills of an untried and freshly anointed monarch seeking to rally the nation behind him. While most Moroccans were drawn in by a media blitz contrived to rouse nationalist fervor, cooler heads opposed the war. UNFP leader Mehdi Ben Barka condemned the conflict as a diversion from more serious problems, and called on Moroccans not to fight their Algerian "brothers" who were in the midst of an experiment in Arab socialism. After hundreds of casualties on both sides, a cease-fire was finally negotiated in November 1963 with the help of the Organization of African Unity. Although the Moroccan army had made a good showing in the field, it kept none of the spoils of victory, and the border problem remained unresolved. Moroccans, furious at this stinging setback, began to feel a widening gulf between themselves and their Algerian neighbors, who were waxing rich from gushing oil revenues. These differences soon hardened into a permanent hostility, and a bitter animosity now poisoned the atmosphere between the two neighbors, leading directly to the Western Sahara crisis of 1975.[8]

PLOTS, COUNTERPLOTS, AND THE ALIENATION OF THE LEFT

Tensions mounted in the period 1962–1965 as the UNFP became more outspoken in its opposition to the monarchy, turning Mehdi Ben Barka, the popular head of the party and pied piper of the younger generation, into the archenemy of the regime. The contrast between the revival of the old makhzan and its autocratic ways, on the one hand, and the fresh breezes blowing in from the Arab socialist regimes in the East on the other, frustrated Ben Barka and his followers. They looked to newly independent Algeria's socialist-leaning nonalignment as an alternative model of governance that differed profoundly from Morocco's conservative and Western-oriented monarchy. Even little Tunisia was following a progressive path under the leadership of Habib Bourguiba and his socialist-oriented neo-Destour political organization. Reading the political *Zeitgeist* and fearful of a resurgence of colonialism, Ben Barka urged Moroccans to recognize their unanimity with other recently liberated Third World nations and to build ties of solidarity with them. Meetings and discussions with revolutionary leaders such as Ho Chi Minh, Fidel Castro, and Che Guevara had radicalized his thinking even more. When the project for a new constitution was announced in 1962, Ben Barka immediately called for its boycott, declaring that "the primary task of the Moroccan people is to battle this totally feudal regime."[9]

Ben Barka's fiery intellectualism and his wide popularity frightened King Hassan II and alarmed Morocco's new Western allies, themselves caught up in Cold War antimonies that situated personalities such as Ben Barka on the far side of the political fence. Moreover, Ben Barka's high-profile activities around the globe that associated Morocco with international revolutionary movements of a Communist flavor came precisely at the moment when Hassan II was seeking rapprochement with the West. After Oufkir's secret services uncovered a plot to kill the king allegedly hatched among members of the disbanded ALN, the regime used this incident to begin open warfare with its opponents on the left, foremost among them Ben Barka.

In July 1963, following a good showing by the UNFP in the first parliamentary elections, a massive arrest of five thousand UNFP militants took place, catching in its net even moderate UNFP leaders such as Abderrahim Bouabid and Abderrahmane Youssoufi. The sudden crackdown announced a new, more violent phase in the monarchy's confrontation with the left and a blatant disregard of the political aspirations of a rising middle class attracted to Ben Barka's populism.[10] During the winter of 1963–1964, a sensational trial of over two hundred UNFP detainees took place, during which eleven prominent leaders of the party accused of participating in the alleged plot against the king were sentenced to death, including Ben Barka. Meanwhile, the now outlawed leader fled abroad and was condemned in absentia. The obvious intention of the trial was to break the back of the UNFP, although Hassan II later denied that he held any personal animosity toward his former professor. In August 1964, Hassan II pardoned the condemned men, but Ben Barka refused to return to Morocco.

The saga of his dramatic exile ended on October 29, 1965, when he was kidnapped on a Paris street and then "disappeared." The full circumstances of his death have never come to light, although the implication of Moroccan, French, and other "foreign" agents in the affair has often been made. General Oufkir (after he was conveniently dead!) was mentioned most often as the chief architect of Ben Barka's abduction, though this, too, has never been proven. As for King Hassan II, he innocently denied all knowledge of the affair, swearing that he had been confronted with "a fait accompli" regarding the fate of Ben Barka. For nearly fifty years, a strict wall of silence has enveloped the death of this most passionate figure of mid-century politics whose presence on the world stage was felt far beyond Morocco, and whose disappearance left a deep and lasting wound in the national psyche made worse by secrecy, falsehood, and innuendo.[11]

The politics of resistance were not confined to the intellectual elites, but filtered down through the ranks of society and eventually burst out into the streets. In the vanguard of the politicized masses was the UNEM (the Moroccan National Students' Union), whose members repeatedly went out on strike in the period 1962–1965. University students had been aggressively wooed by Ben Barka since the early days of the UNFP and formed a core group among its cadres. The yearly congress of the UNEM was often the scene of raucous demands for democratization, the purging of colonialism, and the placing of limits on the powers of the king. When the leadership of the UNFP was rounded up in 1963 for "plotting" against the monarchy, the UNEM rose up with a roar, calling for the "abolition of the regime." The state, for its part, used coercive tactics to try to bring the students to heel, including beatings, arrests and disappearances of leading figures in the student movement. There was no quarter given to the student left and its leadership was hounded relentlessly; Hamid Berrada, a UNEM official-in-exile, echoed Ben Barka's position about the pointlessness of the "war of the sands," and he, too, was condemned to death in absentia.[12]

High school students (*lycéens*) were not officially part of the UNEM, but they, too, heeded its call for top-to-bottom political and social change. When, early in 1965, the Minister of Education instituted new rules regarding secondary school admissions, lycées in Rabat, Casablanca, and other big cities became staging areas for spirited demonstrations against the regime, reaching a crescendo on March 21, 1965, when a student-organized protest in Casablanca quickly devolved into three days of running street battles in which students were joined by thousands of workers laid off during the economic recession of 1964, as well as inhabitants of Casablanca's sprawling bidonvilles. Ripping up trees and paving stones, breaking shop windows and burning cars and busses, the rioters treated the regime to a frightening scene of urban chaos. The coalition of students and the workers organized by the UMT was especially threatening to the authorities, and seemed to portend a coming social revolution. The city was paralyzed and the king was openly denounced in a massive display of civil disobedience. The riots were brutally put down three days later by security forces fortified with phalanxes of tanks and armored vehicles under the direction of Oufkir, who circled the city in a helicopter, at the cost of hundreds of lives.

The strikes spread to other cities: Rabat, Settat, Khouribga, Meknes, and Kénitra were caught up in the antigovernment fervor. When historian Mohamed El Ayadi, at the time a high school student, demonstrated in the Rabat madina, he was expressing a new political awareness: "For me, as well as for the majority of my peers, the first step in our political socialization happened spontaneously in the street, before taking on a more organized and self-conscious form at the university in 1968." Hassan II felt especially betrayed by this youthful opposition and vented his anger on the young, educated Moroccans who were taking to the streets for lack of jobs: "Allow me to tell you," he said on national television, "there is no greater danger to the state than the so-called intellectual; it would have been better for you to be illiterate." Schools and university campuses across the country were shut down, but a dangerous precedent had been set; the concept of popular protest was now securely entrenched in the public mind as a legitimate means of showing dissatisfaction with an otherwise distant, unresponsive, and impenetrable regime.[13]

In the aftermath of the March 1965 riots, the king dismissed the parliament and suspended the Constitution of 1962, putting in place a state of emergency that would last for more than five years. The political parties were now in serious remission, and the main arenas for political dialogue switched to informal settings, in the universities, in the salons of the educated elite, among émigrés and students in France, and within the rank and file of the trade unions who were closely allied with the left. The UNEM had served as an incubator for a new generation of activists, predecessors to an even more ultra-politicized cadre that appeared in the late 1960s, inspired by youthful militancy worldwide and especially the Paris uprisings of May 1968. Impregnated with revolutionary ideology, the "New Left" (*al-yasar al-jadid* in Arabic) rejected affiliation with any of the old political parties who were indelibly marked by their compromises with the authoritarian regime. Many in the New Left were communists who left the PCM when, in a bid to gain legal status and recognition from the monarchy, the PCM entered parliament under the new name of the Party of Liberalism and Socialism (PLS). Deflated by this defection, groups of leftists split from the PLS and went underground. Student uprisings continued into the 1970s, with the universities perpetually on strike and hundreds of activists arrested and sent to jail, including prominent leaders of the UNFP. In 1973, the departments of social science (history, philosophy, sociology) in the government-controlled universities were "Arabized" by fiat, changing the curriculum in fundamental ways, in a crude and obvious attempt to foster a more conservative atmosphere within academia and to dampen enthusiasm for the radicalizing influences filtering in from Europe.

In the forefront of the far left was the organization Ila al-Amam ("To the Forefront"), a political faction composed of young intellectuals such as Abraham Serfaty, Abdellatif Laâbi, and Ahmed Herzenni, vehemently opposed to the king, who considered themselves "the avant-garde" of a popular revolution.[14] Repression of Ila al-Amam was immediate and violent, carried out by security forces working under the direction of the Ministry of the Interior. In the early 1970s, countless militants were arrested and put on trial, and many incarcerated for years, including the charismatic Serfaty, a mining engineer turned political activist. Born in 1926 in Casablanca to a Jewish family, Serfaty trained at the prestigious École des Mines in Paris where he became an ardent Communist. After independence, he returned home and became a government adviser on mining engineering and a university professor. In 1970, he left the Communist Party and co-founded Ila al-Amam; pursued by the authorities, he went underground in 1972 but was captured two years later and held at the notorious Derb Moulay Cherif prison in Casablanca used for "interrogating" suspects where he was repeatedly tortured. In 1977, in a public show trial, he was condemned to life imprisonment with five of his comrades for "attacking the security of the state." Serfaty's beliefs won him seventeen years in confinement and a front place in the ranks of those who opposed the increasing autocracy of King Hassan's rule.[15] His imprisonment and the jailing of his colleagues marks the beginning of a dark period in Moroccan history popularly known as *les années de plomb*, "the years of lead" (roughly 1975–1990), in which many hundreds of Moroccans entered into a Golgotha of suffering kept hidden from the rest of society.

Throughout these violent confrontations, Hassan II relied increasingly on the army and the police as the backbone of his regime, integrating senior officers into his expanding network of royal patronage. In 1964, General

Oufkir was named Minister of the Interior in addition to his central role in the intelligence services, thus tightening the link between the army, the state, and the security apparatus. Hassan II privileged the army above all other institutions in society, and by 1971, the FAR had grown into a formidable force of fifty-seven thousand men. The king regarded the army as the true cross-section of the nation, believing that through it, he had established a tie to the Moroccan people that the unruly political parties had denied him. Cozened and patronized by the king, given favors, gifts of money, land, and promotions, the top brass of the army formed a praetorian guard that was the envy of the rest of society. Hassan's confidence in the military explains his readiness to impose the "state of emergency" in 1965 that represented a final turning away from a fictitious democracy toward an unadulterated authoritarianism. The rupture between the parties of the left and the palace consummated by the 1965 state of emergency concentrated overwhelming authority in the hands of the king, established the military and secret services as his principal tool for keeping civilian politicians in line, and stifled the national debate on issues of much-needed reform.[16]

AN ECONOMY IN DISARRAY

The crisis in the political arena was matched by ongoing turmoil in the economic sphere. Independent Morocco had inherited a host of problems from the Protectorate, as well as certain benefits. On the positive side, it was endowed with a modern infrastructure, some industrial capacity, and the beginnings of a mechanized agricultural sector. On the negative side, the grip of "neocolonialism" was still secure, in the form of foreign control of capital and assets, a weak and dependent agricultural base, and pervasive underdevelopment in both city and countryside, where, according to Ben Barka, "a majority of the population is kept in misery and ignorance."[17] For political reasons, many elements of the former colonial system were kept in place, especially in the countryside where feudal notables still held sway, largely because of the monarchy's need to preserve the privileges of the rural elites who were its most reliable base of support.[18] Perhaps the most vexing economic problem was the vast disparity between the modern agricultural sector and the traditional one, where "antique" forms of production were still in use: the use of wooden plows pulled by undernourished animals surprised even seasoned foreign development experts.

FIGURE 26. King Muhammad V on a U.S.-made Caterpillar tractor, demonstrating the benefits of mechanized farming in "Operation Plowshare," a government program aimed at increasing agricultural productivity among small farmers. (Courtesy of the Library of Congress Prints and Photographs Division)

Distorted patterns of land ownership were at the root of the problem. In 1956, 1.3 million hectares of land in the modern sector were held by fifty-nine hundred Europeans and twelve hundred Moroccans, each with an average holding of 170 hectares, while 1.4 million Moroccan families farmed 6.5 million hectares in the traditional sector, with 90 percent farming an average holding of less than two hectares. Meanwhile, some five hundred thousand Moroccan peasants were absolutely landless, working as *fellahs de khemmas*, or tenant farmers, in a system inherited from precolonial times. Cereal production did not nearly meet the demands of local consumption, for its cultivation had been abandoned over time in favor of high value export crops, such as citrus and vegetables. Recognizing the severity of the problem, the leftist government of Abdallah Ibrahim (1958–1960) opted for a major program of agrarian reform aimed at bringing modern techniques to the farmer, including mechanized plowing and chemical fertilizers to boost cereal production. This ambitious plan, dubbed "Operation Plowshare," failed when it became apparent that it caused an increase, not a reduction, in peasant indebtedness. By 1961, the program was shut down, and Abdallah Ibrahim was dismissed.[19]

Radical innovations in the countryside did not appeal to the monarchy, who feared the effects of social dislocation on its rural power base. Accordingly, only sixteen thousand hectares of former colonial holdings, a bare minimum, were redistributed to farmers between 1956 and 1960. Instead of indulging in sweeping land reform similar to that which followed the Egyptian Revolution of 1952, the monarchy quietly bought up the land of departing French settlers piece by piece, keeping it for itself, reselling it to other big landowners, or redistributing it to its clients in the government or the army. As one observer noted: "What the Moroccan government has called land reform is a misnomer for a repossession program of land owned by European settlers."[20] Meanwhile, traditional agriculture languished and experienced diminishing yields, while the rural population kept growing.

By 1970, the Moroccan economy, from the viewpoint of the working classes, was in dire straits. Economic indicators showed a steady and steep decline from 1956 onward, marked by low productivity, rising unemployment, weak savings and investment, and an unfavorable balance of payments. A stagnant industrial sector compounded the problem, and consecutive five-year plans ushered in with fanfare ended in disappointment. Poor people were experiencing a constant decrease in living standards while prices kept rising. The price of sugar (a basic commodity for the tea-drinking Moroccan worker) doubled in the period August 1963–May 1964, and in roughly the same period, the cost of living rose by 11.5 percent. Meanwhile, wages for urban workers had been frozen since 1956 and the demographic situation was becoming critical: the annual population growth rate was 3.3 percent, overall unemployment stood at 45 percent but went as high as 60 percent in rural areas, the cities were filling with migrants from the countryside, and migration to Europe failed to absorb the surplus. Moreover, the flight of capital abroad created pressure on currency reserves, and after 1968, Morocco began borrowing steadily from the International Monetary Fund (IMF). Fifteen years after independence, according to economist Abdul Aziz Belal, Morocco was faced with "enormous needs in terms of creating jobs, education, training, and improving the quality of life of the mass of its population." While official economic policy was ostensibly liberal, in fact, it was a form of state-directed capitalism aimed at expanding private wealth to benefit the few.[21]

Economic malaise was not only a matter of statistics, it was also etched on the surface of daily life. In the winter of 1971, in the streets of Rabat, mendicants sprawled on the narrow sidewalks, their legs and arms outstretched, forming a tangled obstacle course for the passer-by. Children peddled cigarettes, one by one, on the terrace of the Hotel Balima; oranges cost three cents a kilo in the *suq* in Salé, and twenty cents would buy a bulging sack so heavy that two people had to carry it. Rents were low but so were wages; ten dollars a week bought the services of a full-time housekeeper. Peace Corps volunteers, French *cooperants*, hippies who came to roost, lived in a luxury unattainable at home. The elite was safely hidden away behind high walls in the posh garden suburb of Souissi, while working people huddled four and five to a room in the *quartiers populaires*. Gracious public parks built under the French had become dangerous wastelands of broken trees inhabited by feral cats, country roads were single-lane affairs made for donkey carts and meandering tourists, while ancient *tirailleurs*, some still wearing odd bits of their old army uniforms, sat in dusty cafés and dozed in the sun. Inequality was woven into the texture of the quotidian and misery was its omnipresent face. The situation in Morocco, if one could only read it properly, was rife for an explosion.

A SEASON OF COUPS

Despite the overall gloomy atmosphere, the end of the sixties witnessed a small economic boom, powered by the monarchy's decision to invest state resources in capital development. Under Hassan's determined direction, an ambitious program of dam construction begun in 1968 boosted the amount of irrigated land available for growing export crops; the price of phosphates, of which Morocco was now the chief global exporter, rallied and began to rise; and tourism, targeted as a major growth industry, stimulated a flow of foreign currency. Without abundant oil, Morocco could not develop heavy industry, but concentrated instead on import substitution along with agricultural modernization; as a result, the economy enjoyed an unexpected annual growth rate of 5.6 percent after 1968. While the king gained some popularity from these successes, there was little "trickle down"; the main beneficiaries were still a narrow elite, and to a certain extent, an evolving urban middle class. The extravagant lifestyles of palace favorites and government officials and their families, and especially of the "golden youth" of Casablanca who engaged in unabashedly open consumption on a scale unimaginable to most Moroccans, were offensive to the working and professional classes. The seething resentment that would burst out in the abortive coups of 1971 and 1972 could be read as attempts by the middle social levels to influence basic understandings about the distribution of wealth and the exercise of power. These sentiments were especially strong within the army, where self-appointed "keepers" of morality, often from of rural backgrounds and newly integrated into the urban middle class, were conscious of their position as public guardians and were deeply offended by the growing social disparities.[22]

The king declared an end to the state of emergency in July 1970 and immediately promulgated a new constitution approved by referendum (98.5 percent in favor) that gave the throne virtually unlimited powers. The Istiqlal and the UNFP united into the "Kutla," or national bloc, but boycotted the elections, leaving the way open for the makhzan to fill the seats of the parliament with its own, hand-picked members. Meanwhile, Ila al-Aman organized on the far left, and a new group of religious extremists, the Shabiba Islamiyya (Islamic Youth) quietly congealed on the right, but both were beyond the bounds of political give-and-take. No one was misled to believe that this flurry of activity had in any way changed the fundamental calculus of politics in Morocco, or that the palace had rescinded its role at its head; by all accounts, "the king was the unchallenged master of the system."[23]

The explosion, when it came, took place where it was least expected – in the ranks of the supposedly loyal army command. If there was any single factor that ignited the first coup of July 10, 1971, it was the accumulated evidence of unpunished corruption in high places: ministers on the take, illegal land transfers, enormous kickbacks from foreign companies to members of the royal inner circle. In the summer of 1971, the situation reached a tipping point, and a group of top army officers, led by Lieutenant Colonel M'hamed Ababou, head of the military academy at Ahermoumou, and General Mohamed Medbouh, Director of the Royal Military Household, a man widely respected for his honesty and rectitude, decided to take matters into their own hands. What motivated these high-ranking officers to act? Though their reasons were undoubtedly complex, evidence points to their disgust with the deteriorating moral climate. Members of a proud officer caste, mostly veterans of World War II and Indochina (with the exception of Ababou), it seems that the inner circle that directed the 1971 coup (who never had a chance to speak out) believed that decadence at the top was leading the country down the path of ruin, and it was their duty to act.[24]

FIGURE 27. The Skhirat coup, July 1971, as seen through the lens of a U.S. Peace Corps volunteer who witnessed the attack on the headquarters of Moroccan Radio and Television (RTM) by rebel soldiers: (a) loyalists defending the radio station; (b) a rebel soldier is detained; (c) and roughly tossed into a waiting truck; (d) rebel cadets, now prisoners, are driven away. (Courtesy of Ron Cardoos, RPCV Morocco, 1970–1972)

They made their move on the occasion of the Hassan's forty-second birthday party held at the beach-side palace at Skhirat on July 10, 1971, where hundreds of male guests, including the entire government and heads of the diplomatic corps, were assembled to eat, drink, and play golf. Twelve hundred young cadets from Ahermoumou were driven to the palace in a convoy, given live ammunition, and ordered "not to allow anyone to escape." On entering the interior of the palace, the cadets were greeted by a sumptuous banquet prepared for the royal invitees, the like of which they had probably never seen; in a rage, they upended the heavily laden tables, knocking over pyramids of delicacies and trodding on plates and glasses. In the pandemonium that followed, government ministers, diplomats, and the personal physician of the king were pitilessly massacred.[25] Somehow, Hassan II and his immediate family, including his brother Prince ʿAbdallah and eight-year-old-son, Crown Prince

Muhammad, managed to escape, through a combination of luck and quick-wittedness.

Invested on the spot by the king with full military and civilian powers, General Oufkir took charge. Meanwhile, the Moroccan people stood by in amazement and watched as events unfolded via national radio and TV, even as its headquarters were being beseiged by the rebels. In Rabat, the great wooden gates of the Casbah were swung shut and barred for the first time in recent memory, closing its inhabitants within as army trucks rumbled through the streets below. Noisy antiroyalist demonstrations broke out here and there, but for the most part, people were fearful, mute, and impassive. By midnight, Oufkir informed the king that Ababou and Medbouh were dead, and that troops loyal to the monarchy had restored order. But the toll was a heavy one: more than 100 guests killed and 125 wounded; among the rebels, 150 dead and 900 held in custody. Three days later, on July 13, ten surviving rebel officers were shot on an empty lot south of Rabat, as the king reportedly watched from a distance through binoculars.[26] The coup was over, but in its aftermath, ordinary Moroccans asked how Hassan's favorites had turned into such a pack of wolves, and whether anyone left in the army was worthy of trust. The seeds of suspicion were cast far and wide. They also asked why so many of the plotters were Berbers, as indeed they were, what role the all-knowing Oufkir might have played in events, and how the coup could possibly have taken place without his knowledge.[27]

With the king isolated, the army discredited, and the political parties in disarray, Morocco seemed to be a rudderless ship adrift in a sea of troubles. The crisis worsened on August 16, 1972, when a Royal Air Maroc Boeing 727 carrying home Hassan II and his brother Prince ʿAbdallah from an official visit to France was attacked by four U.S.-supplied F-5 fighter jets from the base at Kénitra, as it entered Moroccan air space. Once again, luck was with the king. The American-trained pilots of the F5s failed to deliver the *coup de grâce*, permitting the king's bullet-riddled passenger jet to land safely at Rabat-Salé airport with its royal cargo intact. This time, the all-powerful Oufkir was identified as the chief plotter, along with two other high-ranking Air Force officers, one of whom was Mohamed Amekrane, commandant of the Kénitra air force base.[28] That evening, Oufkir was summoned to the palace at Skhirat where Hassan awaited him; at his side was Ahmed Dlimi, another shadowy henchman soon to succeed Oufkir as Minister of the Interior. Oufkir never left the palace alive.

Was he assassinated, or was his bullet-riddled corpse the result of "suicide," as Hassan II later claimed in his memoirs?[29] A succession of mysteries surround these sensational events. For example, Oufkir's motives in fomenting the second coup were not at all clear. Was he, too, unsettled by the excesses of the regime? Did he have secret desires to complete the royal housecleaning and become a Moroccan Robespierre? The truth about these matters is buried with him. Meanwhile, Hassan II's white-hot wrath was vented on Oufkir's immediate family. His wife and six children, the youngest only a toddler, once intimates of the palace, were taken to a remote desert outpost where they were incarcerated for fifteen years in appalling conditions. The Oufkir family made their escape in 1987, only to be recaptured and held under house arrest for four more years until 1991, when they were finally set free.[30]

As for the pilots who participated in the assassination attempt, eleven were condemned to death after a brief trial, and thirty-five others were sentenced to jail terms ranging from three to twenty years, while 117 others were acquitted. Those with longer sentences were transferred to Tazmamart prison, a secret hell in the southeastern desert, where they were joined by the condemned of Skhirat. Treatment of these prisoners was hidden from public view until 1992, when, after eighteen years of solitary confinement, the living dead reemerged from their desert prison and began to tell their stories. But not until after the demise of Hassan II were their testimonies published for the first time in Morocco, and the full extent of the injustices committed against them revealed to a shocked and disbelieving Moroccan public.

The two failed coups, accompanied by pervasive corruption, repression, and political turmoil, shook the monarchy to its very foundations and exposed the fragility of its claim to legitimacy. Respect for the king had reached a nadir; for some, it appeared that Hassan's days were numbered, while for others, his two hair's-breadth escapes were a sign of his indelible charisma. The advanced degree of social and political decay demonstrated by the two attempts was profoundly disturbing. Stripped of his closest advisers, shattered by public revelations of his personal failures, Hassan II entered a period of deep self-reflection during which he reexamined the underpinnings of his rule. Characteristically, this period of introspection was followed by one of decisive action. He resumed a dialogue with the opposition parties in order to widen his base of support, and purged the army of doubtful elements. He personally assumed the position of Minister of Defense and reorganized the structure of the FAR, multiplying its operational units to prevent any concentrations of coercive force.[31] And most important of all, he revitalized ties with the conservative Islamic establishment, in an effort to use it as a counterweight to the secularized military higher-ups and the political parties that had failed him. This strategy led the

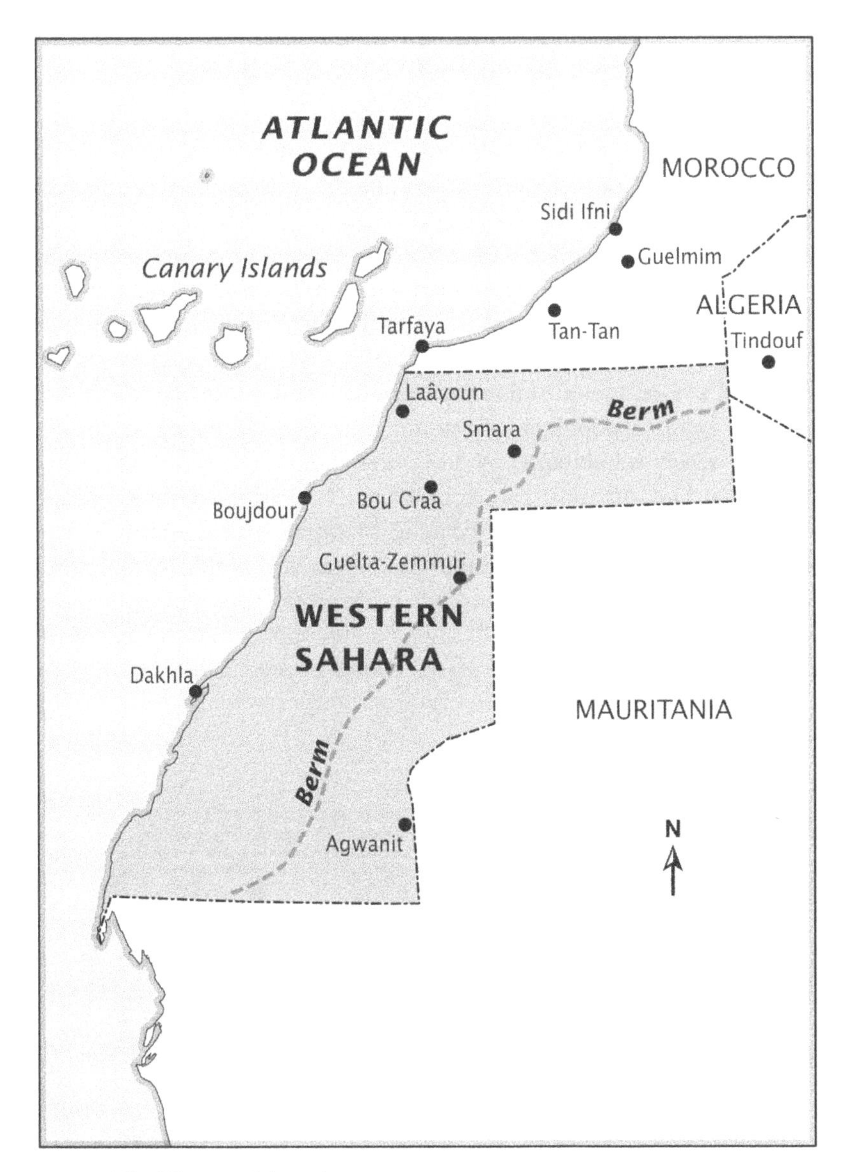

MAP 3. The Western Sahara in 1979

monarch down a new path that would ultimately strengthen the position of the religious element both within and outside the government. At the same time, he turned outward in search of new avenues through which he might rebuild a national consensus, using the "cause" of the Western Sahara as a convenient launching pad to rehabilitate his reputation.

THE WAR IN THE WESTERN SAHARA AND THE "SACRED UNION"

Seizing on the issue of Morocco's "lost" Saharan territories, the king made their recovery a point of national honor and the centerpiece of his domestic politics in the years following the failed coups. Morocco's claim to the Western Sahara was rooted in historical memory harking back to the days of the nineteenth-century patriot Ma al-ʿAynayn; it was also a main component of the Istiqlal's vision of a "Greater Morocco" adopted by the monarchy at independence. During the colonial period, Spain occupied the vast territory of 266,000 square kilometers that included (according to a Spanish census of 1974) a population of about 74,000 that jumped to 330,000 Sahrawis when inhabitants of the surrounding territories (Morocco, Mauritania, and Algeria) were counted in.[32] When Mauritania became independent in 1961 with the backing of other African states, a large chunk of Morocco's imagined Saharan domain was permanently excised. But when Spain in 1971 announced its intention to withdraw from its Saharan possessions, Hassan II saw a new opportunity to revive the Saharan issue, and engaged in various tactics to press a Moroccan claim.

FIGURE 28. Women volunteers in the hundreds were mobilized to join in the Green March in November 1975. Brought by train to key rallying points, women figured prominently in government-staged demonstrations supporting Morocco's claim to the contested Saharan territories. (Bruno Barbey/Magnum Photos)

Rich deposits of phosphates had been discovered in the Western Sahara in 1962, offering an additional enticement. Moroccan ambitions, however, ran directly counter to the hopes of the Sahrawi people and their newly formed military arm, the Polisario Front (the Popular Front for the Liberation of Saguia el Hamra and Río de Oro), whose goal was national self-determination. Both Mauritania and Algeria made known their objection to Morocco's plans, but Hassan II was undeterred.[33]

In May 1975, with the Caudillo Francisco Franco on his deathbed, Spain promised to leave the Sahara "in the shortest time possible," prompting Hassan II to act unilaterally.[34] In great secrecy, he personally planned the "Green March," a massive wave of 350,000 Moroccan volunteers armed "only with their Qur'ans" and their red and green banners of Morocco and Islam. This human flood surged across the frontier on November 6, 1975, uprooting border signs to demonstrate their belief that the Western Sahara should be Moroccan.[35] Ordinary Moroccans rallied to the king's side, and a torrent of popular patriotism erased growing doubts about his competency to rule. Only the extreme left proclaimed its support for Sahrawi independence in a stunning act of defiance, thus deepening its own political isolation. All other organized groups, however, rode the wave of enthusiasm, allowing the king to announce the formation of a "sacred union" of political parties who believed that Moroccan ownership of the Western Sahara was a non-negotiable and natural right. In one brilliant stroke, Hassan II had cornered his political opponents, boosted the flagging spirits of the military, hastened a Spanish withdrawal, assumed a spot on the world stage, and garnered an attention, prestige, and a legitimacy he had not experienced in years. In the aftermath of the march, the UN granted administrative authority, but not sovereignty, to both Morocco and Mauritania over the Spanish Sahara, but the Mauritanians soon withdrew, leaving Morocco in *de facto* control.

The Polisario, however, remained firm in its commitment to total independence, backed by the promise of Algerian aid. On December 19, 1975, the Polisario declared war on Morocco, and Hassan II found himself embroiled in a desert conflict for the second time in his kingship. The confrontation quickly took on the profile of other Cold War clashes: the "revolutionary," anticolonial forces of Algeria and its Sahrawi clients on one side, and "reactionary" Morocco, backed by large shipments of military equipment from the United States, on the other. The war assumed even greater international éclat when the Polisario, warmly embraced by the Third World movement, launched a propaganda offensive against the

FIGURE 29. More than 350,000 volunteers backed King Hassan II's claim to the Western Sahara, crossing the border between Morocco and the former Spanish territory in the "Green March" of November 1975, armed only with their Qur'ans, the national flag, and the photo of the king. (Bruno Barbey/Magnum Photos)

monarchy. Other African states swiftly came to its side, favoring the cause of "Africa's last colony" over Morocco's irredentist claims. To many in the developing world, it was a struggle between the forces of an old-style, selfish, and land-hungry nationalism versus the will of an oppressed people yearning to be free.

Meanwhile, the war was going badly for the Moroccans. Rejecting methods of conventional warfare, the Sahrawis adopted guerrilla techniques that brought them surprising success. Bouncing over familiar terrain in their ubiquitous Land Rovers, they confounded their adversaries with their lightning mobility. Polisario forces entered Moroccan territory in January 1979 and seized the border town of Tan-Tan, capturing hundreds of Moroccan soldiers and carting them off to prison camps inside Algeria, where they were incarcerated for years. This phase of the war culminated in October 1979, with the bloody battle of Smara, where more than a thousand men on each side were killed. By the end of the decade, the balance sheet for Morocco was not especially favorable: crushing military setbacks, an inability to exploit the rich phosphates of the newly acquired territory because of the war, and diplomatic isolation. In 1978, U.S.

government specialists estimated that the Saharan war was costing Morocco about one million dollars a day.[36]

Stunned by the negative accounting, Morocco changed tactics and decided to fortify a reduced security zone instead of attempting to clear a limitless expanse of open desert. The method of building a series of "berms," or defensive walls along the Moroccan-Algerian border, gave the army greater control over the battlefield, tipping the balance in Morocco's favor. Eventually, the Moroccans were able to gain control over most of the territory, allowing King Hassan to negotiate a UN-backed cease-fire in 1989 intended to be followed by a referendum according to which the Sahrawis would choose between integration with Morocco or independence. But an end to the problem was not yet in sight. Hassan's concerns regarding the terms of a referendum, on the one side, and the Polisario's adamant refusal to back down on its demand for unconditional and full independence, on the other, turned the Saharan situation into a never-ending stalemate. Moreover, more than one hundred thousand Sahrawis who had fled the Moroccan invasion in 1976 still languished in camps inside the Algerian border, creating a permanent refugee population under the care of international humanitarian organizations.[37]

FIGURE 30. Crown Prince Sidi Muhammad, the future Muhammad VI, was trained for the duties of kingship from a very young age. Here he is seen at a rally in the desert, preparing to address volunteers assembled to join the Green March, November 1975. (Abbas/Magnum Photos).

Nevertheless, the political gains of the Saharan affair for the regime were considerable. By creating an atmosphere of national emergency over the Sahara, the king was able to build a consensus across the political spectrum that reified the monarchy as the pre-eminent pole of Moroccan national unity. Yet the Saharan issue was a double-edged sword, for in associating possession of these remote territories so closely with the matter of royal legitimacy, Hassan II raised the stakes for the future. After more than three decades of war in which the army has taken many losses, failure on the part of the makhzan to accept anything short of full integration of the territory into Morocco would be unacceptable, for it would raise the specter of an "amputated" kingdom and a weakened throne. Hassan II bequeathed to his son and successor Muhammad VI an open and troublesome dossier – "a war he could not win, but could not afford to lose."[38]

HASSAN THE UNIFIER

The Saharan issue also presented challenges on the domestic front. On the global scale, the war had brought Hassan II closer to the West, including the United States, as well as to conservative Arab states that supplied him with money and arms. He used this moment to push for the "Moroccanization" of the economy, by transferring to political loyalists and high-ranking military officers state-held assets, agricultural lands, and enterprises that were more than 50 percent foreign owned. The operation encompassed thousands of enterprises and changed overnight the proportion of Moroccan-owned industrial enterprises from 18 to 55 percent. Most of this wealth was now concentrated in the hands of thirty-six major families who controlled two-thirds of the moroccanized economy; suddenly, Morocco became a country with a sizeable class of multimillionaires. Moreover, in the period 1973–1977, the country experienced another economic boom, with an annual growth rate of 7.3 percent per year, a new record, financed primarily by borrowing from abroad. These economic measures, coupled with the Saharan triumph, collectively revived the king's fortunes and gave him the opportunity to declare himself as "Hassan the Unifier," the leader who single-handedly brought the nation together. Moreover, the necessity of integrating the new southern territories into the Moroccan economy required the building of expensive infrastructure where none had previously existed, as well as the provision of services to a neglected Sahrawi population. On the average, the Moroccan government spent six times more on the Sahrawis in the period 1977–1980 than on the rest of the Moroccan people.[39]

This shift in priorities was not appreciated by most of the population, for it did little to help solve endemic problems of poverty and political nonparticipation. The "national pact" observed during the Saharan conflict was broken in 1978, when 130,000 teachers went out on strike to protest working conditions, followed by phosphate miners, transport workers, industrial workers, and even the ground crew of Royal Air Maroc. Workers formed a new national union, the CDT (Democratic Confederation of Workers) that broke with the UMT and its parent organization, the Istiqlal, for its "reprehensible collaboration with management and reactionism."[40] Tensions within the working class grew incrementally when a severe drought at the beginning of the 1980s required large-scale imports of wheat, elevating the price of bread and couscous, the daily fare of the average Moroccan, which had been regularly subsidized for years. Under pressure from the IMF, the government was forced to adopt an austerity program that removed subsidies, raising the price of basic foodstuffs about 30 percent. In response, the CDT and its allied party, the USFP (Socialist Union of Popular Forces), a party that evolved out of the UNFP in 1975, organized a general strike in Casablanca on June 20, 1981; this strike soon degenerated into a popular uprising. Strike action was a new phenomenon in Morocco, according to its organizers, because it brought together the unemployed, industrial workers, public servants, students, and self-employed shopkeepers, a broad cross-section of the working and lower middle classes who were fed up with the conditions of daily life. The crowd set fire to cars and looted the shops. The police lost control of the situation when rioters advanced toward them throwing rocks and crying "Kill us! Kill us."[41]

Hassan II had to call out the army to restore calm, but the signals coming from the mob were clear; namely, the hunger for change was no longer confined to rebellious high school youth as it was in 1965, but had infected the new urban middle classes as well. As one observer remarked: "The country had undergone a profound change in its demography, in the composition of its social classes, and in the mentality of its citizens."[42] The state could no longer solve social problems by crushing them with brutal force alone. The response of the king was to not repeat his error of the 1960s when he put absolute coercive power into the hands of one man. Instead, he separated military, gendarmerie, and Ministry of the Interior functions into separate dossiers and used them in tandem to quell the revolt. He assigned the Interior portfolio to Driss Basri, a French-trained lawyer who did not shrink from using strong-arm tactics to end the 1981 riots. Basri's efficiency won him a place at the king's side as the chief planner of the campaign of repression carried out throughout the 1980s and 1990s. A shrewd operator within the labyrinth of the makhzan, Basri presented himself as a loyal servant of the king, saying once that he had filled his head with secrets, locked them in, and had given the key to Hassan II. His ministry was an abode of power with walls thickened by corruption, and his somber figure overshadowed the last two decades of Hassan's reign until he was removed by Muhammad VI in 1999, to a vast public sigh of relief.

More "bread riots" occurred during the 1980s, as the government sought to manage its economic troubles through debt restructuring under the watchful eye of the World Bank. Slowly, after years of stagnation, the makhzan began to work its way out of the economic morass, but not without making difficult choices that came down especially hard on an increasingly militant urban underclass. Fiscal matters took precedence over social ones, with salary freezes for government employees and the elimination of food subsidies for the masses. Every time popular outbursts acted as a safety valve for discontent, the authorities struck back hard. Riots in Nador in the Rif in January 1984 turned into a bloodbath in which dozens were killed and supposedly secretly buried at night by the police. On each occasion, the government forced its way to a solution by cowing the public with a sense of *hayba* (fear), which became the elemental tie between the king and his people.[43]

Wallowing in heavy debts, operating according to tactics of extreme repression, the regime was on autopilot, playing the political game according to familiar rules of reward and punishment, cooptation and isolation, tension and stalemate, that had become its habitual *modus operandi*. The exterior face of political life manifested an eerie calm that hardly betrayed the ferment taking place beneath the surface. But there was indeed an important groundswell underway, much of it beyond the eyes and ears of the makhzan, that was about to burst into the public arena. The awakening of civil society in the 1980s, completely outside the paralytic embrace of either the government or the political parties, was the novel factor. As Morocco turned the corner toward the last decade of the century, Hassan the Unifier found himself confronted by a new combination of social forces, far less easily manipulated than the old, that demanded a change in strategy and outlook. The era of liberalization was at hand, and Hassan II was impelled to respond.

7

The Second Age of Hassan II

The Velvet Glove (1975–1999)

Following the triumph of the Green March and the consolidation of the "sacred union," Hassan II came to the conclusion that allegiance to the state could coexist with moderate expressions of opposition. Public opinion took the lead in showing him that the iron fist was no longer the most efficient instrument of rule, and that allowing criticism and dissent might even be healthy for the regime. The rise of an Islamist movement and other signs of social ferment helped to speed the progressive emergence of a civil society occupying the open space between the individual and the state, as human rights and civic associations, feminist and professional organizations, Berberist groups, and other special interests proliferated in the public sphere. The question was, how to allow this effervescence to go forward without causing an explosion.[1]

In a related development, the parties of the left, excluded from power for more than a generation, gained new life and rejoined the political process, with both the USFP (a radical splinter group of the UNFP formally declared in 1975) and the PPS (the Party of Progress and Socialism, the former Communist Party reborn under yet another new name) reentering the political arena. They were joined by older parties of the center and the right, complicating even further the intricate mosaic of Moroccan party politics. The 1984 elections, with its multiparty participation, confirmed the necessity for government by coalition, an arrangement that allowed the king to continue in his role as grand master of the political game, variously balancing, co-opting, distancing, and integrating the pieces on the chessboard, depending on the circumstances.

THE RISE OF MODERN POLITICAL ISLAM

A critical development of the 1980s was the reemergence of Islam as a salient factor in politics. The admixture of religion and politics in Morocco has roots deep in the past and the interweaving of the two is an ongoing theme in Moroccan history, especially given the duality of the king's claim to legitimacy: a political function, based on his control of a monopoly of coercive power, and a religious function, due to his prophetic lineage and his leadership of the community of the faithful. The fusion of the religious and the political in his personhood is symbolized by the motto of the nation: "God, Nation, and King." (*Allah, watan, malik*). As political scientist Malika Zeghal notes, "this fusion ... is a historically constructed political fiction that might become contested, albeit one that has great mobilizing and legitimizing power." The monarch, despite all of his galvanizing potential, has never held absolute control over the definition of Islam, leaving an open space for other contenders.[2] In the precolonial period, we noted the political instability generated when the sufi shaykh Muhammad al-Kattani contested the legitimacy of Sultan 'Abd al-Hafiz as an example of the kind of dissent that religious personalities could muster against an all-powerful makhzan. Religiously motivated interventions in politics were common in the early twentieth century as well: 'Allal al-Fasi's vision of the postcolonial Moroccan state included an important place for the moral authority of Islam, to be exercised by an educated, modernized, and essentially apolitical ulama.[3]

In the era of Hassan II, the Islamist option as a political force first showed itself in the universities in the late 1960s, mainly as a counterbalance to groups advocating ideologies of the left. In 1969, 'Abd al-Karim Mouti' founded the al-Shabiba al-Islamiyya (Islamic Youth) organization. Mouti' was a former UNFP member who veered sharply in the opposite direction and created a rabidly antileftist movement inspired by the thinking of Sayyid Qutb, intellectual light of the Muslim Brotherhood in Egypt in the 1950s. Between the years 1972 and 1975, the Shabiba occupied the space in the universities vacated by the UNEM when it was repressed by the regime. The Shabiba had a clandestine, paramilitary wing whose penchant for violence hastened its demise when it was involved in the assassination of the popular labor leader Omar Benjelloun in 1975. After this event, Mouti' had to flee Morocco, but he left behind elements of a radical Islamist organization that were later enfolded into other groups.

Closely related with the growing Islamist challenge were the questions of Arabization in the schools and religious education. The ideology of the

Istiqlal supported the teaching of Arabic as far back as the free school movement of the 1920s. After independence, the aim of the party was complete Arabization, but the chaos within the educational system in the 1960s slowed the changeover from French to Arabic. In the late 1970s, Islamic education and Arabic language became required subjects in the public schools. Hassan II, who was completely bilingual, encouraged this development, in the hope that teaching Islamic subjects would counterbalance the rise in leftist agitation. At the same time, in 1973 departments of Islamic studies were created at the universities, often replacing departments of philosophy, allowing for an influx of Islamic-leaning students that eventually led to their takeover of the UNEM. By 1992, Arabization of the secondary school curriculum was complete and the humanities faculties were well on their way to being completely Arabicized. The introduction of compulsory Islamic education benefited pro-Islamist activists, who monopolized the training of teachers and the writing of school curricula. Following these changes, the universities became a vortex of Islamist student activism, with frequent and often bloody clashes between secular students and their Islamist opponents.[4]

By the 1990s, new Islamic organizations had arisen from the embers of the Shabiba. Foremost among them was a group headed by the charismatic Abdessalam Yassine, a former high school teacher who adopted the persona of a sufi mystic and acquired a large and devoted personal following. Shaykh Yassine took advantage of Morocco's multiple disruptions of the early seventies – political repression, economic woes, a lack of jobs, and social malaise – to garner a following and boldly attack the king personally. In a public letter sent to Hassan II in 1974 entitled "Islam or the Deluge," Yassine called on the monarch to repent, mend his ways, and "return to God." The shaykh's self-styled role as "holy chastiser" was based on his adoption of the timeworn trope of the simple wise man admonishing the wayward prince. But his letter went beyond that, for it was not simply a lesson in proper behavior; rather, it was a specific indictment of the king that catalogued his political errors and questioned his religious sincerity, with the implied warning that divine punishment was at hand. Naturally, the king was not receptive to the schoolteacher's reproach, and Yassine's impetuousness earned him three years in a mental hospital. His major "crime" was the explicitly subversive assertion that the monarch was not the sole source of religious legitimacy in the state, and even a humble shaykh could take a stand and criticize his actions.[5]

By censuring Hassan II in this publicly ostentatious manner, Yassine was drawing a clear connection between himself and the figure of

Muhammad b ʿAbd al-Kabir al-Kattani, the sufi shaykh who had harshly criticized Sultan ʿAbd al-Hafiz for his failure to halt European incursions in the first decade of the twentieth century. At that time of national crisis, al-Kattani had also adopted a stance of religious authority and moral rectitude, coupled with public indignation toward the mistakes of the sultan. However, al-Kattani's cruel fate was withheld from Yassine, who reemerged from his incarceration in sound health, only to be immediately placed under house arrest. However, his confinement did not prevent him from building his movement, al-ʿAdl wa-l-Ihsan (Justice and Good Deeds, founded in 1987), and from writing tracts infused with messianic excitement and the message that history was on his side. Concurrently, the influence of his ideas was felt in the public sphere through street demonstrations, the pronouncements of his acolyte-daughter Nadia, and later, through the internet and other forms of new media.

Alarmed by the seemingly mass appeal of Yassine, the monarchy outlawed his organization in 1990, but interest in Islamist organizations whose discourse was infused with religious fervor did not recede. At the same time, some Islamic militants realized that in order to gain a foothold in the system, their tactics had to change. Morocco's support for the United States in the Gulf War of 1991–1992 against Iraq's Saddam Hussein was an opportunity and a moment of inspiration. Public opposition to Morocco's pro-Western stance provoked angry street demonstrations in Fez, Casablanca, Tangier and Kénitra, calling attention to the fact that large segments of the population were more drawn to Islamic solidarity than they were to a policy that favored the West.[6] Wishing to control this sentiment without resorting to violence, the king adopted a new strategy in the 1990s that would integrate moderate Islamist parties into the political sphere, so long as they did not call into question the legitimacy of the monarchy.[7] Soon a range of parties emerged out of the remnants of already existing Islamic groups, ready to follow the rules of the game as outlined by Hassan II.

Foremost among them was the PJD, the Justice and Development Party, a loose coalition of groups that formed a political party in 1998. Before being allowed to join the political field, its organizers had to agree to a list of rules: "recognition of the concept of Commander of the Faithful, renunciation of violence, recognition of the Maliki religious school, and the legitimacy of Moroccan territorial integrity"; in sum, the vital components of the national creed, as defined by Hassan II.[8] Made up of elements from across the Islamist spectrum, the PJD was headed by Abdelilah Benkirane, an engineer who dressed in Western style and spoke both

French and Arabic. Whereas relations between the king and shaykh Yassine had been based on bitter antagonism, the connection between the monarchy and the PJD was based on a cautious civility, creating a situation unprecedented in Moroccan politics. The PJD's modest showing in the 1997 elections certified its need for "respectability," while reassuring liberal and secular-leaning Moroccans that there really was no reason for alarm, for the PJD was only one among multiple contenders. It seemed that the king had cleverly managed to steer between the dangerous extremes of banning the Islamists from political life, on the one hand, and allowing them free rein, on the other. Unlike neighboring Algeria, where in 1991 the state came undone over the question of Islamism, the Moroccan monarchy adopted a different and wiser course, neutralizing the religious factor and gradually introducing it into institutionalized political space.[9]

THE POLITICIZATION OF WOMEN'S ISSUES

The political opening of the 1980s also gave birth to a movement aimed at improving women's status and enhancing their legal rights. As the political parties emerged from the shadows and claimed their reward for having participated in the "sacred union" associated with the Western Sahara war, women party activists were assigned the task of campaigning to attract female votes in the hotly contested legislative elections that followed. Soon the number of women active in politics led to an expansion of women's energies into areas of feminist concern. There were few prior models to guide these women, for the history of the women's movement in Morocco is barely written, as are the historic, but often muted, roles women played in public life.[10]

During the Protectorate period, sociologist Jacques Berque remarked on "the outstanding economic dignity of the women" in the Berber villages of the High Atlas (not noticing, perhaps, that they were doing the lion's share of the backbreaking work); in urban settings, modernizing men understood the value of educating girls. By the 1930s, a few young women began to engage publicly in political discussions and embryonic women's groups were springing up under the aegis of the nationalist movement, mainly for the purpose of propagating its ideology. Because of widespread female illiteracy, politically aware women were few and far between, they were almost always closely allied with powerful men, and they were rarely given decision-making authority. Women played an active role in the War of Liberation in a variety of tasks, evading the police, carrying weapons, teaching literacy classes, and raising the consciousnesses of other women, but never in the forefront of leadership.[11]

The cautious integration of women into public life took a leap forward at mid-century, as economic factors began to shape behavior. Modernization theory visualized a positivist role for the Moroccan woman as "educator" of the modern family, as partner to a monogamous husband (polygamy was in fact declining), and as participant in the work force. A 1952 census estimated that one in eight women worked outside the home for wages as domestics, factory workers, or in the handicrafts industry, a marked increase over the prewar period.[12] The dark side of women's work was exposed by a 1951 study into the "reserved" quarter of Bousbir in Casablanca by two French researchers, influenced by Simone de Beauvoir's groundbreaking pro-feminist book, *The Second Sex* (1949). In a precise and richly documented report, they concluded that three to six thousand women were employed as prostitutes in Bousbir, and that perhaps thirty thousand women in Casablanca earned income through the sex trade.[13] Buried in the turmoil that preceded independence, this study presents data on the historical exploitation of poor women in one of its most extreme forms.

In contrast, the situation of elite and middle-class women had changed dramatically. The arrival of U.S. soldiers during World War II, the introduction of American and French films, the invasion of Egyptian cinema in the early 1950s, the proliferation of newspaper advertising, women's magazines, radio and TV, had changed women's self-perception and their relations with men by commodifying femininity and introducing new styles in dress and comportment. Fatima Mernissi, in her absorbing personal memoir, *Dreams of Trespass*, catalogues her mother's campaign to rid herself of her veil by shrinking it out of existence. But these external changes did not necessarily signal a move toward women's equality. Women were still unorganized, atomized, and legally embedded within the family-based patriarchal system. The severe repression of the political parties of the left after 1965 was especially dampening for the growth of a women's movement, since most female organizations were affiliated with the progressive political parties that fell afoul of the makhzan. However, young women continued to be active through student organizations such as the UNEM, where feminist leader Aïcha Belarbi, Morocco's ambassador to the European Commission in 2000, received her first political education.[14]

The most significant shift came in the period 1975–1989, as women became more active within the resuscitating political parties of the left.

Rather than launching a fruitless frontal assault on the male-dominated political system, women adopted more subtle and inventive methods. One approach was "secular," using party and public platforms to argue that the subordination of women was not a class issue, but rather a gender one, infringing on universally ordained standards of human rights. Another approach, popular among religious women, was to advocate for change on the basis of *ijtihad*, the doctrine of reform within the framework of Islamic law. Mapping yet another tactic, the ADFM (Democratic Association of Moroccan Women), once affiliated with the PPS, wrenched itself free from the grip of its parent organization and became a separate entity, pursuing its own course of action independent of party politics. Other groups did the same on both the right and left of the political spectrum. These various approaches were effective in widening the arena in which women's issues were debated in the face of stiff resistance from the political class as a whole.[15]

After 1989, in step with developments on the world scene that encouraged feminist activism on a global scale, a quiet revolution began to take hold in Moroccan women's personal lives. Increased education, opportunities for employment, the growth of urbanization, the rise in the age of marriage, a dramatic drop in fertility, the growth of the nuclear family, the emergence of the notion of "individual" identity as opposed to a family-oriented, male-controlled one, were factors that improved the position of women from all walks of life and all degrees of religious conviction. By 1995, twenty-two women's associations had registered with the Ministry of Social Affairs, and five others were in the early stages of formation, almost all located in major urban centers.[16]

Despite these changes, the state continued to be ambivalent in its attitude toward women's rights. While the legal system of Morocco was secularized overall, as of 1999, women remained subject to an unreformed *Mudawwana*, the religiously inspired and conservative Family Code that was fast becoming the target of efforts to substantially improve women's legal status.[17] Meanwhile, other forces were working in their favor, especially on the international level. Moroccan participation in the UN-sponsored World Conferences on Women in 1975, 1980, 1985, and 1995 sharpened organizing tactics and reinforced the regime's eagerness to present a progressive face to the world-at-large on women's issues. In his last days, in a striking turnaround, King Hassan II said that the problems raised by women's groups were fair, that their demands were relevant, and that they represented "a bulwark" against the Islamist "danger."[18]

At the close of the century, reform of the Family Code was on the table and four ministerial portfolios were in the hands of women. In retrospect, it is clear that women stood at the juncture of a greater effort to open up the political terrain to new actors, subjects, and institutions by widening the circle of debate to interest groups that formerly stood outside. By interweaving the question of women's rights with the larger question of human rights, women's groups also helped to reinvigorate and re-center political life by starting a conversation about the "forgotten souls" of Moroccan society, such as abused and abandoned children, battered wives, drug users, underage maids, prostitutes, unmarried mothers; in other words, the exploited, the marginalized, and the rejected who traditionally were silenced. In sum, the women's movement not only advanced the cause of women; it also had the electric effect of opening up the political field to new forms of debate associated with a more inclusive political culture.

BERBER CULTURAL REVIVAL

The development of the campaign for Berber cultural rights in Morocco followed closely in the footsteps of the women's movement as it sought to achieve recognition. It, too, grew from an informal collectivity of intellectuals with modest goals seeking to preserve aspects of a threatened Berber identity in the 1970s, to a nationwide experiment in cultural rehabilitation by the year 2000. The constituency for Berber activism in Morocco is potentially huge; 40 to 45 percent of the population are Berber speakers, and almost every Moroccan, as King Hassan II once famously said, has Berber "cells." Since the 1980s, pro-Berber organizations have gathered momentum by promoting their cause within the context of the controlled opening taking place across the political spectrum. Moreover, Berber appeals to all Moroccans to accept cultural diversity resonated with other marginalized groups seeking recognition, such as the tiny (about two thousand souls) but firmly entrenched Jewish community. The voice of the Amazigh (Berber) movement became incrementally louder during this period, adding its claims to the long list of unresolved societal problems demanding the state's attention.

It was not always that way. In the early years of independence, still reverberating with the wickedness of France's "divide and rule" policies under the Protectorate, Moroccans – both those who identified as Berbers and those who did not – rejected the notion that there was any value in preserving Berber difference. Berbers entered the highest levels of state service as nationalists, confidants of the king, generals, and politicians, but not as Berbers *per se*. Moreover, the monarchy, in its own inimitable way, managed to co-opt the Berber "personality" and make it part of the constellation of attributes of the royal family, diluting it, so to speak, into impuissance. As a result, ordinary Berbers were submerged in a larger, Arabo-Islamic identity reified by nationalist rhetoric and in particular by ʿAllal al-Fasi and the Istiqlal, who insisted on the "Moroccanness" of all citizens. As Berbers moved from rural areas to cities, losing their tribal attachments in the process, they also seemed to leave behind their "Berber" selves, no longer speaking their language or wearing their distinctive dress. Young men who went to school in the urban setting quickly replaced Berber with Arabic, leaving the first language behind as a "jargon" of the home, to be used when speaking to wives and mothers. This transformation was inadvertently reinforced by a kind of ethnographic scholarship that read ethnicity more as a correlative of kinship structure, and less as an attitude of mind.[19]

Startled by the rapid deterioration in the use of Berber language, in the 1980s Moroccan intellectuals of Berber background began to agitate actively to preserve their heritage. At a talk on Berber linguistics given at the Faculty of Letters in Rabat in the late 1980s by Ahmad Boukous (today director of IRCAM, the Royal Institute for Amazigh Culture), the overflow audience filled the auditorium and spilled into the central courtyard, eager to catch a few words on a topic long suppressed. The newfound enthusiasm for Berber studies surprised everyone, academics as well as people outside the academy, eliciting responses ranging from lively enthusiasm to dire warnings of ethnic fragmentation. The problems of reviving a language that was not written and had no agreed-upon alphabet, and whose literature was mostly oral, were formidable. While the focus was mainly on the revival and preservation of Tamazight (the collective name for a group of closely related Berber dialects), other topics were not ignored; Berber visionaries spoke of Tamazgha, or Amazighland, extending from the Siwa oasis in Egypt, across the Maghrib to the Canary Islands, and as far south as Niger and Mali, all places where Berber speakers are found.[20]

In 1991, a group of Berber cultural organizations issued the "Charter of Agadir" that denounced "the systematic marginalization of Amazigh language and culture," and called for making Tamazight an official language of Morocco. Their goal was to develop a curriculum for teaching the language and to press for its introduction into the schools and the mass media. However, pushing for Berber rights was still considered by some a subversive activity, engendering strong opposition, even among Berber intellectuals. On May 1, 1994, seven members of the Tilelli (Freedom) Cultural Association, all teachers, were arrested in the town of Guelmim when they unfurled banners in favor of Berber language rights. Their harsh treatment in detention and their trial and conviction provoked an avalanche of protest among the general public that did more for the cause of Berber rights than all previous events.

Always the astute politician, King Hassan II sensed the direction in which popular opinion was moving and jumped on the Berber bandwagon. During his Throne Day speech on August 20, 1994, broadcast on Moroccan television, he announced that Berber dialects "were a component of our authentic history"; in so doing, he formally brought the notion of cultural and linguistic pluralism squarely under the national tent.[21] The makhzan speedily announced plans to begin television news programs in Berber, and in a further development, the king issued a royal decree in 1995 calling for the teaching of Berber in the public schools, signaling the seriousness of his intention to reintroduce Tamazight into the nation's linguistic family. The plan aroused considerable heat among Islamists, who considered it a threat to the supremacy of Arabic and Arabic language studies, as well as a manifestation of Western ideas of cultural "diversity" aimed specifically at "weakening Islam."[22]

But the program for strengthening Amazigh cultural rights was already inserted into the royal portfolio, and the carping from the sidelines was simply ignored. In neighboring Algeria, authorities viewed the Berber factor as unpredictably dangerous and tried to contain it, often infringing on basic human rights; in Morocco, on the other hand, the state co-opted the movement on its own terms, and the king, symbol of the nation, was presented as the preeminent defender of Berber rights.[23] Unlike Algeria, the makhzan did not prevent Moroccans from attending the First World Amazigh Congress, held in August 1997 in the Canary Islands, which gave the movement a broad transnational cast. Instead, it tried to reach a détente with Berberism and use it to reinforce its own program of controlled liberalization. Even though many Berber activists resented the self-serving logic behind the king's tactics and protested against what they called "cooptation" by the makhzan, leaders of the movement argued that fully achieving their goals meant reaching a cultural and political understanding with the state. That the Amazigh factor has become a permanent feature of the Moroccan reality is no longer in doubt; the question moving forward was how and to what extent would its ambitious program be realized.

NEW VOICES: THE PRESS, LITERATURE, AND THE CINEMA

Since the early 1930s, a vibrant and engaged press has animated political life in Morocco. *Maghreb*, the political journal published by the founders of the Istiqlal in 1932, set the standard with its well-written articles on politics, society, and the economy. The postindependence regime prided itself from the early years of statehood on its policy of "freedom of the press"; in comparison with its Maghribi neighbors, Morocco's newspapers were generally unfettered. The Istiqlal founded the first party newspaper, *al-ʿAlam* in Arabic, in 1946, and its French counterpart *L'Opinion* appeared in 1965; meanwhile, almost every other emerging party, group, and association produced its own broadsheet. Since 1971, the official point of view has been represented by the daily *Le Matin du Sahara*, but alongside it are a plethora of other newspapers representing various factions, creating a concert that is not always euphonious, but is rarely dull. Still, the number of readers of newspapers, like the book-reading public, remains small; average daily sales of newspapers in 2000 in a population of thirty million was an unimpressive four hundred thousand copies. As if to compensate, in the 1990s the growth of weekly magazines (*hebdomadaires*) covering politics, the economy, culture, and society was explosive.

The impact of this journalistic cornucopia on the public mind has been incalculable, especially as literacy has increased and political life has "opened up." Nevertheless, egregious examples of censorship still occurred; newspapers were shut down, editors censored and exiled, and red lines of a dubious rationality were capriciously drawn. The most daring sector of this journalistic free-for-all, and the one most closely watched, was that of the so-called economic journals. *Le Journal*, an initiative of Ali Amar and the youthful Abubakr Jamaï, launched in 1997 during the period of political transition to greater freedom known as the *Alternance* (see later in this chapter) was most representative of this genre. In the late 1990s, *Le Journal* became the news magazine of choice for educated Moroccans, exposing corruption, questioning authority, disinterring the past and pinpointing inherited half-truths, providing the substance of countless dinner table conversations and academic postmortems. The provocative nature of this revue became too much for certain members of the political elite to bear, and after 2001, its editors were subjected to repeated harassment.[24]

Similar trends delineate changes in literary life and the world of publishing. Up until the 1970s, publication of books in both French and Arabic was strictly limited, because of the high rate of illiteracy, the small size of a reading public, and the price of books relative to other basic goods. Most books were imported from France or the Middle East, crowding out local production. As university education spread and Arabization took hold, demand leaped upward. The number of publishing houses increased, and the list of available titles reached into the hundreds. By the 1990s, itinerant vendors blanketed the sidewalks of Rabat's main boulevard with books, newspapers, and magazines, their wares perused by students, office workers, *flaneurs*, and curious foreign tourists. The array of topics was striking: history, literature, social criticism, and political essays coexisted alongside popular subjects such as cooking, fashion, and lifestyle magazines in both French and Arabic.

Moroccans have shown increasing experimentation in their literary tastes, particularly in the domain of fiction. Pioneers of the Moroccan novel, like Driss Chraïbi (*Le Passé Simple*, 1954) are lauded for breaking with colonial molds and creating a new "national" literature. In Arabic fiction, Abdelkarim Ghallab was a pioneer with his *Dafanna al-Madi* (*The Buried Past*, 1966), a story about the Moroccan resistance before independence. According to social critic Abdou Filali-Ansary, the generation of Chraïbi and Ghallab focused on "the ways and means by which underdevelopment and historical retardation might be overcome ... through voluntary, rational, and coordinated efforts," and their main preoccupation was with the question of how intellectuals might contribute to nation-building.[25] Many writers were Marxists concerned with the uplifting of the collectivity; their work was often informed by a stark and sometimes brutal social realism, as well as a yearning for greater personal freedom.

A rash of leftist literary journals played their part in establishing the parameters of an evolving public taste. *Souffles*, founded by leftist intellectual Abdellatif Laâbi in 1966, became a meeting place for the most inspired writers, both Moroccan and foreign. The writings of major prophets to the generation of the sixties such as Foucault, Kristeva, and Derrida appeared in its pages in translation, as Laâbi and his compatriots wrestled with the question of the writers' moral responsibility to society. Throughout the worst of the "years of lead," Laâbi continued to publish experimental writing and especially the works of members of Ila al-Amam, such as Serfaty, Mohamed Bedouin, Abdelfattah Fakihani and Mohamed Talbi, skirting the frontiers of the forbidden. *Souffles* finally folded in 1972, following the arrest, torture and imprisonment of its editor. The organ of the Moroccan Writers' Union, *Afaq*, founded in 1963, stayed within acceptable bounds and fared somewhat better, while *Lamalif*, a monthly founded by Zakya Daoud in 1963 that served as a roundtable for the most important thinkers and social scientists of the 1960s and 1970s, survived for over two decades, until it was banned in 1988.[26]

By the end of the 1990s, Moroccan literary production had come into its own, with dozens of novels and books of nonfiction published each year in French and Arabic. The variety of genres was impressive: police procedurals, biographies, historical fiction, feminist literature, and a literature of social protest exposing evils such as pedophilia, the use and abuse of child labor, incest, and other subjects previously hidden from public view. Most significant was the wave of prison literature that began to appear in the 1990s, in the form of testimonials and fictionalized accounts revealing the repressed memories of the victims of the "years of lead" who were either "disappeared" or imprisoned without trial. This outburst represented a landmark moment for Moroccan literature as a whole, locating it within a global dialogue about intellectual freedom and human rights that crossed borders and blurred older categories of racial, linguistic, and national difference.

The medium of cinema has also recorded many of the changes taking place over the past half-century in Moroccan social and cultural life. The history of moviemaking in Morocco is a long one, reaching back to precolonial times, when Moroccans were involved simply as objects in the camera's eye. The Lumière brothers shot footage in Morocco in 1896 that was shown at the palace in Fez to an attentive Sultan ʿAbd al-ʿAziz, himself an ardent cinéaste. After 1912, Protectorate authorities encouraged a cinematic industry that produced films glorifying the colonial project. In the 1930s, as the official mood shifted away from celebrating conquest to promoting the economy, documentary films and newsreels began to appear, produced by the Centre Cinématopographique Marocain (CCM), founded in 1944. This colonial institution, like many others, continued after independence, forming the armature for a new generation of filmmakers who documented the "successes" of the young nation. Meanwhile, foreign filmmakers kept arriving, drawn by Morocco's rich urban and rural landscapes: Orson Welles's *Othello* (1949), Jacques Becker's *Ali Baba and the Forty Thieves* (1954), and Alfred Hitchcock's *The Man Who Knew Too Much* (1955), were all shot on location in Morocco. Famous American directors such as John Huston, Robert

Wise, Francis Ford Coppola, and Martin Scorsese were drawn to Morocco's visual exoticism, producing full-length films for an international public in the 1960s and 1970s.[27]

However, locally produced feature films were still a rarity. Until the 1980s, the Moroccan moviegoing public was treated to a steady if bland diet of spaghetti westerns and foreign-made action films of the "B" variety (Bruce Lee was a particular favorite) screened mainly in the big cities. The discovery that cinema could be used as a platform for expressing oppositional points of view broadened the audience for film as a forum for social commentary. Leftist literary journals such as *Souffles*, as well as the party newspapers, began to publish film criticism, inspiring Moroccan directors to strike out on their own. In an effort to catch up with this trend, a state-run "Support Fund" was established in the early 1980s that made it possible for Moroccan directors, using a combination of public and private funds, to mount full-length productions. State financing helped to produce films such as M. A. Tazi's *The Big Trip* (1981), a Moroccan road movie that introduced the themes of poverty and social malaise. Tazi's next major film, *Looking for a Husband for My Wife* (1993), the comic story of a Fez merchant who makes a mess of his married life, broke all records for attendance and showed that a Moroccan-made film appealing to middle-class audiences could become a box-office success.[28]

Films that captured the complexity of life in contemporary Morocco continued to dominate the field. Farida Benlyazid's *The Door to the Sky* (1988), the story of a migrant woman's return home from France, and Nabil Ayouch's *Ali Zaoua, Prince of the Streets* (2000), a deeply felt account of street children in Casablanca, are examples of a genre built on Moroccans' rapid and often disorienting immersion in modernity. Films depicting social issues, such as problems of life in the diaspora, the culture clash between generations, the confrontation of the religious versus the nonreligious, marked a definite turning away from postcolonial themes of nation-building. In the course of this transition, the attitude of the state was ambivalent. On the one hand, it supported and "tolerated" the treatment of oppositional and even subversive topics, exercising restraint in terms of censorship; on the other hand, astute film directors knew that a "red line" existed (at the discretion of the state) that could not be crossed. Moreover, the CCM was criticized for showing favoritism and biased judgment in its choice of which films to support. State-sponsored cultural activities are often subject to political pressure, and Morocco is no exception.[29]

OPENING THE DOOR TO THE SECRET GARDEN

The larger context for these important changes was a major shift in public acknowledgement of the centrality of the issue of human rights. While word of egregious and severe violations by the regime had been floating around since the 1970s, appeals to the authorities for a clarification were always met with a wall of silence. In those rare cases when a response was forthcoming, it was usually that Morocco was not in violation of international norms, that it held no political prisoners, and that the prison at Tazmamart was "a figment of the imagination," despite mounting evidence to the contrary.[30] By one account, the confessional avalanche began because of the efforts of Christine Daure, who later became the wife of Abraham Serfaty. A French school teacher who first came to Morocco in 1962, ten years later Daure sheltered two militants on the run, one of whom was Serfaty. After his trial and imprisonment in Kénitra in 1977, she began to agitate for better treatment for the prisoners held in the Kénitra jail. Meanwhile, the appearance in Paris in 1980 of letters describing the desperate conditions in the as yet unknown prison at Tazmamart increased concern about violations of human rights within the Moroccan penal system.[31]

In 1984, an Association for the Defense of Human Rights in Morocco (ASDHOM) was founded in Paris; its voice, amplified with Daure's help, was heeded in French political circles, reaching as high as Danièlle Mitterand, wife of the French President, opening the door to direct pressure on Hassan II at the very highest level. In 1986, Christine Daure returned to Morocco, married Serfaty while he was still in prison, and agitated for justice. In 1988, a group of intellectuals led by Omar Azziman, a professor of law, and Mahdi el-Mandjra, an influential voice from the leftist PPS, founded the Moroccan Organization of Human Rights (OMDH). Soon after, another group of liberals created the AMDH (Moroccan Association of Human Rights). Both groups had ties abroad, and Western governments – usually at the insistence of their own human rights organizations, and in the glare of articles published in the international press – began to pressure Morocco about its human rights record and the so-called secret garden holding an unknown number of detainees.

The escape in 1987 of the children of General Oufkir, innocent victims of Hassan's wrath, from their desert prison, and the publication in 1990 of Gilles Perrault's exposé of corruption within the tight circle of the king entitled *Notre ami le roi* (Paris, 1990), were turning points that forced the regime to examine its image in the eyes of the world. Using information from Daure-Serfaty and her associates within the human rights movement, Perrault's book created a near panic in the palace and severely strained Moroccan-French relations. A traveler arriving at Casablanca airport in those days watched helplessly as her luggage was turned topsy-turvy by a zealous customs official engaging in a fruitless search for forbidden materials. The concerted effort to achieve literary purity failed, however, as clandestine copies of the book slipped into Morocco in countless ways. Fraught with sensationalism and unsubstantiated accusations as well as some horrifying truths, the book finally tore the veil off the regime's façade of indifference.[32]

In response to these events, in 1990 the government formulated its own human rights agenda and created the Consultative Council for Human Rights (CCDH) to serve as the official vehicle of a new policy of amnesty and reconciliation, or as Abdallah Laroui put it, to start "its democratic apprenticeship." A Ministry of Human Rights was formed in 1993 and Omar Azziman was appointed at its head, and that same year, Morocco ratified the UN Convention Against Torture. Announcing that he was "turning the page on political prisoners," in September 1991 the king released inmates of detention centers, prisons, and desert tombs where some had been held in near-total isolation since the 1971 coup. On September 13, 1991, Abraham Serfaty, the symbol of a justice system gone awry, was freed from jail and exiled to France on a visa technicality. In October 1991, as the ghosts of Tazmamart emerged from their decades-long incarceration and began to tell their stories, a disbelieving Moroccan public emitted a collective gasp.[33]

An indelible sign that times had really changed was the Tabit Affair. In 1993, Mustapha Tabit, the mighty and seemingly untouchable police commissioner of Casablanca, was found guilty of raping hundreds of falsely detained women and then videotaping his misdeeds; later, it was revealed that he sold the tapes to an international pornography ring. Suspicions about his activities had been circulating for years, but when precise accusations resurfaced in 1993, a decision was made at the highest level not to bury the case but rather to use it as the starting point for a show trial and a purge of the police. Judgment was swift; Tabit was publicly tried and executed on August 9, 1993, and sixteen others who participated in the cover-up were given jail terms from two years to life imprisonment. Before the Tabit affair, the Moroccan press depicted the country as a "land without crime" and the police as an institution beyond reproach; but the unfolding events in this sordid affair, closely followed by the news media that published lurid photos and even more graphic descriptions of Tabit's crimes, demonstrated to the Moroccan public that even the police, long considered inviolate, were now not above the law.[34]

The Tabit affair was the opening salvo of a sweeping and overzealous "cleanup campaign" (*campagne d'assainissement*) commanded by Minister of the Interior Basri in 1995 that went to excess and completely backfired, giving the battle against corruption a bad name. Directed initially against drug dealers, *contrabandistes*, and tax evaders, in due course hundreds of innocent people were thrown into jail, viable businesses were forced into bankruptcy, people lost their jobs, and decent lives were ruined, according to newspaper and other personal accounts of the period. In fact, most of the victims were later amnestied, but without compensation for their losses. According to political observers Mohamed Tozy and Beatrice Hibou, the campaign was seriously misrepresented to the public. Rather than an effort to "remoralise" business practices as was reported in the press (for "corruption," they conclude, is an integral part of the system), it was a move to assert state control over emerging social categories that could become a future source of dissidence. In sum, the "cleanup" was "a modern *harka*" designed to "redefine the norm," discipline potential troublemakers, and "assert the primacy of the central power."[35]

In the public mind, the "cleanup campaign" was yet one more example of an arbitrary regime manipulating the judicial system for its own ends, without concern for the human toll. By the time of Hassan's death, it was clear that the discourse of human rights had entered the lexicon of every politically aware Moroccan. People were awakened to the disturbing fact that international norms of justice had somehow become diluted and even eliminated altogether within their own society. This realization was the source of deep anger and resentment. It was no longer possible to argue for special dispensations because of matters of state security, or to shift responsibility to the victims, or to insist that international standards of human rights were somehow contrary to Islamic cultural values; rather, it was a time of accounting, when the new King Muhammad VI had to face squarely the moral failings of his predecessor. Hassan II's offer of a modest indemnity to a small percentage of the survivors of his dungeons without any public hearings, while granting immunity to the perpetrators without extracting confessions, was the strongest indication of his unyielding state of mind. But this approach was highly unsatisfactory to the outraged victims, who in 1999 organized a public declaration calling for an formal apology, reparations, criminal procedures against the torturers, and an accounting of all those who had disappeared. As the century ended, the carapace of indifference that had so long covered up the issue of human rights had finally been removed.[36]

THE ROYAL ROAD TO REFORM

In the last decade of his rule until his death in July 1999, King Hassan II piloted a sharp turnaround in public policy that surprised his people and won him recognition on the international front. After decades of rigid authoritarian rule in which regime opponents received the harshest treatment, Morocco seemed to transform itself into a model among Arab states for promoting political reform. The atmosphere of change was complemented by a variety of factors that included the end of the Cold War, a resurgent global Islam, the outbreak of civil war in Algeria, the ongoing domestic economic crisis, and greater public access to information through the internet. Yielding to popular demand and international pressure, the king made known his determination to recast Morocco's image along more modern, open, and tolerant lines, while preserving its "specificity" and the tradition-based allure that nourished its uniqueness for generations.[37] The extent to which he succeeded in this quest, his calculated motives for pursuing it, the actual achievements of this "transition," and the impression it made on the Moroccan public, are the bench marks according to which the final phase of his rule must be judged.

Just as in Morocco's first age of reform in the nineteenth century, this new age of reform began with intrusions from the outside world that deeply affected the monarchy's attitude toward domestic politics. The word "democratization" has often been used in connection with these changes, and certainly greater transparency in politics was a characteristic of the period of transition, particularly in regard to elections. However, to assert that Morocco began to follow a "democratic" path along Western lines is a distortion of reality, for in fact the authoritarian nature of the monarchy did not disappear, nor did the king yield any of his exceptional powers. Rather, additional mechanisms were put in place that allowed for greater freedom of action from individuals and groups wishing to enter the public sphere. That is to say, the basic *modus operandi* of the regime did not change; it continued to govern by the old methods of "divide and rule," with occasional episodes of harsh treatment, much to the disappointment of its subjects/citizens. Yet it is also true that the opening up of a space to accommodate new social forces and modes of political activism offered a safety valve that was long overdue.

The decade began with the constitutional reform of 1993 that empowered parliament to challenge appointments and debate government proposals. It also inserted the concept of human rights into official discourse. The preamble to the new Constitution stated that "The Kingdom of Morocco reaffirms its attachment to human rights as they are universally recognized." This revision and the liberal sentiments it expressed gave new life to the opposition parties, who formed themselves into a political bloc (*Kutla*) as a prelude to reentering the political fray. The Kutla then began extended negotiations with the king regarding the terms allowing its participation in the government.

Meanwhile, between 1993 and 1997, a series of "governments of technocrats" signaled an effort to move away from an older model of rule by mandarins closely vetted by the ominous Basri, to a new mode of government based on competence and fresh thinking. These years also saw a determined campaign to get the economy under control through a rigorous austerity program. But these innovations did not mean that the coercive power of the makhzan was in any way diminished, or that the "sacred institution" of the monarchy was circumscribed. Understanding that, the parties of the left refused to enter into a coalition that maintained vestiges of the *ancien regime* (namely Basri), despite the king's invitation.[38]

Hassan II persisted in his reform plans by pushing for an amendment to the constitution that would change the electoral laws. Signed into law in 1996, the amendment created a bicameral legislature that allowed voters to elect all the members of a lower house (instead of only two-thirds), while an upper house, chosen indirectly by regional assemblies and professional organizations, enabled favorites of the king and parties that had not succeeded at the ballot box to participate in legislative rule. More important, however, was the unwritten understanding that the king would name a prime minister from the party having an electoral majority. The 1997 elections were marred by multiple accusations of fraud, yet Abderrahmane Youssoufi, seventy-four-year-old secretary of the USFP and a lifelong opponent of the regime, agreed to head a government of "Alternance," or opposition, at Hassan's request. At this stage, the king was already quite ill and facing his own mortality; it is assumed that his invitation to Youssoufi was motivated largely by a desire to assuage his political opponents and assure a smooth transition after his death.[39]

In retrospect, the task assigned to Youssoufi appears unreasonable because of the difficult conditions imposed on him by the palace. The presence of Driss Basri at the Ministry of the Interior was a psychological necessity for the king but obnoxious to the prime minister, who abhorred working with the principal architect of the "years of lead." Four other "sovereign" ministries were also filled at the discretion of the king: Foreign Affairs, Religious Affairs, Human Rights, and Defense, further circumscribing the authority of the prime minister. Saddled with a team he did not choose, Youssoufi also had to deal with the discordant noise of multiple political parties, each clamoring for a seat at the table. When the dust cleared following cabinet selection, the Youssoufi government emerged as an unmanageable herd of seven parties with forty ministers in all, and only thirteen from Youssoufi's own party.

Despite this unwieldy mix, the aging prime minister persevered, understanding that after a forty-year hiatus, he had been chosen to represent an openness and integrity in the governing equation that had been missing since independence. His relations with the king and other ministers were publicly characterized with words such as "consensus" and "dialogue," and other expressions indicative of the "new order." In his favor were palpable advances in freedom of expression, in women's equality, in religious and ethnic tolerance, buttressed by the strong timber of human rights. Supporting his flanks were intellectuals and militants from the sixties generation – committed reformers such as Habib al-Malki and Khalid Alouia – who were also ready to participate in the experiment in loosening the grip of absolutism on the levers of power. Building on this tender growth, Youssoufi was determined to advance the transition while helping to maintain the stability the palace so much desired. Moreover, as a dyed-in-the wool-patriot, Youssoufi felt that he had little maneuverability, for he had "given his word" to the king.

The Alternance, for all its shortcomings, was an important step in demonstrating to the Moroccan people the possibilities inherent in challenging the system of non-democratic rule that had dominated Moroccan politics since mid-century. It won favor from both right and left, for it introduced new political practices that would benefit the Islamists as well as the secular opposition. Its failings aside, the Alternance marked, according to one observer, an "extraordinary change in tone, in climate, and especially, in mentality."[40] This change was personified on September 30, 1999, when an ailing but triumphant Abraham Serfaty returned home to a heroes' welcome. Even more significant was Muhammad VI's firing, on November 9, 1999, of the much hated Driss Basri as Minister of the Interior, four months after the death of King Hassan II, raising the all-important question of the future role of the Ministry of the Interior in relation to politics and the functioning of the state.

Morocco seemed to have truly entered a period of "transition," but it was a transition directed from above that served, first and foremost, the purposes of the monarchy. While Hassan II in the last decade of his life deliberately started down the path of political reform, the process was only in its beginning stages and far from complete. From the perspective of the elite, the pace of change may have seemed dizzying; for Morocco's friends on the outside, such as the United States, it may have appeared measured and hopeful; but for the majority of the Moroccan people, it was still far too slow. Whether Hassan's motives for instituting changes were rooted in *realpolitik* or remorse, or simply the desire to guarantee his legacy, we do not know. His own sense of history was acute and he was always keenly aware of the mood of the times. The method of the regime was to proceed with the greatest caution while maintaining complete control over the tempo of reform – an attitude made apparent by its ambiguity, its foot-dragging concerning the exculpation of the crimes of the past, and the reluctant, deliberate, and carefully managed pace of change.

MOROCCO IN THE WORLD

It is a truism that domestic and international policies reflect each other in a Janus-like fashion. In the first period of Hassan's rule, Morocco's internal political paralysis and its ongoing economic difficulties shaped its stance vis-à-vis the wider world. As we have seen, initially, Hassan II followed in the footsteps of his father, who traced a nonaligned stance in the early years of statehood; later, desperately in need of foreign aid and cognizant of preexisting realities, Hassan II executed a sharp turnabout by placing his confidence in the West.

By 1964, the value of Morocco's trade with the European Economic Community (EEC) was ten times that of trade with the Eastern Bloc. The EU, successor to the EEC, was and remains to this day Morocco's most important trading partner, receiving 65 percent of Morocco's total exports in 2009.[41] In 1969, at France's insistence, Morocco was given "Associate" status in the EEC, but the conditions of association did not work in Morocco's favor, especially regarding the price of agricultural exports. Farm products were Morocco's main source of revenue until 1973, when it received an unexpected but very short-term windfall in the form of a precipitous rise in the price of phosphates. A second agreement signed with the EEC in 1976 brought more financial aid, allowing Morocco to draw heavily from European lenders, so that by the mid-1980s it had run up a considerable debt. By 1983, foreign exchange reserves were at an all-time low, having been depleted by the costs of the Saharan war and the trauma of the global oil shocks of the early 1980s. External debt was 70 percent of GDP, and the debt service had climbed to 42 percent of annual exports.[42]

The threat of financial collapse forced Morocco to comply with a series of structural readjustment programs mandated by the IMF that reshaped its economy, including the selling-off to the private sector of government monopolies in which the king was often a principal shareholder. Wealthy Moroccan investors were encouraged to buy into these formerly state-run companies, exaggerating even more an already distorted concentration of capital within the elite strata. Hassan II's petition in 1987 to make Morocco a full member of the EEC was based on the argument that he had "liberalized" the Moroccan economy and committed his government to a "democratic" multiparty system. These arguments collapsed before the weight of European opinion (most sharply enunciated by the French far right) that an Arab-Islamic state in Africa could not reasonably be considered part of Europe. Unspoken but palpably in the air was the fear that EEC membership for Morocco would augment the already robust migration of Moroccan workers to Europe. The false perception that North Africans in general were a source of crime and labor unrest gave thrust to the anti-Moroccan crusade. On July 30, 1987, the *Financial Times* wrote that Hassan's application "was greeted in the European media with a mixture of incredulity, scorn and the kind of racial jibe which many educated Arabs have come to expect from Western countries."[43]

Privatization accelerated after 1991 under the watchful eye of the makhzan, as the "jewels" of the economy, according to Clement Henry, were parsed out to friends of the king: "... in league with foreign owners, principally French banks, the king's men thus controlled over three-quarters of the private sector's total assets."[44] By disengaging the state from the economy, Hassan II was able to develop new political clienteles while satisfying European investors that Morocco had truly followed the path of liberal reform. As a result, a European free trade agreement signed in 1996 brought rich benefits in terms of development aid. But it came at a high social cost; namely, inflation and the bifurcation of the Moroccan labor force into a well-paid professional class and an underpaid, informal workforce, exacerbating Morocco's already critical social problems.

Embedded in this swing to "neoliberalism" was the almost mystical belief that economic development would "trickle down" and eventually lead to greater prosperity and wider participation in the political process through the recruitment of new stakeholders in the middle class. But globalization, as Shana Cohen has pointed out, has another, less lovely face: the shrinking of the public sector required by international lenders produced widespread unemployment, especially among university graduates, creating a permanently disruptive and dangerous threat to social stability. By 1999, it was clear that chronically inadequate government policies in the economic sphere had failed to keep up with the needs of a youthful population demanding jobs, services, and educational opportunities, creating a permanent and unresolved cancer within the body politic.[45]

The connection between internal and external affairs was equally evident in Morocco's relations with the West. Morocco's ties to NATO and with the United States grew increasingly friendly over the years under Hassan II's careful management. Considering himself an "adviser" to American Presidents, he dutifully made the voyage across the Atlantic numerous times, to golf, horseback ride, and party with every American head of state from John F. Kennedy to Bill Clinton. Morocco was one of the first countries to invite U.S. Peace Corps volunteers, who began to arrive in 1963. Built on the legacy of memories, mostly positive, of the American landings during World War II that brought chewing gum, be-bop, nylons and lipstick, enhanced by the U.S. Food for Peace (PL 480) program during the Cold War that distributed countless sacks of flour stamped with the logo of friendly shaking hands, by the 1970s, a store of rosy images relating to America had penetrated the Moroccan imagination.

On the military front, the United States steadily supplied arms to Morocco for its Saharan war, and in return, Morocco became a consistent supporter of U.S.-Middle East policies that were often distasteful to other Arab States. Hassan II played a crucial role in the post-Camp David efforts to sustain the peace process, capitalizing on the regime's long and mostly positive history with its own Jewish minority by maintaining contacts with high Israeli officials as well as with the Palestine Liberation Organization (PLO).[46] U.S. Moroccan strategic cooperation became less important once the Cold War ended, but Morocco was still seen by many U.S. lawmakers as a "bulwark" of stability in an otherwise volatile area. And as the "war on terror" spread its dark cloud across the region after September 11, 2001, Morocco became America's "first friend" in supporting the U.S. counterterrorism campaign.[47]

At the same time, King Hassan II showed a strong streak of independence from the West, the best example being his interactions with Libya's Muʿammar al-Qaddafi, *bête noir* of successive Washington administrations. Before the two leaders signed a cooperative accord at Oujda in August 14, 1984, they had regarded each other with "undisguised contempt." But the reality of regional policies, namely, Algeria's unvarnished support for the Polisario and Morocco's subsequent isolation, made Morocco and Libya into strange bedfellows. The short-lived alliance with the Libyan dictator was one of the less fortuitous foreign policy ventures of Hassan's reign, indicating the extent to which the Saharan issue had become the touchstone defining Morocco's relations with its Maghribi neighbors. The sauve Hassan had little stomach for the mercurial Libyan dictator. The alliance ended suddenly and badly in 1984, with Radio Rabat calling al-Qaddafi "an imbecile tyrant."[48] With Habib Bourguiba, Tunisia's President-for- Life, whose tenure as head of state roughly paralleled his own, Hassan II claimed to have had a "close friendship," but in fact it was a relationship that fluctuated between mutual respect and intense animosity.[49] Both were French-trained lawyers, both preserved their ties with France after independence, both came to Algeria's rescue during its bloody revolution, both shared a pragmatic approach to power, and though Bourguiba was a confirmed republican, he too ruled with an iron fist. But the ups-and-downs of inter-Maghribi politics wore heavily on them

FIGURE 31. King Hassan II welcomes Algerian President Houari Boumedienne and Foreign Minister Abdelaziz Bouteflika to Morocco in 1972, in a rare moment of amity between the two nations. (Abbas/Magnum Photos)

both and impeded the forging of a smooth and lasting Moroccan-Tunisian détente.[50]

Toward Algeria, Morocco's supposed "brother," relations were poisoned by the ongoing Saharan dispute, blocking a trans-Maghribi understanding that might have opened up doors to regional economic cooperation. King Hassan reportedly said that the most vexing external relations of his reign were with Algeria, with whom Morocco shared so much culturally and historically, but so little politically. A short-lived Arab Maghreb Union (AMU) came into being with the signing of the Treaty of Marrakesh in 1988, having as its goal the setting up of a North African "Common Market" among the supposedly complementary economies of the region. But chronic underlying tensions, both personal and political, tore the agreement apart; in 1994, a terrorist attack in Marrakesh, suspected by Morocco of being Algerian-inspired, led to the closing of the Moroccan-Algerian border and the freezing of the AMU.[51]

In the inter-Arab sphere, Hassan II considered his relations with other Arab and Islamic states to be especially close and "natural." Morocco sent token contingents to support the Arab side in both the 1967 and 1973 Arab-Israeli wars, and Hassan II was a leading actor in the Islamic Conference, chairing the al-Quds (Jerusalem) Committee dedicated to preserving the Arab character of the Holy City. His engagements with Arab states tended to favor ties with the monarchies that most closely resembled his own: the Gulf royals, or King Hussein of Jordan, whose death preceded Hassan's by only a few months. The Moroccan monarch's moderate stance on Arab-Israeli issues and his adherence to the ceremonies of royal privilege did not win him great popularity in the Arab socialist heartland. To his Arab critics, he responded acerbically by saying that Arab leaders had neither the ability to make war against Israel, nor the willingness to make peace. After the collapse of the Arab Maghreb Union in 1994 and the stalemate following the Oslo Accords, Hassan II increasingly pointed his antennae toward Europe, building his most important relations economically and politically on a North–South axis rather than across the region.

King Hassan's actions on the diplomatic front were wide-ranging, often unpredictable, but never tentative. He saw himself as a leading actor on the world stage, perhaps the most prominent statesman in the region at the time of his death, because of the range of his relationships, his closeness with the West, his contacts with the former Soviet Union and China, and his forays into African politics where he was among the founders of the Organization of African States. Like Anwar Sadat, his value abroad far outshone his currency at home. Yet, for the most part, his foreign activities were motivated by practical domestic concerns: preserving his vision of the national territory, finding the resources to compensate for budgetary shortfalls, assuring the prestige and survival of the monarchy. His actions in the foreign field contributed to strengthening the monarchical institution by broadening its base and its capacities, with the result that a diplomatic dimension lacking under his father now enhanced the royal persona: Hassan the Unifier was joined by Hassan the World Leader, creating a model of international statesmanship for his successor to follow.

On July 25, 1999, in what the *New York Times* described as a "scene of tumult," two million mourners lined the streets of Rabat to say goodbye to the king that many Morocans knew as their only ruler. After thirty-eight years on the throne, Hassan II finally succumbed to the maladies that had weakened him in his final years. A panoply of world leaders followed the cortège: President Bill Clinton, former President George H. W. Bush, President Jacques Chirac of France, Palestinian leader Yasir Arafat, and Ehud Barak, Prime Minister of Israel, along with a clutch of kings and princes. Ordinary Moroccans poured into Rabat from all over the country, many of them walking on foot along blocked highways from as far away as Casablanca, sixty miles away. The juxtaposition of this torrent of emotion for the defunct monarch with the memory of his harsh practices and his inability to deal with Morocco's most pressing social problems introduces us to the central dilemma of his years in power.

While the world press lionized the defunct king as "a sage" and "worldly Muslim leader," a "peacemaker" and a "visionary," most Moroccans thought of him as a stern and forbidding father who used the rod more often than the gentle word. Yet the acknowledgment of his achievements was inescapable, even from his most determined critics. In 1961, Hassan II took the formless clay of the state handed to him by his father, and molded it into something that most Moroccans came to recognize as singularly their own. During his years in power, he shaped an entity that would live beyond his own life span, embossed with the attributes of a modern and functioning nation-state. While his people may have not always loved their king, they had become enamored of the concept of Kingship, seeing it as the governmental form that best suited their needs as a nation, albeit with a long list of complaints, caveats, and modifications.

Late in his life, Hassan II opened his eyes to the dynamic nature of the state as an evolving political institution, along with the prospects for its reform. At that point, putting aside his essential conservatism and bringing to bear his deep understanding of the mechanics of the Moroccan political system, he sought practical ways of moving forward. Too little and too late, according to his critics, and perhaps this is true. It may be that his most grievous error was his failure to discern the swiftness with which his country and his people were changing. Yet during his tenure, the attributes of power inscribed in the monarchical order did not fail him; rather, his principal dilemma concerned the manner and pace at which royal influence should be applied. The ideological underpinnings of the monarchy remained intact, despite the sharps jabs directed at it from left and right, from republican militants, on the one hand, and Islamist sympathizers, on the other. Indeed, the idea of the monarchy emerging from Hassan's incumbency was more firmly implanted in the Moroccan reality than ever before. It was in the political arena, in the pragmatic and day-to-day juggling of the limited assets and built-in constraints that Hassan II was handed, that he faced his greatest challenges. As Morocco moved forward to a new century under a new king, the need for far-reaching changes to satisfy the demands of a restless people was undisputable, but the fundamental *raison d'être* of the system inherited by Hassan II, recrafted by his genius, and passed on to his successor, was hardly brought into question.

8

Summation

In Search of a New Equilibrium

The year 1999 and the death of Hassan II marked a watershed in Moroccan history. The outpouring of public grief at his funeral revealed a nation profoundly moved by the disappearance of this larger-than-life and often unloved father figure. While some mourned the passing of the *ancien regime*, others quietly rejoiced at the opportunity for greater political freedom within the framework of institutionalized monarchical rule. The new King Muhammad VI seemed to breathe fresh life into the political process because of his youthfulness and open style, and hopes ran high that the reforms initiated by his father would deepen and accelerate. But the realities of temporal politics soon intervened: the shock of 9/11 coupled with attacks in Casablanca in 2003 provided the brake that opponents of change were seeking. In 2003, in response to the increase in radical militancy, the new king pronounced that the "era of leniency" was over, raising the question of whether or not reform would continue at the same pace as before.

The Arab Spring of 2011 reopened the debate in an explosive manner, raising once again the question of reform, this time focusing especially on changes to the constitution that would limit the powers of the king. Once again the knotted problem of the monarch's dual and intertwined attributes as both religious and temporal leader of the nation became a topic of public discussion. But as Rémy Leveau warned some years ago, the crux of the political struggle in Morocco is not over ideology in all its competing forms, but rather over tactics and accommodation of interests: "Morocco's most important institutional problems are not really constitutional," he said, "rather, they concern the interaction and power-sharing between the monarchy and Morocco's political parties."[1] The king's central symbolic role, his special privileges, his overwhelming authority in governmental affairs, the blurring of the line between his personal wealth and the treasure of the state, all of these questions hung in the balance, appended to matters of a more ideological nature. Meanwhile, the political life of the nation goes on, revitalized by the emergence of a popular voice seeking a greater role in politics. It is not the role of the historian to predict the future, but rather to try to clarify the past and render it useful in thinking through the complexities of the present. But certain continuities stand out from our account of the past 170 years of Moroccan history that might serve as markers for finding a route through the current confusion, as well as providing guideposts to the future.

The narrative we have chosen to represent the flow of Moroccan history over the past two centuries revolves around three principal axes: the monarchy, the state (not always easily distinguished from the monarchy), and society. An overarching theme of this narrative has been the interlacing of relations among these three centers, and how their interactions form the substratum of Moroccan history in the modern period. Each in its own way was a prime mover, sometimes acting in isolation, but more often moving in tandem with the others, interweaving interests and negotiating compromises. It is a principal thesis of this book that these compromises were reached less on the basis of ideology and more on the basis of material necessity and pragmatic goals. While inherited traditions, cultural templates, and conceptual frameworks are important, it is the stuff of the every day, the materials at hand, and the opportunities and threats of the moment, that have to a large extent determined the course of modern Moroccan history. Moreover, as methods of communication have become more complex, as the possibilities for networking and exchange have multiplied, the historian's task of identifying the major trends and devising an appropriate analysis of them has become increasingly difficult. Yet in a synthetic political history such as this, a key question remains: How may we understand the fit between single events and the *long durée*, and what are the terms of analysis that undergird the framework we have chosen? Why this particular narrative and not another?

In political and diplomatic history, the state is by necessity the main actor who controls the agenda and orchestrates, more than other players, the principal performances. The makhzan/state as we know it is an institution hardened by experience and replete with its own rules, regulations, and traditions. Continuity and resistance to change are its earmarks, along with an acute awareness of its own unassailable position at the heart of the

Moroccan body politic. How the state construed its role historically is the core issue of any political accounting of Morocco, as we have often pointed out here. Inherited beliefs about what the state/sultanate should represent, usually articulated in religiocultural terms, have received a preponderant amount of attention from students of Moroccan history. But as we have argued throughout, alongside these factors, of equal if not greater importance, are the raw materials of political decision making that are contextually transparent and recoverable by means of a thorough search through the closet of history.

Take, for example, the relationship between the state and its territory. Over the period of our discussion, Moroccan monarchs have wrestled with the problem of settling the contested boundaries of the state as an essential ingredient in establishing both the physical and perceptual parameters of national identity. But territorial issues also intersect with the pragmatic need to make the state more secure and less vulnerable to outside interference. Not surprisingly, it was always the closest neighbor, Algeria, who was at the heart of these disputes. In the age of jihad, the quandary over the defense of western Algeria led to humbling defeats that initiated the first age of reform; at the turn of the last century, the loss of territory to French colonial troops crossing from Algeria into Morocco presaged the coming of the Protectorate. In the independent state, the wars in the desert have repeatedly pitted the Moroccan army against the forces of Algeria and muddied relations between the two. The historical continuities that permeate the border issue explain the saliency of Moroccan-Algerian relations in recent Moroccan history, and why this topic constantly returns. Intense feelings about questions of territorial integrity have been a centerpiece of foreign relations for a very long time, exaggerated by popular sentiment and manipulated by the monarchy in order to win recognition for its diplomatic skills at home and abroad.

The relationship between the state and the monarchy is a second key theme. The monarchy – not the constitution, or the parliament, or the people – is the main source of legitimacy in the Moroccan polity. The monarch's role as the symbolic center has grown incrementally over time, becoming, in the age of Hassan II, the source of immense authority. But this pole has also fluctuated over time, and though the institution of the monarchy, more than any other, is built on a pedestal of belief, it is also an institution that has demonstrated an astonishing ability to be responsive to the changing times. We should recall the nineteenth century, when the position of the sultan was in a state of constant renegotiation; indeed, at times sultanic power was reduced to a mere modicum of respect rather than inducing the terrifying awe of a later period. By instrumentalizing this authority and using it in tandem with other coercive means, Hassan II was able to force the modernization of the state without having to rely on other institutions such as parliament or the religious establishment. This political masterstroke, while bringing about changes long overdue, weakened complementary political forces and bolstered the supposition that reform could only come as an emanation of the sovereign will. But in practice, the attrition of the political parties and the stagnation of meaningful political activity were corollaries of the incremental growth in kingly authority. The steady accrual of royal power, traced historically, demonstrates how the hopes of those invested in the democratic process despaired of ever achieving parity with the state. But it was in the arena of practical politics, not in the sphere of ideology, where the monarchy delivered its most virtuoso performance, and it is in the realm of the quotidien that the role of the monarchy becomes most historically relevant.

Another trend we have marked is toward the centralization of state institutions. The increasing visibility and omnipresence of the state was a global phenomenon that emerged in the nineteenth century and gathered momentum in the twentieth. In the precolonial period, the makhzan exercised intermittent control over tribes that sometimes resisted, sometimes acquiesced in their submission; already, the tendency toward domination from the center is evident under Sultan Hassan I. The integrating actions of Lyautey as he laid the foundation for the Protectorate are well documented. In the independent makhzan that followed, both Muhammad V and Hassan II incrementally reinforced many of the structures and mechanisms of control instituted by the colonial power. Electoral reforms, the implementation of new varieties of governance in the rural areas, the management of urban space, the growth of municipalities, the expansion of bureaucracies, were decisive actions that brought subjects under the umbrella of the state. The taming of the forests and fields, the building of dams and irrigation systems, the creation of agricultural plans, were counterparts to this centralizing and disciplining trend that were observable in the natural world. New environmental histories locate and document these trends, demonstrating the step-by-step accumulation of measures that added up to a massive focalization of power in the apparatus of the state.

Alongside centralization was the mechanism of co-optation. Co-optation was a phenomenon that penetrated all of the principal institutions of public life and it, too, can be historically traced. Co-optation is a social style that has permeated Moroccan politics for centuries; one has only to look at

Sultan Hassan I's treatment of dissident tribes, or his manipulations of the Fez bourgeoisie, to find tell-tale signs of its presence. In the modern period, it has been especially decisive in filling out the arsenal of the state. The army and the police, as we have seen, were absorbed and gradually made into instruments of state policy through gifts, favoritism, and special treatment. The old makhzan in the nineteenth century was beset by the problem of finding the resources needed to pay for military reform; the new makhzan was bedeviled by the problem of finding the rewards that would keep the army, now firmly established, within its fold. The setbacks of the failed coups of 1971 and 1972 brought the loyalty of the army into question, highlighting the fact that military insurrection was an ever-present possibility. Neutralizing the army after the fall of Oufkir in 1972 by the redistributing its power among multiple centers was an innovation of Hassan II, forced upon him by circumstances. Whether the army is completely inside or outside the tent today is a critical question, occulted by the veneer of a steady professionalization.

The ulama, too, have also been increasingly absorbed through a historical process; from their nineteenth century role as spoilers of reform under Sultan ʿAbd al-ʿAziz, they have been gradually taken in and converted into a tool of the central power. Schools and the educational system have also been harnessed to the bureaucracy, and school curricula at every level reflect the conservative norms of society. The state has also shown a sustained ability to control the economy; the chaotic response to the nineteenth century debt crisis was not repeated in the twentieth, as Hassan II, wielding his extraordinary powers, imposed strictures on taxation, trade, and investment though various phases of debt restructuring in the 1980s and 1990s. This aspect of control spread from economic matters to class formation, making the state to a large extent the progenitor of a new middle class. Co-opting this class has also become a project of the makhzan: will professionals who comprise the expanding middle stratum of society continue to value stability over freedom of action, or will they escape the state's tutelage and opt for something different?

While the state as prime mover dominates the historical narrative, on the opposite side of the balance sheet are the people and their social institutions. We have repeatedly pointed to a deeper social reality not always easy to locate as an underlying current within the historical process. The example of the riot or urban revolt as an ongoing theme in Maghribi history emerging out of popular sentiment is an apt one. Mass demonstrations, such as the Green March, are occasions for transformative collective action, while anti-government street demonstrations provide a counterpoint to makhzan policies of repression and "divide and rule." From the revolt of the Fez tanners in 1874 to the urban riots of Casablanca in 1965 and 1981 to the 20 February Movement of the 2011 Arab Spring, Moroccans have demonstrated for recognition and social justice in the face of sometimes overwhelming coercive power.

The "tradition" of the demonstration is more than simply street theater; in a non-democratic setting, it is a political maneuver of an exemplary type, evoking past glories as well as the present complaints of the common people. Youth who took part in the Casablanca riots of 1965 acknowledge that the street demonstrations unleashed by that event were a "school" for learning about political activism. Their testimonies after the fact were a kind of "witnessing" in which people's memories trumped the bland official accounts that screened out popular grievances. By memorializing these events through informal means, young people came to see insurrectional behavior as an instrument of political culture that is deeply rooted in society. Critical of authority, disorganized politically, divided in their loyalties, yet sharing a consensus that the future must somehow be better than the past, Morocco's youth have become a group-in-formation that uses the street as its party headquarters.

The press is another institution that has, to a large extent, escaped the confines of the state and has increasingly become a vehicle for popular expression over time. From its humble beginnings in the late nineteenth century, to its role in the nationalist movement, to its impact as an arm of party politics in the 1950s, the Moroccan press has developed into a vibrant, contentious, and informative locus of information and public debate. The press more than any other institution in society has pushed for the recovery of a buried past that often confutes established opinion. In the absence of a genuinely critical contemporary historiography, newspapers and magazines have been the vehicle of choice for rewriting recent political history. By publishing memoirs, reviews, and news analyses that provide a counterpoint to "official" accounts that glorify the monarchy, the press has disseminated information that contests the restrictive pro-makhzanian discourse that has monopolized the field since independence. Press exposés on the "years of lead," or on the kidnapping of Ben Barka, fill the void between official dogma and suppressed memory. Writing in the press, when not subjected to censorship, has offered the plurality of perspectives necessary for a balanced accounting of the past.

The resurgence of civil society in all its forms is another manifestation of change that enriches historical discussion and constitutes a continuous theme. While informal social structures of the nineteenth century have received some attention from historians, there is much to be learned from the study of groups that systematically resisted the state in the course of modern Moroccan history. Urban militias, saintly lineages, sufi orders, secret societies, trade unions, civic associations, radical leftists, women's organizations, all comprise entities whose histories need to be reanalyzed and retold in the light of a positive dynamic of social change. Finding these phenomena tucked away in the recesses of the past has only begun; stories about the prostitutes of Bousbir, the *goumis* of World War II, women revolutionaries, Moroccan Jewish communists, Berber poets, all considered "peripheral" by those in rule, contribute to a re-centered narrative characterized by diversity and inclusiveness.

Historians do not make social revolutions, nor can they heal the iniquities of the past, but they can help reorient the imagination and suggest new avenues for research and action by providing examples from the archives of memory. In the "new" Morocco in search of an equilibrium between the all-powerful state and its restless citizens, the elements of a freedom-loving tradition embedded in historical discourse are the vital components for the construction of a revised connection with the past. The appearance of novel perspectives from every direction, native and foreign, written and oral, are the signs of a society in mutation. The Moroccan state has lost control of the minds of its citizens, if it ever held it, and that fact has helped to incite the ferment we witness today. A decentered and pluralistic history is part of that ferment, constituting one of the mainstays of a truly democratic society in which people make their own choices about which narratives they choose to believe. History from below is difficult to write, especially in the absence of sources, and when questioning and innovation are not encouraged by a regime that up to now has regarded history as its own sacred territory. Recovered memories can produce a Pandora's box of images that are difficult to restrain. But this, too, is changing in an era of renewal, in which historical inquiry in all its forms becomes vital to the consciousness of a new generation.

9

Postscript

The Long Decade of Muhammad VI (2000–2011)

The Moroccan people were deeply affected by the dramatic events of the Arab Spring in the first months of 2011. The king's response to the popular uprising that shook the country in February and March of 2011 marked a new chapter in Morocco's modern history, in which the monarchy's inventiveness, flexibility, and will to survive were severely tested. Muhammad VI's deft handling of the crisis was the result of a decade-long inculcation in the practices of monarchical rule, acquired through skillful manipulation of the elite classes, the political parties, and the mass movements played out in the street, that make up the fractured and highly mobile Moroccan political scene.

The first months of Muhammad VI's rule were characterized by bold acts that set the tone for a decisive departure from the past. The ascent of the youthful king to the throne offered opportunities to introduce far-reaching changes in public perceptions of the monarchy, with the new king's age and accessibility raising hopes for a more equitable balance between the regime and its people. Immediately upon acceding to power, he placed his stamp on public affairs by positioning the complementary concepts of political liberalization and respect for human rights at center stage. By all accounts, King Muhammad VI's desire to clean up the residual grievances from the "years of lead" was genuine. In August 1999, he set up a Royal Commission to study the payment of indemnities to former political prisoners, and on September 13, 1999, Morocco's most famous political prisoner, Abraham Serfaty, along with his wife Christine Daure-Serfaty, was allowed to return home. In October 1999, he visited the north of Morocco, a notoriously fractious region shunned by his father, and with one stroke, returned the densely populated Rif to the national fold after years of isolation and neglect. On November 9, 1999, an even more startling act was the firing of the much-hated Interior Minister Driss Basri, symbol of state secrecy and oppression under Hassan II. This bold move set the stage for a reorganization of the security apparatus, raising hopes for a rapprochement between the forces of order and a deeply alienated public.

The figure of the king acquired a new humanity, as the thick veil of secrecy thrown over the personal life of Hassan II was cast aside. In the spring of 2002 Muhammad VI married Salma Bennani, a modern, educated woman from a well-known Fasi bourgeois family, and a year later, she delivered their first child, Prince Hassan, now heir to the throne. For the first time, Moroccans saw the face of the king's consort – a redheaded beauty – plastered over the pages of the foreign and national press. Morocco now had a "royal family" centered on a "first couple" whose images, desires, and habits were publicly scrutinized in a closely managed campaign in the popular media. Moroccans learned facts about the royal family they had never before known: the location of their many residences, the annual budget of the royal household, their preferences, and their pastimes.

The new king also surrounded himself with a cadre of advisers of a totally new cast: friends from school, business associates, and graduates from the most prestigious French and American universities and professional schools, who were assigned to crucial posts in the palace and government and wielded immense power in his name. A dense and interlocking web of royal commissions, institutes, councils, and foundations sprang up, manned by comrades and protégés of Muhammad VI, and answering to him alone. Key posts were filled by talented loyalists, such as palace spokesman Hassan Aourid (a school friend) Interior Minister Chakib Benmousa (École polytechnique and MIT), Tourism Minister Adil Douiri (École nationale des ponts et chaussées and Harvard). Their mission was broad but well defined: to modernize an outdated infrastructure, to build barriers against the threat from religious extremists, to launch a "war on poverty" that would ameliorate the appalling conditions in which many Moroccans lived, to encourage foreign investment, to build bridges to Morocco's friends in Europe and the United States, and to help preserve the material and spiritual bedrock on which the monarchy rested.

Uppermost in the king's mind was the plan to increase social mobilization by closing the books on the "years of lead." King Hassan II had tried to clean the slate, but at his death, the job was only half-done. The 1998 government of Alternance represented something of a détente with the regime's old opponents on the left, but it left unanswered the question of reparations for the victims of makhzan brutality. Under pressure from former prisoners and following the publication of harrowing accounts of their travail, such as *Tazmamart cellule 10* of Ahmed Marzouki, the makhzan felt compelled to respond. Muhammad VI assumed responsibility for this dossier, and in 2003 created the Equity and Reconciliation Commission (ERC) for the sole purpose of exposing victims' stories to the public eye and arranging compensation for them. His charge to the ERC was to bring the truth to light, but "without judging my father," and without citing names of perpetrators. Human rights activist Driss Benzekri was appointed to head the commission to the chagrin of many of his former associates and fellow prisoners, who saw his cooperation as a form of capitulation.

The ERC worked for nearly two years, recording and videotaping testimony from thousands of victims, creating a record of individual abuses and cases of disappearance, locating sites of torture as well as the secret burial places of the dead. The nation stood transfixed as these revelations unfolded in the media. But the identities of the torturers were never revealed, the name of Hassan II was never invoked, and no punishments were meted out to the perpetrators. In December 2005, the ERC delivered its final report, calling for a reform of the judicial system that would obviate a return to the iniquities of old, but these recommendations were never acted upon. Instead, on January 6, 2006, Muhammad VI received the families of the victims and accepted the regime's responsibility for their suffering, according them a "noble amnesty." Overall, nearly ten thousand victims of the "years of lead" received indemnities totaling more than $200 million.

Despite its shortcomings, Morocco's experience with the ERC was revolutionary in the Arab world, establishing judicial norms that were widely praised at home and abroad. However, turning the page on the "years of lead" did not mean that human rights issues disappeared from the political agenda. Human rights advocacy in Morocco continued both under the umbrella of the state and outside of it; a National Human Rights Council (CNDH) commands the field, organizing humanitarian efforts, reporting on abuses, defending children's and prisoners' rights, and acting as a standardbearer in Arab and international fora. The regime's progressive stance on human rights has paid multiple political dividends, allowing it to coopt and neutralize many of its former adversaries on the left. But after 2003, when the temperature of the Islamist threat rose and the regime began to confront militants now located mainly on the right, norms of conduct embraced during the campaign to repair the damage of the years of lead were allowed to lapse. By mid-decade, many Moroccans were wondering if, in the sphere of human rights, the more things had changed, the more they had remained the same.

The fear of a new descent into repression was implicit in the second platform of Muhammad VI's early years, when he was willingly recruited into the international "war on terror" waged by the West against Muslim extremists. While a virulent religious opposition had been part of the Moroccan scene since the 1980s, with the diatribes of Shaykh Abdessalam Yassine receiving the most attention, the danger of a religiously based insurgency did not really come home to Morocco until 2001, when security forces revealed the presence of cells of the al-Qaʿida-linked group Salafiyya Jihadiyya dispersed around the country. In the intense manhunt that followed, thousands of populist preachers and their followers were seized and thrown into prison, reawakening for many Moroccans the nightmare of the harsh repressions of the past. Suicide bombings on May 16, 2003, in Casablanca carried out by members of the Salafiyya Jihadiyya mainly from the Sidi Moumen bidonville of Casablanca killed forty-five people and injured scores more, deepening Morocco's involvement with the growing problem of international terrorism. While aimed principally at Jewish and foreign (Spanish) targets, the bombings traumatized the Moroccan public at large. A massive public relations effort was launched, leading with the slogan "Don't touch my country!" in an concerted effort to galvanize public opinion against the security threat. Popular feeling was inflamed further by the Madrid train bombings of March 11, 2004, allegedly planned and executed with Moroccan participation. Parallel to these events, the government initiated a campaign of severe repression directed against Islamist militants that continued unabated from 2003 onward, orchestrated by the flamboyant General Hamidou Laanigri, head of the National Security organization until his fall from power in September 2006.

Meanwhile, Morocco became implicated in America's "war on terror," with allegations surfacing that sites in Morocco were being used for the "rendition" of detainees suspected of terrorist activities. The BBC reported on September 28, 2006, that the nongovernmental AMDH, along with Amnesty International and Human Rights Watch, were claiming that a "black site" at the beach town of Temara was being used to interrogate and torture prisoners. The Moroccan Ministry of Justice denied knowledge of such a place, but the negative image of official involvement in torture now circulated widely in the local and international press. Many Moroccans felt that by engaging in the "war on terror" Muhammad VI was fighting America's war, and that Morocco should play a more neutral role.

Indeed, the degree to which the press would be allowed to critique the regime became another bone of contention between the monarchy and human rights activists. Press freedom promoted by Hassan II reached a high point in the late 1990s, when a spate of new periodicals appeared that exposed formerly hushed-up subjects to the public gaze, even at the risk of being censored. And censored they were, with increasing severity during the reign of Muhammad VI, who was in many ways more thin-skinned than his father.

The case of *Le Journal* is instructive. When it first appeared in 1997, its editors Ali Amar, Abubakr Jamaï, and Hassan Mansouri immediately showed their political mettle by giving an interview to the head of the Polisario. The magazine was shut down for the first time in 2000, but soon reappeared with an article denouncing the Washington, DC, real estate capers of the then Moroccan ambassador to the United States, Mohamed Benaïssa. In 2001, *Le Journal* was slapped with a five hundred thousand dirham fine in connection with the Benaïssa case that put a huge hole in its finances; nevertheless, the editors persevered, inciting even greater anger from the powers-that-be for their unrelenting attacks on corruption in high places. When Abubakr Jamaï was compelled to flee Morocco in 2007 or be subject to prosecution, the life span of Le *Journal* entered its final stages; former editor Ali Amar announced the magazine's demise in 2010, naming as its cause the campaign of "financial asphyxiation" mounted against it by the regime. News magazines of a satiric nature, like Ali Mrabet's *Demain* and *Doumane*, suffered reprisals for showing "a lack of respect for the King," and Rachid Niny, editor of the high circulation daily *al-Masa'*, was arrested for publishing "disinformation." While some news magazines like *Tel Quel* managed to endure, others fell by the wayside. By the end of the decade, it was clear that the brief honeymoon between the activist press and Muhammad VI had come to an end.

Another topic carried over from the previous era was the issue of Berber rights, and the place of Berber language (Tamazight) and culture in the Moroccan national diadem. King Muhammad VI took on this cause as a third item in his campaign to correct lapses of the past, recognizing the argument that the suppression of Berber culturalism was widely construed as an infringement of human rights. He was also personally open on this topic, since his close friend Hassan Aourid was a standard-bearer for the

Amazigh cause. In March 2000, over two hundred intellectuals led by Berber university professor Mohamed Chafik published a "Berber Manifesto," insisting on the presence of "Amazighity" in Morocco since pre-Islamic times, while frontally attacking the ideology of Islamo-Arabism that had served as a cornerstone of nationalist discourse since the early days of the Istiqlal. The Manifesto made a series of demands, including a call to make Tamazight an official language alongside Arabic. In May 2000, a congress of Amazigh activists held at Bouznika laid the foundations of the movement, but when a second national congress was planned for June 2001 with the aim of creating a Berber political party, opposing voices condemned the movement as "racist," "xenophobic," and "separatist," and a danger to the integrity of the nation, and the congress was abruptly cancelled.

With more than 40 percent of Moroccans still identifying with their Berber roots, Muhammad VI understood the volatility of the topic and stepped in. On October 17, 2001, at Ajdir, the Rifian village of the Berber nationalist hero ʿAbd al-Karim al-Khattabi, Muhammad VI announced the creation of the IRCAM, and appointed Muhammad Chafik as its first director. The mission of this institute was to publicize the Berber element in Moroccan culture through programs of research, conferences, and publications generously supported by the state. But the IRCAM soon adopted a more aggressive platform when in 2003 Chafik was replaced by Ahmed Boukous, another widely respected academic. Under Boukous' guidance, the IRCAM pushed for changes such as the adoption of a Berber alphabet (Tifinagh), making it possible for the first time to develop textbooks and school curricula that would bring the demand for a state-sponsored program of Berber language instruction into the realm of reality.

With the debate focusing on the question of Berber language, officials faced a serious challenge. Studies have shown that many Moroccan students, even those who complete high school, are weak in reading and writing formal Arabic (*fusha)*, while mastery of French is an accomplishment usually confined to the educated elites. The addition of Berber to this already indigestible linguistic mix presented a daunting problem for planners, who were wallowing under a welter of demands to modernize an overcharged and under-funded school system. In 2006, a coalition of dozens of pro-Berber associations presented a report to the United Nations about the situation in Morocco, protesting against "official denial of the Amazigh reality, constitutional discrimination and exclusion, oppressive Arabization, and prevention of activities by Amazigh associations and intimidations" while condemning the IRCAM as an "instrument of the makhzan created to squelch the Amazigh movement." As the Berber movement split into warring factions, the Berber language issue became yet another arena in which the forward momentum of the early years of Muhammad VI's reign appeared to grind to a halt.

A fourth platform of the new regime was the reform of the Mudawwana, or Code of Family Law. Steps toward the rewriting of the family code began under Hassan II, but the project became ensnared in the question of the religious legitimacy of the monarchy and its conservative responsibility to uphold principles of Muslim law. Supported by a modernizing faction who felt that outmoded traditional practices clashed with the mood of the times, the new king decided to make reform of the Mudawwana a pillar of his social policy. One of his first acts, on August 20, 1999, was to make a speech in which he questioned the rationale behind subjecting women to second-class citizenship in a country headed toward "progress and prosperity." Spurred on by his words, women's groups took to the street in well-organized marches in Rabat and Casablanca in March 2000 to urge the reform of the family code. Rather than being upstaged by the activist civic associations, the king decided to appoint a royal commission made up of a variety of actors – law professors, ulama, jurists, feminists – to consider the issue and draft a new family code. Meeting behind closed doors for months, the commission failed to reach consensus and presented two separate plans to Muhammad VI, who exercised his authority by choosing the more liberal version. The new Mudawwana was presented to parliament in September 2003 and passed after a brief debate, but there was no doubt in the public mind that the ultimate guarantor of this new law was the monarch himself, backed by his prestige as Commander of the Faithful and head of the Islamic community.

The new family code was by most accounts revolutionary. The legal age of marriage was raised to eighteen, each member of the married couple was equal in the court of law, and women could no longer be repudiated without the couple appearing before a judge. The code created divorce by mutual consent and allowed women to initiate divorce proceedings, even without cause. The law also protected the rights of women who were divorced or repudiated, allowing them to keep their possessions and children without being thrown into the street, and placed severe constraints on polygamy. While the Mudawwana was not secular law, its greatest innovation was its establishment of the legal rights of married women as their own agents in a court of law. The code was received with enthusiasm by women activists, who saw it as a giant leap forward. But it soon became apparent that application of the code was uneven, as judges unfamiliar with its terms, or ideologically opposed to them, impeded its implementation. Moreover, rural women were far less familiar with it than urban women, and Islamist groups stood against it on political grounds. In a July 3, 2007, interview with the German magazine *Der Speigel*, Nadia Yassine, daughter of Shaykh Yassine, said that the new Mudawwana favored the "small secular elite" who supported the king: "The king has passed a law for women who go to high school," she declared, "but not for average people in the countryside." Recognizing these problems, progressive women's organizations took the lead in sponsoring the dissemination of the code in *darija* (spoken Moroccan Arabic) as well as in the Berber dialects used by rural women.

Dramatic reforms created a sense of a progressive opening during the early years of Muhammad VI's reign, but the mood of optimism soon faded as "business as usual" took hold. The arena of electoral politics is yet another example of good intentions giving way to political pragmatism and old habits of divide and rule. The experience of the Alternance of the late 1990s demonstrated that transparent elections could generate an atmosphere of confidence in the regime. But it was soon apparent that despite the opening posited by the Alternance, further structural changes in the mechanisms of rule were needed. Some kind of political "transition" was clearly in the offing, but it was not the fundamental realignment that many had hoped for. Sweeping powers remained the monarch's alone: the appointment of ministers, including the prime minister, the right to dissolve parliament and legislate in its absence, the ability to declare a state of emergency and to revise the constitution by national referendum. These and other entrenched practices kept the prerogatives of absolute rule intact.

Staging regular elections appeared to be yet another mechanism cloaking the monarchy in a mantle of democratization, without giving up any real measure of royal authority. The elections of September 2002 brought this reality home with striking clarity. The first elections to be held in the post-Basri era, the government took advantage of the current of fresh air and organized a successful campaign to get out the vote, brandishing the slogan, "The future is in your hands." The results of wider participation – 51 percent of the eligible electorate went to the polls – were evident in the stunning victory of the PJD, the Islamist party, over all other contenders. The PJD success marked the end of the government of Alternance of Youssoufi and the emergence of the pro-Islamists as the single most important force in parliament. Despite their victory, the king chose as his prime minister Driss Jettou, a businessman and loyalist who handed out ministerial posts to the old parties of the Alternance, excluding the PJD and ignoring its victory at the polls.

Working against the backdrop of the May 2003 terrorist attacks, Jettou remained in office for five years, directing a program of rapid modernization piloted by the king without parliamentary interference. On the positive side, unlike Algeria, where Islamist leaders were violently purged from political life, in Morocco after 2002 Islamist politicians were allowed to participate in government, but they were held in close check by the understanding that discretion was the key to their political survival. The unwritten accord between the palace and the Islamists assured social peace while maintaining the façade of inclusiveness, allowing the king to point with pride to a record of transparency and electoral fairness unusual in the Arab world.

With encouragement from the palace, parties began to jockey for position for the next electoral trial held on September 7, 2007, with the palace again mounting an energetic publicity campaign to mobilize Moroccans for the forthcoming vote. Despite these efforts, only 37 percent of the eligible electorate turned out this time. The restrained number of voters delivered a stunning defeat to the PJD in favor of the Istiqlal, prompting yet another swing in the electoral pendulum. With the Istiqlal now the dominant party in the parliament, the king appointed its leader Abbas al-Fassi as prime minister at the head of a coalition government made up of a multitude of small and ineffectual parties, many of them pro-royalist. This return to the past both startled and relieved Moroccans, especially those who feared the PJD victory erroneously prognosticated in the press. Yet, at the same time, the low voter turnout was worrisome: Why such indifference to electoral politics?

Despite the effort by the makhzan to build credibility by using elections as a touchstone of democratization, the Moroccan electorate chose to desist from voting, exposing the fallacies of the makhzan's strategy. People deplored the alphabet soup of parties, the vacuity of their platforms, the lack of clear policies or projects, their puppetlike obedience to the palace, the whiff of corruption that emanated from backroom deals, and the suspicion that votes were still being bought. In short, the electorate demonstrated a genuine disillusionment with party politics, convinced that the immense social and economic problems that plagued the country would not find their solution through the electoral or legislative processes. Most troubling of all was the indifference of young people. The "depoliticization" of youth was a trend that accelerated after 2000, according to surveys conducted by academic researchers, who found that

FIGURE 32. Demonstrations by unemployed university graduates protesting limited job opportunities were a common sight in the streets of Rabat in 2008. (Collection Susan Gilson Miller)

the majority of Moroccan youth made no distinction between left and right, deplored the lack of "moral" content in political life, and favored the religiously oriented parties. The poor turnout for the 2007 vote was an early warning sign of the cynicism and the widespread disillusionment with party politics among youth that burst out into the open during Spring 2011.

The political transition of the first decade of Muhammad VI's rule was also accompanied by sweeping changes in the economic sphere, marked by improvement in the regime's ability to manage growth and investment. But this transition, too, was managed from above with an eye to strengthening the structural underpinnings of *le pouvoir*, as the regime was commonly called. The practice of placing technocrats in key economic posts begun under Hassan II was accentuated under the new king, a businessman *par excellence*, whose personal fortune was estimated by *Forbes Magazine* at around $2.5 billion in 2009, five times greater than that of the Queen of England. The king's economic advisers emulated his aggressive business style, turning their backs on the "nationalist" economic policies of the 1960s and 1970s, and adopting instead an IMF-approved fiscal discipline designed to attract direct foreign investment and reorient Morocco toward European markets. Privatization had already begun under Hassan II, who championed the opening of the Casablanca stock market in the 1990s and invited foreign participation in Moroccan enterprises. These trends gained momentum under Muhammad VI, who became Morocco's chief economic ambassador abroad, selling the "new-old" Morocco as a good place to invest.

The Moroccan economy is heavily export-oriented; lacking energy reserves and food security, it must import both, creating a permanent trade deficit. The annual gap between exports (about $15 billion in 2008) and imports (about $35 billion) is partially filled by revenues from tourism and remittances from Moroccans living abroad. Morocco's impressive growth rate in recent years (4.2 percent in 2010) is fueled by foreign capital sunk mainly in projects in telecommunications, banking, insurance, hotels, and port facilities, such as the huge Tanger-Med facility on the Mediterranean coast between Tangier and Tetuan, soon to be the largest port in Africa. Seventy-five percent of Morocco's exports go to Europe, and France is by far Morocco's biggest foreign investor and trading partner, a relationship fanned by the friendship between King Muhammad VI and former French President Jacques Chirac. Next comes Spain, and in third place, the countries of the Gulf: Bahrain, Qatar, Kuwait and Saudi Arabia. Lagging behind are the United States and China, although trade with these two giants is on the increase. French investment is omnipresent in Morocco's economy in every sector from the national airline to the yoghurt industry, leading Driss Basri to say in 2004 that "France has bought everything."

Among nonstate actors, the World Bank has played a key role in Morocco, generously opening its coffers for development projects. After 2007, the IMF under Dominique Strauss-Kahn, a great friend of Morocco, joined the parade, helping to burnish Morocco's image as a potential economic powerhouse. But in fact, the Moroccan economy remains fragile and sensitive to fluctuations in the global economy, and its heavy dependence on foreign investment for growth is a chief cause for worry. Moreover, the agricultural sector, though not as important as it once was, is still the primary employer and subject to sharp swings due to the weather, reinforcing fears of vulnerability. The anxieties of a large population living below the poverty line – the official figure is 15 percent but most observers agree the number could be double that – compounded by a 30 percent unemployment rate, contributed to the turmoil and anger expressed in the street demonstrations of Spring 2011.

Economic troubles are at the heart of the massive human outflow that has characterized Moroccan life for decades. Moroccan emigration after independence was largely a movement of workers seeking factory jobs in the booming postwar European economy; in recent years, it has turned into a classic brain drain, as Moroccans have become better educated and seek salaries commensurate with their experience. Doctors, engineers, scientists, and technicians trained in Morocco or abroad make up the movement. Morocco is the largest supplier of émigrés to Europe and the Americas among the countries of the Middle East, surpassing Algeria, Turkey, and Egypt; in 2007, nearly five million Moroccans lived abroad, not counting political exiles and "clandestine" migrants who live "below the radar." Nearly three million Moroccans live in Europe, not counting children, with the majority in France and Spain, creating a huge overseas constituency that maintains ties with the homeland. Moroccans in the hundreds of thousands reside permanently in the Netherlands, Belgium, Italy, the United Kingdom, and Germany. About three hundred thousand Moroccans live in the Arab East, with Libya in the lead (where the effects on them of the 2011 revolution are as yet unknown), while in the countries of the Gulf, Moroccan women hold service jobs in health and education. As of this writing, over one hundred thousand Moroccans live in the United States, and another eighty thousand are settled in Canada, the majority concentrated in French-speaking Montreal. The North American émigrés are especially well qualified in terms of education, with Moroccans now holding teaching and research posts at some of North America's most prestigious universities.

The future impact of this variegated and increasingly important overseas community is imponderable. Denied voting rights, but courted and tabulated by the regime, they could wield considerable economic and political influence in the future. The "return" of certain émigrés to management posts within Morocco under Muhammad VI has significantly shaped government policy, with their advanced expertise being felt in the telecommunications, tourist, and banking sectors. Recognizing the potential richness of this human resource, King Muhammad VI created the Hassan II Foundation for Moroccans living abroad in an effort to keep émigrés "within the family," and he has deftly shepherded this cohort, who generally feel exceptional loyalty to country and king. State-sponsored projects help maintain close ties. Each year, the Moroccan government sends hundreds of imams to Europe during Ramadan to act as "religious ambassadors"; it offers aid to Islamic associations in Europe; and it has made the "annual summer return" an occasion for celebration through the improvement of port and customs facilities.

Linkages forged with émigré communities are only one part of a larger diplomatic offensive launched by Muhammad VI to strengthen ties with the wider world. He has carefully pursued foreign policy lines laid down by his father, clinging closely to friendships in the West, maintaining low-key relations with Israel, while warmly embracing his fellow royals in Jordan and the Gulf. The most difficult issue handed on by Hassan II to his son is the Saharan case; at his death, a cease-fire was still in force in preparation for a referendum on the territory's future. But agreement in principle on who would vote in this referendum was never reached, and the UN proved to be incapable of ending the deadlock. Meanwhile, the Sahara officially remains non-Moroccan, to the chagrin of nearly all Moroccans, vexed by the massive financial and human investments made in the contested territory over the past thirty-five years. Since 2008, the United States has pushed for Saharan "autonomy," but this plan has been rejected both by the Polisario, who want full independence, and by most Moroccans, who demand full integration. Meanwhile, practically speaking, the Sahara has been fully absorbed from the Moroccan perspective, leaving the regime open to the charge from erstwhile friends in Africa and Asia that it has acted in a high-handed and "neocolonial" manner.

Consultation on the Saharan issue is only one aspect of an increasingly close relationship with the United States, especially in the military/security sphere. Morocco's position at the entry to the Mediterranean has transfixed American military strategists for decades, while its supportive stance on the "war of terror," its lukewarm yet positive attitude toward Israel, its tough opposition to Islamic extremism, its dedication to some form of democratization, and its pro-business king, are additional factors that have endeared it to American policy makers. In 2004, the United States and Morocco signed a sweeping free trade agreement that mutually lowered most tariffs and raised the promise of greater U.S. direct investment in the Moroccan economy. As a result, U.S. – Moroccan trade is steadly increasing. The most recent evidence that Morocco under Muhammad VI is a solid ally of the United States came in 2007, when U.S. President George W. Bush announced that Morocco would allow the construction of a U.S. military base at Tan-Tan to serve as a staging area for Africom, the newly created U.S. military force aimed at policing terrorist movements in Africa.

Relations with Algeria, however, remain poor at best. The border between the two countries is closed, despite persistent efforts from the Moroccan side to reopen it. The Algerians have remained steadfast in their refusal to do business, using as a pretext Morocco's intransigence on the Saharan issue; meanwhile, Algerian citizens eager to dip into the shopping cornucopia of Morocco's northern coastal cities are kept at bay, with smuggling replacing legal business operations. Relations with Spain have also had their difficulties, with the "lost" territories of Ceuta and Melilla constituting a permanent stumbling block to otherwise mostly friendly ties. In July 2002, an armed incident between Moroccan and Spanish troops broke out on the rocky, goat-inhabited Island of Perejil (in English, "Parsley"; and in Tamazight, "Tura") located in the Strait of Gibraltar close to Morocco. This confrontation perturbed relations between the two countries until it was settled by international mediation. The incident revealed once again that the Moroccan ambition to recover territories long held by Spain on the Mediterranean coast would remain a sticking point in Spanish-Moroccan relations for the foreseeable future.

Morocco is seen in the West as an "island of stability" in an otherwise turbulent region, despite its endemic poverty, illegal drug trade, residual corruption, runaway population increase, disaffected youth, political paralysis, variable economy, and government of "enlightened" authoritarianism. King Muhammad VI is viewed as the centerpiece of this variagated mosaic, personifying a widespread belief in the indispensability of monarchical rule to the continuity of peace and stability. In the first decade of his rule, King Muhammad VI managed to convince a majority of Moroccans that they should put aside the near-mystical dread they felt toward his predecessor and instead, embrace the monarchy as a source of compassion, competence and professionalism, seeing it as the crucial cement of national unity and the best form of governance for Morocco. For many of his subjects, but not all, Muhammad VI fulfilled the prototype of the "citizen monarch," dear to his people, sharing their values and aspirations, despite his slow but steady reversion to many of the autocratic practices of the past.

This aura of calm was abruptly disrupted by the events of the winter and spring of 2011, when the uprisings that began in Tunisia and Egypt rolled across North Africa. The tumult of the Arab Spring that caused heads to roll further East brought people out into the streets to protest a whole range of grievances: the lack of jobs, official corruption, the thwarting of Berber rights, and most of all, the long-sleeping issue of the monarchy's monopolization of politics. A big rally in Rabat and other cities on February 20, 2011, marked the beginning of a youth-led movement that was patently opposed to the royal monopoly on power. Once again, the old dilemma between preserving tranquility versus limiting royal authority raised its ugly head. Using social media to direct the rising tide of popular feeling, the February 20 Movement kept up a rolling wave of protests in major cities across the country throughout the spring of 2011. In March, demonstrations turned violent, with considerable damage to government property and banks, and dozens of casualties. Calling for jobs, democracy, and constitutional reform, the February 20 Movement orchestrated the demonstrations but showed surprising restraint, rarely openly attacking the personhood of the king. Backed by a small but militant group of educated and successful businessmen, the February 20 Movement represented an innovative coalition of young people and certain members of the upwardly mobile, secularized, and Westernized middle class.

Heeding the seriousness of the demands, and fearing a replication of the upheaval taking place elsewhere in the Middle East, Muhammad VI reacted on March 9, 2011, by announcing the creation of a commission to draft a new constitution. Charging it to work with haste, he set out the guidelines for a new compact, promising among other things that in the future, the prime minister would be chosen from the majority party and would wield effective executive powers. At the same time, he appointed a consultative committee to serve as a liaison between the drafters, the political parties, and other civic groups, in order to supply ideas and offer feedback. It is still unclear if any debate or genuine exchange of views ever took place between this body and the drafters, who, like previous constitutional commissions, worked *in camera*.

On June 17, 2011, the king announced details of the draft constitution in a televised speech to the nation. Groups on the left, including the February 20 Movement, rejected the document, saying it did not go far enough, while mainstream political parties, including the PJD, endorsed it with enthusiasm. On July 1, the constitution was approved by 98.5 percent of voters, with nearly ten million votes cast, representing close to 75 percent of the eligible electorate. The new constitution tackled many of the issues that had roiled the public sphere since Muhammad VI's ascent to power, such as the place of Islam, reconfirmed as the state religion, and the status of Tamazight, now recognized as an "official" language alongside Arabic.

The most important innovations, however, were the limitations on the king's ability to intervene in day-to-day politics. While the king's role as "supreme arbiter" of political life remained unquestioned, the new constitution enhanced the legislative powers of the parliament and increased the independence of the judiciary, moving at least in spirit toward a separation of powers. What it did not do was to unequivocally limit the king's preponderant influence over public affairs, or move Morocco closer to becoming a parliamentary monarchy; in other words, it stopped short of remaking Muhammad VI into "a king who reigns but does not rule."

On November 25, parliamentary elections yielded a clear victory for the PJD, with the Islamist party capturing 107 of the 395 seats. On November 29, 2011, Abdelilah Benkirane, head of the PJD and a one-time member of the Shabiba Islamiyya, was named prime minister, promising to defend a "controlled democracy" and "personal freedoms." Meanwhile, the anemic 45 percent rate of participation in the elections signaled that many Moroccans still felt alienated from politics and preferred to stay home on election day. Members of the February 20 Movement loudly boycotted the elections, while others voiced their disillusionment with the political parties and expressed doubts about their ability to tackle deeply rooted social problems.

Nevertheless, there was a wide consensus that Muhammad VI's rapid response to the demand for constitutional reform had kept his regime from experiencing the life-threatening spasms felt elsewhere in the Arab world. His political nimbleness coupled with other strategic gestures, such as doubling food subsidies, opening up new government jobs, and increasing the salaries of civil servants, tipped the balance in his favor, at least for the time being. Once again, the monarchy mastered a situation in which the institutional channels for expressing the popular will remain chronically blocked. Moreover, while the king's swift and decisive action seems to have momentarily succeeded in restoring calm, there is no doubt that "the street" and the politically engaged classes will continue to press for change. Clearly, the main grievances of the protestors – and of most Moroccans – concerning quality-of-life issues have not yet been met, neither by social measures nor by constitutional reform. As of this writng, the following questions are quietly but insistently posed: Will the PJD be able to succeed where so many others have failed? Can the Islamists provide a means to lead Morocco out of its unending crises? And most important of all: How long will the patience of the Moroccan people continue to be tried?

Key Abbreviations

AIU	Alliance Israélite Universelle
AMDH	Moroccan Association of Human Rights
AMU	Arab Maghreb Union
CAM	Moroccan Action Committee
CCDH	Consultative Committee of Human Rights
CDT	Democratic Confederation of Workers
CNDH	National Council of Human Rights
ERC	Equity and Reconciliation Commission
FAR	Royal Moroccan Armed Forces
FDIC	Front for the Defense of Constitutional Institutions
IHEM	Moroccan Institute for Higher Education
IRCAM	Royal Institute for Amazigh Culture
MP	Popular Movement
OMDH	Moroccan Organization of Human Rights
PAM	Party of Authenticity and Modernity
PCM	Moroccan Communist Party
PDI	Democratic Party for Independence
PJD	Justice and Development Party
PLS	Party of Liberation and Socialism
PPS	Party of Progress and Socialism
SARD	Sahrawi Arab Democratic Republic
SFIO	French Section of the Workers International
UGEM	General Union of Moroccan Students
UMT	Moroccan Union of Workers
UNEM	National Union of Moroccan Students
UNFP	National Union of Popular Forces
USFP	Socialist Union of Popular Forces

Glossary of Arabic Terms

ʿadl. pl. ʿudul notary
amin, pl. umana Government tax collector, overseer, head of a professional corporation
ʿaskar nizami The modernized professional army of the later nineteenth century
baraka Mystical power of saints and sharifs; miracle-working abilities
bayʿa Oath of allegiance to the sultan
bled (Ar., bilad) Countryside, rural area
dahir Royal decree
dhimmi A non-Muslim, Jew or Christian
fatwa Legal opinion issued by one of the ulama
fiqh Islamic jurisprudence
habous, hubus, habus Religious endowment in perpetuity
harka Military expedition to the interior
hectare (fr.) Piece of land of about 2.5 acres
hurm A sacred sanctuary
islah (pl. islahat) Reform, religious and political
jaysh, gish Tribal military contingents offered in return for tax exemption
khalifa "Deputy," heir apparent to the throne
khutba The Friday prayer in the mosque
latif A prayer for divine intervention in times of distress
millah, mellah Jewish quarter of the Moroccan city
madina The old city, the walled section of a town
mahalla Army troop on the march
makhzan Lit. storehouse or treasury; in Morocco, *makhzan* signifies the government or the state
marabout, (Ar. murabit) Holy man, saint

maks Non-Qur'anic taxes that raised popular resentment
mujahid Warrior in defense of Islam
mithqal Sum of money equal to ten dirhams (c. 1900)
pasha Governor of a large town
qa'id Governor of a rural area
salafi A member of the Muslim reform movement founded by Muhammad 'Abduh
shariah Islamic law
sharif, pl. shurafa Nobility; descendant of Prophet Muhammad
siba Dissidence, territory not under mahzan control
tabor A military unit of varying size, between three hundred and twelve hundred men
tajir, pl. tujjar A member of the merchant class
tamazight The main dialect of Berber in Morocco
tanzimat The Ottoman reform movement of the nineteenth century
tartib A universal tax on wealth paid in cash
umma The Muslim community or nation
'ushr, pl. a'shar Qur'anic tax of one-tenth on agricultural produce
za'im Charismatic political leader
zakat A Qur'anic tax of 2.5 percent paid on capital goods and livestock
zawiya A religious lodge or retreat; a religious order

French Résidents-Généraux in Morocco, 1912–1956

1912–1925	Louis Hubert Gonzalve Lyautey
1916–1917	Henri Gouraud (Acting)
1925–1929	Théodore Steeg
1929–1933	Lucien Saint
1933–1936	Auguste Henri Ponsot
1936	Marcel Peyrouton
1936–1943	Charles Hippolyte Noguès
1943–1946	Gabriel Puaux
1946–1947	Eirik Labonne
1947–1951	Alphonse Pierre Juin
1951–1954	Augustin Léon Guillaume
1954–1955	Francis Lacoste
June 1955–August 1955	Gilbert Yves Édmond Grandval
August 1955–November 1955	Pierre Boyer de Latour
1955–1956	André Louis Dubois

Sultans and Kings of the ʿAlawite Dynasty, 1664–2012

1664–1672	Rashid
1672–1729	Ismaʿil
1727–1729	Ahmad al-Dahabi
1729–1745	ʿAbdallah b. Ismaʿil
1757–1790	Muhammad III b. ʿAbdallah
1790–1792	Yazid b. Muhammad
1792–1793	Hisham b. Muhammad
1793–1822	Sulayman b. Muhammad
1822–1859	ʿAbd al-Rahman b. Hisham
1859–1873	Muhammad IV b. ʿAbd al-Rahman
1873–1894	Hassan I b. Muhammad
1894–1907	ʿAbd al-ʿAziz b. Hassan
1907–1912	ʿAbd al-Hafiz b. Hassan
1912–1927	Yusuf b. Hassan
1927–1953	Muhammad V b. Yusuf (deposed)
1953–1956	Muhammad b. ʿArafa
1955–1962	Muhammad V b. Yusuf
1962–1999	Hassan II b. Muhammad
1999–	Muhammad VI b. Hassan

Notes

1. The Closing of the Era of Jihad (1830–1860)

1. C.-A. Julien, *History of North Africa: Tunisia, Algeria, Morocco, from the Arab Conquest to 1830*, transl. John Petrie, ed. C. C. Stewart (London: Routledge & Kegan Paul, 1970), 126.
2. A. Laroui, *The History of the Maghrib* (Princeton: Princeton University Press, 1977), 275–9.
3. Mohamed El Mansour gathered from various sources a rough estimate of population size between the years 1771 and 1825 in his *Morocco in the Reign of Mawlay Sulayman* (Wisbech, UK: MENAS Press, 1988), 6.
4. On al-Zayani, see M. El Mansour, "The Makhzan's Berber: Paths to Integration in Pre-Colonial Morocco," in *Berbers and Others: Beyond Tribe and Nation in the Maghrib*, K. E. Hoffman and S. G. Miller, eds. (Bloomington: University of Indiana Press, 2010), 63–79.
5. Laroui, *History*, 276.
6. al-Zayani, *Al-Tarjumana al-kubra fi akhbar al-ma'mur barran wa-bahran* (Rabaṭ: Wizarat al-Anba, 1967), 131–2.
7. On the building of Essaouira, also known as Mogador, see Mina al-Mghari, *Madinat mukadur-al-sawira ; Dirasa tarikhiyya wa-athariyya* (Rabat: Dar Abi Ragrag lil-taba'a wa-al-nashr, 2006).
8. F. Harrak, "State and Religion in Eighteenth Century Morocco: The Religious Policy of Sidi Muhammad b. 'Abd Allah, 1757–1790." Ph.D. diss., School of Oriental and African Studies, University of London, 1989.
9. El Mansour, *Mawlay Sulayman*, 22.
10. A. Jabarti, *Napoleon in Egypt: Al-Jabarti's Chronicle of the First Seven Months of the French Occupation, 1798* (Princeton: Markus Wiener, 1993).
11. El Mansour, *Mawlay Sulayman*, 67.
12. Ibid., 189. On the plague of 1818, see Dr. H. J. P. Renaud, "La Peste de 1818 d'après des documents inédits," *Hespéris* 3,1 (1923): 13–35.
13. The best introduction to the motives and events surrounding the French landing in Algiers (despite its near-complete dependency on published French sources) is still C.-A. Julien, *Histoire de l'Algérie contemporaine, 1827–1871* (Paris: Presses Universitaires de France, 1964), chs. 1 and 2. See also L. Addi, "Colonial Mythologies: Algeria in the French Imagination," in *Franco-Arab Encounters: Studies in the Memory of David Gordon*,

L. C. Brown and M. Gordon, eds. (Beirut: American University of Beirut Press, 1996), 93–105.

14. A. K. Bennison., *Jihad and Its Interpretations in Pre-Colonial Morocco: State-Society Relations During the French Conquest of Algeria* (London and New York: Routledge Curzon, 2002), 47; M. Kenbib, "The Impact of the French Conquest of Algeria on Morocco (1830–1912), in *North Africa: Nation, State, and Region*, E. G. H. Joffé, ed. (London and New York: Routledge, 1993), 38.
15. A. al-Nasiri, *Kitab al-Istiqsa li-akhbar duwal al-Maghrib al-aqsa*, 8 vols., M. Hajji, B. Bu Talib, A. Tawfiq, eds. (Casablanca: al-Najah, 2001–2005) 8: 39–41.
16. al-Nasiri, *Kitab al-Istiqsa*, 8:43.
17. C. H. Churchill, *The Life of Abdel Kader, Ex-Sultan of the Arabs of Algeria: Written from His Own Dictation, and Comp. From Other Authentic Sources* (London: Chapman and Hall, 1867), 2.
18. al-Nasiri, *Kitab al-Istiqsa*, 8:51.
19. Churchill, *The Life of Abdel Kader*, 25.
20. Ibid., 62.
21. Julien, *L'Algérie contemporaine*, 105.
22. Churchill, *The Life of Abdel Kader*, 78.
23. F. Harrak, "Mawlay Isma'il's Jaysh al-'Abid: Reassessment of a Military Experience," in *Slave Elites in the Middle East and Africa*, M. Toru and J. E. Philips, eds. (London and New York: Kegan Paul International, 2000), 185–190.
24. El Mansour, *Mawlay Sulayman*, 26; the quote is from the Moroccan Minister Muhammad b. Idris al-'Amrawi.
25. al-Nasiri, *Kitab al-Istiqsa*, 8:47–50.
26. Bennison, *Jihad*, 115.
27. al-Nasiri, *Kitab al-Istiqsa*, 8:61.
28. Ibid., 8:62. See also L. Valensi, *Fables de la mémoire: la glorieuse bataille des trois rois* (Paris: Editions Seuil, 1992), 98–100.
29. S. G. Miller, "Crisis and Community: The People of Tangier and the French Bombardment of 1844: The Purim of 'Las Bombas'," *Middle Eastern Studies* 27, 4 (1991): 583–96. The quotations are from Dr. A.-H. Warnier, *Campagne du Maroc, 1844: Journal d'Auguste-Hubert Warnier, chirurgien-major, attaché à l'état-major du prince de Joinville*, H-R. d'Allemagne, ed. (Paris: Nouvelle revue rétrospective, 1899), 99; and from an unpublished Purim scroll in the possession of the author.
30. 'Abd al-Qadir was imprisoned in France until 1853, when he was finally permitted to leave for the East, eventually settling in Damascus. For an account of his later career, see B. Étienne, *Abdelkader* (Paris: Hachette, 1994), esp. pp. 208–12, 221–52.
31. J. McDougall, *History and the Culture of Nationalism in Algeria* (Cambridge: Cambridge University Press, 2006), 177–183.
32. F. Cooper, "Conflict and Connection: Rethinking Colonial African History," *American Historical Review* 99, 5 (1994), 1532–3.

33. S. G. Miller, ed. and transl., *Disorienting Encounters: Travels of a Moroccan Scholar in France in 1845–1846: The Voyage of Muhammad as-Saffar* (Berkeley: University of California Press, 1992), 193–4.
34. J. Gallagher and R. Robinson. "The Imperialism of Free Trade," *The Economic History Review*, New Series, 6, 1 (1953): 1–15.
35. F. R. Flournoy, *British Policy toward Morocco in the Age of Palmerston (1830–1865)* (London and Baltimore: P. S. King and Johns Hopkins Press, 1935), 31–36.
36. K. Ben Srhir, *Britain and Morocco During the Embassy of John Drummond Hay, 1845–1886* (London and New York: Routledge Curzon, 2005), 59.
37. E. Burke, III, *Prelude to Protectorate in Morocco: Precolonial Protest and Resistence, 1860–1912* (Chicago: University of Chicago Press, 1976), 26–27.
38. Flournoy, *British Policy toward Morocco in the Age of Palmerston*, 236 n. 1, based on statistics provided by consular reports from Tangier printed in the *Parliamentary Papers*.
39. Ibid.,197; R. Carr, ed., *Spain: A History* (Oxford and New York: Oxford University Press, 2000), 214; N. Erzini, "Hal Yaslah Li-Taqansut [Is He Suitable for Consulship?]: The Moroccan Consuls in Gibraltar in the Nineteenth Century," *Journal of North African Studies* 12, 4 (2007): 521.
40. al-Nasiri, *Kitab al-Istiqsa*, 8:107.
41. *Diary of a Witness*, trans. B. Keating (Memphis, TN: White Rose Press: 1988), 388–9.
42. Flournoy reports that the British investors in the 1861 Moroccan loan were fully repaid by 1883 at the handsome rate of 8 percent interest: *British Policy toward Morocco in the Age of Palmerston*, 212; see also J. D. Hay, L. A. E. Drummond Hay Brooks, and A. E. Drummond Hay, *A Memoir of Sir John Drummond Hay: Sometime Minister at the Court of Morocco: Based on His Journals and Correspondence* (London: J. Murray, 1896), 214–20. For calculating the value of nineteenth-century British pounds at today's prices, see http://www.measuringworth.com. See also J.-L. Miège, *Le Maroc et l'Europe (1830–1894)*, 4 vols. (Rabat: Editions La Porte, 1989): 2 :374–82.
43. G. Ayache, "Aspects de la crise financière au Maroc après l'expédition espagnole de 1860," in *Études d'histoire marocaine* (Rabat: SMER, 1983), 97–138.
44. al-Nasiri, *Kitab Istiqsa*, 8: 116–17.
45. Hay, Brooks, and Drummond Hay, *A Memoir*, 218.
46. K. Pomeranz, *The Great Divergence: China, Europe, and the Making of the Modern World Economy* (Princeton: Princeton University Press, 2000), 15.

2. Facing the Challenges of Reform (1860–1894)

1. B. Dennerlein, "South-South Linkages and Social Change: Moroccan Perspectives on Army Reform in the Muslim Mediterranean in the Nineteenth Century," *Comparative Studies of South Africa and the Middle East* 27, 1 (2007): 52–61.
2. The *bayʿa*, or the election of a sultan, was the end point of a complex negotiation among various social forces that, by dint of custom and religious law, were entitled to participate in the process of selection. The contractual nature of royal

authority was made explicit through this process, since the ulama who "elected" the sultan were in theory representatives of the *umma*, or community of believers. On the death of the reigning sultan, the ulama in each imperial city hastened to confer the bay'a on a successor in order to head off a hiatus in rule. Before the nineteenth century, rarely did the process of eliciting the bay'a allow for an amicable resolution of differences of opinion. The process of electing the sultan often became the chaotic arena for the playing out of competing objectives among various groups and individuals, each with its own pretensions to power. But by mid-century, the sultanate had accrued sufficient authority to make the process of transition proceed more smoothly. For a discussion of the concept from an anthropologist's perspective, see H. Munson, Jr., *Religion and Power in Morocco* (New Haven: Yale University Press, 1993): 38–39.

3. al-Nasiri, *Kitab al-Istiqsa*, 8:149; B. Dennerlein, "Legitimate Bounds and Bound Legitimacy; The Act of Allegiance to the Ruler (Bai'a) in 19th Century Morocco," *Welt des Islams* 41, 3 (2001): 287–310.
4. A. Laroui, *Les origines sociales et culturelles du nationalisme marocain (1830–1912)* (Paris: François Maspero, 1977), 77–81.
5. G. Ayache, "Aspects de la crise financière au Maroc," in *Études d'histoire marocaine* (Rabat: SMER, 1983), 97.
6. M. Ennaji, *Expansion européenne et changement social au Maroc: (XVIe–XIX siécles)* (Casablanca: Editions Eddif, 1996), 60–72.
7. T. K. Park, "Inflation and Economic Policy in 19th Century Morocco: The Compromise Solution," *The Maghreb Review* 10, 2–3 (1985): 51–56. See also al-Nasiri's comments on inflation in 1845, which he blames on the increasing number of foreign merchants trading in the Moroccan ports: *Kitab al-Istiqsa*, 8:66; and on the re-evaluation of the currency under Sultan 'Abd al-Rahman, see *Kitab al-Istiqsa*, 8:79.
8. P. Alarcón, *Diary of a Witness* (Memphis, TN: White Rose Press, 1988) 454.
9. al-Nasiri, *Kitab al-Istiqsa*, 8:136.
10. T. K. Park, "Colonial Perceptions of Precolonial Administration: Creating the Illusion of Failure," unpublished paper. By permission of the author.
11. S. G. Miller, ed. and trans., *Disorienting Encounters: Travels of a Moroccan Scholar in France in 1845–1846: The Voyage of Muhammad as-Saffar* (Berkeley: University of California Press, 1992), 42–48.
12. For a close description of the functioning of the central government, see E. Aubin, *Morocco of Today* (London: J. M. Dent & Co, 1906), 158–81.
13. K. Ben-Srhir, *Britain and Morocco during the embassy of John Drummond Hay, 1845–1886* (London and New York: Routledge Curzon, 2005), 235–9. Ben-Srhir makes a strong case that these fiscal reforms were British-inspired and that Drummond Hay's exceptional personal influence was crucial to winning the sultan's agreement. But it could also be argued that the notion of reform was already "in the air" and Hay's proposals were falling on receptive ground. On the organization of the umana, see N. H. Tawzani, *al-Umana bi-al-Maghrib fi 'ahd al-Sulṭan Mawlay al-Hasan (1290–1311/1873–1894): Musahamah fi dirasat al-nizam al-mali bi-al-Maghrib* (Rabat: Kulliyat al-Adab wa-l-'Ulum al-Insaniyya, 1979), 33–37.

14. A. Ibn Zaydan, *Ithaf alam al-nas bi-jamal akhbar hadirat Miknas*, 5 vols. (Rabat: al-Matbaʿa al-Wataniyya, 1929) 3: 379–89.
15. Tawzani, *al-Umana*, 295–6.
16. M. Lahbabi, *Le gouvernement marocain a l'aube du XXe siècle* (Rabat: Editions Techniques Nord-Africaines, 1958), 136–8. E. Aubin, *Morocco of Today* (London: J. M. Dent, 1906), 169.
17. Laroui, *Les origines*, 155.
18. Quoted in J. Dakhlia, "Dans la mouvance du Prince: la symbolique du pouvoir itinérant au Maghreb," *Annales: ESC* 43, 3 (1988), 735.
19. D. Nordman, "Les Expeditions de Moulay Hassan; essai statistique," *Hespéris-Tamuda* 19 (1980–81): 123–52, and especially, 148–9. Also on the harka, see A. El Moudden, "État et société rurale à travers la harka au Maroc du XIXe siècle," *Maghreb Review* 8, 5–6 (1983): 141–5; M. Aafif, "Les Harkas hassaniennes d'après l'oeuvre d'A. Ibn Zidane," *Hespéris-Tamuda* 19 (1980–81): 153–68.
20. Dakhlia, "Dans la mouvance du Prince," 735–60.
21. al-Nasiri, *Kitab al-Istiqsa*, 8: 215.
22. French colonial social scientists posited the image of a Morocco perpetually divided between two competing zones, an area under government control (*bled makhzen*), and the tribal "lands of dissidence," (*bled siba*). Inaccurate in the extreme, this stereotype became an touchstone of colonial policy making, masking the complexity of state structures and smoothing over the vastness of human interactions that took place within them.
23. A. El Moudden, "Looking Eastward: Some Moroccan Tentative Military Reforms with Turkish Assistance (18th–Early 20th Centuries)," *Maghreb Review* 19 (1994): 237–45.
24. A. K. Bennison, "The 'New Order' and Islamic Order: The Introduction of the Nizami Army in the Western Maghrib and its Legitimation, 1830–1873," *International Journal of Middle East Studies* 36 (2004): 591–612.
25. Ibid., 600. See also K. Fahmy, *All the Pasha's Men: Mehmed Ali, His Army, and the Making of Modern Egypt* (Cambridge: Cambridge University Press, 1997).
26. Hay, Brooks, and Drummond Hay, *A Memoir*, 232.
27. *Encyclopédie du Maroc/Maʿalamat al-Maghrib* (Sala: l'Association des auteurs marocains pour la publication, 2005), s.v. "Muhammad b. ʿAbd al-Rahman b. Hisham," 21: 7017–19.
28. G. Ayache, "L'apparition de l'imprimerie au Maroc," in *Études d'histoire marocaine*, 139–58.
29. W. J. Rollman, *The "New Order" in a Pre-Colonial Muslim Society: Military Reform in Morocco, 1844–1904*, Ph.D. diss., University of Michigan, 1983, 574–75.
30. On the the tattooing of conscripts, see E. Amster, "The Many Deaths of Dr. Emile Mauchamp: Medicine, Technology, and Popular Politics in Pre-Protectorate Morocco, 1877–1912," *International Journal of Middle East Studies* 36:3 (2004): 417.
31. Bennison, "The 'New Order,'" 603–07.
32. al-Nasiri, *Kitab al-Istiqsa*, 8: 121.

33. W. Rollman, "Military Officers and the 'Nidham al-Jadid' in Morocco, 1844–1912: Social and Political Transformations," *Réforme par le haut, réforme par le bas: la modernisation de l'armée aux 19e et 20e siècles. Quaderni di Oriente Moderno* 23:5 (2004): 217.
34. M. Manuni, *Mazahir yaqazat al-Maghrib al-hadith*, 2 vols. (Rabat: Manshurat wizarat al-awqaf wa-al-shu'un al-islamiyya wa-al-thaqafiyya, 1973) 1: 156–78. On the *makina*, see Rollman, *The New Order*, 704–06; for a detailed account of the Italian-run arms factory in Fez, see B. Simou, *Les réformes militaires au Maroc de 1844 à 1912* (Rabat: Université de Mohammed V, Faculté des lettres et des sciences humaines, 1995): 237–84.
35. *Ma'alamat al-Maghrib* (*Encyclopédie du Maroc*) s.v. "al-Jibbas, Mahammad," 9: 2912–15; K. Ben Srhir, "Britain and Military Reforms in Morocco During the Second Half of the Nineteenth Century," in *Réforme par le haut, réforme par le bas: la modernisation de l'armée aux 19e et 20e siècles*, O. Moreau and A. El Moudden, eds. (Rome: Instituto per l'Oriente Nallino, 2004), 105–07.
36. J. Berque, *L'Intérieur du Maghreb: XVe–XIXe siècle* (Paris: Gallimard, 1978), 497; Miège, *Le Maroc et l'Europe*, 4: 139; S. G. Miller and Amal Rassam, "Moroccan Reaction to European Penetration During the Late Nineteenth Century: The View from the Court," *Revue de l'Occident musulman et de la Méditerranée* 36, 2 (1983), 51–63; W. B. Harris, *Tafilet: The Narrative of a Journey of Exploration in the Atlas Mountains and the Oases of the North-West Sahara* (Edinburgh: W. Blackwood and Sons, 1895), 208–09.
37. D. Nordman, "Les expeditions de Moulay Hassan," 127. The practice of the mahalla was not confined to Morocco. *Deys* (Algeria) and *beys* (Tunisia) also used this method of asserting their sovereignty. For a description of this region by a European who claimed to be "the first" to journey there, see W. B. Harris, "A Journey to Tafilet," *The Geographical Journal*, 5:4 (April 1895), 319–35.
38. M. Kenbib, "Structures traditionelles et protections étrangères au Maroc au XIXème siècle," *Hespéris-Tamuda* 22 (1984): 81; by the same author, "Système impérial et bourgeoisie comparadore au Maroc au 19ème siècle," *Revue d'histoire Maghrebine/Al-Majalla al-Tarikhiyya al-Magharibiyya* 41 (1986): 90–91; Miège, *Le Maroc et l'Europe*, 2: 403–07.
39. H. C. M. Wendel, "The Protégé System in Morocco," *The Journal of Modern History* 2:1 (March 1930): 59.
40. Kenbib, "Structures traditionelles," 84.
41. Miège, *Le Maroc*, 2: 554–555.
42. M. Kenbib, "Structures traditionelles," 94–95.
43. A. Green, *Moses Montefiore: Jewish Liberator, Imperial Hero* (Cambridge, MA: Harvard University Press, 2010), 135.
44. The *Bulletin of the AIU*, cited in Miege, *Le Maroc*, 2:570.
45. Always the shrewd politician, Montefiore no doubt added the reference to Christians to solidify the alliance between his own brand of Jewish humanitarianism and the high moral purpose of his British Anglican counterparts. A. Green, "Rethinking Sir Moses Montefiore: Religion, Nationhood, and International Philanthropy in the Nineteenth Century," *The American Historical Review* (June 2005): 631–58.

46. L. Loëwe, ed., *Diaries of Sir Moses and Lady Montefiore, a Facsimile of the 1890 Edition*, 2 vols. (London: The Jewish Historical Society of England, 1983), 2: 45–46.
47. A translation of the dahir into English is found in T. Hodgkin, *Narrative of a Journey to Morocco in 1863 and 1864* (New York: Arno Press, 1971), 121–122. The Arabic text is in *al-Watha'iq*, 9 vols. (Rabat: al-Maktaba al-malkiyya) Document #540, 4: 291. The circular letter to governors is in the same source, Document #541, 4:294.
48. M. Kenbib, *Juifs et musulmans au Maroc, 1859–1948* (Rabat: Université Mohammed V, Faculté des lettres et sciences humaines, 1994): 159; Miege, 2: 568 n. 4.
49. Green, *Montefiore*, 314; al-Nasiri, *Kitab Istiqsa*, 8: 129
50. M. al-Manuni, "Mulakhadhat hawla baʿda rudud faʿl al-mugharaba tujah al-daʿwa ila islah fi al-qarn 19, min khilal wathiqa mawduʿiya," *Majallat kulliyat al-adab wa-al-ʿulum al-insaniyya bi-al-Ribat* (1982): 145–53.
51. K. J. Perkins, *A History of Modern Tunisia* (Cambridge: Cambridge University Press, 2004): 36.
52. E. F. Cruickshank, *Morocco at the Parting of the Ways; The Story of Native Protection to 1885* (Philadelphia: University of Pennsylvania Press, 1935), chs. 5 and 6.
53. Miège, *Le Maroc*, 3:163; 4:47; Kenbib, "The Impact of the French Conquest," 43–44.
54. S. G. Miller and A. Rassam, "The View from the Court: Moroccan Reactions to European Penetration During the Late 19th Century," *International Journal of African Historical Studies* 16:1 (1983): 31, 37.
55. H. de la Martinière, "Au Maroc: Le règne de Moulai-El-Hassan." *Revue de deux mondes* 64:4, (1894): 398.
56. E. de Amicis, *Morocco, Its People and Places*, transl. M. H. Lansdale, 2 vols. (Philadelphia: H. T. Coates & Co,1897), 2: 44–45.
57. A.J.P. Taylor, "British Policy in Morocco, 1886–1902," *The English Historical Review*, 66 (July 1951): 342–74.
58. J. Berque, *L'Intérieur du Maghreb*, 474–5; J.-L. Miège, "Hassan Ier et la crise marocaine au XIXe siècle," in *Les Africains*, 3 vols., C.-A. Julien et al., eds. (Paris: Jeune afrique, 1977) 3: 238.
59. al-Nasiri, *Kitab Istiqsa*, 8: 75.
60. R. Guyot, R. Le Tourneau, and L. Paye, "La Corporation des tanneurs et l'industrie de la tannerie à Fès," *Hespéris* 21:1–2 (1935): 167–240.
61. Berque, *L'Interieur du Maghreb*, 489–92.
62. A. Sebti, "Chroniques de la contestation citadine: Fès et la revolte des tanneurs (1873–1874)," *Hespéris-Tamuda* 24:2 (1991): 99.
63. al-Nasiri, *Kitab al-Istiqsa*, 8: 220 n. 337.
64. On this point, see the article of M. El Ayadi, "Du fondementalisme d'état et de la *nasiha* sultanienne: à propos d'un certain réformisme makhzenien, *Hespéris-Tamuda* 39:2 (2001), 85–107.
65. S. E. Holden, *The Politics of Food in Modern Morocco* (Gainesville: University Press of Florida, 2009), ch. 1.
66. al-Nasiri, *Kitab al-Istiqsa*, 8: 221.

3. The Passing of the Old Makhzan (1894–1912)

1. F. Weisgerber, *Au seuil du Maroc moderne* (Rabat: Éditions La Porte, 1947), 63. Ba Ahmad's younger brother was made *allaf*, or Minister of War; he was described by Weisgerber as a *bon-vivant* about forty years old, "as indolent as a dormouse and as proud as a peacock" (*op. cit.*, p. 70).
2. W. B. Harris, *Morocco That Was* (Edinburgh and London: W. Blackwood and Sons, 1921), 50–53.
3. E. Aubin, *Morocco of Today* (London: J. M. Dent & Co., 1906), 320. Aubin was the *nom de plume* of Léon Descos, a French diplomat and travelwriter whose account of Morocco in the years 1902–1903 shows penetrating insight into societal themes. F. Pouillon, ed., *Dictionnaire des orientalistes de langue française* (Paris: Karthala, 2008), 27.
4. A. Laroui, *Les Origines sociales et culturelles du nationalisme marocain, 1830–1912* (Paris: F. Maspero, 1977), 337–8.
5. Aubin, *Morocco of Today*, vi–vii.
6. Ibid., 127.
7. Ibid., 11–12. G. Veyre, *Au Maroc : dans l'intimité du Sultan* (Paris: Librairie Universelle, 1905), 11–12.
8. P. Jacquier, M. Pranal, and F. Abdelouahab, *Le Maroc de Gabriel Veyre: 1901–1936* (Paris: Kubik, 2005), and esp. pp. 20–21, photographs taken by Sultan ʿAbd al-ʿAziz.
9. L. Arnaud, *Au temps des "mehallas" ou le Maroc de 1860 à 1912* (Casablanca: Éditions Atlantides, 1952), 71, 129, 132.
10. Aubin, *Morocco of Today*, 127.
11. Weisgerber, *Au seuil du Maroc moderne*, 118; Laroui, *Origines*, 340.
12. E. Burke, III, *Prelude to Protectorate in Morocco: Precolonial Protest and Resistance, 1860–1912* (Chicago: University of Chicago Press, 1976), 54.
13. Aubin, *Morocco of Today*, 77.
14. A. Asʿad, "Al-nidham al-jiba'i lil-tartib fi ʿahd al-sultan al-mawlay al-Hasan al-awl," in *Le Maroc de l'avènement de Moulay Abdelaziz à 1912*, 3 vols. (Mohammedia: Université d'été, juillet 1987), 2:167–175.
15. N. Michel, *Une économie de subsistances: Le Maroc précolonial.* 2 vols. (Cairo: Institut d'archéologie orientale, 1997) 1: 85–92; *Maʿalamat al-Maghrib*, s.v. "tartib," 7: 2316; A. Ibn Zaydan, *Ithaf aʿlam al-nas bi-jamal akhbar hadirat Miknas*, 5 vols. (Rabat: al- Matbaʿa al-Wataniyya, 1929)1: 394–6; A. Tawfiq, *Al-Mujtama al-maghribi fi al-qarn al- tasiʾ ʿashar: Inultan, 1850–1912* (Rabat: Kulliyat al-Adab wa-al-ulum al-Insaniyya, 1983), 599–604; E. Michaux-Bellaire, "Les impôts marocaines," *Archives marocaines* 1 (1904): 56–96. See M. al-Manuni, *Mazahir*, 2: 85–100 for the text of the dahir and related documents; Aubin, *Morocco of Today*, 203–05; G. Saint-René-Taillandier, *Les origines du Maroc français; Récit d'une mission, 1901–1906* (Paris: Plon, 1930), 158–65.
16. Arnaud, *Au temps des "mehallas,"* 126.
17. Weisgerber, "Les tribus du Maroc," National Library and Archives, Rabat, Fonds du Protectorat, Dossier F 126.
18. Burke, *Prelude to Protectorate*, 56–57.

19. Ibid., 71–75; P. Guillen, "La resistence du Maroc à l'emprise française au lendemain des accords franco-anglais de 1904," *Revue de l'Occident musulman et de la Méditerranée* 8 (1970): 115–22; and by the same author, *L'Allemagne et le Maroc de 1870 à 1905* (Paris: Presses universitaires de France, 1967), 653–97.
20. Laroui, *Origines*, 340; K. Brown, *People of Salé: Tradition and Change in a Moroccan City, 1830–1930* (Cambridge, MA: Harvard University Press, 1976), ch. 8; and by the same author, "L'évolution de la société de Salé et la pression européenne au XIXe siècle," in *Le Maroc de l'avènement de Moulay Abdelaziz à 1912* (Mohammédia: Université d'été, 1987), 3: 107–14.
21. S. E. Holden, "Famine's Fortune: The Pre-Colonial Mechanisation of Moroccan Flour Production," *Journal of North African Studies* 15, 1 (2010): 71–84; N. Michel, *Une économie de subsistances*, 2: chs. 7 and 8.
22. R. Bourqia, "Vol, pillage et banditisme dans le Maroc du XIXe siècle," *Hespéris Tamuda* 29, 2 (1991): 191–226.
23. David Hart, *Banditry in Islam: Case Studies from Morocco, Algeria, and the Pakistan North West Frontier* (Wisbech, UK: MENAS Press, 1987).
24. Aubin, *Morocco of Today*, 89–108; 322–40; Burke, *Prelude to Protectorate*, 62–65; R. E. Dunn, "Bu Himara's European Connexion; The Commercial Relations of a Moroccan Warlord," *Journal of African History* 21:2 (1980): 235–53; P. R. Venier, "French Imperialism and Pre-Colonial Rebellions in Eastern Morocco, 1903–1910," *Journal of North African Studies* 2:2 (1997): 58–59; ʿA al-Timsimani-Khaluk, "Watha'iq ʿan al- fattan al-daʿi Bu Himara," *Revue Dar al-Niaba* 1:4 (1984): 35–37.
25. W. R. Rollman, *"The 'New Order' In a Pre-Colonial Muslim Society: Military Reform in Morocco, 1844–1904,"* Ph.D. diss., University of Michigan, 1983, 800.
26. Aubin, *Morocco of Today*, 335; W. J. Rollman, "Military Officers and the 'Nidham al-Jadid' in Morocco, 1844–1912: Social and Political Transformations," *Quaderni di Oriente Moderno* 5 (2004): 217; R. E. Dunn, "The Bu Himara Rebellion in Northeast Morocco Phase I," *Middle Eastern Studies* 17:1 (1981): 31–48; and by the same author, *Resistance in the Desert: Moroccan Responses to French Imperialism 1881–1912* (London: Croom Helm; Madison: University of Wisconsin Press, 1977), 125–129; M. Kenbib, "Contrebande d'armes et 'anarchie' dans le Maroc précolonial (1844–1912), *Revue Dar al-Niaba* 1:4 (1984): 8–13.
27. F. Harrak, "State and Religion in Eighteenth Century Morocco: The Religious Policy of Sidi Muhammad b.ʿAbd Allah, 1757–1790," Ph.D. diss., School of Oriental and African Studies, University of London, 1989, 176–7; R. T. Forbes, *The Sultan of the Mountains: The Life Story of Raisuli* (New York: H. Holt and Co., 1924); Arnaud, *Au temps des "mehallas,"* 215–30; E. Michaux-Bellaire, "Le Cherif Moulay Ahmed Ben Mohammed Ben Abdallah Er resouni," *Revue du monde musulman* 5 (1908): 503–11; M. Kenbib, "Protégés et brigands dans le Maroc du XIXe siècle et début du XXe," *Hespéris Tamuda* 29:2 (1991): 244–5; A. Temsamani Khalouk, "Les Coups de Raïssouni (1895–1907)," *Revue Dar al-Niaba* 19/20 (1988): 1–30.

28. B. Tuchman, "Perdicaris Live or Raisuli Dead," in *A Sense of History: The Best Writing from the Pages of American Heritage*, B. Dobell, ed. (New York: Houghton Mifflin, 1985), 548–60; Arnaud, *Au temps des "mehallas,"* 218–21; A. Benjelloun, "Raïssouni: brigand, collaborateur ou résistant?" *Revue d'histoire maghrébine* 26 (1999): 197–203. This incident was the inspiration for a Hollywood potboiler, *The Wind and the Lion* (1975), in which the famously corpulent al-Raysuni was portrayed by dashing Scottish actor Sean Connery and Perdicaris was feminized and played by Candice Bergen.
29. R. Forbes, *Sultan of the Mountains*, ix; and the review by E. E. Mavrogordato in the *Times Literary Supplement* no. 1165 (May 15, 1924): 297.
30. A. Temsemani-Khaluk, *Al-haraka al-raysuniyya min khilal al-watha'iq al-maghribiyya, 1909–1925*, 2 vols. (Tangier: Saliki, n.d.)
31. This story is retold by S. Bazzaz, "Heresy and Politics in Nineteenth Century Morocco," *Arab Studies Journal* (2002/2003): 66–86.
32. See the perceptive monograph by S. Bazzaz, *Forgotten Saints: History, Power, and Politics in the Making of Modern Morocco*, Harvard Middle Eastern Monographs 41 (Cambridge, MA: Harvard University Press, 2010).
33. J. Cagne, *Nation et nationalisme au Maroc: Aux racines de la nation marocaine* (Rabat: Dar Nashr al-Ma'rifa, 1988): 434; E. Michaux-Bellaire, "Une tentative de restauration Idrissite à Fès," *Revue du monde musulman* 5 (1908): 402–23. The quotation from al-Hajwi is found in Laroui, *Origines*, 378. For more precise details on the rise the Hafiziyya, see Burke, *Prelude to Protectorate*, ch. 5.
34. R. Dunn, *Resistance in the Desert*, 48, 83, 117, 204–10; D. Nordman, "L'armée d'Algérie et le Maroc; le dynamisme de la conquête (fin du XIXe siècle–début du XX siècle)," in J. Frémeaux et al., *Armées, guerre et politique en Afrique du Nord: XIXe–XXe siècles* (Paris: Presses de l'Ecole normale supérieure, 1977): 33–51.
35. Nordman, "L'armée d'Algérie," 42, citing A. Le Révérend, *Lyautey écrivain* (Paris: Ophrys, 1976), 203.
36. G. Salmon, "Une opinion marocaine sur la conquête du Touat," *Archives marocaines* 1 (1904): 416–24; M. Abitbol, "Jihad et nécessité; le Maroc et la conquête française de Soudan occidental et de la Mauritanie," *Studia Islamica* 63 (1986): 172–7; al-Moutabassir, "Ma El 'Ainin Ech-Changuity," *Revue du monde musulman* 1 (1907): 343–51; F. Correale, "Ma' al-'Aynayn, il Marocco e la resistenza alla penetrazione coloniale (1905–1910)," *Oriente Moderno* 78, 2 (1998): 227–78; S. Sayagh, *La France et les frontières maroco-algériennes 1873–1902* (Paris: Éditions CNRS, 1986): 79–102; Laroui, *Origines*, 384.
37. The diplomatic moves of this period are covered in detail in Burke, *Prelude to Protectorate*, 75–89; see also G. Saint-René-Taillandier, *Les origines du Maroc français*, 356–60; Guillen, *L'Allemagne et le Maroc*, 837–50; A. G. P. Martin, *Quatre siècles d'histoire marocaine: Au Sahara de 1504 à 1902, au Maroc de 1894 à 1912* (Rabat: Éditions La Porte, 1994), 424; for a Moroccan perspective, Ibn Zaydan, *Ithaf*, 1: 396 and al-Manuni, *Mazahir*, 2: 191–232. See also Cagne, *Nation et nationalisme*, 385–98, in which the author lists "consultations" under prior sultans, pointing out that this practice was not new.

38. J-C. Allain, "Le Maroc dans les relations internationales: au temps d'Algeciras (1906–1912)," in *Le Maroc de l'avènement de Moulay Abdelaziz à 1912*, 3: 131–144; and in the same volume, S. Ihraï, "La conference d'Algéciras de 1906," 3:193–201; al-Manuni, *Mazahir*, 2: 191–232; on the American role, see P. Potter, "The Origin of the System of Mandates under the League of Nations," *American Political Science Review* 16:4 (1922): 579.
39. Miège, *Le Maroc*, 3: 469–92; J. Erckmann, *Le Maroc moderne* (Paris: Challamel Ainé, 1885), 183–84; L. Karow, *Neuf années au service du Maroc (1900–1908)*, translated by M. and J.-L. Miège (Rabat: Éditions La Porte, 1998).
40. J. Baida and V. Feroldi, *Présence chrétienne au Maroc, XIXème–XXème siècles* (Rabat: Éditions Bouregreg, 2005), 16–33; Aubin, *Morocco of Today*, 37–38; M. Kenbib, "Les Conversions dans le Maroc contemporain (1860–1956): Présentation et étude d'un corpus, " in *Conversions islamiques: Identités religieuses en Islam méditerranéen*, M. García-Arenal, ed. (Paris: Maisonneuve et Larose, 2002), 369–76.
41. J. G. Katz, *Murder in Marrakesh: Émile Mauchamp and the French Colonial Adventure* (Bloomington: Indiana University Press, 2006); E. Amster, "The Many Deaths of Dr. Emile Mauchamp: Medicine, Technology, and Popular Politics in Pre-Protectorate Morocco, 1877–1912," *International Journal of Middle East Studies* 36:3 (2004): 409–28.
42. Arnaud, *Au temps des "mehallas,"* 240.
43. Burke, *Prelude to Protectorate*, 122–3; Laroui, *Origines*, 385–99; A. Tawfiq, "Ta'ammulat fi al-bay'a al-Hafiziyya," in *Le Maroc de l'avènement de Moulay Abdelaziz à 1912*, 1: 335–47; A. al-Kattani, *Mufakahat dhawi al-nubl wa-al-ijada hadrat mudir jaridat al-Sa'ada* (Fez: s.n., 1326), 5–10, a pamphlet written by Muhammad al-Kattani's younger brother, 'Abd al-Hayy, and directed against critics of the Fez bay'a. The last battle is described by Weisgerber, *Au seuil du Maroc moderne*, 186–92.
44. Weisgerber, "Les tribus," unpaged.
45. "*Wa-lakin al-fatq kana fawq qudrat al-ratiq*," Ibn Zaydan, *Ithaf*, 1: 454.
46. Bazzaz, "Heresy and Politics," 66–86.
47. C. A. Bayly, *The Birth of the Modern World, 1780–1914: Global Connections and Comparisons* (Malden, MA: Blackwell, 2004), 172; on the impact of modernity on port cities of the Muslim Mediterranean, see M. J. Reimer, "Ottoman-Arab Seaports in the Nineteenth Century: Social Change in Alexandria, Beirut, and Tunis," in *Cities in the World System*, R. Kasaba, ed. (Westport, CT: Greenwood Press, 1991), 135–56.
48. S. G. Miller, "Making Tangier Modern: Ethnicity and Urban Development," in *Jewish Culture and Society in North Africa*, E. Benichou Gottreich and D. Schroeter, eds. (Bloomington, University of Indiana Press, 2011), 128–49.
49. M. Kenbib, "1767–1957: Du 'paradis des drogmans' à la cité 'internationale,' *Tribune juive (Montreal)* 2, 5 (1994): 62–73; S. G. Miller, "Apportioning Sacred Space in a Moroccan City: The Case of Tangier, 1860–1912," *City & Society* 13, 1 (2001): 57–83; and, by the same author, "The Beni Ider Quarter of Tangier; Hybridity as a Social Practice," in S. G. Miller and

M. Bertagnin, eds., *The Architecture and Memory of the Minority Quarter in the Muslim Mediterranean City* (Cambridge, MA: Aga Khan Program in Islamic Architecture, Graduate School of Design, 2010), 138–73.

50. B. Meakin, *The Moorish Empire, a Historical Epitome* (London: S. Sonnenschein, 1899), 535; L. Mercier, "La Presse arabe au Maroc," *Revue du monde musulman* 7 (1909): 128–33. Laroui, *Origines*, 380–81: K. Ben Ghabrit, "S. E. El Hadj Mohammed El Mokri: Grand Vizir de l'Empire chérifien," *France-Maroc* 2:5 (15 May 1918): 141–3; *Maʿalamat al-Maghrib*, s.v. "al-Jibbas, Mahammad," 8: 2912–15.
51. J. Baida, "Rasaʿil maftuha ila al-salatinayn al-Mawlay ʿAbd al-ʿAziz wa-al-Mawlay ʿAbd al-Hafiz," in *Mélanges offerts au Professeur Brahim Boutaleb*, ed. A. Kaddouri (Rabat: Faculté des lettres et sciences humaines, 2001): 493–529.
52. J. Baida, *La Presse marocaine d'expression française: Des origines à 1956* (Rabat: Faculté des lettres et des sciences humaines, 1996): 31–87; by the same author, "La presse tangéroise: relais de communication dans le Maroc précolonial," in *Miroirs maghrébins*, Susan Ossman, ed. (Paris: CNRS éditions, 1998), 21–28, and "La pensée réformiste au Maroc à la veille du Protectorat," *Hespéris Tamuda* 39:2 (2001): 52; Laroui, *Origines*, 381.
53. F. Abdulrazak, "The Kingdom of the Book: The History of Printing as an Agency of Change in Morocco between 1865 and 1912, " Ph.D. diss., Boston University, 1990, 234; al-Manuni, *Mazahir*, 2: 375–85; M. al-Kattani, *Nasihat ahl al-Islam: Tahlil islami ʿilmi li-awamil suqut al-dawla al-islamiyya wa-ʿawamil nuhudiha* (Rabat: Maktabat Badr, 1989); Laroui, *Origines*, 328–33.
54. R. Bourqia, "Droit et pratiques sociales: le cas des *nawazil* au XIXe siècle," *Hespéris Tamuda* 35, 2 (1997): 131–45; al-Manuni, *Mazahir*, 2: 327–328; J. Abun-Nasr, "The Salafiyya Movement in Morocco: The Religious Bases of the Moroccan Nationalist Movement," St. Antony's Papers, 16, A. Hourani, ed., *Middle Eastern Affairs*, 3 (London: Chatto & Windus, 1963): 98.
55. M. Ibn al-Hajj, *ʿUlama al-Maghrib al-muʿasirin* (Casablanca: al-Jadida, 1992): 272–8; on *Salwat al-Anfas*, see E. Lévi-Provençal, *Les Historiens des Chorfas: Essai sur la littérature historique et biographique au Maroc du XVIe au XXe siècle* (Paris: Larose, 1922), 280–6; S. Bazzaz, "Reading Reform Beyond the State: *Salwat al-Anfas*, Islamic Revival and Moroccan National History," *Journal of North African Studies* 13:1 (2008): 1–13.
56. *Maʿalamat al-Maghrib*, s.v. "al-Hajwi, Muhammad b. al-Hasan," 10: 3337–3338; M. Gouvion Saint-Cyr and E. Gouvion Saint-Cyr, *Kitab aayane al-Maghrib al-Aksa: Equisse générale des Moghrebs de la Genése à nos jours et livre des grands du Maroc*, 2 vols. (Paris: Librairie orientaliste Paul Geuthner, 2001), 1: 265–70; A. Bin 'Addadah, *Al-fikr al-islahi fi 'ahd al-himaya: Muhammad ibn al-Hasan al-Hajwi namudhajan* (Beirut: Markaz al-Thaqafi al-'Arabi, 2003); M. al-Hajwi, "Al-Qawl al-fasl fi aqsa amad al-haml," in *Thalath rasa'il: tajdid 'ulum al-din* (Salé: Matbaʿat al-thaqafa, 1357/1938); Abun-Nasr, "The Religious Bases," 98.

4. France and Spain in Morocco: The Early Years of the Protectorates (1912–1930)

1. G. Stuart, *The International City of Tangier*, 2nd ed. (Stanford, CA: Stanford University Press, 1955): 89–90; 127–30; G. H. Bennett, "Britain's Relations with France After Versailles: The Problem of Tangier, 1919–23," *European History Quarterly* 24 (1994), 53–84; C. Spencer, "The Spanish Protectorate and the Occupation of Tangier in 1940," in *North Africa, Nation, State and Region*, George Joffé, ed. (London: Routledge, 1993), 91–101; S. Sueiro, "L'Espagne et la 'question marocaine': La politique méditerranéenne de Primo De Rivera (1923–1930)," in *Matériaux pour l'histoire de notre temps: Colonisations en Afrique* (1993): 15–17.
2. L. Brunot and E. Malka, eds., *Textes judéo-arabes de Fès: Textes, transcription, traduction annotée* (Rabat: École du Livre, 1939): 206; F. Weisgerber, *Au seuil du Maroc moderne* (Rabat: Éditions La Porte, 1947): 284–293.
3. W. A. Hoisington, *Lyautey and the French Conquest of Morocco* (Basingstoke, UK: Macmillan, 1995), 45; M. Gershovich, *French Military Rule in Morocco: Colonialism and Its Consequences* (London: Frank Cass, 2000), 65.
4. D. Rivet, *Le Maghreb à l'épreuve de la colonisation* (Paris: Hachette, 2002), 216.
5. Hoisington, *Lyautey*, 6; quoted from H. Lyautey, *Lettres de Tonkin et de Madagascar (1894–1899)* 2 vols. (Paris: A. Colin, 1920), 1: 71.
6. W. B. Harris, *France, Spain and the Rif* (New York, London: Longmans Green, E. Arnold, 1927), 188; the text of the Treaty of Fez is found in *L'Afrique française*, 22:6 (June 1912): 219–20; D. Rivet, *Le Maroc de Lyautey à Mohammed V: Le double visage du Protectorat* (Paris: Denoël, 1999), 136.
7. A. Scham, *Lyautey in Morocco; Protectorate Administration, 1912–1925* (Berkeley: University of California Press, 1970), 55–75; W. Hoisington Jr., "Designing Morocco's Future: France and the Native Policy Council, 1921–25," *Journal of North African Studies* 5:1 (2000): 63–65.
8. H. Prost, "Le développement de l'urbanisme dans le Protectorat du Maroc de 1914 à 1923," in *L'Urbanisme aux colonies et dans les pays tropicaux: Communications et rapports du congrés international de l'urbanisme aux colonies et dans les pays de latitude intertropicale*, 2 vols., J. Royer, ed. (Nevers: Fortin, 1932) 1: 59–108; G. Wright, *The Politics of Design in French Colonial Urbanism* (Chicago: University of Chicago Press, 1991): 85–160; P. Rabinow, *French Modern: Norms and Forms of the Social Environment* (Chicago: University of Chicago, 1995): ch. 9; and, by the same author, "France in Morocco: Technocosmopolitanism and Middling Modernism," *Assemblage* 17 (April 1992): 55; J.-L. Cohen and M. Eleb, *Casablanca: Mythes et figures d'une aventure urbaine* (Paris: Hazan, 1998): 75–85.
9. D. Rivet, *Lyautey et l'institution du protectorat français au Maroc*, 3 vols. (Paris: L'Harmattan, 1988) 3: 147 n. 716; S. G. Miller, "Of Time and the City: Clifford Geertz on Urban History," *Journal of North African Studies* 14, 3 (2009): 479–90.
10. H. de la Casinière, *Les municipalités marocaines: Leur développement, leur legislation* (Casablanca: Imprimérie de la Vigie Marocaine, 1924), 12–14; Hoisington, *Lyautey*, 129; Rivet, *Le Maroc*, 227–39.

11. O. Abi-Mershed, *Apostles of Modernity: Saint-Simonians and the Civilizing Mission in Algeria* (Stanford, CA: Stanford University Press, 2010), ch. 5; M. Le Glay, *Nouveaux récits marocains de la plaine et des monts* (Paris: Berger-Levrault, 1932).
12. Hoisington, *Lyautey*, 50–53; K. Perkins, *Qaids, Captains, and Colons: French Military Administration in the Colonial Maghrib, 1844–1934* (New York: Africana Publishing, 1981); R. Bidwell, *Morocco under Colonial Rule: French Administration of Tribal Areas, 1912–1956* (London: Frank Cass, 1973), 157.
13. On the battle of El Herri, see the first-person account by J.-M. Pichon, *Le Maroc au début de la guerre mondiale: El-Herri: Vendredi, 13 novembre 1914* (Paris: Lavauzelle, 1936), cited in M. Gershovich, "Stories on the Road from Fez to Marrakesh: Oral History on the Margins of National Identity," *Journal of North African Studies* 8, 1 (2003): 43–58; D. Maghraoui, "From 'Tribal Anarchy' To 'Military Order': The Moroccan Troops in the Context of Colonial Morocco," in *Réforme par le haut, réforme par le bas: La modernization de l'armée aux 19e et 20e siècles*, O. Moreau and A. El Moudden, eds. (Rome: Instituto per l'Oriente, C. A. Nallino, 2004), 235–236.
14. Hoisington, *Lyautey*, ch. 4; Gershovich, *French Military Rule*, 787.
15. *L'Afrique française*, 27:1–2 (Jan–Feb 1917): 18, quoted in Hoisington, *Lyautey*, 103. Al-Hiba continued to harass French forces under the banner of jihad until his death in 1919.
16. J. El Adnani, "Le Caïd El Glaoui et la Tijaniyya sous l'ordre colonial français," in *Pouvoir central et caïdalité au sud du Maroc*, A. El Moudden, A. Ammalek, A. Belfaïda, eds. (Rabat: Université Mohammed V, 2010): 7–20; Hoisington, *Lyautey*, 107.
17. H. Gaillard, *La réorganisation du gouvernement marocain* (Paris: Comité de l'Afrique Française, 1916), 21–48.
18. Rivet, *Lyautey*, 2: 146–53.
19. M. Benhlal, *Le collège d'Azrou: Une élite berbère civile et militaire au Maroc, 1927–1959*, (Paris: Karthala, 2005), see the preface by D. Rivet, and ch. 9; Rivet, *Lyautey*, 2 : 245–52; M. Jadda, *Bibliographie analytique des publications de l'Institut des Hautes Études Marocaines* (Rabat: Faculté des lettres et des sciences humaines, 1994): 24; M. Bekraoui, *Les marocains dans la grande guerre, 1914–1919* (Rabat: Annajah, 2009): 225–37; M. Gershovich, "A Moroccan St. Cyr," *Middle Eastern Studies* 28:2 (1992) : 231–57.
20. S. G. Miller, "Gender and the Poetics of Emancipation: *The Alliance Israélite Universelle* in Northern Morocco, 1890–1912," in *Franco-Arab Encounters*, L. C. Brown and M. Gordon, eds. (Beirut: American University of Beirut Press, 1996): 229–58.
21. S. Segalla, *The Moroccan Soul: French Education, Colonial Ethnology, and Muslim Resistance, 1912–1956* (Lincoln: University of Nebraska Press, 2009): 51–53; Benhlal, *Le collège d'Azrou*, 5: for a comparison of Morocco and Tunisia in this period, see P. Vermeren, *École, élite et pouvoir au Maroc et en Tunisie au XXe siècle* (Rabat: Alizés, 2002), 13–110; and by the same author, "La mutation sociale de l'enseignement supérieur musulman sous le protectorat au Maroc," in *Parcours d'intellectuels maghrébins: Scolarité,*

formation, socialisation et positionnements, Aïssa Kadri, ed. (Paris: Karthala 1999), 43–60; J. Baida, "Situation de la presse au Maroc sous le 'Proconsulat' de Lyautey (1912–1925)," *Hespéris-Tamuda* 30, 1 (1992): 67–92; J. Damis, *The Free School Movement in Morocco, 1919–1970*, Ph.D. diss., Fletcher School of Law and Diplomacy, 1970, 65–70; on training women in the handicrafts, see H. Irbouh, *Art in the Service of Colonialism: French Art Education in Morocco 1912–1956* (London: I. B. Tauris, 2005), ch. 5.

22. *Archives marocaines* published between 1904 and 1936 is still a precious source of information about Morocco for the early years of the twentieth century. See E. Burke, III, "La mission scientifique au Maroc: Science sociale et politique dans l'âge de l'impérialisme," in *Actes de Durham: Récherches récentes sur le Maroc moderne, 13–15 juillet 1977* (Rabat: BESM, 1979) : 37–56; F. Houroro, *Sociologie politique coloniale au Maroc: Cas de Michaux Bellaire* (Casablanca: Afrique Orient, 1988), 14–22, 141–6.
23. M. Jadda, *Bibliographie analytique*, 39; G. Deverdun, "Institut des Hautes Études Marocaines (IHEM)" *Encyclopaedia of Islam, Second Edition, Brill Online*, accessed January 30, 2011, at http://www.brillonline.nl/subscriber/entry?entry=islam_SIM-8703; Segalla, *Moroccan Soul*, 119–23; Rivet, *Lyautey*, 3: 246; P. Vermeren, *École, élite et* pouvoir, 38–40.
24. R. Fogarty, *Race and War in France: Colonial Subjects in the French Army, 1914–1918* (Baltimore: Johns Hopkins University Press, 2008): 78.
25. Ibid., 79–80, 215. Rivet, *Lyautey*, 2: 79.
26. Gershovich, *French Military Rule*, 172–5; M. Bekraoui, *Les marocains dans la grande guerre*, 65–66, 127, 149; R. Fogarty, *Race and War in France*, 38.
27. Quoted in Bekraoui, *Marocains dans la grand guerre*, 157.
28. Ibid.
29. A. Hammoudi, "Aspects de la mobilisation populaire à la campagne vus à travers la biographie d'un Mahdi mort en 1919," in *Islam et politique au Maghreb*, E. Gellner and J.-C. Vatin, eds. (Paris: CNRS, 1981): 47–55.
30. D. S. Woolman, *Rebels in the Rif; Abd El Krim and the Rif Rebellion* (Stanford, CA: Stanford University Press, 1968), 5; Rivet, *Lyautey*, 3: 254.
31. A. Bachoud, *Los españoles ante las campañas de marruecos* (Madrid: Espasa-Calpe, 1988), 79–94.
32. V. Sheean, *An American among the Riffi* (New York: Century, 1926), 154–86.
33. W. Harris, *France, Spain and the Rif*, 69–70; Rivet, *Lyautey*: 3: 255.
34. Woolman, *Rebels in the Rif*, 83–111: F. J. Romero Salvadó, *The Spanish Civil War: Origins, Course and Outcomes* (New York: Palgrave Macmillan, 2005), 20.
35. C. R. Pennell, "Women and Resistance to Colonialism in Morocco: The Rif, 1916–26," *Journal of African History* 28, 1 (1987): 112; and by the same author, *A Country with a Government and a Flag: The Rif War in Morocco, 1921–1926* (Boulder, CO: L. Rienner, 1986), chs. 7 and 8; and "The Rif War: Link or Cul-De-Sac? Nationalism in the Cities and Resistance in the Mountains," *Journal of North African Studies* 1, 3 (1996): 242–3; D. M. Hart, *The Aith Waryaghar* (Tucson: University of Arizona Press, 1976): 375–94, and, by the same author, "De 'Ripublik' à 'République'," in *Abd el-krim et la république du Rif: Actes du colloque international d'études*

historiques et sociologiques, 18–20 janvier 1973 (Paris: F. Maspero, 1976): 35–45.

36. G. Ayache, "Les implications internationales de la guerre du Rif, (1921–1926)," *Études d'histoire marocaine* (Rabat: SMER, 1979): 379; Rivet, *Lyautey*, 3: 253–310.
37. Harris, *France, Spain and the Rif*, 239.
38. Hart, *Aith Waryaghar*, 394–403; D. Rivet, "Le commandment français et ses reactions vis-à-vis du mouvement rifian, 1924–1926," in *Abd el-Krim et la république du Rif*, 118–31; S. E. Fleming and A. K. Fleming, "Primo de Rivera and Spain's Morocco Problem, 1923–27," *Journal of Contemporary History* 12,1 (1977), 92.
39. D. H. Slavin, "The French Left and the Rif War, 1924–25: Racism and the Limits of Internationalism," *Journal of Contemporary History*, 26:1 (1991):10; R. Gallissot, "La parti communiste et la guerre du Rif," in *Abd el-krim et la république du Rif*, 237–57.
40. Harris, *France, Spain and the Rif*, 239, 246–7.
41. Woolman, *Rebels in the Rif*, 208.
42. Z. Daoud, *Abdelkrim: Une épopée d'or et de sang* (Paris: Sèguier, 1999): 349–87; A. al-Fasi, *The Independence Movements in Arab North Africa* (Washington, DC: American Council of Learned Societies, 1954), 301–14.
43. J. Berque, *French North Africa: The Maghrib between Two World Wars* (London: Faber, 1967): 169.
44. G. Ayache, *Les origines de la guerre du Rif* (Rabat: SMER, 1981): 331–41.
45. Rivet, *Lyautey*, 3: 7–11; A. Mejri, *Les socialistes français et la question marocaine (1903–1912)* (Paris: L'Harmattan, 2004), 193–200.
46. Y. Knibiehler, G. Emmery, and F. Leguay, *Des français au Maroc: La présence et la mémoire, 1912–1956* (Paris: Denoël, 1992), 43; A. Ayache, *Le mouvement syndical au Maroc*, 2 vols. (Paris: L'Harmattan, 1982), 1: 12–14.
47. M. Thomas, "Albert Sarraut, French Colonial Development, and the Communist Threat, 1919–1930," *The Journal of Modern History* 77 (December 2005): 919–20.
48. Rivet, *Lyautey*, 3: 134, 146.
49. W. D. Swearingen, *Moroccan Mirages: Agrarian Dreams and Deceptions, 1912–1986* (Princeton: Princeton University Press, 1987), 20; and by the same author, "In Pursuit of the Granary of Rome: France's Wheat Policy in Morocco, 1915–1931," *International Journal of Middle East Studies* 17, 3 (1985): 347–50; J. Gadille, "La colonisation officielle au Maroc," *Les cahiers d'outre-mer* 8 (Oct–Dec 1955): 306–309; P. Pascon, *Capitalism and Agriculture in the Haouz of Marrakesh* (London: KPI, 1986), ch. 2; D. K. Davis, *Resurrecting the Granary of Rome: Environmental History and French Colonial Expansion in North Africa* (Athens: Ohio University Press, 2007), ch. 5.
50. D. Rivet, *Lyautey*, 3:26. Knibiehler et al., *Des français au Maroc*, 44.
51. M. Nahon, *Notes d'un colon du Gharb* (Casablanca: Société d'éditions marocaines, 1925); see also the first-person accounts of settler life collected by Y. Knibiehler et al., in *Des français au Maroc*, 119–56.

52. W. Swearingen, "In Pursuit of the Granary of Rome," 363: M. Kleiche, "Aux origines du concept de développement: Quand l'irrigation devient enjeu de réforme agricole: Nouvelle mise en ordre du paysage rural marocain dans l'entre-deux-guerres," *Herpéris-Tamuda* 39:2 (2001): 179–89.
53. D. Rivet, *Maghreb*, 282.
54. J. Berque, *French North Africa*, 164–84; D. Rivet, *Le Maroc*, 242–50.
55. Ayache, *Mouvement syndical*, 1:17, 24.
56. Ibid.
57. Rivet, *Lyautey*, 3: 311; Berque, *French North Africa*, 170.
58. See, for example, the heated argument of nationalist Mohammed Hasan al-Ouezzani against the characterization of Lyautey as the "architect of modern Morocco" in *Le Protectorat: Crime de Lèse-Nation* (Fez: Fondation Mohamed Hassan Ouezzani, 1992), 5–10.

5. Framing the Nation (1930–1961)

1. E. Gellner, "Do nations have navels?" *Nations and Nationalism* 10 (1996): 367; E. Manela, "A Man Ahead of His Time? Wilsonian Globalism and the Doctrine of Preemption," *International Journal* 60:4 (2005): 1117–18.
2. J. Berque, *French North Africa: The Maghrib Between Two World Wars* (New York: Praeger, 1967), 65.
3. Berque, *French North Africa*, 67; W. A. Hoisington, "Designing Morocco's Future: France and the Native Policy Council, 1921–25," *Journal of North African Studies* 5:1 (2000): 78–80: P. Vermeren, *École, élite et pouvoir au Maroc et en Tunisie au XXe siècle* (Rabat: Alizés, 2002): 11, 25; R. Montagne, "Un rapport secret sur les Jeunes marocains dans les années vingt," *Revue d'histoire maghrébine* 131 (2008): 141–2.
4. *Plan de réformes marocaines, élaboré et présenté à S. M. Le Sultan, au gouvernement de la République française et à la Résidence Générale au Maroc par le Comité d'Action marocaine* (n.p.: Édition française, 1934), ix.
5. K. Brown, "The Impact of the Dahir Berbère in Salé," in *Arabs and Berbers; From Tribe to Nation in North Africa*, E. Gellner and and C. Micaud, eds. (Lexington, MA: D.C. Heath, 1972): 204; H. Rachik, *Symboliser la nation: Essai sur l'usage des identités collectives au Maroc* (Casablanca: Le Fennec, 2003), 66–67: J. P. Halstead, *Rebirth of a Nation: The Origins and Rise of Moroccan Nationalism, 1912–1944* (Cambridge, MA: Harvard University Press, 1967), 161–77; J. Damis, "The Origins and Significance of the Free School Movement in Morocco, 1919–1931," *Revue de l'occident musulman et de la Méditerranée* 19–20 (1975): 75–99.
6. M. Bekraoui, "Les étudiants marocains en France à l'époque du Protectorat, 1927–1939," in *Présences et images franco-marocaines au temps du protectorat*, J.C. Allain, ed. (Paris: l'Harmattan, 2003), 89–111.
7. Berque, *French North Africa*, 76. Vermeren, *École, élite et pouvoir*, 110; M. Sijelmassi and M. al-Saghir Janjar, *Le Maroc au XXe siècle: Fresque historique des hommes, des femmes et des grands événements du siècle* (Casablanca: Éditions Oum, 2001), 125.

8. Hoisington, "Designing Morocco's Future: France and the Native Policy Council, 1921–25," 86.
9. C. R. Ageron, "La politique berbère du Protectorat marocain de 1913 à 1934," *Revue d'histoire moderne et contemporaine* 18:1 (1971): 51–53; E. Burke III, "The Image of the Moroccan State in French Ethnological Literature: New Light on the Origins of Lyautey's Berber Policy," in *Arabs and Berbers*, 175–99; P. Lorcin, *Imperial Identities: Stereotyping, Prejudice and Race in Colonial Algeria* (London and New York: I. B. Tauris, 1995), *passim.*
10. Ageron, "La politique berbère," 63.
11. J. Halstead, *Rebirth of a Nation*, 276–7 for the full text of the dahir.
12. H. Rachik, *Symboliser la nation*, 64. C. Ageron, "La politique berbère," 79–80; K. Brown, "The Impact of the Dahir Berbère," 209–13.
13. W. L. Cleveland, *Islam against the West: Shakib Arslan and the Campaign for Islamic Nationalism* (Austin: University of Texas Press, 1985), 95; Ageron, "La politique berbère," 83.
14. Ibid., 83, 85; For a provocative discussion of the historical reinterpretation of the dahir, see D. M. Hart, "The Berber Dahir of 1930 in Colonial Morocco: Then and Now (1930–1996)," *Journal of North African Studies* 2:2 (1997): 11–33.
15. E. Balibar, "The Nation Form: History and Ideology," in *Race, Nation, Class: Ambiguous Identities*, E. Balibar and I. M. Wallerstein, eds. (London: Verso, 1991), 87–88; W. Hoisington, "Cities in Revolt: The Berber Dahir (1930) and France's Urban Strategy in Morocco," *Journal of Contemporary History* 13:3 (1978): 444; see also J. Wyrtzen,"Colonial State-Building and the Negotiation of Arab and Berber Identity in Protectorate Morocco," *International Journal of Middle East Studies* 43:2 (2011), 227–49.
16. J. Halstead, *Rebirth of a Nation*, 194; C.A. Julien, *Le Maroc face aux impérialismes: 1415–1956* (Paris: Éditions J.A., 1978), 170–1.
17. R. Rézette, *Les partis politiques marocains* (Paris: A. Colin, 1955), 267–90.
18. J. Berque, *French North Africa*, 180–1; E. G. H. Joffé, "The Moroccan Nationalist Movement: Istiqlal, the Sultan, and the Country," *The Journal of African History* 26:4 (1985): 294; C. Stewart, *The Economy of Morocco, 1912–1962*, Harvard Middle Eastern Monographs 12 (Cambridge, MA: Harvard University Press, 1964): 142.
19. F. Mernissi, *Dreams of Trespass: Tales of a Harem Girlhood* (Reading, MA: Addison-Wesley, 1994): 118–22. Wearing the jallaba by women was frowned on by social conservatives because it too closely resembled the male garment.
20. H. Rachik, *Symboliser la Nation*, 82–85, 97–112; J. Halstead, *Rebirth of a Nation*, 203–4; A. Aouchar, *La presse marocaine dans la lutte pour l'indépendance (1933–1956)* (Casablanca: Wallada, 1990): 60.
21. Halstead, *Rebirth*, 233; R. Landau, "Moroccan Profiles: A Nationalist View," *Middle East Journal* 7:1 (1953): 50; H. Bleuchot, *Les libéraux français au Maroc, 1947–1955* (Paris: Éditions Ophrys, 1973): 27.
22. Halstead, *Rebirth of a Nation*, 145–9; Aouchar, *La presse marocaine*, 29–38.
23. ʿA. al-Fasi, *The Independence Movements in Arab North Africa* (Washington, DC: American Council of Learned Societies, 1954); 139; Comité d'action marocaine, *Plan de réformes marocaines*, 21, 128–9.

24. Rézette, *Les partis politiques marocains*, 69, 87–90.
25. Halstead, *Rebirth of a Nation*, 242–4.
26. S. E. Fleming, "Spanish Morocco and the Alzamiento Nacional, 1936–1939: The Military, Economic and Political Mobilization of a Protectorate," *Journal of Contemporary History* 18:1 (1983): 30.
27. J. Halstead, *Rebirth of a Nation*, 258; C. R. Halstead, "A 'Somewhat Machiavellian' Face: Colonel Juan Beigbeder as High Commissioner in Spanish Morocco, 1937–1939," *Historian* 37:1 (1974): 46–66; C. Spencer, "The Spanish Protectorate and the Occupation of Tangier in 1940," in *North Africa: Nation, State, and Region*, E. G. H. Joffé, ed. (London: Routledge, 1993), 103–4; Rézette, *Les partis politiques marocains*, 113–29. The theme of *convivencia* was elaborated by the colonial writer Tomás García Figueras: see G. Jensen, "The Peculiarities of 'Spanish Morocco': Imperial Ideology and Economic Development," *Mediterranean Historical Review* 20:1 (2005): 81–102; Cleveland, *Islam Against the West*, 143–4, 155–6; J. Baïda, "Perception de la periode nazie au Maroc: Quelques indices de l'impact de la propagande allemande sur l'état d'esprits des marocains," in *Marocains et Allemands: La perception de l'autre*, A. Bendaoud and M. Berriane, eds. (Rabat: Faculté des lettres et des sciences humaines, 1995): 13–19; Aouchar, *La presse marocaine*, 33, 73; W. A. Hoisington, *The Casablanca Connection: French Colonial Policy, 1936–1943* (Chapel Hill: University of North Carolina Press, 1984), 146–7.
28. D. Rivet, *Le Maghreb à l'épreuve de la colonization* (Paris: Hachette, 2002), 272.
29. See many evocative passages of domestic life in this era in F. Mernissi, *Dreams of Trespass, passim.*
30. D. Rivet, "Hygiénisme colonial et médicalisation de la société marocaine au temps du Protectorat français (1912–1956)," in *Santé, médecine et société dans le monde arabe*, E. Longuenesse, ed. (Paris: l'Harmattan, 1995), 105–8.
31. S. G. Miller, "The Sleeping Fetus," *Encyclopedia of Women & Islamic Cultures*, Suad Joseph, ed., 6 vols. (Leiden: Brill, 2006): 3: 421–4.
32. Rivet, "Hygiénisme colonial," 113; R. Pourquier, "La santé et l'hygiéne publiques," *L'Encyclopédie colonial et maritime*: *Le Maroc*, 3rd ed. (Paris: l'Encyclopédie Colonial et Maritime, 1941), 165–167.
33. R. Gallissot, *Le patronat européen au Maroc: Action sociale, action politique (1931–1942)* (Casablanca: EDDIF, 1990): 55–58, 71–74; A. Ayache, *Le mouvement syndical au Maroc*, 3 vols. (Paris: L'Harmattan, 1982), 1:85; R. Montagne, *Naissance du prolétariat marocain* (Paris: Peyronnet, 1952), 135–40.
34. Ayache, *Le mouvement syndical*, 1: 143, 185; Stewart, *The Economy of Morocco*, 141; M. Kenbib, "Le Général de Gaulle et les nationalistes marocains (1940–1946)," *Espoir* 80 (1992): 85; D. Rivet, *Le Maroc de Lyautey à Mohammed V : Le double visage du protectorat* (Paris: Denoël, 1999), 136. Moroccans were not officially allowed to join unions until the 1950s, although many had informally joined before that time; see al-Fasi, *Independence Movements*, 173–5.

35. M. Abitbol, *The Jews of North Africa During the Second World War* (Detroit: Wayne State University Press, 1989): 56–101: Joffé, "The Moroccan Nationalist Movement," 301–2.
36. 'A. al-Fasi, *Independence Movements*, 213.
37. B. T. Edwards, *Morocco Bound: Disorienting America's Maghreb, from Casablanca to the Marrakech Express* (Durham, NC: Duke University Press, 2005), 30.
38. E. N. Sangmuah, "Sultan Mohammed Ben Youssef's American Strategy and the Diplomacy of North African Liberation, 1943–61," *Journal of Contemporary History* 27:1 (1992): 131; L. B. Blair, *Western Window in the Arab World* (Austin: University of Texas Press, 1970), 96–97; E. Roosevelt, *As He Saw It* (New York: Duell, Sloan and Pearce, 1946): 109–112; Hassan II, *La memoire d'un roi: Entretiens avec Eric Laurent* (Paris: Plon, 1993), 18; M. Kenbib, "L'impact americain sur l'nationalisme marocaine (1930–1947), *Hespéris Tamuda* 37–38 (1988–1989): 207–23.
39. Kenbib, "Le Général de Gaulle et les nationalistes marocains," 85, 88; Hoisington, *Casablanca Connection*, 200–14.
40. Rivet, *Le Maroc*, 359–61.
41. D. Zisenwine, *The Emergence of Nationalist Politics in Morocco: The Rise of the Independence Party and the Struggle against Colonialism after World War II* (New York: Tauris, 2010), 24.
42. 'A. al-Fasi, *Independence Movements*, 113.
43. P. Rabinow, *French Modern: Norms and Forms of the Social Environment* (Chicago: University of Chicago Press, 1995), 2–4; R. Pinta, "La lutte contre la misère au Maroc en 1945," *Bulletin économique et social du Maroc* 8:28 (1946): 285.
44. D. Rivet, *Le Maroc*, 148–9, 217–23.
45. M. Ben Barka, *The Political Thought of Ben Barka: Revolutionary Option in Morocco,* [*sic*] *Political Articles, 1960–1965* (Havana: Tricontinental, 1968), 44.
46. R. Landau, "Moroccan Profiles," 50, 53; J. and S. Lacouture, *Le Maroc à l'épreuve* (Paris: Éditions du Seuil, 1958), 134–5.
47. 'A. al-Fasi, *Independence Movements*, 266–83, for a discussion of the ramifications of the visit from the Istiqlal perspective.
48. Landau, *Moroccan Drama*, 285; D. Rivet, quoting Balafrej in *Le Maroc*, 397.
49. A. Ayache, "Mouvements urbains en milieu colonial: les événements de Casablanca des 7 et 8 décembre 1952," in *Mémorial Germain Ayache*, 'Umar Afa, ed. (Rabat: Université Mohammed V, Faculté des lettres et sciences humaines, 1994), 59–68.
50. M. Aouad and M. Awad, *Les trente glorieuses, ou, l'âge d'or du nationalisme marocain, 1925–1955: Témoignage d'un compagnon de Mehdi Ben Barka* (Rabat: Éditions LPL, 2006), 262–86.
51. M. Sijelmassi and M. al-Ṣaghir Janjar, *Le Maroc au XXe siècle*, 138; Landau, *Moroccan Drama*, 310.
52. Quoted in Rivet, *Le Maroc*, 424.
53. G. Delanoë, *Lyautey, Juin, Mohammed V, fin d'un Protectorat* (Casablanca: Eddif, 1993): 162–163.

54. On the colonial troops who participated in the war in Indochina, see N. Delanoë, *Poussières d'Empires* (Casablanca: Tarik, 2002).
55. W. A. Hoisington, *The Assassination of Jacques Lemaigre Dubreuil: A Frenchman between France and North Africa* (London and New York: Routledge, 2005), and, by the same author, "Commerce and Conflict: French Businessmen in Morocco, 1952–55," *Journal of Contemporary History* 9, 2 (1974): 49–67; Landau, *Moroccan Drama*, 367–8.
56. N. Bouzar, *L'armée de libération nationale marocaine, [1955–1956]: Retour sans visa, journal d'un résistant maghrébin* (Paris: Publisud, 2002), 177–80; L. J. Duclos, "The Berbers and the Rise of Moroccan Nationalism," in *Arabs and Berbers*, 224–9.
57. *Ma'alamat al-Maghrib*, s.v "Al- Muqri, Muhammad," 21: 7235.
58. Joffé, "The Moroccan Nationalist Movement," 297–8; R. Bidwell, *Morocco under Colonial Rule: French Administration of Tribal Areas, 1912–1956* (London: Cass, 1973), 307–28.
59. P. Vermeren, *Histoire du Maroc depuis l'indépendance* (Paris: Découverte, 2006), 20–21.Vermeren leans heavily on M. Monjib, *La monarchie marocaine et la lutte pour le pouvoir: Hassan II face à l'opposition nationale, de l'indépendance à l'état d'exception* (Paris: l'Harmattan, 1992), ch. 1.
60. Rivet, *Le Maroc*, 420–1.
61. R. Leveau, *Le fellah marocain, défenseur du trône*, 2nd ed. (Paris: Presses de la Fondation nationale des sciences politiques, 1985); part I.
62. See L. Cerych, *Fin d'un régime colonial: Sociologie du conflit franco-marocain (1930–1956)* (Bruges: De Tempel, 1964), 50.
63. M. J. Willis, "The Military in Maghrebi Politics," unpublished paper presented at the Middle East Studies Association Conference, November 2003, 4. My thanks to Prof. Willis for his permission to make use of this work.
64. Vermeren, *Histoire du Maroc*, 26; R. Leveau, *Le sabre et le turban: L'avenir du Magheb* (Paris: F. Bourin, 1993), 207.
65. J. Waterbury, *The Commander of the Faithful: The Moroccan Political Elite – A Study in Segmented Politics* (New York: Columbia University Press, 1970); 245, 254–6; *Tel Quel on line*, http://www.telquel-online.com/341/maroc2_341.shtml, accessed on June 28, 2011. The FDIC was founded in 1958 but did not compete in parliamentary elections until 1963.
66. A. Boukhari, *Le secret: Ben Barka et le Maroc: Un ancien agent des services spéciaux parle* (Neuilly-sur-Seine [France]: Lafon, 2002), 26; Vermeren, *Histoire du Maroc*, 41; *Tel-Quel* on line, http://www.telquel-online.com/162/index_162.shtml. Accessed on June 24, 2011.
67. Morocco refused to sign the Eisenhower Doctrine, designed to stop the spread of Communism in the Middle East and North Africa, and the United States, under pressure from the nationalists, agreed to close all U.S. bases in Morocco in the early 1960s. C. Gallagher, *The United States and North Africa: Morocco, Algeria, and Tunisia* (Cambridge, MA: Harvard University Press, 1963), 240–1.
68. C. Geertz, Review of *The Commander of the Faithful* by John Waterbury, *Middle Eastern Studies* 7:2 (May 1971): 251–5.

6. The First Age of Hassan II: The Iron Fist (1961–1975)

1. R. Leveau, "The Moroccan Monarchy: A Political System in Quest of a New Equilibrium," in *Middle East Monarchies: The Challenge of Modernity*, J. Kostiner, ed. (Boulder, CO: Lynne Rienner, 2000), 117.
2. M. Monjib, *La monarchie marocaine et la lutte pour le pouvoir: Hassan II face à l'opposition nationale, de l'indépendance à l'état d'exception* (Paris: l'Harmattan, 1992), 234–5, 240.
3. The quote is from R. Landau, *Hassan II, King of Morocco* (London: Allen & Unwin, 1962), 84; see also Z. Daoud and M. Monjib, *Ben Barka* (Paris: Éditions Michalon, 1996), 281–2; J. Waterbury, *The Commander of the Faithful; The Moroccan Political Elite – a Study in Segmented Politics* (New York: Columbia University Press, 1970), 258.
4. Monjib, *La monarchie marocaine*, 239–52.
5. This would include the Spanish coastal enclaves of Ceuta, Melilla and Ifni, as well as Mauritania and Spanish Sahara.
6. D. Ashford, "The Irredentist Appeal in Morocco and Mauritania," *The Western Political Quarterly* 15:4 (1962): 641–51; Monjib, *La Monarchie marocaine*, 248–50.
7. I. W. Zartman, *Morocco: Problems of New Power* (New York: Atherton Press, 1964), 23–60.
8. Hassan II, *Memoire d'un roi: Entretiens avec Eric Laurent* (Paris: Plon, 1993), 85–86; Monjib and Daoud, *Ben Barka*, 300.; K. Farsoun and J. Paul, "War in the Sahara: 1963," *MERIP Reports* no. 45 (March 1976): 13–16; M. Ben Barka, *The Political Thought of Ben Barka: Revolutionary Option in Morocco, Political Articles, 1960–1965* (Havana: Tricontinental, 1968), 183–186; Vermeren, *Histoire du Maroc depuis l'independence* (Paris: La Decouverte, 2002), 38–39.
9. Daoud and Monjib, *Ben Barka*, 276, 299. For a brief biography of Ben Barka, see, A. Ouardighi, *L'itinéraire d'un nationaliste: Mehdi Ben Barka, 1920–1965: Une biographie* (Rabat: Éditions Moncho, 1982). For his political writing, especially on Third World issues, see the collection edited by R. Gallissot and J. Kergoat, *Mehdi Ben Barka: De l'indépendance marocaine à la Tricontinentale* (Paris: Karthala, 1997) and R. Jean, *Problèmes d'édification du Maroc et du Maghreb; Quatre entretiens avec el Mehdi Ben Barka*, Tribune Libre, 52 (Paris: Plon, 1959).
10. B. Belouchi, *Portraits d'hommes politiques du Maroc* (Casablanca: Afrique Orient, 2002), 65; *Tel Quel on line*, "Cheikh el-Arab: Itineraire d'un heros sans gloire," http://www.telquel-online.com/111/sujet3.shtml. Accessed on June 27, 2011; Leveau, "The Moroccan Monarchy," 118.
11. Hassan II, *Mémoire d'un roi*, 105–7; D. Guérin, *Ben Barka, ses assassins: Seize ans d'enquête* (Paris: Plon, 1982); a recent account by a former member of the Moroccan secret service (CAB1) is A. Boukhari, *Raisons d'états: Tout sur l'affaire Ben Barka et d'autres crimes politiques au Maroc* (Casablanca: Ed. Maghrébines, 2005); Vermeren, *Histoire du Maroc*, 47–48. Some quarters claim that both the CIA and the Mossad were implicated in the plot, although without offering conclusive proof.

12. C. H. Moore and A. Rothschild, "Student Unions in North African Politics," *Daedelus* 97:1 (1968): 29; Waterbury, *Commander of the Faithful*, 214–15; M. Bennouna, *Héros sans gloire: échec d'une révolution, 1963* (Casablanca: Tarik, 2002).
13. Vermeren, *Histoire du Maroc*, 45–46. J. Waterbury, "The Coup Manqué," in *Arabs and Berbers: From Tribe to Nation in North Africa*, E. Gellner and C. Micaud, eds. (Lexington, MA: DC Heath, 1972), 414–15; M. Benhlal, "Le Syndicat comme enjeu politique au Maroc (1955–1981)," in *Le Mouvement ouvrier maghrébin*, N. Sraïeb, ed. (Paris: CNRS, 1985), 228: The quotations from El Ayadi and Hassan II appeared in *Tel Quel* #169, http://www.telquel-online.com/169/sujet1.shtml,"Casablanca, le 23 mars 1965," accessed on July 8, 2011. See also M. El Ayadi, "Les mouvements de la jeunesse au Maroc: L'émergence d'une nouvelle intelligentsia politique durant les années soixante et soixante-dix," in *Émeutes et mouvements sociaux au Maghreb; Perspective comparée*, D. Le Saout and M. Rollinde, eds. (Paris: Karthala, 1999), 201–30.
14. Vermeren, *Histoire du Maroc*, 52–53.
15. C. Daure-Serfaty, *Letter from Morocco* (East Lansing: Michigan State University Press, 2003); A. Serfaty and M. Elbaz, *L'insoumis: Juifs, marocains et rebelles* (Paris: Desclée de Brouwer, 2001); *Tel Quel online*, "Témoignages. Abraham Serfaty, par ses Compagnons," http://www.telquelonline.com/335/maroc2_335.shtml, accessed on June 29, 2011.
16. M. J. Willis, "The Military in Maghrebi Politics," unpublished paper presented at the Middle East Studies Association Conference, November 2003, 6; see also ʿA. al-Marini, *al-Jaysh al-maghribi ʿabr al-tarikh* (Rabat: Dar al-Nashr al-Maʿrifa, 1997).
17. Ben Barka, *Political Thought*, 18.
18. A. Doumou, "The State and Legitimation in Post-Colonial Morocco," in *The Moroccan State in Historical Perspective, 1850–1985*, A. Doumou, ed. (Dakar, Senegal: CODESRIA, 1990), 65–66.
19. W. D. Swearingen, *Moroccan Mirages: Agrarian Dreams and Deceptions, 1912–1986* (Princeton: Princeton University Press, 1987), 143–145; H. Van Wersch, "Rural Development in Morocco: 'Operation Labour,'" *Economic Development and Cultural Change* 17:1 (1968): 33.
20. Van Wersch, "Operation Labour," 47; Ben Barka, *Political Thought*, 49; W. D. Swearingen, "Morocco's Agricultural Crisis," in *The Political Economy of Morocco*, I. W. Zartman, ed. (New York: Praeger, 1987), 159–72.
21. Ben Barka, *Political Thought*, 96–97; A. Belal and A. Agourram, "L'economie marocaine depuis l'independence," *Annuaire de l'Afrique du Nord* 8, (1969): 145, 154, 155.
22. Vermeren, *Histoire du Maroc*, 55; Leveau, "Moroccan Monarchy," 126.
23. J. Waterbury, "The coup manqué," 399.
24. Profiles of the main actors in the putsch are found in Waterbury, "The coup manqué," 418–420; for a sketch of Ababou, see http://www.telquel-online.com/373/couverture_373.shtml, "Portrait-Enquête. L'homme qui a voulu tuer Hassan II," accessed on July 5, 2011.
25. A detailed account of the bloodbath is found in Waterbury, "The coup manqué," 406–13; see *Paris Match*, no. 1159 (July 24, 1971, with remarkable

photographs); *Jeune Afrique*, no. 550, July 20, 1971; *L'Express*, no. 1045 (July 19–25, 1971). More recent eyewitness accounts are found in the post-prison narratives of participants in the coup who survived: A. Binebine, *Tazmamort: Récit* (Paris: Denoël, 2009); M. Raïss, *De Skhirat à Tazmamart: Retour du bout de l'enfer* (Maroc: Afrique Orient, 2002); A. Marzouki, *Tazmamart Cellule 10* (Casablanca: Tarik, 2000). See also *Tel Quel online*, http://www.telquel-online.com/359/couverture_359.shtml, "Histoire. Les minutes d'un anniversaire sanglant," accessed on July 5, 2011; *New York Times*, "Hassan II of Morocco Dies at Seventy," July 24, 1999.

26. Waterbury, "The coup manqué," 413.
27. A. Coram, "The Berbers and the Coup," in *Arabs and Berbers*, 425–30.
28. It has been rumored that leading politicians from the Istiqlal, the UNFP, and a clandestine organization headed by Muhammad "Fqih" Basri called "Tanzim," were in secret conversation with Oufkir, but so far, there is no concrete proof of this allegation. http://www.telquel-online.com/244/maroc3_244.shtml, "Interview Mohamed Aït Kaddour. "Quand nous étions révolutionnaires," accessed on July 21, 2011.
29. Hassan II, *The Challenge: The Memoirs of King Hassan II of Morocco* (London: Macmillan, 1978) 154; S. Smith, *Oufkir, un destin marocain* (Paris: Hachette, 2002), 342–366.
30. M. Oufkir and M. Fitoussi, *Stolen Lives: Twenty Years in a Desert Jail* (New York: Talk Miramax Books/Hyperion, 2001); see also *Tel Quel*: http://www.telquel-online.com/244/maroc3_244.shtml, "L'affaire du Boeing: Révélations sur le putsch de 72," accessed on July 5, 2011.
31. Willis, "The Military in Maghebi Politics," 14.
32. S. Hughes, *Morocco under King Hassan* (Reading, U.K.: Ithaca, 2001), 234; The Sahrawis' tribal ancestors are the Beni Hassan of Yemeni origin; they speak an Arabic dialect known as Hassaniyya. For the most part, they were traders and pastoralists, wandering in wide arcs across the Western Sahara without paying much heed to the borders of Morocco, Algeria, and Mauritania. See S. Zunes and J. Mundy, *Western Sahara : War, Nationalism, and Conflict Irresolution* (Syracuse, NY: Syracuse University Press, 2010), ch. 4.
33. J. B. Weiner, "The Green March in Historical Perspective," *Middle East Journal* 33, 1 (1979): 22.
34. J. Damis, "King Hassan and the Western Sahara," *The Maghreb Review* 25, 1–2 (2000), 16.
35. See Hughes's colorful eyewitness account, *Morocco under King Hassan*, 240.
36. J. Gretton, "The Western Sahara in the International Arena," *The World Today* 36, 9 (1980): 343, 349; J. Mundy, "Neutrality or Complicity? The United States and the 1975 Moroccan Takeover of the Spanish Sahara," *Journal of North African Studies* 11:3 (2006): 275–303; R. B. Parker, *North Africa: Regional Tensions and Strategic Concerns* (Westport, CT: Praeger, 1987), 29. The Moroccans detained Algerian prisoners at a military camp near Rabat, where they remained for years.
37. The Wikipedia article on this topic is soundly documented: http://en.wikipedia.org/wiki/Sahrawi_refugee_camps, accessed on July 8, 2011; see also J. Harding, "Behind the Sandwall; Review of Toby Shelley, *Endgame for the*

Western Sahara: What Future for Africa's Last Colony? (London: Zed, 2004)," *The London Review of Books* (February 23, 2006), 8–11; R. B. Khoury, "Western Sahara and Palestine: A Comparative Study of Colonialisms, Occupations, and Nationalisms," *New Middle Eastern Studies*, 1 (2011): 1–20.

38. Damis, "Western Sahara," 30; *Tel Quel online*, http://www.telquelonline.com/198/sujet1.shtml, "La vérite sur la Marche Verte," accessed on July 24, 2011.
39. K. Mohsen-Finan, *Sahara Occidental: Les enjeux d'un conflit régional* (Paris: CNRS, 1997), 86–87; P. Vermeren, *Histoire du Maroc*, 66–68.
40. M. Benhlal, "Le Syndicat comme enjeu," 237.
41. Ibid., 241.
42. Ibid., 243
43. Vermeren, *Histoire du Maroc*, 83–84; on the Nador riots, see *Tel Quel online*, "La révolte des "awbach," http://www.telquel-online.com/259/maroc5_259.shtml, accessed on July 8, 2011.

7. The Second Age of Hassan II: The Velvet Glove (1976–1999)

1. "Civil society" is a term defined in various ways. The definition put forward by the London School of Economics' Centre for Civil Society suits our purposes : "Civil society refers to the arena of uncoerced collective action around shared interests, purposes and values ... its institutional forms are distinct from those of the state, and market, though in practice, the boundaries between state, civil society, and market are often complex, blurred and negotiated.... Civil societies are often populated by organizations such as registered charities, development and non-governmental organizations, community groups, women's organizations, faith-based organizations, professional associations, trade unions, self-help groups, social movements, business associations, coalitions and advocacy groups." See also James Sater, "The Dynamics of State and Civil Society in Morocco," *Journal of North African Studies* 7:3 (2002): 101–18.
2. M. Zeghal, *Islamism in Morocco: Religion, Authoritarianism, and Electoral Politics* (Princeton: Markus Wiener, 2008), xiv–xv.
3. ʿA. al-Fasi, *Difa ʿan al-shariʿa* (Rabat: Maktabat al-Risala, 1966), 300, quoted in Zeghal, *Islamism*, 69–76; M. Tozy, "Monopolisation de la production symbolique et hiérarchisation du champ politico-religieux au Maroc," *Annuaire de l'Afrique du Nord* 18 (1979): 228–31.
4. M. El Ayadi, "Between Islam and Islamism: Religion in the Moroccan Public School," unpublished paper, n.d.; M. Tozy, "Réformes politiques et transition démocratique," *Maghreb Machrek* 164 (1999): 80.
5. M. Tozy, *Monarchie et Islam politique au Maroc* (Paris: Presses de la Fondation nationale des sciences politiques, 1999), 198; Zeghal, *Islamism*, 79–142, and esp. pp. 98–116.
6. M. Bennani-Chraïbi and R. Leveau, *Soumis et rebelles: Les jeunes au Maroc* (Paris: CNRS, 1994), 257–85.
7. The building of the Hassan II mosque in Casablanca, announced by the king in July 1988 and inaugurated in 1993, was aimed at demonstrating Hassan's

mastery over the Islamic field. Built at the cost of $600 million tithed from every segment of the Moroccan population, the mosque was a massive public works project employing thousands of workers. Not everyone greeted this Maoist-style fund drive with joy; shopkeepers prominently displayed their certificate of donation, more out of fear of being tithed again than out of pride in giving. Even middle class professors grumbled at the obligatory nature of the collection. A gargantuan structure with a minaret seven hundred feet tall sprawling across the Casablanca seafront, Hassan's achievement had manifold purposes, according to French historian Pierre Vermeren: the mosque branded "New York–like" Casablanca with an unmistakably Islamic feel, it soaked up millions of unspent dirhams at a time of runaway inflation, and it reminded the faithful of the Sultan/King's preeminence in the religious sphere. See his *Histoire du Maroc depuis l'independence* (Paris: La Decouverte, 2002), 95–97.

8. Zeghal, *Islamism*, 178.
9. M. Zeghal and F. Fergosi, *Religion et politique au Maghreb: Les exemples tunisien et marocain*, *Policy Paper 11*, K. Mohsen-Finan, ed. (Paris: Institut français des relations internationales (IFRI), (2005), 32–33; see also F. Laroui, "Democracy and Islam in the Maghreb and Implications for Europe," in *The Other Muslims: Moderate and Secular*, Z. Baran, ed. (New York: Palgrave, 2010) 71–79.
10. For example, the nationalist militant Malika al-Fasi was instrumental in drafting the 1944 Manifesto of Independence, but her name does not appear among the list of signatories. L. Akharbach and N. Rerhaye, *Femmes et Politique* (Rabat: Éditions Le Fennec, 1992), 17–26.
11. J. Berque, *Structures sociales du Haut-Atlas* (Paris: PUF, 1955), 347. A. Belarbi, "Le mouvement associatif feminine," *Prologues*, 9 (May 1997), 28–33.
12. D. Rivet, *Le Maroc de Lyautey à Mohammed V* (Paris: Denoél, 1999), 319. A. Baker, *Voices of Resistance: Oral Histories of Moroccan Women* (Albany: State University of New York Press, 1998), *passim.*
13. J. Mathieu, P. H. Maury, and A. Arrif, *Bousbir: La prostitution dans le Maroc colonial : ethnographie d'un quartier reservé* (Aix-en-Provence; Paris: IREMAM; Paris-Méditerranée, 2003) 11–35. See also C. Taraud, *La prostitution coloniale: Algérie, Tunisie, Maroc (1830–1962)* (Paris: Payot, 2003).
14. Belarbi, "Mouvement associatif," 30: F. Mernissi, *Dreams of Trespass: Tales of a Harem Girlhood* (Reading, MA: Addison-Wesley, 1994), 118.
15. R. Naciri, "Engaging the State: The Women's Movement and Political Discourse in Morocco," in *Missionaries and Mandarins: Feminist Engagement with Development Institutions*, C. Miller and R. Shahrashoub Razavi, eds. (London: Intermediate Technology Publications and the United Nations Research Institute for Social Development, 1998), 87–111; Sater, "The Dynamics of State and Civil Society in Morocco," 106.
16. Belarbi, "Mouvement feminin," 31.
17. A reformed and far more liberal Family Code incorporating significant changes in many important areas of women's status was promulgated by King Muhammad VI in 2004.

18. Naciri, "Engaging the State," 102, 105.
19. K. Brown, "A Few Reflections on 'Tribe' and 'State' in Twentieth-Century Morocco," in *Tribes and Power: Nationalism and Ethnicity in the Middle East*, F. Abdul-Jabar and H. Dawod, eds. (London: Saqi, 2003), 206.
20. B. Maddy-Weitzman, "Contested Identities: Berbers, 'Berberism' and the State in North Africa," *Journal of North African Studies* 6:3 (2001): 25.
21. Ibid., 32, quoting BBC Monitoring, Summary of World Broadcasts 4, The Middle East, August 23, 1994: 19–20.
22. Ibid., 34; M. Bensadoun, The (Re)fashioning of Moroccan National Identity," in B. Maddy Weitzman and D. Zisenwine, eds., *The Maghrib in the New Century* (Gainsville: University of Florida Press, 2007), 18.
23. See J. Goodman's account of the 1984 Berber Spring trial of Algerian activists, "Imazighen on Trial; Human Rights and Berber Identity in Algeria, 1985," in *Berbers and Others: Beyond Tribe and Nation in the Maghrib*, K. E. Hoffman and S. G. Miller, eds. (Bloomington: Indiana University Press, 2010): 103–125; S. Slyomovics, "Self-Determination as Self-Definition: The Case of Morocco," in *Negotiating Self-Determination*, H. Hannum and E. Babbitt, eds. (Lanham, MD: Lexington Books, 2006), 135–57.
24. Slyomovics, "Self-Determination," 138–9.
25. Quoted in *Écritures marocaines contemporaines* (Maroc: Printemps, 2001), 14.
26. Z. Daoud, *Les années Lamalif: 1958–1988, trente ans de journalisme au Maroc* (Casablanca: Tarik, 2007); V. Orlando, *Francophone Voices of the "New" Morocco in Film and Print: (Re)Presenting a Society in Transition* (New York: Palgrave Macmillan, 2009), 10, 21–24.
27. F. Ramirez, "Le stéréotype ambigu: Aspects de la représentation du Maroc dans le cinéma colonial," in *Présences et images franco-marocaines au temps du Protectorat*, J.-C. Allain, ed. (Paris: l'Harmattan, 2003), 179–93; M. D. Jaïdi, *Histoire du cinema au Maroc: Le cinéma colonial* (Casablanca: Najah al-Jadida, 2001); R. Armes, "Cinema in the Maghreb," in *Companion Encyclopedia of Middle Eastern and North African Film*, Oliver Leaman, ed. (London: Routledge, 2001), 426; K. Dwyer, *Beyond Casablanca: M. A. Tazi and the Adventure of Moroccan Cinema* (Bloomington: Indiana University Press, 2004), 122–4.
28. Dwyer, *Beyond Casablanca*, 155–6, and "Chronology," unpaged.
29. K. Dwyer, "Moroccan Cinema and the Promotion of Culture," *Journal of North African Studies* 12:3 (2007): 278; by the same author, *Beyond Casablanca*, 281–3, and esp. n. 21, p. 395; B. Edwards, "*Marock* in Morocco: Reading Moroccan Films in the Age of Circulation," *Journal of North African Studies* 12:3 (2007): 287–307.
30. S. E. Waltz, "Interpreting Political Reform in Morocco," in *In the Shadow of the Sultan: Culture, Power and Politics in Morocco*, R. Bourqia and S. G. Miller, eds. (Cambridge, MA: Harvard University Press, 1999), 282.
31. C. Daure-Serfaty, *Letter from Morocco* (East Lansing: Michigan State University Press, 2003), xi–xiii: *Tel Quel online*, "Hassan II a facilité mon marriage," http://www.telquel-online.com/365/interrogatoire_365.shtml, accessed on July 16, 2011.

32. Waltz, "Interpreting Political Reform," 292; Vermeren, *Histoire du Maroc*, 91–95.
33. A. Laroui, *Le Maroc et Hassan II: Un témoignage* (Québec: Presses Inter Universitaires, 2005), 162. The genre of Moroccan prison literature is extensive; among the most memorable is Ahmed Marzouki's *Tazmamart, Cellule 10* (Casablanca: Tarik, 2000). In English, Prix de Goncourt–winning author Tahar Ben Jelloun used the memories of a former prisoner to write a controversial fictionalized account of this same prison entitled *This Blinding Absence of Light* (New York: New Press, 2002); for an anthropologist's view of the prison experience and its memorialization, see S. Slyomovics, *The Performance of Human Rights in Morocco* (Philadelphia: University of Pennsylvania Press, 2005).
34. *Tel Quel online*, "Tabit, La vraie histoire," http://www.telquel online.com/281/couverture_281.shtml, accessed on July 16, 2011; Jonathan Smolin, "Moroccan Noir: The Genesis of the Arabic Police Novel," unpublished paper by permission of the author. Prof. Smolin informs me that he believes no one associated with the Tabit affair is still in jail. (July 2011); for an unusual perspective on the affair as it was reflected in popular culture, see A. Lakhsassi, "Scandale national et chansons populaires," in *Miroirs maghrébins*, S. Ossman, ed. (Paris: CNRS Editions, 1998), 99–119.
35. M. Tozy and B. Hibou Tozy, "Une lecture d'anthropologie politique de la corruption au Maroc: Fondement historique d'une prise de liberté avec le droit," *Hespéris-Tamuda* 39:2 (2001): 226–233; *Tel Quel On-line*, "Assainissement: Dix ans après," http://www.telquel-online.com/179/eco_sujet_179.shtml, accessed on July 20, 2011.
36. Slyomovics, *Performance of Human Rights*, 22.
37. E. G. H. Joffé, "Morocco's Reform Process: Wider Implications," *Mediterranean Politics* 14:2 (2009): 151–64; A. Maghraoui, "Monarchy and Political Reform in Morocco," *Journal of Democracy* 12:1 (2001): 73.
38. M. Cherkaoui and D. Ben Ali, "The Political Economy of Growth in Morocco," *The Quarterly Review of Economics and Finance* 46 (2007): 746.
39. Vermeren, *Histoire du Maroc*, 97–105; J. P. Ketterer, "From One Chamber to Two: The Case of Morocco," *Journal of Legislative Studies* 7:1 (2001): 135–50.
40. B. Belouchi, *L'Alternance, les mots et les choses* (Casablanca: Afrique Orient, 2003), 34.
41. World Trade Organization Country Profiles, http://stat.wto.org/CountryProfile/WSDBCountryPFView.aspx?Country=MA&Language=E, accessed on July 19, 2011.
42. A. Rhazaoui, "Recent Economic Trends: Managing the Indebtedness," in *The Political Economy of Morocco*, I. W. Zartman, ed. (New York: Praeger, 1987), 141; in the same volume, R. Pomfret, "Morocco's International Relations," 173–85; see also C. Dawson, *EU Integration with North Africa: Trade Negotiations and Democracy Deficits in Morocco* (New York: St. Martin's Press, 2009).
43. J. Marks, "The Concept of Morocco in Europe," in *Morocco and Europe*, E. G. H. Joffé, ed. (London: SOAS, 1989), 15; and, in the same publication, B. Boutaleb, "Morocco and Europe: From Protectorate to Independence,"

60–64; see also M. Catusse, "L'entrée en politique des entrepreneurs marocains: Formation d'une catégorie sociale et réforme de l'ordre politique dans le cadre de la libéralisation économique," *EIU Working Paper RSC 2001/25* (European University Institute, 2001), 16.

44. C. M. Henry, "Crises of Money and Power: Transitions to Democracy?" in *Islam, Democracy and the State in North Africa*, J. Entelis, ed. (Bloomington: Indiana University Press, 1997), 199.
45. S. Cohen, "Alienation and Globalization in Morocco: Addressing the Social and Political Impact of Market Integration," *Comparative Studies in Society and History* 45:1 (2003): 168–189; Maghraoui, "Monarchy and Political Reform," 76; S. Tangeaoui, *Les entrepreneurs marocains: Pouvoir, société et modernité* (Paris: Karthala, 1993), 161–2.
46. B. Maddy-Weitzman, "Israel and Morocco: A Special Relationship," *The Maghreb Review* 21:1–2 (1996): 36–48.
47. J. Damis, *U.S. Arab Relations: The Moroccan Dimension* (Washington, DC: National Council on U.S-Arab Relations, 1986).
48. J. Entelis, "Libya and its North African Policy," in D. Vandewalle, ed., *Libya since 1969: Qadhafi's Revolution Revisited* (New York: Palgrave Macmillan, 2008), 181.
49. Hassan II, *The Challenge: The Memoirs of King Hassan II of Morocco* (London: Macmillan, 1978), 172.
50. O. Bendourou, "Bourguiba et le Maroc," in *Habib Bourguiba: La trace et l'héritage*, M. Camau and V. Geisser, eds. (Paris: Karthala, 2004), 499.
51. B. Stora, "Maroc-Algérie, retour du passé et écriture de l'histoire," *Vingtième Siècle: Revue d'histoire* 68 (2000): 109–18; and, by the same author, "Le Maroc et l'Algérie: Reflexions sur des relations complexes, difficiles," *Les Cahiers de l'Orient* 58 (2000): 11–24.

8. Summation: In Search of a New Equilibrium

1. R. Leveau, "The Moroccan Monarchy: A Political System in Quest of a New Equilibrium," in *Middle East Monarchies: The Challenge of Modernity*, Joseph Kostiner, ed. (Boulder, CO: Lynne Rienner, 2000), 122–23.

Bibliography of Works Cited

Plan de Réformes marocaines. Élaboré et présenté à S.M. le Sultan, au gouvernement de la République française, et à la Résidence générale au Maroc par le Comité d'Action Marocaine. n.p., 1934.

Écritures marocaines contemporaines. Maroc: Printemps, 2001.

Aafif, Mohamed. "Les Harkas hassaniennes d'après l'oeuvre d'A. Ibn Zidane." *Hespéris-Tamuda* 19 (1980): 153–68.

Abdulrazak, Fawzi. "*The Kingdom of the Book: The History of Printing as an Agency of Change in Morocco between 1865 and 1912*." Ph.D. diss. Boston University, 1990.

Abi-Mershed, Osama. *Apostles of Modernity: Saint-Simonians and the Civilizing Mission in Algeria*. Stanford, CA: Stanford University Press, 2010.

Abitbol, Michel. "Jihad et nécessité: Le Maroc et la conquête française de Soudan occidental et de la Mauritanie." *Studia Islamica* 63 (1986): 159–77.

The Jews of North Africa During the Second World War. Detroit: Wayne State University Press, 1989.

Les Commercants du roi: Tujjar al-Sultan: Une élite économique judéo-marocaine au XIXe siècle; lettres du makhzen, traduites et annotées, 1998. Paris: Maisonneuve et Larose, 1998.

Abun-Nasr, Jamil. "The Salafiyya Movement in Morocco: The Religious Bases of the Moroccan Nationalist Movement." In *Middle Eastern Affairs*, edited by Albert Hourani. London: Chatto & Windus, 1963.

Addi, Lahouari. "Colonial Mythologies: Algeria in the French Imagination." In *Franco-Arab Encounters: Studies in the Memory of David Gordon*, edited by L. C. Brown and M. Gordon. Beirut: American University of Beirut Press, 1996.

Ageron, Charles Robert. "La Politique berbère du protectorat marocain de 1913 à 1934." *Revue d'histoire moderne et contemporaine* 18:1 (1971): 50–90.

Akharbach, Latifa, and Narjis Rerhaye. *Femmes et politique*. Casablanca: Najah al-Jadid, 1992.

Alarcón, Pedro Antonio de. *Diary of a Witness*. Translated by Bern Keating. Memphis, TN: White Rose Press, 1988.

Allain, J-C. "Le Maroc dans les relations internationales: au temps d'Algeciras (1906–1912)." In *Le Maroc de l'avènement de Moulay Abdelaziz à 1912*. Mohammedia: Kingdom of Morocco, Summer University, 1987.

Amster, Ellen. "The Many Deaths of Dr. Emile Mauchamp: Medicine, Technology, and Popular Politics in pre-Protectorate Morocco, 1877–1912." *International Journal of Middle East Studies* 36:3 (2004): 409–28.

Aouad, M'hammed, and Maria Awad. *Les Trente glorieuses, ou, l'age d'or du nationalisme marocain, 1925–1955: Témoignage d'un compagnon de Mehdi Ben Barka*. Rabat: Éditions LPL, 2006.

Aouchar, Amina. *La Presse marocaine dans la lutte pour l'indépendance (1933–1956)*. Casablanca: Wallada, 1990.

Armes, Roy. "Cinema in the Maghreb." In *Companion Encyclopedia of Middle Eastern and North African Film*, edited by Oliver Leaman. London: Routledge, 2001.

Arnaud, Louis. *Au Temps des "mehallas": Ou, le Maroc de 1860 à 1912*. Casablanca: Éditions Atlantides, 1952.

As'ad, 'Abd al-Majid. "Al-nidham al-jiba'i lil-tartib fi 'ahd al-sultan al-Mawlay al-Hasan al-awl." In *Le Maroc de l'avènement de Moulay Abdelaziz à 1912*. Mohammedia: Kingdom of Morocco, Summer University, 1987.

Ashford, Douglas. "The Irredentist Appeal in Morocco and Mauritania." *The Western Political Quarterly* 15:4 (1962): 641–51.

Aubin, Eugene. *Morocco of Today*. London: J. M. Dent & Co., 1906.

Ayache, Albert. *Le Mouvement syndical au Maroc*. Paris: L'Harmattan, 1982.

"Mouvements urbains en milieu colonial: Les événements de Casablanca des 7 et 8 décembre 1952." In *Mémorial Germain Ayache*, edited by 'Umar Afa. Rabat: Université Mohammed V, Faculté des lettres et sciences humaines, 1994.

Ayache, Germain. "Aspects de la crise financiére au Maroc aprés l'expedition espagnole de 1860." In *Études d'histoire marocaine*. Rabat: SMER, 1983.

"L'apparition de l'imprimerie au Maroc." *Hespéris-Tamuda* 5 (1964): 143–61.

Les Origines de la guerre du Rif. Rabat: SMER, 1981.

"Les Implications internationales de la guerre du Rif (1921–1926)." In *Études d'histoire marocaine*. Rabat: SMER, 1983.

Bachoud, Andrée. *Los españoles ante las campañas de Marruecos*. Madrid: Espasa-Calpe, 1988.

Baïda, Jamaa. "Situation de la presse au Maroc sous le 'Proconsulat' de Lyautey (1912–1925)." *Hespéris-Tamuda* 30:1 (1992): 67–92.

"Perception de la periode nazie au Maroc: quelques indices de l'impact de la propagande allemande sur l'état d'esprits des marocains." In *Marocains et allemands: La perception de l'autre*, edited by A. Bendaoud and M. Berriane. Rabat: Faculté des lettres et des sciences humaines, 1995: 13–19.

La Presse marocaine d'expression française: Dès origines à 1956. Rabat: Faculté des lettres et des sciences humaines, 1996.

"La Presse tangéroise: Relais de communication dans le Maroc précolonial." In *Miroirs Maghrébins*, edited by Susan Ossman. Paris: CNRS, 1998.

"Rasa'il maftuha ila al-salatinayn al-Mawlay 'Abd al-Aziz wa-l-Mawlay 'Abd al-Hafiz." In *Mélanges offerts au Professeur Brahim Boutaleb*, edited by Abdelmajid Kaddouri. Rabat: Faculté des lettres et sciences humaines, 2001.

"La Pensée réformiste au Maroc à la veille du Protectorat." *Hespéris Tamuda* 39:2 (2001): 49–69.

and Vincent Feroldi. *Présence chrétienne au Maroc, XIXème–XXème siècles.* Rabat: Éditions Bouregreg, 2005.

Baker, Alison. *Voices of Resistance: Oral Histories of Moroccan Women.* Albany: State University of New York Press, 1998.

Balibar, Etienne. "The Nation Form: History and Ideology." In *Race, Nation, Class: Ambiguous Identities*, edited by Etienne Balibar and Immanuel Maurice Wallerstein. London: Verso, 1991.

Bayly, C. A. *The Birth of the Modern World, 1780–1914: Global Connections and Comparisons.* Malden, MA: Blackwell, 2004.

Bazzaz, Sahar. "Heresy and Politics in Nineteenth Century Morocco." *Arab Studies Journal* (2002/2003): 66–86.

"Reading Reform Beyond the State: *Salwat Al-Anfas*, Islamic Revival, and Moroccan History." *Journal of North African Studies* 13:1 (2008): 1–13.

Forgotten Saints: History, Power, and Politics in the Making of Modern Morocco, Harvard Middle Eastern Monographs 41. Cambridge, MA: Harvard University Press, 2010.

Bekraoui, Mohammed. "Les étudiants marocains en France à l'époque du Protectorat, 1927–1939." In *Présences et images franco-marocaines au temps du Protectorat*, edited by Jean-Claude Allain. Paris: L'Harmattan, 2003.

Les marocains dans la Grande Guerre, 1914–1919. Rabat: Annajah, 2009.

Belal, Abdel Aziz, and A. Agourram. "L'Économie marocaine depuis l'independence." *Annuaire de l'Afrique du Nord* 8 (1969): 145–68.

Belarbi, Aïcha. "Le mouvement associatif féminin." *Prologues: Revue maghrebine du livre* 9 (May 1997): 28–33.

Belouchi, Belkassem. *Portraits d'hommes politiques du Maroc.* Casablanca: Afrique Orient, 2002.

L'alternance, les mots et les choses. Casablanca: Afrique Orient, 2003.

Ben Barka, Mehdi. *The Political Thought of Ben Barka: Revolutionary Option in Morocco. Political Articles, 1960–1965.* Havana: Tricontinental, 1968.

Ben Barka, Mehdi, and Raymond Jean. *Problèmes d'édification du Maroc et du Maghreb: Quatre entretiens avec El Mehdi Ben Barka.* Paris: Plon, 1959.

Ben Ghabrit, Kaddour. "S.E. El Hadj Mohammed El Mokri: Grand Vizir de l' Empire chérifien." *France-Maroc* 2:5 (1918): 141–43.

Ben Jelloun, Tahar. *This Blinding Absence of Light.* Translated by Linda Cloverdale. New York: New Press, 2002.

Ben Srhir, Khalid. "Britain and Military Reforms in Morocco during the Second Half of the Nineteenth Century." In *Réforme par le haut, réforme par le bas: La modernisation de l'armée aux 19e et 20e siècles*, edited by Odile Moreau and Abderrahmane el Moudden. Rome: Instituto per l'Oriente C.A. Nallino, 2004.

Britain and Morocco during the Embassy of John Drummond Hay, 1845–1886. London: Routledge Curzon, 2005.

Bendourou, Omar. "Bourguiba et le Maroc." In *Habib Bourguiba: La trace et l'héritage*, edited by Michel Camau and Vincent Geisser. Paris: Karthala 2004.

Benhlal, Mohamed. "Le Syndicat comme enjeu politique au Maroc (1955–1981)." In *Le Mouvement ouvrier maghrébin*, edited by Noureddine Sraïeb. Paris: CNRS, 1985.

Le Collège d'Azrou: Une élite berbère civile et militaire au Maroc, 1927–1959. Paris: Karthala, 2005.

Benjelloun, Abdelmajid. "Raïssouni: Brigand, collaborateur ou résistant?" *Revue d'histoire maghrébine* 26 (1999): 197–203.

Bennani-Chraïbi, Mounia, and Rémy Leveau. *Soumis et rebelles: Les jeunes au Maroc*. Paris: CNRS, 1994.

Bennett, G.H. "Britain's Relations with France after Versailles: The Problem of Tangier, 1919–23." *European History Quarterly* 24 (1994): 53–84.

Bennison, Amira K. *Jihad and Its Interpretations in Pre-Colonial Morocco: State-Society Relations During the French Conquest of Algeria*. London: Routledge Curzon, 2002.

"The 'New Order' and Islamic Order: The Introduction of the Nizami Army in the Western Maghrib and Its Legitimation, 1830–1873." *International Journal of Middle East Studies* 36 (2004): 591–612.

Bennouna, Mehdi. *Héros sans gloire: Échec d'une révolution, 1963–1973*. Casablanca: Tarik, 2002.

Bensadoun, Mickael. "The (Re)Fashioning of Moroccan National Identity." In *The Maghrib in the New Century*, edited by Bruce Maddy-Weitzman and Daniel Zisenwine. Gainsville: University of Florida, 2007.

Berque, Jacques. *Structures sociales du Haut-Atlas*. Paris: Presses universitaires de France, 1955.

French North Africa: The Maghrib between Two World Wars. New York: Praeger, 1967.

L'Intérieur du Maghreb: XVe–XIXe siècle. Paris: Gallimard, 1978.

Bidwell, Robin L. *Morocco under Colonial Rule: French Administration of Tribal Areas 1912–1956*. London: Cass, 1973.

Bin-'Addadah, Asiya. *Al-fikr al-islahi fi 'ahd al-himaya: Muhammad ibn al-Hasan al-Hajwi namudhajan*. Casablanca: al-Markaz al-thaqafi al-'arabi, 2003.

Binebine, Aziz. *Tazmamort: Récit*. Paris: Denoël, 2009.

Blair, Leon Borden. *Western Window in the Arab World*. Austin: University of Texas Press, 1970.

Bleuchot, Hervé. *Les Libéraux français au Maroc, 1947–1955*. Paris: Éditions de l'Université de Provence; Éditions Ophrys, 1973.

Boukhari, Ahmed. *Le Secret: Ben Barka et le Maroc: Un ancien agent des services spéciaux parle*. Neuilly-sur-Seine [France]: Lafon, 2002.

Raisons d'états: Tout sur l'affaire Ben Barka et d'autres crimes politiques au Maroc. Casablanca: Maghrébines, 2005.

Bourqia, Rahma. "Vol, pillage et banditisme dans le Maroc du XIXe siècle." *Hespéris Tamuda* 29:2 (1991): 191–226.

"Droit et pratiques sociales: Le cas des nawazil au XIXe siècle." *Hespéris Tamuda* 35:2 (1997): 131–45.

Boutaleb, Brahim. "Morocco and Europe: From Protectorate to Independence." In *Morocco and Europe*, edited by George Joffé. London: SOAS, 1989.

Bouzar, Nadir. *L'armée de libération nationale marocaine, [1955–1956]: Retour sans visa, journal d'un résistant maghrébin*. Paris: Publisud, 2002.

Brown, Kenneth. "The Impact of the Dahir Berbère in Salé." In *Arabs and Berbers: From Tribe to Nation in North Africa*, edited by Ernest Gellner and Charles Micaud. Lexington, MA: D.C. Heath & Co., 1972.

People of Salé: Tradition and Change in a Moroccan City, 1830–1930. Cambridge, MA: Harvard University Press, 1976.

"L'evolution de la société de Salé et la pression européenne au XIXe siècle." In *Le Maroc de l'avènement de Moulay Abdelaziz à 1912*. Mohammédia: Kingdom of Morocco, Summer University, 1987.

"A Few Reflections on 'Tribe' and 'State' in Twentieth-Century Morocco." In *Tribes and Power: Nationalism and Ethnicity in the Middle East*, edited by Faleh Abdul-Jabar and Hoshem Dawod. London: Saqi, 2003.

Brunot, Louis, and Elie Malka. *Textes judéo-arabes de Fès: Textes, transcription, traduction annotée*. Rabat: École du Livre, 1939.

Burke III, Edmund. "The Image of the Moroccan State in French Ethnological Literature: New Light on the Origins of Lyautey's Berber Policy." In *Arabs and Berbers: Ethnicity and Nation-Building in North Africa*, edited by Ernest Gellner and Charles Micaud. Lexington, MA: D.C. Heath & Co., 1972.

Prelude to Protectorate in Morocco: Precolonial Protest and Resistance, 1860–1912. Chicago: University of Chicago Press, 1976.

"La Mission scientifique au Maroc: Science sociale et politique dans l'âge de l'impérialisme." In *Actes de Durham: Recherches récentes sur le Maroc moderne, 13–15 Juillet 1977*. Rabat: Bulletin économique et sociale du Maroc, 1979.

Cagne, Jacques. *Nation et nationalisme au Maroc: Aux racines de la nation marocaine*. Rabat: Dar Nashr al-Ma'rifa, 1988.

Carr, Raymond, ed. *Spain: A History*. New York: Oxford University Press, 2000.

Casinière, H. de la. *Les municipalités marocaines: Leur développement, leur législation*. Casablanca: Imprimerie de la Vigie Marocaine, 1924.

Catusse, Myriam. *L'entrée en politique des entrepreneurs marocains: Formation d'une catégorie sociale et réforme de l'ordre politique dans le cadre de la libéralisation économique*. EUI Working Paper No. 2001/25, 2001.

Cerych, Ladislav. *Fin d'un régime colonial: Sociologie du conflit franco-marocain (1930–1956)*. Bruges: De Tempel, 1964.

Cherkaoui, Mouna, and Driss Ben Ali. "The Political Economy of Growth in Morocco." *The Quarterly Review of Economics and Finance* 46 (2007): 741–61.

Churchill, Charles Henry. *The Life of Abdel Kader, Ex-Sultan of the Arabs of Algeria: Written from His Own Dictation, and Comp. From Other Authentic Sources*. London: Chapman and Hall, 1867.

Clancy-Smith, Julia. "The Maghrib in the Mediterranean World in the Nineteenth Century: Illicit Exchanges, Migrants, and Social Marginals." In *The Maghrib in Question, Essays in History & Historiography*, edited by Michel Le Gall and Kenneth Perkins. Austin: University of Texas Press, 1997.

Cleveland, William L. *Islam against the West: Shakib Arslan and the Campaign for Islamic Nationalism*. Austin: University of Texas Press, 1985.

Cohen, Jean-Louis, and Monique Eleb. *Casablanca: Mythes et figures d'une aventure urbaine*. Paris: Hazan, 1998.

Cohen, Shana. "Alienation and Globalization in Morocco: Addressing the Social and Political Impact of Market Integration." *Comparative Studies in Society and History* 45:1 (2003): 168–89.

Cooper, Frederick. "Conflict and Connection: Rethinking Colonial African History." *American Historical Review* 99:5 (1994): 1516–45.

Coram, A. "The Berbers and the Coup." In *Arabs and Berbers: From Tribe to Nation in North Africa*, edited by Ernest Gellner and Charles Micaud. Lexington, MA: D.C. Heath & Co, 1972.

Correale, F. "Ma' al-ʿAynayn, il Marocco e la resistenza alla penetrazione coloniale (1905–1910)." *Oriente Moderno* 78:2 (1998): 227–78.

Cruickshank, Earl F. *Morocco at the Parting of the Ways: The Story of Native Protection to 1885*. Philadelphia: University of Pennsylvania Press; 1935.

Dakhlia, Jocelyne. "Dans la mouvance du prince: La symbolique du pouvoir itinérant au Maghreb." *Annales:ESC* 43:3 (1988): 735–60.

Damis, John. "The Free School Movement in Morocco, 1919–1970." Ph.D. diss., Tufts University, 1970.

"The Origins and Significance of the Free School Movement in Morocco, 1919–1931." *Revue de l'Occident musulman et de la Méditerranée* 19–20 (1975): 75–99.

U.S. Arab Relations: The Moroccan Dimension. Washington, DC: National Council on U.S-Arab Relations, 1986.

"King Hassan and the Western Sahara." *The Maghreb Review* 25: 1–2 (2000): 13–30.

Daoud, Zakya. *Abdelkrim: Une épopée d'or et de sang*. Paris: Séguier, 1999.

Les Années Lamalif: 1958–1988, Trente ans de journalisme au Maroc. Casablanca: Tarik, 2007.

and Maâti Monjib. *Ben Barka*. Paris: Michalon, 1996.

Daure-Serfaty, Christine. *Letter from Morocco*. East Lansing: Michigan State University Press, 2003.

Davis, Diana. *Resurrecting the Granary of Rome*. Athens: Ohio University Press, 2007.

Dawson, Carl. *EU Integration with North Africa: Trade Negotiations and Democracy Deficits in Morocco*. London: I.B. Tauris, 2009.

De Amicis, Edmondo. *Morocco, Its People and Places*. Translated by Maria Hornor Lansdale. 2 vols. H.T. Coates & Co: Philadelphia, 1897.

Delanoë, Guy. *Lyautey, Juin, Mohammed V, fin d'un Protectorat*. Paris: L'Harmattan, 1988.

Delanoë, Nelcya. *Poussières d'Empires*. Casablanca: Tarik, 2002.

Dennerlein, Bettina. "Legitimate Bounds and Bound Legitimacy: The Act of Allegiance to the Ruler (Baiʿa) in 19th Century Morocco." *Welt des Islams* 41:3 (2001): 287–310.

"South-South Linkages and Social Change: Moroccan Perspectives on Army Reform in the Muslim Mediterranean in the Nineteenth Century."

Comparative Studies of South Asia, Africa and the Middle East 27:1 (2007): 52–61.
Doumou, Abdelali. *The Moroccan State in Historical Perspective, 1850–1985*. Dakar, Senegal: CODESRIA, 1990.
Duclos, Louis-Jean. "The Berbers and the Rise of Moroccan Nationalism." In *Arabs and Berbers: From Tribe to Nation in North Africa*, edited by Ernest Gellner and Charles Micaud. Lexington, MA: DC Heath, 1972.
Dunn, Ross E. *Resistance in the Desert: Moroccan Responses to French Imperialism 1881–1912*. Madison: University of Wisconsin Press, 1977.
"Bu Himara's European Connexion: The Commercial Relations of a Moroccan Warlord." *Journal of African History* 21:2 (1980): 235–53.
"The Bu Himara Rebellion in Northeast Morocco, Phase I." *Middle Eastern Studies* 17:1 (1981): 31–48.
Dwyer, Kevin. "Moroccan Cinema and the Promotion of Culture." *Journal of North African Studies* 12:3 (2007): 277–86.
Edwards, Brian. "*Marock* in Morocco: Reading Moroccan Films in the Age of Circulation." *Journal of North African Studies* 12:3 (2007): 287–307.
Morocco Bound: Disorienting America's Maghreb, from Casablanca to the Marrakech Express. Durham, NC: Duke University Press, 2005.
El Adnani, Jilali. "Le Caïd El Glaoui et la Tijaniyya sous l'order colonial français." In *Pouvoir central et caïdalité au sud du Maroc*, edited by A. El Moudden, A. Ammalek, A. Belfaïda. Rabat: Université Mohammed V, 2010.
El Ayadi, Mohammed. "Les Mouvements de la jeunesse au Maroc: L'émergence d'une nouvelle intelligentsia politique durant les années soixante et soixante-dix." In *Émeutes et mouvements sociaux au Maghreb: Perspective comparée*, edited by Didier Le Saout et Marguerite Rollinde. Paris: Karthala, 1999.
"Du fondamentalisme d'état et de la nasiha sultanienne: À propos d'un certain reformisme makhzenien." *Hespéris Tamuda* 39:2 (2001): 85–107.
El Mansour, Mohamed. *Morocco in the Reign of Mawlay Sulayman*. Wisbech, UK: Middle East and North African Studies Press Limited, 1990.
"The Makhzan's Berber: Paths to Integration in Pre-Colonial Morocco," in *Berbers and Others: Beyond Tribe and Nation in the Maghrib*, edited by K. E. Hoffman and S. G. Miller. Bloomington: University of Indiana Press, 2010.
El Moudden, Abderrahman. "État et société rurale à travers la harka au Maroc du XIXe siècle." *The Maghreb Review* 8:5–6 (1983): 141–45.
"Looking Eastward: Some Moroccan Tentative Military Reforms with Turkish Assistance (18th-Early 20th Centuries)." *The Maghreb Review* 19:2–3 (1994): 237–45.
Ennaji, Mohammed. *Expansion européenne et changement social au Maroc: (XVIe–XIXe siécles)*. Casablanca: Éditions Eddif, 1996.
Entelis, John. "Libya and Its North African Policy." In *Libya since 1969: Qadhafi's Revolution Revisited*, edited by Dirk Vandewalle. New York: Palgrave Macmillan, 2008.
Erckmann, Jules. *Le Maroc moderne*. Paris: Challamel Ainé, 1885.
Erzini, Nadia. "Hal yaslah li-taqansut (Is He Suitable for Consulship?): The Moroccan Consuls in Gibraltar in the Nineteenth Century." *Journal of North African Studies* 12:4 (2007): 517–29.

Etienne, Bruno. *Abdelkader: Isthme des isthmes (barzakh al-barazikh)*. Paris: Hachette, 1994.

Fahmy, Khaled. *All the Pasha's Men: Mehmed Ali, His Army, and the Making of Modern Egypt*. Cambridge: Cambridge University Press, 1997.

Farsoun, Karen, and Jim Paul. "War in the Sahara: 1963." *MERIP Reports* 45 (1976): 13–16.

Al-Fasi, 'Allal. *The Independence Movements in Arab North Africa*. Washington, DC: American Council of Learned Societies, 1954.

Fleming, Shannon E. "Spanish Morocco and the Alzamiento Nacional, 1936–1939: The Military, Economic and Political Mobilization of a Protectorate." *Journal of Contemporary History* 18:1 (1983): 27–42.

and Ann K. Fleming. "Primo De Rivera and Spain's Moroccan Problem, 1923–27." *Journal of Contemporary History* 12:1 (1977): 85–99.

Flournoy, Francis. *British Policy toward Morocco in the Age of Palmerston (1830–1865)*. Baltimore: The Johns Hopkins University Press, 1935.

Fogarty, Richard Standish. *Race and War in France: Colonial Subjects in the French Army, 1914–1918*. Baltimore: Johns Hopkins University Press, 2008.

Forbes, Rosita Torr. *The Sultan of the Mountains: The Life Story of Raisuli*. New York: H. Holt and Company, 1924.

Gadille, Jacques. "La Colonisation officielle au Maroc." *Les Cahiers d'Outre-Mer* 8 (October–December 1955): 305–22.

Gaillard, Henri. *La Réorganisation du gouvernement marocain*. Paris: Comité de l'Afrique Française, 1916.

Gallagher, Charles F. *The United States and North Africa: Morocco, Algeria, and Tunisia*. Cambridge, MA: Harvard University Press, 1963.

Gallagher, John, and Ronald Robinson. "The Imperialism of Free Trade." *The Economic History Review* new ser., 6:1 (1953): 1–15.

Gallissot, René. "Le Parti communiste et la guerre du Rif." In *Abd El-Krim et la République du Rif: Actes du colloque international d'études historiques et sociologiques, 18–20 Janvier 1973*. Paris: F. Maspero, 1976.

Le Patronat européen au Maroc: Action sociale, action politique (1931–1942). Casablanca: EDDIF, 1990.

and Jacques Kergoat. *Mehdi Ben Barka: de l'indépendance marocaine à la Tricontinentale*. Paris:Saint-Denis: Karthala; Institut Maghreb-Europe, Université Paris 8, 1997.

Geertz, Clifford. "Review of *the Commander of the Faithful* by John Waterbury." *Middle Eastern Studies* 72 (1971): 251–55.

Gellner, Ernest. "Do Nations Have Navels?" *Nations and Nationalism* 2:3 (1996): 366–79.

Gershovich, Moshe. "A Moroccan Saint-Cyr." *Middle Eastern Studies* 28:2 (1992): 231–57.

French Military Rule in Morocco: Colonialism and Its Consequences. Portland, OR: F. Cass, 2000.

"Stories on the Road from Fez to Marrakesh: Oral History on the Margins of National Identity." *Journal of North African Studies* 8:1 (2003): 43–58.

Goodman, Jane. "Imazighen on Trial: Human Rights and Berber Identity in Algeria, 1985." In *Berbers and Others: Beyond Tribe and Nation in the*

Maghrib, edited by K. E. Hoffman, and S. G. Miller. Bloomington: Indiana University Press, 2010.
Gouvion Saint-Cyr, Marthe, and Edmond Gouvion Saint-Cyr. *Kitab aâyane al-Marhrib 'l-akça= equisse générale des Moghrebs de la genèse à nos jours et livre des grands du Maroc*. 2 vols. Paris: Librairie orientaliste Paul Geuthner, 2001.
Green, Abigail. *Moses Montefiore: Jewish Liberator, Imperial Hero*. Cambridge, MA: Belknap Press of Harvard University Press, 2010.
Gretton, John. "The Western Sahara in the International Arena." *The World Today* 36:9 (1980): 343–50.
Guérin, Daniel. *Ben Barka, ses assassins: Seize ans d'enquête*. Paris: Plon, 1982.
Guillen, Pierre. *L'Allemagne et le Maroc de 1870 à 1905*. Paris: Presses universitaires de France, 1967.
"La Résistence du Maroc à l'emprise française au lendemain des accords franco-anglais de 1904." *Revue de l'Occident et de la Méditerranée* (1970): 115–22.
Guyot, R., Le Tourneau, R. and L. Paye. "La Corporation des tanneurs et l'industrie de la tannerie à Fès." *Hespéris* 21:1–2 (1935): 167–240.
al-Hajwi, Muhammad b. al-Hajj al-Hassan. "Al-Qawl al-fasl fi aqsa amad al-haml." In *Thalath rasa'il: Tajdid 'ulum al-din*. Salé: Matba'a al-thaqafa, 1357/1938.
Halstead, Charles R. "A 'Somewhat Machiavellian' Face: Colonel Juan Beigbeder as High Commissioner in Spanish Morocco, 1937–1939." *Historian*, 37:1 (1974): 46–66.
Halstead, John P. *Rebirth of a Nation; the Origins and Rise of Moroccan Nationalism, 1912–1944*, Harvard Middle Eastern Monographs 18. Cambridge, MA: Harvard University Press, 1967.
Hammoudi, Abdallah. "Aspects de la mobilisation populaire à la campagne vus à travers la biographie d'un Mahdi mort en 1919." In *Islam et politique au Maghreb*, edited by Ernest Gellner and J.-C. Vatin. Paris CNRS, 1981.
Harding, Jeremy. "Behind the Sandwall: Review of Toby Shelley, *Endgame for the Western Sahara: What Future for Africa's Last Colony*? (London: Zed, 2004)." *The London Review of Books*, February 23, 2006: 8–11.
Harrak, Fatima. "State and Religion in Eighteenth Century Morocco: The Religious Policy of Sidi Muhammad b.ʿAbd Allah, 1757–1790." Ph. D. diss., The School of Oriental and African Studies, University of London, 1989.
"Mawlay Ismaʿil's Jaysh al-ʿAbid: Reassessment of a Military Experience." In *Slave Elites in the Middle East and North Africa*, edited by M. Toru and J. E. Philips. London: KPI International, 2000.
Harris, Walter B. *Tafilet: The Narrative of a Journey of Exploration in the Atlas Mountains and the Oases of the North-West Sahara*. Edinburgh: W. Blackwood and Sons, 1895.
"A Journey to Tafilet." *The Geographical Journal* 5, 4 (1895): 319–35.
France, Spain and the Rif. New York: Longmans Green, 1927.
Hart, David M. *The Aith Waryaghar*. Tucson: University of Arizona Press, 1976.
"De 'Ripublik' à 'République'." In *Abd El-Krim et la République du Rif: Actes du colloque international d'études historiques et sociologiques, 18–20 janvier 1973*. Paris: Maspero, 1976.

Banditry in Islam: Case Studies from Morocco, Algeria, and the Pakistan North West Frontier. Wisbech, UK: MENAS Press, 1987.

"The Berber Dahir of 1930 in Colonial Morocco: Then and Now (1930–1996)." *Journal of North African Studies* 2:2 (1997): 11–33.

Hassan II. *The Challenge: The Memoirs of King Hassan II of Morocco*. London: Macmillan, 1978.

La Mémoire d'un roi: Entretiens avec Eric Laurent. Paris: Plon, 1993.

Hay, John Drummond, Louisa Annette Edla Drummond Hay Brooks, and Alice Emily Drummond Hay. *A Memoir of Sir John Drummond Hay: Sometime Minister at the Court of Morocco: Based on His Journals and Correspondence*. London: J. Murray, 1896.

Henry, Clement M. "Crises of Money and Power: Transitions to Democracy?" In *Islam, Democracy and the State in North Africa*, edited by John Entelis. Bloomington: Indiana University Press, 1997.

Hodgkin, Thomas. *Narrative of a Journey to Morocco*. New York: Arno Press, 1971.

Hoisington, William A. "Commerce and Conflict: French Businessmen in Morocco, 1952–55." *Journal of Contemporary History* 9:2 (1974): 49–67.

The Casablanca Connection: French Colonial Policy, 1936–1943. Chapel Hill: University of North Carolina Press, 1984.

Lyautey and the French Conquest of Morocco. New York: St. Martin's Press, 1995.

"Designing Morocco's Future: France and the Native Policy Council, 1921–25." *Journal of North African Studies* 5:1 (2000): 63–108.

The Assassination of Jacques Lemaigre Dubreuil: A Frenchman between France and North Africa. London and New York: Routledge, 2005.

Holden, Stacy E. *The Politics of Food in Modern Morocco*. Gainesville: University Press of Florida, 2009.

"Famine's Fortune: The Pre-Colonial Mechanisation of Moroccan Flour Production." *Journal of North African Studies* 15:1 (2010): 71–84.

Houroro, Faouzi. *Sociologie politique coloniale au Maroc: Cas de Michaux Bellaire*. Casablanca: Afrique Orient, 1988.

Hughes, Stephen O. *Morocco under King Hassan*. Reading, UK: Ithaca, 2001.

Ibn al-Hajj, M. *Ulama' al-Maghrib al-mu'asirin*. Casablanca: al-Jadida, 1992.

Ibn Zaydan, 'Abd al-Rahman. *Ithaf 'alam al-nas bi-jamal akhbar hadirat Miknas*. al-Tabah 1. 5 vols. Rabat: al-Matba'a al-Wataniyya, 1929.

Ihraï, Saïd. "La Conference d'Algeciras de 1906." In *Le Maroc de l'avènement de Moulay Abdelaziz à 1912*. Mohammedia: Kingdom of Morocco, Summer University, 1987.

Irbouh, Hamid. *Art in the Service of Colonialism: French Art Education in Morocco, 1912–1956*. London: I. B. Tauris, 2005.

al-Jabarti, Abd al-Rahman. *Napoleon in Egypt: Al-Jabarti's Chronicle of the First Seven Months of the French Occupation, 1798*. Princeton: M. Wiener, 1993.

Jacquier, Philippe, Gabriel Veyre, Marion Pranal, and Farid Abdelouahab. *Le Maroc de Gabriel Veyre: 1901–1936*. Paris: Kubik, 2005.

Jadda, M'hamed. *Bibliographie analytique des publications de l'Institut des Hautes Études Marocaines*. Rabat: Faculté des lettres et des sciences humaines, 1994.

Jaïdi, Driss. *Histoire du cinéma au Maroc: Le cinéma colonial*. Rabat: Almajal, 2001.
Jensen, Geoffrey. "The Peculiarities of 'Spanish Morocco': Imperial Ideology and Economic Development." *Mediterranean Historical Review* 20:1 (2005): 81–102.
Joffé, E. G. H. "The Moroccan Nationalist Movement: Istiqlal, the Sultan, and the Country." *The Journal of African History* 26:4 (1985): 289–307.
"Morocco's Reform Process: Wider Implications." *Mediterranean Politics* 14:2 (2009): 151–64.
Julien, Charles-André. *History of North Africa: Tunisia, Algeria, Morocco, from the Arab Conquest to 1830*. Translated by John Petrie. Edited by C. C. Stewart. London: Routledge & Kegan Paul, 1970.
Le Maroc face aux impérialismes: 1415–1956. Paris: Éditions J. A., 1978
and Charles Robert Ageron. *Histoire de l'Algérie contemporaine*. Paris: Presses universitaires de France, 1964.
Karow, Leonhard. *Neuf années au service du Maroc (1900–1908)*. Translated by Monique Miège and J.-L. Miège. Rabat: Éditions La Porte, 1998.
al-Kattani, 'Abd al-Hayy b. 'Abd al-Kabir. *Mufakahat dhawi al-nubl wa-al-ijada hadrat mudir jaridat al-sa'ada*. Fez: 1326.
al-Kattani, Muhammad b. Ja'far. *Nasihat ahl al-Islam: Tahlil islami 'ilmi li-awamil suqut al-dawla al-islamiyya wa-'awamil nuhudiha*. Rabat: Maktabat Badr, 1989.
Katz, Jonathan G. *Murder in Marrakesh: Émile Mauchamp and the French Colonial Adventure*. Bloomington: Indiana University Press, 2006.
Kenbib, Mohammed. "Structures traditionelles et protections étrangères au Maroc au XIXème siècle." *Hespéris-Tamuda* 22 (1984): 79–101.
"Contrebande d'armes et 'anarchie' dans le Maroc précolonial (1844–1912)." *Revue Dar al-Niaba* 1:4 (1984): 8–13.
"Système impérial et bourgeoisie comparadore au Maroc au 19ème siècle." *Revue d'histoire maghrébine* 41 (1986): 86–100.
"L'impact americain sur l'nationalisme marocaine (1930–1947). *Hespéris Tamuda* 37–38 (1988–1989): 207–23.
"Protegés et brigands dans le Maroc du XIXe siècle et début du XXe." *Hespéris Tamuda* 29:2 (1991): 227–48.
"Le Général de Gaulle et les nationalistes marocains (1940–1946)." *Espoir* 80 (1992): 84–92.
"The Impact of the French Conquest of Algeria on Morocco (1830–1912)." In *North Africa: Nation, State, and Region*, edited by E. G. H. Joffé. London: Routledge, 1993.
Juifs et Musulmans au Maroc, 1859–1948. Rabat: Université Mohammed V, 1994.
"1767–1957: Du 'Paradis des Drogmans' à la cité 'Internationale.'" *Tribune juive (Montreal)* 2:5 (1994): 62–73.
"Les Conversions dans le Maroc contemporain (1860–1956): Présentation et étude d'un corpus." In *Conversions islamique: Identités religieuses en Islam Méditerranéen*, edited by Mercedes García-Arenal. Paris: Maisonneuve et Larose, 2002.

Ketterer, James P. "From One Chamber to Two: The Case of Morocco." *Journal of Legislative Studies* 7:1 (2001): 135–50.
Khalouk Temsamani, A. "Les Coups de Raïssouni (1895–1907)." *Dar al-Niaba* 19/20, (1988): 1–30.
Khoury, Rana B. "Western Sahara and Palestine: A Comparative Study of Colonialisms, Occupations, and Nationalisms." *New Middle Eastern Studies* 1 (2011): 1–20.
Kleiche, Mina. "Aux origines du concept de développement. Quand l'irrigation devient enjeu de réforme agricole: nouvelle mise en ordre du paysage rural marocain dans l'entre-deux-guerres." *Hespéris Tamuda* 39:2 (2001): 175–94.
Knibiehler, Yvonne, Geneviève Emmery, and Françoise Leguay. *Des Français au Maroc: La présence et la mémoire, 1912–1956*. Paris: Denoël, 1992.
Lacouture, Jean, and Simonne Lacouture. *Le Maroc à l'épreuve*. Paris: Éditions du Seuil, 1958.
Lahbabi, Moḥammad. *Le Gouvernement marocain à l'aube du XXe siècle*. Rabat: Éditions Techniques nord-africaines, 1958.
Lakhsassi, Abderrahmane. "Scandale national et chansons populaires." In *Miroirs Maghrébins*, edited by Susan Ossman. Paris: CNRS, 1998.
Landau, Rom. "Moroccan Profiles: A Nationalist View." *Middle East Journal* 7:1 (1953): 45–57.
Hassan II, King of Morocco. London: Allen & Unwin, 1962.
Laroui, Abdallah. *The History of the Maghrib*. Princeton: Princeton University Press, 1977.
Les Origines sociales et culturelles du nationalisme marocain, 1830–1912. Paris: Maspero, 1977.
Le Maroc et Hassan II: Un temoignage. Québec: Presses Inter Universitaires, 2005.
Laroui, Fouad. "Democracy and Islam in the Maghreb and Implications for Europe." In *The Other Muslims: Moderate and Secular*, edited by Zeyno Baran. New York: Palgrave, 2010.
Le Glay, Maurice. *Récits marocains de la plaine et des monts*. Paris: Berger-Levrault, 1948.
Leveau, Rémy. *Le Fellah marocain, défenseur du trône*. Paris: Presses de la Fondation nationale des sciences politiques, 1985.
Le Sabre et le turban: L'avenir du Maghreb. Paris: Éditions F. Bourin, 1993.
"The Moroccan Monarchy: A Political System in Quest of a New Equilibrium." In *Middle East Monarchies: The Challenge of Modernity*, edited by Joseph Kostiner. Boulder, CO: Lynne Rienner, 2000.
Lévi-Provençal, Evariste. *Les Historiens des chorfas: Essai sur la littérature historique et biographique au Maroc du XVIe au XXe siècle*. Paris: Larose, 1922.
Loewe, Louis, Dr., ed. *Diaries of Sir Moses and Lady Montefiore, a Facsimile of the 1890 Edition*. London: The Jewish Historical Society of England, 1983.
Ma'alamat al-Maghrib/Encyclopédie du Maroc. 24 vols, edited by Ahmed Toufiq and Mohamed Hajji. Salé: L'Association des Auteurs Marocains pour la Publication, 1989–2008.
Maddy-Weitzman, Bruce. "Israel and Morocco: A Special Relationship." *The Maghreb Review* 21:1–2 (1996): 36–48.

"Contested Identities: Berbers, 'Berberism' and the State in North Africa." *Journal of North African Studies* 6:3 (2001): 23–47.
Maghraoui, Abdeslam. "Monarchy and Political Reform in Morocco." *Journal of Democracy* 12:1 (2001): 73–86.
Maghraoui, Driss. "From 'Tribal Anarchy' to 'Military Order': The Moroccan Troops in the Context of Colonial Morocco." In *Réforme par le haut, réforme par le bas: La modernisation de l'armée aux 19e et 20e siècles*, edited by Odile Moreau and Abderrahmane El Moudden. Rome: Istituto per l'Oriente, C.A. Nallino, 2004.
Manela, Erez. "A Man Ahead of His Time? Wilsonian Globalism and the Doctrine of Preemption." *International Journal* 60:4 (2005): 1115–1124.
al-Manuni, Muhammad. "Mulakhadhat hawla ba'da rudud fa'l al-mugharaba tujah al-da'wa ila islah fi al-qarn 19, min khilal wathiqa mawdu'iya." *Majallat kulliyat al-adab wa-al-'ulum al-insaniyya bi-al-Ribat* (1982): 145–53.
Mazahir yaqzat al-maghrib al-hadith. 2 vols. Casablanca: al-Mudaris, 1985.
al-Marini, 'Abd al-Haqq. *Al-jaysh al-maghribi 'abr al-tarikh*. Rabat: Dar al-Nashr al-Ma'rifa, 1997.
Marks, Jon. "The Concept of Morocco in Europe." In *Morocco and Europe*, edited by George Joffé. London: SOAS, 1989.
Martin, A. G. P. *Quatre siècles d'histoire marocaine: Au Sahara de 1504 à 1902, au Maroc de 1894 à 1912*. Rabat: Éditions La Porte, 1994.
Martinière, H. de la. "Au Maroc: Le règne de Moulai-El-Hassan." *Revue de deux mondes* 4:125 (1894): 398–436.
Marzouki, Ahmed. *Tazmamart Cellule 10*. Casablanca: Tarik, 2000.
Mathieu, Jean, P. H. Maury, and Abdelmajid Arrif. *Bousbir: La prostitution dans le Maroc colonial: ethnographie d'un quartier rèservè*. Aix-en-Provence; Paris: IREMAM; Paris-Méditerranée, 2003.
McDougall, James. *History and the Culture of Nationalism in Algeria*. Cambridge and New York: Cambridge University Press, 2006.
Meakin, Budgett. *The Moorish Empire, a Historical Epitome*. London: S. Sonnenschein, 1899.
Mejri, Abdelkrim. *Les Socialistes français et la question marocaine (1903–1912)*. Paris: L'Harmattan, 2004.
Mercier, P-L. "La Presse arabe au Maroc." *Revue du monde musulman* 7 (1909): 128–33.
Mernissi, Fatima. *Dreams of Trespass: Tales of a Harem Girlhood*. Reading, MA: Addison-Wesley, 1994.
Mghari, Mina. *Madinat mukadur-al-sawira: Dirasa tarikhiyya wa-athariyya*. Rabat: Dar Abi Ragrag lil-taba'a wa-l-nashr, 2006.
Michaux-Bellaire. E. "Les Impots marocaines." *Archives marocains* 1 (1904): 56–96.
"Le Cherif Moulay Ahmed Ben Mohammed Ben Abdallah Er Resouni." *Revue du monde musulman* 5 (1908): 503–11.
"Une Tentative de restauration Idrissite à Fès." *Revue du monde musulman* 5 (1908): 393–423.

Michel, Nicolas. *Une économie de subsistances: Le Maroc précolonial.* 2 vols. Le Caire: Institut d'archéologie orientale, 1997.

Miège, J-L. "Hassan Ier et la crise marocaine au XIXe siècle." In *Les Africains*, edited by C.-A Julien et al. Paris: Jeune Afrique, 1977.

Le Maroc et l'Europe (1830–1894). 4 vols. Rabat: Éditions La Porte, 1989.

Miller, Susan Gilson. "Crisis and Community: The People of Tangier and the French Bombardment of 1844 (the Purim of Las Bombas)." *Middle Eastern Studies* 27:4 (1991): 583–96.

Ed. and transl. *Disorienting Encounters: Travels of a Moroccan Scholar in France in 1845–1846: The Voyage of Muhammad as-Saffar.* Berkeley: University of California Press, 1992.

"Gender and the Poetics of Emancipation: The Alliance Israélite Universelle in Northern Morocco, 1890–1912." In *Franco-Arab Encounters*, edited by L. Carl Brown and Matthew Gordon. Beirut: American University of Beirut, 1996.

"Apportioning Sacred Space in a Moroccan City: The Case of Tangier, 1860–1912." *City & Society* 13:1 (2001): 57–83.

"The Sleeping Fetus." *In Encyclopedia of Women & Islamic Cultures*, edited by Suad Joseph. 6 vols. Leiden: Brill, 2006; 3: 421–24.

"The Mellah of Fez: Reflections on the Spatial Turn in Moroccan Jewish History." In *Jewish Topographies*, edited by A. Nocke, J. Brauch and A. Lipphardt. London: Ashgate, 2007.

"Of Time and the City: Clifford Geertz on Urban History." *Journal of North African Studies* 14:3 (2009): 479–90.

"The Beni Ider Quarter of Tangier: Hybridity as a Social Practice." In *The Architecture and Memory of the Minority Quarter in the Muslim Mediterranean City*, edited by Susan Gilson Miller and Mauro Bertagnin. Cambridge, MA: Aga Khan Program in Islamic Architecture, Graduate School of Design, 2010.

"Making Tangier Modern: Ethnicity and Urban Development." In *Jewish Culture and Society in North Africa*, edited by E. Benichou Gottreich and D. Schroeter. Bloomington, University of Indiana Press, 2011.

Mohsen-Finan, Khadija. *Sahara Occidental: Les enjeux d'un conflit regional.* Paris: CNRS, 1997.

Monjib, Maâti. *La Monarchie marocaine et la lutte pour le pouvoir: Hassan II face à l'opposition nationale, de l'indépendance à l'état d'exception.* Paris: L'Harmattan, 1992.

Monkachi, Mohamed. *Pour une histoire des femmes au Maroc: Actes du colloque de Kénitra, Faculté des lettres et sciences humaines, 4–5 Avril 1995.* Paris: CEDREF, 1995.

Montagne, Robert. *Naissance du prolétariat marocain, enquête collective exécutée de 1948 à 1950.* Paris: Peyronnet, 1952.

ed. "Un rapport secret sur les jeunes marocains dans les années vingt." *Revue d'histoire maghrébine* 131 (2008): 125–63.

Moore, Clement Henry, and Arlie Rothschild. "Student Unions in North African Politics." *Daedelus* 97:1 (1968): 21–50.

Al-Moutabassir,. "Ma El ʿAinin Ech-Changuity." *Revue du monde musulman* 1 (1907): 343–51.

Mundy, Jacob. "Neutrality or Complicity? The United States and the 1975 Moroccan Takeover of the Spanish Sahara." *Journal of North African Studies* 11:3 (2006): 275–303.

Munson, Henry, Jr., *Religion and Power in Morocco*. New Haven: Yale University Press, 1993.

Naciri, Rabéa. "Engaging the State: The Women's Movement and Political Discourse in Morocco." In *Missionaries and Mandarins: Feminist Engagement with Development Institutions*, edited by C. Miller and R. Shahrashoub. London: Intermediate Technology Publications and the United Nations Research Institute for Social Development, 1998.

Nahon, Moïse. *Notes d'un colon du Gharb*. Casablanca: Société d'éditions marocaines, 1925.

al-Nasiri, Ahmad b. Khalid. *Kitab al-istiqsa li-akhbar duwal al-maghrib al-aqsa*. Edited by M. Hajji, I. Bu Talib, A. Tawfiq. 8 vols. Casablanca: Ministry of Culture, 2001.

Nordman, Daniel. "L'armée d'Algérie et le Maroc: Le dynamisme de la conquête (fin du XIXe siècle-début du XX siècle)," in *Armées, guerre et politique en Afrique du Nord: XIXe–XXe siècles*, edited by D. Nordman, J. Frémeaux, G. Pervillé. Paris: Presses de l'École normale supérieure, 1977.

"Les Expéditions de Moulay Hassan: Essai statistique." *Hespéris-Tamuda* 19 (1980–81): 123–52.

Orlando, Valérie. *Francophone Voices of the "New" Morocco in Film and Print: (Re)Presenting a Society in Transition*. New York: Palgrave Macmillan, 2009.

Ouardighi, Abderrahim. *L'itinéraire d'un nationaliste: Mehdi Ben Barka, 1920–1965: Une biographie*. Rabat: Éditions Moncho, 1982.

Oufkir, Malika, and Michèle Fitoussi. *Stolen Lives: Twenty Years in a Desert Jail*. New York: Talk Miramax Books/Hyperion, 2001.

Park, Thomas K. "Inflation and Economic Policy in 19th Century Morocco: The Compromise Solution." *The Maghreb Review* 10, 2–3 (1985): 51–56.

"Colonial Perceptions of Precolonial Administration: Creating the Illusion of Empire." Unpublished MS, by permission of the author, n.d.

Parker, Richard Bordeaux. *North Africa: Regional Tensions and Strategic Concerns*. New York: Praeger, 1984.

Pascon, Paul, and John R. Hall. *Capitalism and Agriculture in the Haouz of Marrakesh*. London and New York: Routledge & Kegan Paul, 1986.

Pennell, C. R. *A Country with a Government and a Flag: The Rif War in Morocco, 1921–1926*. Boulder, CO: L. Rienner, 1986.

"Women and Resistance to Colonialism in Morocco: The Rif 1916–26." *Journal of African History* 28:1 (1987): 87–106.

"The Rif War: Link or Cul-De-Sac? Nationalism in the Cities and Resistance in the Mountains." *Journal of North African Studies* 1:3 (1996): 234–47.

Perkins, Kenneth J. *Qaids, Captains, and Colons: French Military Administration in the Colonial Maghrib, 1844–1934*. New York: Africana, 1981.

A History of Modern Tunisia. Cambridge: Cambridge University Press, 2004.

Petruccioli, Attilio, ed. *Rethinking [the] Xixth Century City*. Cambridge, MA: Agha Khan Program for Islamic Architecture, 1998.

Pichon, Jean. *Le Maroc au dèbut de la guerre mondiale: El-Herri, vendredi 13 novembre 1914*. Paris: Lavauzelle, 1936.

Pinta, R. "La Lutte contre la misère au Maroc en 1945." *Bulletin économique et social du Maroc* 8:28 (1946): 284–87.

Pomeranz, Kenneth. *The Great Divergence: China, Europe, and the Making of the Modern World Economy*. Princeton: Princeton University Press, 2000.

Pomfret, Richard. "Morocco's International Relations." In *The Political Economy of Morocco*, edited by I. W. Zartman. New York: Praeger, 1987.

Potter, Pitman B. "The Origin of the System of Mandates under the League of Nations." *American Political Science Review* 16:4 (1922): 563–83.

Pouillon, François. *Dictionnaire des orientalistes de langue française*. Paris: IISMM: Karthala, 2008.

Pourquier, R. "La Santé et l'hygiéne publique." In *L'Encyclopédie colonial et maritime: Le Maroc*. Paris: L'Encyclopédie colonial et maritime, 1941.

Prost, Henri. "Le Développement de l'urbanisme dans le protectorat du Maroc de 1914 à 1923." In *L'Urbanisme aux colonies et dans les pays tropicaux; communications et rapports du Congres International de l'urbanisme aux colonies et dans les pays de latitude intertropicale*, edited by J. Royer. Nevers: Fortin, 1932.

Rabinow, Paul. "France in Morocco: Technocosmopolitanism and Middling Modernism." *Assemblage* 17 (April 1992): 52–57.

French Modern: Norms and Forms of the Social Environment. Chicago: University of Chicago, 1995.

Rachik, Hassan. *Symboliser la nation: Essai sur l'usage des identités collectives au Maroc*, Casablanca: Le Fennec, 2003.

Raïss, Mohammed. *De Skhirat à Tazmamart: Retour du bout de l'enfer*. Casablanca: Afrique Orient, 2002.

Ramirez, Francis. "Le Stéréotype ambigu: Aspects de la représentation du Maroc dans le cinéma colonial." In *Présences et images franco-marocaines au temps du protectorat*, edited by Jean-Claude Allain. Paris: L'Harmattan, 2003.

Rassam, Amal and Susan G. Miller. "Moroccan Reaction to European Penetration During the Late Nineteenth Century: The View from the Court." *Revue de l'Occident musulman et de la Méditerranée* 36:2 (1983): 51–61.

Reimer, Michael J. "Ottoman-Arab Seaports in the Nineteenth Century: Social Change in Alexandria, Beirut and Tunis." In *Cities in the World System*, edited by Risat Kasaba. Westport, CT: Greenwood Press, 1991.

Renaud, H. P. J. "La Peste de 1818 au Maroc d'après des documents inédits." *Hespéris* 3 (1923): 13–35.

Rézette, Robert. *Les Partis politiques marocains*. Paris: A. Colin, 1955.

Rhazaoui, Ahmed. "Recent Economic Trends: Managing the Indebtedness." In *The Political Economy of Morocco*, edited by I. W. Zartman. New York: Praeger, 1987.

Rivet, Daniel. "*Le Commandement français et ses réactions vis-à-vis du mouvement rifian. 1924–1926*," in *Abd el-krim et la République du Rif: Actes du colloque international d'études historiques et sociologiques, 18–20 janvier 1973*. Paris: F. Maspero, 1976.

Lyautey et l'institution du protectorat français au Maroc. 3 vols. Paris: L'Harmattan, 1988.

"Hygiénisme colonial et médicalisation de la société marocaine au temps du protectorat français (1912–1956)." In *Santé, médecine et société dans le monde arabe*, edited by Elisabeth Longuenesse. Paris: L'Harmattan, 1995.

Le Maroc de Lyautey à Mohammed V: Le double visage du Protectorat. Paris: Denoël, 1999.

Le Maghreb à l'épreuve de la colonisation. Paris: Hachette, 2002.

Rollman, Wilfrid J. "The 'New Order' in a Pre-Colonial Muslim Society: Military Reform in Morocco, 1844–1904." Ph.D. diss., University of Michigan, 1983.

"Military Officers and the 'Nidham al-Jadid' in Morocco, 1844–1912. Social and Political Transformations." In *Réforme par le haut, réforme par le bas: La modernisation de l'armé aux 19e et 20e siècles. Quaderni di Oriente Moderno* 5 (2004): 205–25.

Romero Salvadó, Francisco J. *The Spanish Civil War: Origins, Course and Outcomes*. Houndmills, Basingstoke, UK, and New York: Palgrave Macmillan, 2005.

Roosevelt, Elliott. *As He Saw It*. New York: Duell, Sloan and Pearce, 1946.

Saint-René-Taillandier, Georges. *Les Origines du Maroc français: Récit d'une mission (1901–1906)*. Paris: Plon, 1930.

Salmon, Georges. "Une opinion marocaine sur le conquête du Touat." *Archives marocaines* 1 (1904): 416–24.

Sangmuah, Egya N. "Sultan Mohammed Ben Youssef's American Strategy and the Diplomacy of North African Liberation, 1943–61." *Journal of Contemporary History* 27:1 (1992): 129–48.

Sater, James. "The Dynamics of State and Civil Society in Morocco." *Journal of North African Studies* 7:3 (2002): 101–18.

Sayagh, Saïd. *La France et les frontières maroco-algériennes, 1873–1902*. Paris: CNRS, 1986.

Scham, Alan. *Lyautey in Morocco: Protectorate Administration, 1912–1925*. Berkeley: University of California Press, 1970.

Schroeter, Daniel J. *Merchants of Essaouira: Urban Society and Imperialism in Southwestern Morocco, 1844–1886*. Cambridge: Cambridge University Press, 1988.

Sebti, Abdelahad. "Chroniques de la contestation citadine: Fès et la revolte des tanneurs (1873–1874)." *Hespéris-Tamuda* 24:2 (1991): 283–312.

Segalla, Spencer D. *The Moroccan Soul: French Education, Colonial Ethnology, and Muslim Resistance, 1912–1956*. Lincoln: University of Nebraska Press, 2009.

Serfaty, Abraham, and Mikhaël Elbaz. *L'insoumis: Juifs, marocains et rebelles*. Paris: Desclée de Brouwer, 2001.

Sheean, Vincent. *An American Among the Riffi*. New York and London: The Century Co., 1926.

Sijelmassi, Mohamed, and Mohammed al-Saghir Janjar. *Le Maroc au XXe siècle: Fresque historique des hommes, des femmes et des grands événements du siècle*. Casablanca: Éditions Oum, 2001.

Simou, Bahija. *Les Réformes militaires au Maroc de 1844 à 1912*. Rabat: Université de Mohammed V, Faculté des lettres et des sciences humaines, 1995.

Slavin, David H. "The French Left and the Rif War, 1924–25: Racism and the Limits of Internationalism." *Journal of Contemporary History* 26:1 (1991): 5–32.

Slyomovics, Susan. *The Performance of Human Rights in Morocco*. Philadelphia: University of Pennsylvania Press, 2005.

"Self-Determination as Self-Definition: The Case of Morocco." In *Negotiating Self-Determination*, edited by Hurst Hannum and Eileen Babbitt. Lanham, MD: Lexington Books, 2006.

Smith, Stephen. *Oufkir, un destin marocain*. Paris: Hachette, 2002.

Spencer, Claire. "The Spanish Protectorate and the Occupation of Tangier in 1940." In *North Africa: Nation, State, and Region*, edited by E. G. H. Joffé. London and New York: Routledge, 1983.

Stewart, Charles F. *The Economy of Morocco, 1912–1962*. Harvard Middle Eastern Monographs, 12. Cambridge, MA: Harvard University Press, 1964.

Stora, Benjamin. "Maroc-Algérie: Retour du passé et écriture de l'histoire." *Vingtième Siècle. Revue d'histoire* 68 (October – December 2000): 109–18.

"Le Maroc et l'Algérie: Reflexions sur des relations complexes, difficiles." *Les Cahiers de l'Orient* 58 (2000): 11–24.

Stuart, Graham H. *The International City of Tangier*, 2nd ed. Stanford, CA: Stanford University Press, 1955.

Sueiro, Susana. "L'Espagne et la 'question marocaine': La politique méditerranéenne de Primo De Rivera (1923–1930)," *Matériaux pour l'histoire de notre temps: Colonisations en Afrique* (1993): 15–17.

Swearingen, Will D. "In Pursuit of the Granary of Rome: France's Wheat Policy in Morocco, 1915–1931." *International Journal of Middle East Studies* 17:3 (1985): 347–63.

Moroccan Mirages: Agrarian Dreams and Deceptions, 1912–1986. Princeton: Princeton University Press, 1987.

"Morocco's Agricultural Crisis." In *The Political Economy of Morocco*, edited by I. W. Zartman. New York: Praeger, 1987.

Tangeaoui, Saïd. *Les Entrepreneurs marocains: Pouvoir, société et modernité*. Paris: Karthala, 1993.

Taraud, Christelle. *La Prostitution coloniale: Algérie, Tunisie, Maroc (1830–1962)*. Paris: Payot, 2003.

Tawfiq, Ahmad. "*Ta'ammulat fi al-bay'a al-Hafiziyya.*" In *Le Maroc de l'avènement de Moulay Abdelaziz à 1912*. Mohammedia: Kingdom of Morocco, Summer University, 1987.

Al-Mujtama al-maghribi fi al-qarn al-tasi' 'ashar: Inultan, 1850–1912. al-Rabat: Kulliyat al-adab wa-al- 'ulum al-insaniyya, 1983.

Tawzani, Na'ima Harraj. *Al-Umana bi-al-Maghrib fi 'ahd al-Sultan Mawlay al-Hasan (1290–1311/1873–1894): Musahama fi dirasat al-nizam al-mali bi-al-Maghrib*. Rabat: Kulliyat al-adab wa-al-'ulum al-insaniyya, 1979.

Taylor, A. J. P. "British Policy in Morocco, 1886–1902." *English Historical Review* 66 (1951): 342–73.

Tazi, M. A., and Kevin Dwyer. *Beyond Casablanca: M.A. Tazi and the Adventure of Moroccan Cinema*. Bloomington: Indiana University Press, 2004.

Thomas, Martin. "Albert Sarraut, French Colonial Development, and the Communist Threat, 1919–1930." *The Journal of Modern History* 77 (2005): 917–55.

Timsimani-Khaluk, A. *Al-Haraka al-raysuniyya min khilal al-watha'iq al-maghribiyya, 1909–1925*. 2 vols. Tangier: Saliki, n.d.

Tozy, Mohamed. "Monopolisation de la production symbolique et hiérarchisation du champ politico-religieux au Maroc." *Annuaire de l'Afrique du Nord* 18 (1979): 219–34.

"Réformes politiques et transition démocratique." *Maghreb-Machrek* 164 (1999): 67–84.

Monarchie et Islam politique au Maroc. Paris: Presses de la Fondation nationale des sciences politiques, 1999.

and Beatrice Hibou. "Une lecture d'anthropologie politique de la corruption au Maroc: fondement historique d'une prise de liberté avec le droit." *Hespéris Tamuda* 39:2 (2001): 215–36.

Tuchman, Barbara W. "Perdicaris Live or Raisuli Dead." In *A Sense of History: The Best Writing from the Pages of American Heritage*, introduction by Byron Dobell. New York: Houghton Mifflin, 1985.

Valensi, Lucette. *Fables de la mémoire: La glorieuse bataille des trois rois*. Paris: Seuil, 1992.

Van Wersch, Herman. "Rural Development in Morocco: 'Operation Labour'." *Economic Development and Cultural Change* 17:1 (1968): 33–49.

Venier, P.R. "French Imperialism and Pre-Colonial Rebellions in Eastern Morocco, 1903–1910." *Journal of North African Studies* 2:2 (1997): 557–67.

Vermeren, Pierre. "La Mutation sociale de l'enseignement supérieur musulman sous le protectorat au Maroc." In *Parcours d'intellectuels maghrébins: Scolarité, formation, socialisation et positionnements*, edited by Aïssa Kadri. Paris: Karthala 1999.

École, élite et pouvoir au Maroc et en Tunisie au XXe siècle. Maroc: Alizés, 2002.

Histoire du Maroc depuis l'indépendance. Paris: Découverte, 2006.

Veyre, Gabriel. *Au Maroc: Dans l'intimité du Sultan*. Paris: Librairie Universelle, 1905.

Waltz, Susan E. "Interpreting Political Reform in Morocco." In *In the Shadow of the Sultan: Culture, Power and Politics in Morocco*, edited by Rahma Bourqia and Susan Gilson Miller. Cambridge, MA: Center for Middle Eastern Studies, Harvard University Press, 1999.

Warnier, A., and Henry-René d'Allemagne. *Campagne du Maroc (1844): Journal d'Auguste-Hubert Warnier, chirurgien-major, attaché à l'état-major du Prince de Joinville*. Paris: Nouvelle revue rétrospective, 1899.

Waterbury, John. *The Commander of the Faithful: The Moroccan Political Elite – A Study in Segmented Politics*. New York: Columbia University Press, 1970.

"The Coup Manqué." In *Arabs and Berbers: From Tribe to Nation in North Africa*, edited by Ernest Gellner and Charles Micaud. Lexington, MA: DC Heath, 1972.

Wazzani, Muhammad Hasan. *Le Protectorat, crime de lèse-nation: Le cas du Maroc*. Fez: Fondation Mohamed Hassan Ouezzani, 1992.

Weiner, Jerome B. "The Green March in Historical Perspective." *Middle East Journal* 33:1 (1979): 20–33.

Weisgerber, F. *Au seuil du Maroc moderne*. Rabat: Éditions La Porte, 1947.

Wendel, H. C. M. "The Protégé System in Morocco." *Journal of Modern History* 2:1 (1930): 48–60.

Woolman, David S. *Rebels in the Rif: Abd El Krim and the Rif Rebellion*. Stanford, CA: Stanford University Press, 1968.

Wright, Gwendolyn. *The Politics of Design in French Colonial Urbanism*. Chicago: University of Chicago Press, 1991.

Wyrtzen, Jonathan. "Colonial State-Building and the Negotiation of Arab and Berber Identity in Protectorate Morocco." *International Journal of Middle East Studies* 43:2 (2011): 227–49.

Zartman, I. William. *Morocco: Problems of New Power*. New York: Atherton Press, 1964.

al-Zayani, Abu al-Qasim b. Ahmad. *Al-Tarjumana al-kubra fi akhbar al-ma'mur barran wa-bahran*. Rabat: Kingdom of Morocco, Ministry of Information, 1967.

Zeghal, Malika. *Islamism in Morocco: Religion, Authoritarianism, and Electoral Politics*. Princeton: Markus Wiener, 2008.

and Franck Fergosi, eds. *Religion et politique au Maghreb: Les exemples tunisien et marocain*, edited by Khadija Mohsen-Finan. Paris: Institut français des relations internationales (IFRI), 2005.

Zisenwine, Daniel. *The Emergence of Nationalist Politics in Morocco: The Rise of the Independence Party, and the Struggle against Colonialism after World War II*. London and New York: Tauris Academic Studies, 2010.

Zunes, Stephen, and Jacob Mundy. *Western Sahara: War, Nationalism, and Conflict Irresolution*. Syracuse, NY: Syracuse University Press, 2010.

Index